JeaTTle

HIDDEN®

Seattle

Including Puget Sound,
the Olympic Peninsula,
and the San Juan Islands

John Gottberg

Ulysses Press®
BERKELEY, CALIFORNIA

Published by:
ULYSSES PRESS
P.O. Box 3440
Berkeley, CA 94703
www.ulyssespress.com

ISSN 1545-5602
ISBN 1-56975-395-4

Printed in Canada by Transcontinental Printing

10 9 8 7 6 5 4 3 2 1

MANAGING EDITOR: Claire Chun
PROJECT DIRECTOR: Lily Chou
EDITORIAL ASSOCIATES: Kate Allen, Laura Brancella, Rachel Rubin,
    Kaori Takee
TYPESETTING: Lisa Kester, James Meetze, Steven Zah Schwartz
CARTOGRAPHY: Pease Press
COVER PHOTOGRAPHY: Getty Images (Pioneer Square)

Distributed in the United States by Publishers Group West
and in Canada by Raincoast Books

The author and publisher have made every effort to ensure the accuracy of information contained in *Hidden Seattle*, but can accept no liability for any loss, injury or inconvenience sustained by any traveler as a result of information or advice contained in this guide.

For Erik (a.k.a. Beefer), a true Seattleite

Write to us!

If in your travels you discover a spot that captures the spirit of Seattle, or if you live in the region and have a favorite place to share, or if you just feel like expressing your views, write to us and we'll pass your note along to the author.

We can't guarantee that the author will add your personal find to the next edition, but if the writer does use the suggestion, we'll acknowledge you in the credits and send you a free copy of the new edition.

ULYSSES PRESS
P.O. Box 3440
Berkeley, CA 94703
E-mail: readermail@ulyssespress.com

What's Hidden?

At different points throughout this book, you'll find special listings marked with a hidden symbol:

◀ HIDDEN

This means that you have come upon a place off the beaten tourist track, a spot that will carry you a step closer to the local people and natural environment of Seattle.

The goal of this guide is to lead you beyond the realm of everyday tourist facilities. While we include traditional sightseeing listings and popular attractions, we also offer alternative sights and adventure activities. Instead of filling this guide with reviews of standard hotels and chain restaurants, we concentrate on one-of-a-kind places and locally owned establishments.

Our authors seek out locales that are popular with residents but usually overlooked by visitors. Some are more hidden than others (and are marked accordingly), but all the listings in this book are intended to help you discover the true nature of Seattle and put you on the path of adventure.

Contents

Maps

OUTDOOR ADVENTURE SYMBOLS

The following symbols accompany national, state and regional park listings, as well as beach descriptions throughout the text.

▲	Camping	🏄	Surfing
🥾	Hiking	🎿	Waterskiing
🚲	Biking	🏄	Windsurfing
🐎	Horseback Riding	🛶	Canoeing or Kayaking
⛷	Downhill Skiing	🚤	Boating
🎿	Cross-country Skiing	🚤	Boat Ramps
🏊	Swimming	🐟	Fishing
🤿	Snorkeling or Scuba Diving		

ONE

The Emerald City

 Rain city? Not today. Last night's storm has washed the air clean, swept away yesterday's curtain of clouds to reveal Mt. Rainier in all its astonishing glory. From the window of your hotel room, you see sailboats dodging ferries on the blue gulf of Puget Sound, and beyond this inland sea, the Olympic Mountains rising like the jagged edge of a logger's snow-tipped saw. Below, downtown Seattle awakens to sunshine, espresso and the promise of a day brimming with discovery for the fortunate traveler.

A jewel of a city—its sapphire waters lapping emerald forests, encircled by a pearl necklace of snow-cloaked peaks—Seattle squeezes into a lean, hourglass shape between Elliott Bay and Lake Washington. The northwesternmost major city in the United States covers only 84 square miles, and its population is less than 600,000; but the greater metropolitan area, reaching from Tacoma to Everett and east to the Cascade foothills, is home to some 3 million Washingtonians. The queen city of Puget Sound is a mere three-hour drive from both Portland, Oregon, and Vancouver, British Columbia; and it's nearer yet to the Pacific Ocean and to the lofty Cascade summits.

Explorers and entrepreneurs, environmentalists and dreamers have long walked the Yellow Brick Road to The Emerald City, as Seattle calls itself. The extraordinary growth of recent decades has slowed in the past few years, but the city continues to sparkle in ways too numerous to count. Yet the city offered no hint of its future prominence when pioneers began arriving on Elliott Bay more than 150 years ago.

Like other settlements around Puget Sound, Seattle survived by farming, fishing, shipbuilding, logging and coal mining. For decades the community hardly grew at all. One whimsical theory has it that because the frontier sawmill town offered a better array of brothels to the region's loggers, miners and fishermen, capital tended to flow into Seattle to fund later investment and expansion.

Whatever the reason, the city quickly rebuilt after the disastrous "Great Fire" of 1889. Eight years later, the discovery of Alaskan gold put Seattle on the map. On July 17, 1897, the ship *Portland* steamed into Elliott Bay from Alaska, bearing its legendary "ton of gold" (actually, nearly two tons), triggering the Klondike Gold Rush. Seattle immediately emerged as chief outfitter to thousands of would-be miners heading north to seek their fortunes.

Today, Seattle remains tied to its traditions. It's so close to the sea that 20-pound salmon are still hooked in Elliott Bay, at the feet of those gleaming, new skyscrapers. It's so near its waterfront that the boom of ferry horns resonates among its buildings and the cries of gulls still pierce the rumble of traffic. But the city's economy has grown beyond the old resource-based industries. International trade, tourism, agriculture, biotechnology and software giants like Microsoft now lead the way. The spotlight has passed from building ships to building airplanes, from wood chips to microchips, from mining coal to cultivating the fertile fields of tourism.

Starbucks, a home-grown company founded by three University of Washington graduates, fueled the international specialty coffee boom; now Seattle considers itself the coffee capital of the world, and visitors can sample an astonishing array of roasts and blends. Nordstrom brought true customer service to the retail industry; Eddie Bauer and REI, two other home-grown institutions, melded flannel and fashion; the city was the test market that proved America would embrace Altoids. In other words, like San Francisco and Los Angeles, Seattle is a good place to see what's coming down the cultural pike.

In the process, one of the nation's most vibrant economies has emerged—despite Boeing's relocation of its head offices to Chicago in 2002 (the aerospace giant still manufactures many of its planes in the Seattle area). You can see that energy in Seattle's highrises, feel it in the buoyant street scene fueled in part by locals' infatuation with espresso. And there is fresh energy beneath your very feet. An "underground" of retail shops (as distinguished from the historic Pioneer Square Underground) has taken shape around the downtown Westlake stations in the Metro Transit Tunnel.

Text continued on page 6.

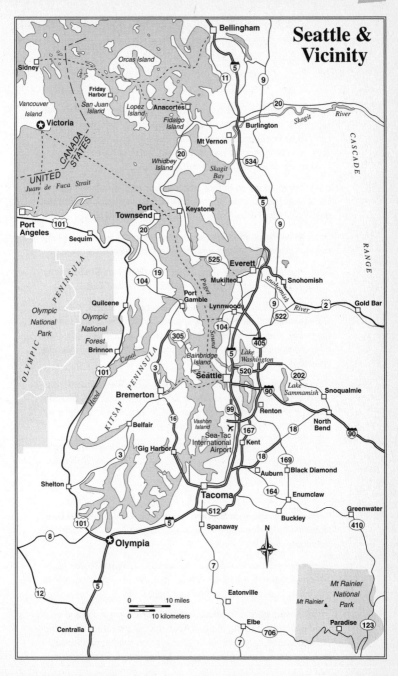

Seattle & Vicinity

Three-day Weekend

Seattle

DAY 1
- Check in. It makes sense to stay downtown, where most of the key sights are located. Driving from other parts of this long, narrow city can be time consuming. If you *do* stay outside of the downtown area, your best bet is to park at Seattle Center and ride the monorail instead of looking for downtown parking.

- If you haven't done so before starting your trip, make reservations for dinner and the theater tonight and the Underground Tour tomorrow. Seattle runs on reservations, and most locals plan far ahead.

- Stroll **Pike Place Market** and the **waterfront** (see the walking tour on pages 60–61) and visit the **Seattle Aquarium** (page 57).

- Rest your feet on a low-cost, scenic **Washington State Ferry** cruise from the Pier 52 terminal to Bremerton and back.

- On terra firma once more, climb the steep hill to the Westlake Center monorail terminal. Ride the monorail to **Seattle Center** (page 86). Visit the **Experience Music Project** (page 88), then take the elevator for the view from the top of the **Space Needle** (page 86).

- Dine atop the Space Needle at the **Sky City Restaurant** (page 91) if you like; alternatively, there are cheap eats at the **Seattle Center Food Court** and numerous wonderful, moderately priced restaurants in nearby Belltown (page 77).

- In the evening, enjoy your choice of Seattle Center performing-arts events, which may range from operas and ballets to stage plays and folk-dancing lessons.

DAY 2
- Stroll down to **Pioneer Square** and take the **Underground Tour** (page 54) for a look at the abandoned city that lies hidden beneath downtown Seattle's streets.

- Above ground, ride the elevator to the top of **Smith Tower** (page 54) and imagine the long-ago time when this mini-skyscraper was the tallest building west of the Mississippi River.

- Wander through the **International District** (page 55) and take your pick from the many small Asian restaurants along Main and Jackson streets for lunch. Feast your eyes on the exotic foodstuffs and fine Asian home furnishings at **Uwajimaya**. Complete your exploration of the district with a visit to the **Wing Luke Asian Museum**.

• For dinner this evening, why not enjoy Seattle's favorite food, alder-grilled salmon, at **Ivar's Salmon House** (page 119) on the Lake Union shoreline? Start driving up there early or take a cab; for a popular tourist restaurant, it's a little tricky to find.

• This could be the evening to check out the city's exceptionally lively nightclub scene. (If you don't feel like dyeing your hair green, simply wear your most authentically grungy camping clothes . . . .)

DAY 3
• Is it raining? If not, this could be an ideal morning for urban hiking on the secluded trails of the **Washington Park Arboretum** and **Foster Island** (page 98).

• If it *is* raining, check out the nearby **Museum of History and Industry** (page 100)—the name may sound boring, but the museum is fascinating.

• For lunch, try one of the interesting, affordable restaurants in the Green Lake area, such as the **Jitterbug** (page 120).

• Sun still shining? How about a bike ride along **Alki Beach** (page 136) in West Seattle, with its old-time California atmosphere and its great views of the Seattle skyline across the bay?

• Still raining? The city has plenty of other good museums to stay dry in. One good bet is the Boeing's **Museum of Flight** (page 134), tracing the century-long history of the Seattle area's largest employer.

• Consider finishing up your Seattle spree with a big-splurge dinner at **Campagne** (page 75) or **Cascadia** (page 77), two of the city's finest restaurants.

Seattle has also achieved national—even global—cultural status. Grunge rock swept the music industry in the early '90s, led by local groups such as Pearl Jam, Nirvana, Soundgarden (named after a Seattle park), Alice in Chains and legendary record label Sub Pop. All these bands still live and work here (except Nirvana, disassembled by the death of grunge king Kurt Cobain), and music fans can hear the next generation of stars in the city's innumerable clubs and small concert halls. And the past and present of Pacific Northwest music is displayed on grand stage at the Experience Music Project, at the foot of the iconic Space Needle.

> With more than two dozen specialty coffee retailers in Seattle, there's literally a coffee shop on every corner.

Civic energy has produced a glorious art museum downtown, a small but lively "people place" in Westlake Park, a spacious convention center and additions to Freeway Park. Private enterprise has added hotels, office towers whose grand lobbies brim with public art, shopping arcades, restaurants and nightclubs.

During the late 1980s, as locals struggled with construction chaos, Seattle's downtown briefly suffered the nickname "little Beirut." (The name was revived in the wake of riots against the World Trade Organization in 1999.) Now, in the early years of the 21st century, downtown Seattle is once more under construction. But this time the atmosphere is one of urban revitalization, as the city has gained a new symphony hall, a plethora of condominiums and several upscale shopping and entertainment complexes.

Seattle's urban energy is admired even by those who bemoan its traffic congestion, suburban sprawl, crime and worrisome air and water pollution. Growth has been the engine of change, and challenges are inherent in change. An example: The city's geography allows it only two north–south arterials, both clogged with vehicles at rush hours. To make matters worse, one of them—Route 99 across downtown's Alaskan Way Viaduct—is acknowledged as a severe hazard should a major earthquake strike the city. Improved mass transit has been a persistent topic of discussion in civic circles, with the result that a significant expansion in light-rail service and an extension of a 40-year-old monorail line—northwest from downtown to the Ballard neighborhood and southwest to West Seattle—are now in the works.

As vibrant as it is, downtown also exhibits the famed Seattle social courtesy and informality. Drivers on many downtown streets still stop to let waiting pedestrians cross (in fact, it's against the law not to do so at street corners and crosswalks); and it's considered impolite to honk your horn. Ask directions of anyone who looks like he knows his way around; he'll almost always do his best to help. Only bankers, lawyers and corporate executives wear suits to work, and not even all of those do. Casual wear is acceptable in almost every social situation; even the symphony and opera draw fans dressed in jeans.

Have goofy weather, growth, gentrification of downtown neighborhoods and a tide of new immigrants—especially from Asia and Eastern Europe—eradicated the old Seattle? Not by a long shot. Pike Place Market's colorful maze is still there to beguile you. Ferry boats still glide like wedding cakes across a night-darkened Elliott Bay. The central waterfront is as clamorous, gritty and irresistible as ever. Pioneer Square and its catacomb-like underground still beckons. The soul of the city somehow endures even as the changes wrought by regional growth accumulate.

By almost any standard, Seattle and its environs still offer an extraordinary blend of urban and outdoor pleasures close at hand. Growth seems only to have spurred a much richer cultural scene in Seattle. There are better restaurants serving original cuisines, more swank hotels and art galleries, superb opera and a vital theater community, and livelier shopping in a retail core sprinkled with public plazas that reach out to passersby with summer noon-hour concerts.

Hidden Seattle will help you explore this fascinating city. Besides taking you to countless popular spots, it will lead to unusual and unique locales. In these pages, you will find our suggestions of places to eat, stay, sightsee and shop, and where to enjoy the outdoors and nightlife. We think you'll find greater Seattle to be a place you can explore for a day, a week or much longer.

There are certain things you won't want to miss during your Seattle visit, and I've covered most of these in my "Three-day Weekend" itinerary. Pike Place Market, Pioneer Square and Seattle Center are at the top of most visitors' lists. The market—a designated National Historic District nearly a century old—offers a public market experience unparalleled

Where to Go

elsewhere in the United States. Pioneer Square, the original city center, offers a glimpse of early-day Seattle, especially to those who join a beneath-the-sidewalks tour of its "underground." Seattle Center, created in 1962 for the city's World's Fair, is home to the iconic Space Needle and the avant-garde Experience Music Project, a new museum celebrating Seattle's harmonic roots.

Seattle is first and foremost a maritime community. You'll begin to understand as you stroll the colorful waterfront, seeing the impressive aquarium and the maritime discovery center; but to really taste the salt air, take a short cruise on the Washington State Ferry, across Puget Sound to Bremerton and back. Then travel a few miles north to the always-active Hiram M. Chittenden Locks on the Lake Washington Ship Canal (through which any boat bound to or from saltwater must pass), and have a twilight drink on Lake Union, whose Center for Wooden Boats is frequently visited by classic tall ships.

There are some marvelous museums in this city—the Seattle Art Museum and its affiliated Seattle Asian Art Museum, the University of Washington's Burke Memorial Museum of anthropology, the city's Museum of History and Industry, the Museum of Flight in the original Boeing Airplane Co. "red barn." In nearby Tacoma, an industrial city now undergoing a cultural renaissance, native-son glass artist nonpareil Dale Chihuly has built a "bridge of glass" over the railroad tracks, linking the city's new Museum of Glass to the Washington State History Museum.

Looming over all is stately Mt. Rainier, easily the highest summit of the Cascade Range, its snow-capped volcanic cone rising from the dense coniferous forests that still shroud the environs of metropolitan Puget Sound. It serves as a reminder that to truly appreciate Seattle, you must get out of the city itself: You must hike the wooded paths, ski the powdery hills, raft the rippling rivers, fish the tidal inlets, kayak the serrated shorelines amid sea birds and orca whales. For Seattle is as much a center for outdoor adventure as it is a thriving, cosmopolitan city.

SEASONS   Don't be daunted by Seattle's reputation for nasty weather. True, it's wet here—but more in the number of gray days than in the actually quantity of precipitation. The city's 37 inches of annual rainfall are less than many other American cities—New York, Miami and Houston, for three examples—but for much of the

Seattle's
Street System

Newcomers to Seattle often find street signs bewildering; the city is divided into several sections, each with different area designations. Here's how the system works: All avenues run north–south and are followed by a geographical indicator (1st Avenue Northwest, 23rd Avenue South); all streets run east–west and are preceded by the direction (East Ward Street, Northwest 65th Street). Exceptions are noted below.

The city's sections are:

Northwest, bounded by Puget Sound on the west, the Lake Washington Ship Canal on the south, and 1st Avenue Northwest on the east.

North, bounded by 1st Avenue Northwest, Denny Way and 1st Avenue Northeast. South of the Canal, the streets have no geographical indicators.

Northeast, bounded by 1st Avenue Northeast, the Canal and Lake Washington.

West, bounded by Puget Sound, the Canal, Denny Way and Queen Anne Avenue.

East, bounded by the Canal, Eastlake Avenue, Route 5, Broadway, Yesler Way and Lake Washington. South of Denny Way, the avenues have no geographical indicators.

Downtown, bounded by Elliott Bay, Denny Way, Melrose Avenue, East Union Street, Broadway and Yesler Way. There are no geographical indicators.

South, bounded by Yesler Way, Lake Washington and Elliott Bay and 1st Avenue South.

Southwest, bounded by Puget Sound, Elliott Bay and 1st Avenue South.

Adding to the confusion is a maze of freeways, bridges and angled streets. But with a map and some experience, the system isn't as difficult as it first appears.

year they are delivered in a gossamer mist that makes an umbrella as useful as sunscreen. Historically, July and August bring the driest, sunniest, warmest (into the 80s) weather, although visitors will usually find ample breaks in the clouds between May and September. In winter, Seattle is decidedly soggy and overcast; temperatures typically run from the mid-30s into the 40s. It's wise to come prepared—spiritually and practically—for whatever mix of dreary and sublime days fate may deliver. An accepting attitude may be the best defense in a region that has been described by this paraphrase of Mark Twain: "The mildest winter I ever spent was a summer on Puget Sound."

The same weather patterns—wet winters, damp and fickle springs and autumns, sunnier summers—are consistent from one end of Puget Sound to the other: south to Olympia, north to Bellingham, west across the Kitsap Peninsula. In fact, precipitation increases steadily as one travels east from the Sound into the Cascade foothills and crests. Rainfall is even heavier on the coast, especially on the western flank of the Olympic Peninsula. The lone exception is a rainshadow area along the northeastern rim of that peninsula, from Port Angeles to Port Townsend, and especially around little Sequim. While Seattle averages less than 40 inches of rain a year, and Forks (on that soggy Olympic coast) about 140 inches, Sequim gets only 15 inches annually.

CALENDAR OF EVENTS

Festivals and events are a big part of life in the Seattle area, especially when the rains disappear and everyone is ready to spend time outdoors enjoying the sun. It seems as if there's at least one major event per weekend from late spring to early fall. Below is a sampling of some of the most popular.

JANUARY **Seattle The Martin Luther King Jr. Birthday Celebration** at Seattle Center honors the memory of the great African-American leader in a party that features step shows, hip-hop dances and African drumming.

FEBRUARY **Seattle** Chinese Americans and other East Asians observe the **Lunar New Year** in a day-long festival in the International District that boasts lion dances, ethnic music, crafts and food. Vietnamese celebrate their new year with the **Tet Festival** at Seattle Center. **Fat Tuesday** is a week-long Mardi Gras–style festival with a parade, arts and crafts, jazz and food. Seattle blooms with demonstration gardens and floral displays during the **Northwest Flower and Garden Show** located at the Seattle Convention Center.

Tacoma & Southern Puget Sound   In Tacoma, **Wintergrass** features bluegrass music and a street dance the last weekend of the month.

Northern Puget Sound & the San Juan Islands   Amateur detectives have a field day during Whidbey Island's **Langley Mystery Weekend,** when local merchants offer clues and prizes to solve a whodunit.

Seattle   The Emerald City honors the Emerald Isle during the **Irish Week Festival,** highlighted by the whimsical St. Patrick's Day parade.   **MARCH**

Olympic Peninsula & Western Puget Sound   Step back in time at the five-day **Port Townsend Victorian Festival,** a celebration of the historic port's heritage with workshops devoted to historic preservation and events portraying Victorian lifestyles.

Northern Puget Sound & the San Juan Islands   Watch a cooking demonstration, enter a mussel-eating contest or compare shellfish chowder recipes at the **Penn Cove Mussel Festival** on Whidbey Island.

Seattle   The walkways of Seattle Center are lined with cherry trees during the **Cherry Blossom Festival,** which celebrates the fleeting beauty of the ethereal *sakura*; expect to see many Japanese Americans dressed in traditional kimonos and other garb.   **APRIL**

Tacoma & Southern Puget Sound   Enjoy spring's early blossoms at the **Daffodil Festival** in Tacoma, Puyallup, Sumner and Orting; it's launched by Tacoma's Junior Daffodil Parade for children and climaxed by a Grand Floral Parade and Floral Marine Parade.

Olympic Peninsula & Western Puget Sound   Bring your umbrella—not necessarily for rain—to watch contestants lure gulls for prizes in Port Orchard's **Seagull Calling Festival.**

Northern Puget Sound & the San Juan Islands   To catch early-spring colors in their natural glory, queue up for the drive through the rich farmlands of La Conner and Mount Vernon during the **Skagit Valley Tulip Festival,** held the first through third weekends of the month.

MAY

Seattle   The **University District Street Fair** packs University Avenue with more than 500 arts-and-crafts booths, food gardens, live-music stages, and unpredictable behavior. May 17 is **Norwegian Independence Day** in the Scandinavian-flavored Ballard district, celebrate with a parade, as well as a crafts fair with storytelling and music at the Nordic Heritage Museum. One of the largest and best attended film fests in the U.S., the **Seattle International Film Festival** draws directors, actors and critics with more than 140 feature films from all over the world in addition to industry forums and premieres. Memorial Day weekend is the unofficial start to the summer season, kicking off the free **Northwest Folklife Festival** at Seattle Center—partly a multi-ethnic celebration, partly a coming-out party for the Birkenstock set since the '70s. Also in May, look for the **International Children's Festival** at Seattle Center; the **Maritime Festival**, with tugboat races on the Waterfront; and the **Pike Place Market Festival**, featuring live music and coffee and beer gardens.

Olympic Peninsula & Western Puget Sound   Bremerton honors its military presence during the **Armed Forces Festival and Parade** with a range of exhibits and concerts, plus a golf tournament. Poulsbo's response to Ballard's Norwegian festival is the **Viking Fest**, a celebration of Scandinavian heritage with a parade, a carnival, food and musical entertainment.

JUNE

Seattle   June is the kickoff month for several concert series that feature artists with national followings: **Summer Nights at the Pier** offers outdoor shows at Pier 62/63 on the Waterfront; **Zoo Tunes** at the Woodland Park Zoo presents folk and pop performances by the likes of Joan Baez, Shawn Colvin and Taj Mahal; the **Summer Festival on the Green** at the Chateau Ste. Michelle winery serves up an eclectic mix of outdoor concerts. Downtown Seattle hosts a summer-long **Out to Lunch** series of midday jazz, classical and rhythm-and-blues concerts at various locations—and they're free. The Filipino community celebrates its cultural heritage with music, dance, food and exhibits during the three-day **Pagdiriwang** festival at Seattle Center. One of Seattle's oldest street festivals (dating from the early '70s) is the zany **Fremont Fair**—you can't miss the naked bicyclists during the Solstice Parade at noon on Saturday, even if you want to. The **Seattle Pride March and Rally**, celebrating Freedom Day and centered around the southeast corner of Volunteer Park, is the Northwest's largest lesbian, gay, bisexual and transgender parade and festival.

Tacoma & Southern Puget Sound Puyallup's **Meeker Days,** named after a pioneer citizen, celebrates regional history with food stands, crafts booths and live music spread across 15 city blocks.

Olympic Peninsula & Western Puget Sound From the last week of June through the first week of July, Bainbridge Island celebrates its laidback lifestyle during **Island Days** with a street dance and one-day strawberry festival.

Northern Puget Sound & the San Juan Islands Salty Sea Days in Everett—in addition to a range of nautical events like outrigger and hydroplane races—boast a carnival, parade, arts-and-crafts show, classic car show, Hawaiian cultural fest and grand fireworks show.

Seattle The July 4th weekend **Heritage Festival** celebrates history, culture and arts with programs on the grounds of Marymoor Park, a 500-acre greensward built around a 1905 pioneer mansion in Redmond. Begun in 1950, the enduring **Seafair** and its crew of Seafair pirates hosts dozens of greater Seattle events, including a whimsical milk-carton derby on Green Lake, a triathlon, Naval and Coast Guard fleet parades, hydroplane races, a Blue Angels air show and a torchlight parade. The city's annual food festival, **Bite of Seattle,** offers the chance to sample food and wine from dozens of restaurants and wineries at Seattle Center; it's coupled with the largest kids' parade in the state. Mid-July brings the annual **UW Summer Arts Festival,** a week-long series of theater, music, dance, film and visual-arts programs, to the campus of the University of Washington. At the **Vashon Island Strawberry Festival,** islanders celebrate rural life and community with parades, food, music, and arts-and-crafts booths. The **Ballard Seafoodfest** challenges you to try lutefisk (that oh-so-Nordic lye-marinated cod dish); for meeker tastes, there's alder-smoked salmon, live music, an arts-and-crafts show, and children's programs. Northwest talent is showcased in Bellevue at the **Pacific Northwest Arts and Crafts Fair,** host to more than 300 artists, craftspeople and performers.

JULY

Tacoma & Southern Puget Sound Eatonville, south of Tacoma, honors slime-time invertebrates at its annual **Slug Festival**—take your turn as a banana-slug jockey in the slug races. Olympia's **Capital Lakefair,** on the banks of Capital Lake, is a family event in the shadow of the State Capitol with food and crafts booths, music, a parade, fireworks and a children's day. Enumclaw hosts the **King County Fair** during the third full week of the month and follows it with the **Pacific Northwest Scottish Highland Games**, a spectacle of Gaelic bagpiping, drumming and dancing, and traditional athletic and sheepdog competitions. Gig Harbor's **Renaissance Faire & Gothic Fantasy**—equestrian games, sword fighting, archery and chess competition—is so much fun, it's held twice: in July and August.

Northern Puget Sound & the San Juan Islands Most small towns have grand **Fourth of July** celebrations. We like the fireworks over La Conner and Oak Harbor. At Camano Island's **Independence Day Parade and Ice Cream Social** in Stanwood, townspeople march in old-time costumes with antique cars, farm implements and fire equipment. The third week of July is **Whidbey Island Race Week**, one of the top-20 sailing regattas in the world; evenings are filled with social events in Oak Harbor. Down island, Greenbank's **Loganberry Festival** celebrates the berry harvest with a pie-eating contest, music, arts and crafts, food and wine. Everett celebrates African and African-American culture at the **Nubian Jam Community Festival**, which honors elders and aims to inspire youth and help the greater community become aware of African-American heritage.

AUGUST   **Seattle**   The free, alternative rock–oriented **Seattle Music Fest**, on West Seattle's Alki Beach, presents local acts as well as sports and other beach events, food and arts-and-crafts displays. Some 200 boats, 30 feet and longer, are on display at Ballard's Shilshole Bay Marina in the **Boats Afloat Show**, an adjunct to the annual mid-January Seattle Boat Show at the Seahawks Exhibition Center.

Tacoma & Southern Puget Sound   Olympia hosts the month-long **Washington Shakespeare Festival** with a troupe of regional and national repertory actors performing four of the Bard's plays. At the foot of Puget Sound in Shelton, the **Polynesian Luau and Heritage Fair** celebrates South Pacific culture—Hawaiian, Samoan, Tongan—with a luau and pig roast, food and craft booths, a dance show, and banana-peeling contests.

Olympic Peninsula & Western Puget Sound   The wise Indian leader for whom this city was named is honored during **Chief Seattle Days** at Suquamish, hosting a traditional salmon bake, Indian arts, canoe races, traditional dancing, and a graveside memorial service for Seattle's namesake, Chief Sealth.

Northern Puget Sound & the San Juan Islands   The official Washington state fair—the **Evergreen State Fair**—is staged in Monroe (east of Everett): farm animals, exhibition halls, carnival rides and big-name entertainment.

Seattle   **Bumbershoot** is one of America's great music festivals, **SEPTEMBER** packing four days of performing arts, film, literary arts, fine arts and crafts, food and children's activities into the Seattle Center. The five-day **Salmon Homecoming Celebration** at the Seattle Aquarium hosts American Indian salmon bakes, music, dancing, storytelling and crafts displays coupled with exhibits on the salmon's life cycle. The **Western Washington Fair**, one of the country's largest, is best known simply as the Puyallup Fair, boasting extensive animal and agricultural exhibits, a large carnival and big-name musical entertainment. Costumed canines accompany their kids, who ride down Kirkland's Park Lane on decorated bicycles, in the annual **Pedals-n-Paws Bike & Dog Parade**. The event kicks off **Taste! Kirkland**, a waterfront festival of food and music.

Tacoma & Southern Puget Sound   The state's capital is port of call for **Olympia Harbor Days**, celebrating maritime heritage with tugboat races, arts and crafts, and music over Labor Day weekend. The next weekend is **Foofaraw**, a day of appreciation for the U.S. military.

Olympic Peninsula & Western Puget Sound   More than 150 unique and classic vessels gather in Port Townsend the second weekend of the month for the **Wooden Boat Festival**, perhaps joined by vintage tall ships and enhanced by demonstrations and lectures, music and fine foods. One week later, grand Victorian homes are open to the public during the **Historic Homes Tour**.

Seattle   **Salmon Days** in Issaquah honor the return of spawning **OCTOBER** salmon with hatchery tours, a salmon bake, live entertainment, arts and crafts and a parade. Writers, publishers and book lovers of all ages converge on the **Northwest Bookfest**, a literary extravaganza at Sand Point's Magnuson Park showcasing author readings, book displays, and children and teen areas.

Tacoma & Southern Puget Sound   Learn how to shuck an oyster at Shelton's **Oysterfest**, which couples the Washington State Seafood Festival with seafood cooking demonstrations, a juried art and photography show, and musical entertainment. At Tacoma's Fort Nisqually, celebrate Halloween in the style of the 19th-century trappers and traders; **Bonfires, Beaver Pelts & Bogeymen** will try to scare you with ghost stories around a roaring fire—straight from 1855.

Olympic Peninsula & Western Puget Sound   During Port Townsend's **Great Kinetic Sculpture Race**, garage-lab inventors show off vehicles that can run on land, through mud and over water.

NOVEMBER   **Seattle**   Eat a sugar skull and dance with a skeleton at the Seattle Center's **Día de Muertos** ("Day of the Dead") Latino celebration. Return a week later to observe **Hmong New Year**, a tradition of immigrant people from the Southeast Asian highlands.

Olympic Peninsula & Western Puget Sound   Bremerton's **Festival of Trees** is not merely about beautifully decorated Christmas trees—there's also a gingerbread village, visits by Santa and Mrs. Claus, arts-and-crafts exhibits, live entertainment and children's activities.

DECEMBER   **Seattle**   Hordes of people gather on the Lake Washington and Elliott Bay shorelines to listen to carolers aboard the festively decorated **Argosy Christmas Ship** and to view the brightly lit private pleasure craft that accompany it. Seattle Center is decked out with an ice-skating rink, Holiday Train display, colorful carousel and arts-and-crafts booths during **Winterfest**.

Tacoma & Southern Puget Sound   Tacoma's Point Defiance Zoo & Aquarium hosts **Zoolights**—450,000 colorful lights depicting zoo animals and nursery rhymes.

▼▼▼▼▼▼▼▼▼▼▼▼
Before You Go

VISITORS CENTERS

Seattle's Convention & Visitors Bureau has an excellent and informative website from which you can order a free visitors guide, lodging guide and calendar of events. ~ www.seeseattle.org. Or write the bureau (Attention: Visitor Information) at One Convention Place, 701 Pike Street #800, Seattle, WA 98101; 206-461-5840.

Your first stop on arrival in Seattle should be the bureau's **Citywide Concierge Service**, adjacent to the elevators on the main floor of One Convention Place. Travel specialists will assist you in making reservations, buying event tickets, arranging transportation and handling other details of your visit. ~ 8th Avenue and Pike Street; 206-461-5888.

If you're planning trips outside of Seattle, you'll want a free copy of the *Washington State Lodging and Travel Guide*, which you can obtain by contacting **Washington State Tourism**. ~ P.O. Box 42500, Olympia, WA 98504; 360-586-2088, 800-544-1800; www.experiencewashington.com.

Many have learned of Washington's charms thanks to poets and writers like Theodore Roethke, Gary Snyder, Annie Dillard, Tom Robbins, Timothy Egan and David Guterson.

For visitors arriving by automobile, Washington provides numerous **Welcome Centers** at key points along the major highways. Visitors can pull off for a stretch, a cup of coffee or juice and plenty of advice on what to see and do in the area. The centers are clearly marked and are usually open during daylight hours throughout the spring, summer and fall.

Large cities and small towns throughout the state have chambers of commerce or visitor information centers; many of those within daytrip range of Seattle are listed in *Hidden Seattle* under the appropriate chapter.

PACKING

Comfortable and casual are the norm for dress in Seattle. You'll want something dressier if you plan to catch a show, indulge in high tea or spend your evenings in posh restaurants and clubs, but for the most part, your topsiders and slacks are acceptable garb everywhere else.

Layers of clothing are your best bet, since the weather can change so drastically any time of year. Even in summer, you'll appreciate having packed a jacket to protect you from nippy Puget Sound breezes or drizzly rains.

Pack long-sleeve shirts, pants and lightweight sweaters and a water-resistant jacket along with your shorts, T-shirts and bathing suit. Bring along those warmer clothes—pants, sweaters, jackets, hats and gloves—in spring and fall, too, since days may be warm but it's rather chilly after sundown. Winter calls for thick sweaters, knitted hats and warm (even down) jackets. It's not a bad idea to call ahead to check on weather conditions.

Sturdy, comfortable walking shoes are a must for sightseeing. If you plan to go for long walks on the beach, bring a pair of lightweight canvas shoes that you don't mind getting wet.

Don't forget your camera for capturing Seattle's marvelous scenery and a pair of binoculars for watching the abundant bird and wildlife. Also pack an umbrella, just in case. (But don't unfurl it for a light drizzle lest you immediately identify yourself as an out-of-towner.) And by all means, don't forget your copy of *Hidden Seattle*!

LODGING
Whatever your preference and budget, you can probably find something to suit your taste with the help of this book. Rooms may be scarce and prices rise during the summer high season, so it's a good idea to book ahead: Conventions can overwhelm the lodging market in cities like Seattle. Off-season rates are often drastically reduced. In general, you can get your best rates on weekends and holidays—or, in rural areas, during the week.

Seattle's Convention & Visitors Bureau has two lodging reservations programs. During the low season (mid-October through March), the **Seattle SuperSaver** (www.seattlesuper saver.com) can get you 70 percent off rack rates at 48 hotels. In peak tourist season (April to mid-October), the **Seattle Hotel Hotline** promises the best available rate. Call the same toll-free number for either option. ~ 800-535-7071.

Especially in downtown Seattle, you will find three principal groups of hotel properties. There are large luxury hotels with exceptional service, lavish Sunday buffets and complete business facilities. There are smaller but equally inviting boutique hotels with charming lobbies, fine restaurants and personalized service. And there are the national franchise motor hotels—Courtyard, Holiday Inn, Ramada, Crowne Plaza—with names and amenities you've come to recognize and respect.

Outside of the city center and international airport areas, you'll find fewer major hotels and more mom-and-pop motels, especially along such highway corridors as old Route 99 north and south of Seattle. Bed-and-breakfast inns have proliferated in many outlying urban neighborhoods as well as charming daytrip destinations, including Whidbey Island and Port Townsend. Backpackers' hostels, and a handful of comfortable pensions based on the European model, accommodate visitors in all price ranges.

Lodging in this book is classified by price. Listed rates are for two people during high season, so if you are looking for low-season bargains, it's good to inquire. *Budget* facilities are generally less than $60 per night and are satisfactory and clean but modest. *Moderate*-priced lodgings run from $60 to $120; what they have to offer in the way of luxury will depend upon where they are located, but they often feature ample rooms and attractive surroundings. At a *deluxe* hotel or resort, you can expect to spend between $120 and $175 for a double; you'll usually find spacious rooms, a fashionable lobby, a restaurant and a few shops. *Ultra-deluxe* properties, priced above $175, are the city's finest, offering all the amenities of a deluxe hotel plus plenty of extras. Whatever the charge, you will be taxed 15.8 percent on top of the quoted rate: 8.8 percent state sales tax and 7 percent (Seattle city) hotel tax.

For an offbeat experience, you might want to try one of Seattle's wheatgrass bars, which serve the ultimate health food drink, clipped fresh and ground into a chlorophyll-laden treat.

DINING

Seafood is a staple in Seattle, and salmon is king. Whether it's poached in herbs or grilled on a stake Indian-style, plan to treat yourself to this regional specialty often. Also, at least once, seek out a restaurant specializing in Pacific Northwest regional cuisine: The goal of these chefs is to prepare hearty meals using only the freshest meat, produce and other ingredients that are organically grown and available locally. Seattle's ethnic restaurant community is particularly strong on Asian cuisine, including Chinese, Japanese, Thai and Vietnamese dishes. With numerous open-air eateries and waterfront restaurants, the city is also blessed with a generous supply of coffee bars serving first-rate espresso and cappuccino.

In this book, restaurants are categorized geographically, with each entry describing the type of cuisine, general decor and price range. Restaurants listed offer lunch and dinner unless otherwise noted. Dinner entrées at *budget* restaurants usually cost under $8 (alcohol, tax and tip not included). The ambience is informal, service usually speedy and the crowd a local one. *Moderate*-priced restaurants range between $8 and $16 at dinner; surroundings are casual but pleasant, the menu offers more variety and the pace is usually slower. *Deluxe* establishments tab their entrées from $16 to $25; the cuisine may be simple or sophisticated, depending on the location, but the decor is plusher and the service more personalized. *Ultra-deluxe* dining rooms, where entrées begin at $25, are often gourmet places where the cooking and service have become an art form. Keep in mind that the state sales tax of 8.8 percent will be added to your bill, and you're expected to tip an additional 15 to 20 percent.

We've made an effort to include places with established reputations for good eating. Breakfast and lunch menus vary less in price from restaurant to restaurant than do the evening offerings. If you are dining on a budget and still hope to experience the best of the bunch, visit at lunch when portions and prices are reduced.

TRAVELING WITH CHILDREN

By all means, bring the kids to Seattle. Besides the many museums, shops and festivals set aside for them, the city also has dozens of parks and beaches, many of which sponsor children's activities during the summer months. Here are a few guidelines that can help make travel with children a pleasure.

Many bed and breakfasts do not accept children, so be sure of the policy when you make reservations. If you need a crib or cot, arrange for it ahead of time. A travel agent can be of help here, as well as with most other travel plans.

If you're traveling by air, try to reserve bulkhead seats where there is plenty of room (unless you want to view a movie). Take along extras you may need, such as diapers, a change of clothing for both yourself and your child, snacks and toys or books. When traveling by car, be sure to carry the extras, along with plenty of juice and water. And always allow plenty of time for getting places.

A first-aid kit is a must for any trip. Along with adhesive bandages, antiseptic cream and something to stop itching, include any medicines your pediatrician might recommend to treat allergies, colds, diarrhea or any chronic problems your child may have. In the city, you'll find all-night grocery, pharmacy or convenience stores that stock these necessities.

When spending time at the beach or in the mountains, take extra care the first few days. Children's skin is especially sensitive to sun, and severe sunburn can happen before you realize it, even on overcast days. Hats for the kids are a good idea, along with liberal applications of sunblock. Be sure to keep a constant eye on children near the water.

Many parks and attractions schedule activities designed just for children. Consult the calendar listings in local newspapers or websites, and/or phone the numbers in this guide to see what's happening during your visit.

Traveling solo grants an independence and freedom different from that of traveling with a partner, but single travelers are more vulnerable to crime and must take additional precautions.

WOMEN TRAVELING ALONE

It's unwise to hitchhike and probably best to avoid inexpensive accommodations on the outskirts of town; the money saved does not outweigh the risk. Bed-and-breakfast inns, youth hostels and YWCAs are generally your safest bet for lodging, and they also foster an environment ideal for bonding with fellow travelers.

Keep all valuables well-hidden and clutch cameras and purses tightly. Avoid late-night treks or strolls through undesirable parts of town, but if you find yourself in this situation, continue walking with a confident air until you reach a safe haven. A fierce scowl never hurts.

These hints should by no means deter you from seeking out adventure. Wherever you go, stay alert, use your common sense and trust your instincts. If you are hassled or threatened in some way, never be afraid to yell for assistance. It's also a good idea to carry change for a phone call and to know a number to call in case of emergency, such as the **King County Sexual Resource**

CINEMATIC SEATTLE

Washington state in general and Seattle in particular have become major locations for full-length feature films by both Hollywood and independent producers. The modern growth of the industry really took off following the 1992 Tom Hanks–Meg Ryan movie, *Sleepless in Seattle*, and the hit television series "Frasier." Since 1992, more than 100 major features have been shot here, and more than twice that many TV series and/or episodes. But the list goes back much further than that, and includes renowned directors like Bernardo Bertolucci, Nora Ephron, David Lynch, David Mamet, Gus Van Sant and local residents Cameron Crowe and the late Stanley Kubrick. These are just some of the major motion pictures filmed in Seattle and environs: *Tugboat Annie* (1933), *It Happened at the World's Fair* (1963), *War Games* (1982), *Say Anything* (1988), *Singles* (1991), *The Vanishing* (1993), *Get Carter* (2000) and *The Ring* (2002).

Center. ~ P.O. Box 300, Renton, WA 98057; 24-hour crisis line: 800-825-7273 (call for advice and referrals); www.kcsarc.org.

For more helpful hints, get a copy of *Safety and Security for Women Who Travel* (Travelers' Tales).

GAY & LESBIAN TRAVELERS

The Capitol Hill neighborhood is the hub of gay life in Seattle, and is the location of most resource and support centers. Check street boxes for the current edition of the weekly *Seattle Gay News* or the monthly *LRC News,* or drop into the **Beyond the Closet Bookstore.** ~ 518 East Pike Street; 206-322-4609. The **Seattle LGBT Community Center** has a wide range of information on gay services and events, and organizes monthly guest-speaker brunches. ~ 1115 East Pike Street; 206-323-5428; www.seattle lgbt.org.

Of the 50 states, Washington is the only one named for a president.

For gay men, the **Gay City Health Project** is wired into all manner of resources for physical and psychological health. ~ 1505 Broadway; 206-860-6969; www.gaycity.org. For women, **The Lesbian Resource Center** is the oldest of its kind in the country. ~ 2214 South Jackson Street; 206-322-3953; www.lrc.net. Young people with sexual lifestyle questions can contact the **Gay Lesbian Bisexual Transgender Youth Information Line.** ~ 206-547-7900. The **Seattle–King County Department of Public Health** offers anonymous HIV/AIDS testing and counseling (206-205-7837, 800-678-1595; www.metrokc.gov/health/apu).

SENIOR TRAVELERS

Senior citizens will find Seattle a hospitable place to visit, especially during the cool, sunny summer months that offer respite from hotter climes elsewhere in the country. Museums and other attractions, even restaurants and hotels, offer senior discounts that can cut a substantial chunk off vacation costs.

The **American Association of Retired Persons** (AARP) offers membership to anyone age 50 or over. AARP's benefits include travel discounts with a number of firms and escorted tours with Gray Line buses. ~ 601 E Street Northwest, Washington, DC 20049; 800-424-3410; www.aarp.org.

Elderhostel offers reasonably priced, all-inclusive educational programs in a variety of Pacific Northwest locations throughout the year. ~ 11 Avenue de Lafayette, Boston, MA 02111; 877-426-8056, fax 617-426-0701; www.elderhostel.org.

Be extra careful about health matters. In addition to the medications you ordinarily use, it's a good idea to bring along prescriptions for obtaining more. Consider carrying a medical record with you—including your medical history and current medical status, as well as your doctor's name, phone number and address. Make sure your insurance covers you while you're away from home.

DISABLED TRAVELERS

Seattle's steep hills, though no rival to San Francisco's, can still create significant problems for travelers who may be wheelchair-bound or otherwise not able-bodied. In downtown Seattle, there are a couple of elevators lifting pedestrians from the Waterfront to Pike Place Market and Belltown (at the west end of Lenora Street). And the wheelchair-accessible bus tunnel between Westlake Center and the International District is a boon to disabled travelers.

Most hotels have special rooms for disabled travelers; many of the newer and better lodgings also offer TDD telephones. Car-rental companies may have hand-controlled cars available, with two to three days' advance notice.

Easter Seals Project ACTION maintains a **National Accessible Travelers' Database** with detailed information on accessible transit services in Seattle and other cities nationwide. Or contact the Easter Seal Society's Seattle office. ~ 175 Roy Street; 206-764-3492, 800-659-6428, TDD 202-347-7385; www.projectaction.easter-seals.org.

Before traveling, get additional information and resource links from the **Society for Accessible Travel and Hospitality**. This group can recommend tour operators, travel agents, companion services and more; annual membership includes a quarterly magazine, *Open World*. ~ 347 5th Avenue #610, New York, NY 10016; 212-447-7284; www.sath.org. The **Travelin' Talk Network** operates a website for disabled travelers and e-mails a monthly newsletter to members. ~ P.O. Box 1796, Wheat Ridge, CO 80034; 303-232-2979; www.travelintalk.net. **The American Foundation for the Blind** provides information on travel with seeing-eye dogs. ~ 800-232-5463; www.afb.org.

FOREIGN TRAVELERS

Passports and Visas Most foreign visitors are required to obtain a passport and tourist visa to enter the United States. Contact your nearest U.S. Embassy or Consulate well in advance to obtain a visa and to check on any other entry requirements. Entry into Canada calls for a valid passport, visa or visitor permit for all foreign visitors except those from the United States, who should carry some proof of citizenship (voter's registration or birth certificate), including two pieces with photo ID. A passport is preferred, but a birth certificate or voter's registration should be sufficient; officially, driver's licenses are no longer considered proof of citizenship, although border guards usually let you pass with one.

Customs Requirements Foreign travelers are allowed to bring in the following: 200 cigarettes (1 carton), 50 cigars or 2 kilograms (4.4 pounds) of smoking tobacco; one liter of alcohol for personal use only (you must be at least 21 years of age to bring in alcohol); and US$100 worth of duty-free gifts that can include an additional quantity of 100 cigars. You may bring in any amount of currency (amounts over US$10,000 require a form). Americans who have been in Canada over 48 hours may take out $400 worth of duty-free items ($25 worth of duty-free for visits under 48 hours). Carry any prescription drugs in clearly marked containers; you may have to provide a written prescription or doctor's statement to clear customs. Meat or meat products, seeds, plants, fruits and narcotics may *not* be brought into the United States.

Driving If you plan to rent a car, an international driver's license should be obtained prior to arrival. United States driver's licenses are valid in Canada and vice versa. Some rental car companies require both a foreign license and an international driver's license along with a major credit card and require that the lessee be at least 25 years of age. Seat belts are mandatory for the driver and all passengers. Children under the age of 5, or under 40 pounds, should be in the back seat in approved child safety restraints. For motorcyclists, a helmet is required.

Currency American money is based on the dollar. Bills in the United States come in six denominations: $1, $5, $10, $20, $50 and $100. Every dollar is divided into 100 cents. Coins are the penny (1 cent), nickel (5 cents), dime (10 cents) and quarter (25 cents); half-dollar and dollar coins are used infrequently. You may not use foreign currency to purchase goods and services in

Parking
Solutions

The best solution to parking in central Seattle is to leave your car behind. That's not always possible; a few strategies will help ease the struggle.

The basic principle is that, the farther from main points of interest you are, the easier and cheaper parking becomes. Especially troublesome spots are the Westlake Center area; Pioneer Square; the waterfront; Pike Place Market; and Capitol Hill. If you have to park in central downtown, expect to pay $4 to $6 an hour—or more—in a parking garage; many garages fill up just before lunch time.

One reasonably priced garage that usually has space is the **IBM Building** (the garage entrance is actually on University between 5th and 6th avenues). ~ 1200 5th Avenue; 206-623-2675. Another similarly priced garage is at the **Washington Athletic Club**. ~ 1409 6th Avenue; 206-622-7900.

Metered parking is available under the **Alaskan Way Viaduct** along the waterfront; most spaces are taken by 10 a.m. **Public Market Parking** often has space, and offers a free hour to those on quick errands. ~ 1531 Western Avenue; 206-621-0469.

Once you reach downtown's edges, price goes down and availability goes up. On 7th Avenue north of the major hotels, several lots offer cheaper deals, including the Key Park at 7th Avenue and Denny Way, which charges $4.50 for a full day if you park before 9 a.m.; the price then rises to $7. ~ 206-443-8400. And up on First Hill, east of downtown, Caplan Parking charges $12 for a full day. ~ 1012 Terry Avenue; 206-623-1792. All these lots are within a ten-minute walk of Seattle Center, Westlake Center and the Washington State Convention & Trade Center.

the United States. Consider buying traveler's checks in dollar amounts. You may also use credit cards affiliated with an American company such as Interbank, Barclay Card, VISA and American Express.

Electricity and Electronics Electric outlets use currents of 110 volts, 60 cycles. To operate appliances made for other electrical systems, you need a transformer or other adapter. Travelers who use laptop computers for telecommunication should be aware that modem configurations for U.S. telephone systems may be different from their European or Asian counterparts. Similarly, the U.S. format for videotapes is different from that in Europe; if you're purchasing a souvenir video, European format may be available upon request.

Weights and Measurements The United States uses the English system of weights and measures. American units and their metric equivalents are as follows: 1 inch = 2.5 centimeters; 1 foot = 0.3 meter; 1 yard = 0.9 meter; 1 mile = 1.6 kilometers; 1 ounce = 28 grams; 1 pound = 0.45 kilogram; 1 quart (liquid) = 0.9 liter.

Transportation

Seattle lies along Puget Sound in the state of Washington, east of the Olympic Peninsula, north–south **Route 5** is its prime arterial; the interstate highway enters Seattle from Olympia and Tacoma to the south and from Everett and Bellingham to the north. **Route 99**, the pre-interstate U.S. highway, more or less parallels Route 5 between Tacoma and Everett and provides an alternate arterial passage for commuter traffic. **Route 405** circumvents downtown Seattle; it branches off Route 5 near Renton and runs north through Bellevue, Kirkland and Bothell before rejoining Route 5 at Lynnwood.

The east–west interstate, **Route 90**, has its western terminus in Seattle; it crosses Lake Washington at Mercer Island and **Route 405** in Bellevue, continuing to Issaquah, Snoqualmie Pass and points east. **Route 520** also crosses the lake, on the Evergreen Point Floating Bridge between the University District, Bellevue and Redmond. **Route 2** crosses Stevens Pass east from Everett, while **Route 410** skirts Mount Rainier heading east from Tacoma.

AIR About 20 miles south of downtown Seattle is **Seattle-Tacoma International Airport** (Sea-Tac). It is served by the following domestic airlines: Alaska Airlines, America West Airlines, American

Airlines, Big Sky, Continental Airlines, Delta Air Lines, Frontier
Airlines, Hawaiian Airlines, Horizon Air, JetBlue Airways, Northwest Airlines, Skywest Airlines, Southwest Airlines, United Airlines, US Airways and several smaller charter airlines. In addition,
numerous foreign airlines are routed through Sea-Tac: Aeroflot,
Air Canada, Asiana, EVA Air, Iberia, KLM Royal Dutch, Lufthansa
and Scandinavian.

A new parking structure has eased gridlock for many travelers, though the main terminal (there are two satellite buildings
linked by light rail) continue in renovation. For general information, call 206-431-4444. There's a visitors information center on
the baggage level of Sea-Tac Airport (206-433-5218; www.port
seattle.org/seatac).

The **Washington State Ferry System** serves Seattle (Pier 50/52) to   **FERRY**
Bainbridge Island, Bremerton and Vashon Island; Seattle (Faunt-
leroy) to Vashon and Southworth (Kitsap Peninsula); Edmonds
to Kingston (Kitsap Peninsula); Whidbey Island to Mukilteo
(near Edmonds) and Port Townsend; and Anacortes to Sidney,
British Columbia, via the San Juan Islands. Most are car ferries.
~ 206-464-6400; www.wsdot.wa.gov/ferries.

The **Victoria Clipper** passenger catamaran service operates
daily trips (two and one half hours) between Seattle (Pier 69) and
Victoria, B.C., and a summer whale-watching excursion to and
from Friday Harbor in the San Juan Islands. ~ 206-448-5000;
www.victoriaclipper.com.

Seattle is served by **Greyhound Bus Lines,** with a downtown ter-   **BUS**
minal at 811 Stewart Street. ~ 800-231-2222; www.greyhound.
com. **Gray Line Airport Express** provides inexpensive shuttle
service between Sea-Tac Airport and downtown hotels. ~ 206-
626-6088.

Rail service in and out of Seattle is provided by **Amtrak** on the   **TRAIN**
Empire Builder, Coast Starlight and *Amtrak Cascades.* Call or
surf for more information on connections from around the country. ~ 800-872-7245; www.amtrak.com.

Most major car-rental businesses have offices at Seattle-Tacoma   **CAR**
International Airport. Rental agencies include **Avis Rent A Car**   **RENTALS**
(800-331-1212), **Budget Rent A Car** (800-527-0700), **Dollar Rent**

A Car (800-800-4000), Hertz Rent A Car (800-654-3131), National Car Rental (800-227-7368) and Thrifty Car Rental (800-367-2277). Ace Extra Car Discount Rentals (800-227-5397) offers low rates and shuttle service to the airport.

PUBLIC TRANSIT

Metro Transit buses provide free transportation in downtown Seattle, and low-cost service throughout greater Seattle and King County. The agency also operates Waterfront Streetcar trolleys between Pier 70 and the International District. ~ 206-553-3000; transit.metrokc.gov.

Then deemed transportation for the future, the Seattle Center Monorail was built for the 1962 World's Fair. It runs between downtown and Seattle Center, at the foot of the Space Needle, every ten minutes, 7:30 a.m. (9 a.m. on weekends) until 11 p.m. ~ 206-441-6038.

The downtown hub for both the Monorail and the bus system is Westlake Center, on Pine Street between 4th and 5th Avenues. The Monorail arrives on an elevated platform above the street-level mall, while buses load in an underground terminal. The buses are uniquely designed so they can switch from diesel to electric power when they enter the subterranean 1.3-mile bus tunnel (between Westlake Center and the International District.

A new monorail—this one a 14-mile Green Line connecting downtown Seattle with the Ballard (northwest) and West Seattle (southwest) neighborhoods—has gained voter approval. Groundbreaking is scheduled for 2005, with completion of the full line four years later.

Three central Puget Sound counties have combined their energies in support of SoundTransit, an agency that provides reliable commuter transportation between Seattle, Tacoma and Everett. An expansion of the light-rail and bus system is ongoing. ~ 800-201-4900; www.soundtransit.org.

TAXIS

Seattle area cab services include Farwest Taxi (206-622-1717), Orange Cab (206-522-8800) and Yellow Cab (206-622-6500).

TWO

History

 A popular theory today suggests that 25,000 years ago, at the end of the last ice age, the seas were 300 feet lower and a stretch of land traversed the Bering Strait. The first humans to arrive on the west coast of North America are thought to have used this "land bridge" to walk from Asia to what is now Alaska. From there, they wandered through Canada and down into Washington in search of a warmer climate. Archaeologists have discovered solid evidence of human existence dating back 10,000 years with the find of Marmes Man, a hunter and gatherer whose skeletal remains (found in eastern Washington) are among the oldest documented in the Western Hemisphere.

Other, more recent evidence of human culture was found at Ozette on the Olympic Coast, the site of one of five major Makah villages. Archaeologists have unearthed well-preserved baskets, harpoons and clothing of the people who lived here an estimated 500 years ago until a mud slide, probably triggered by an earthquake, engulfed and buried the settlement. Because the slide caught the American Indians by surprise, it buried utensils in all stages of use and development. While wooden and textile artifacts have often been destroyed by the region's damp climate, Ozette was beautifully preserved by the great slide. Eleven years of excavation turned up more than 55,000 artifacts, making it possible to paint a complete picture of the early Makah. This find has dwarfed all other projects of its kind and today, 97 percent of all Northwest Coast Indian artifacts are from Ozette.

These ancient people were the ancestors of the numerous tribes that later populated the North American continent. Among them are the Kwakiutl, Haida, Bella Coola, Tlingit, Salish, Yakima, Nez Percé, Paiute, Shoshone, Umpqua and Rogue tribes of the Northwest.

The Indians of Puget Sound were predominantly Salish. The mild climate and abundant resources here led them to a fairly sedentary lifestyle. These native peoples constructed permanent villages from the readily available wood, fished the rich waters, foraged in lush forests and had enough free time to develop ritualized arts and ceremonies, as well as an elaborate social structure. Several families often lived together in "longhouses," wooden buildings as much as 100 feet long and 40 feet wide.

Puget Sound tribes had a wealth of food. Their diets depended on seafood (mostly shellfish and salmon) supplemented by a surplus of potatoes, a common crop for settled tribes. Materialistic and organized, they had time to create beautiful basketry, hats and wooden whale-fin sculptures inlaid with hundreds of sea otter teeth. They were also very resourceful people, taking advantage of the malleable consistency of the western red cedar, using its wood for everything from medicinal teas and ointments to houses and canoes.

EARLY EXPLORATION   In the 1700s, the heads of several European nations interested in expanding their borders sent explorers to claim chunks of the Northwest coast. The explorers also searched continually for the fabled Northwest Passage, which supposedly connected the Pacific and Atlantic oceans by water. The search for the passage actually had begun much earlier. In the late 1500s, Juan de Fuca, the first recorded explorer to sail along the Washington coastline, thought he had discovered it. However, this Greek traveler, who had adopted his Spanish name as well as flag, was mistaken. What he really found was the mouth of Puget Sound, now called the Strait of Juan de Fuca in his honor.

Nearly two centuries later, in 1774 and 1775, the Spanish sent out two more parties. Juan Perez, leader of the former, was the first to describe in-depth the region's natural beauty. The second party, led by Bruno de Heceta and Juan Francisco de la Bodega, was much greater in number, as well as purpose. Heceta went ashore on the coast and claimed the whole Northwest in the name of Spain.

In the mid-1700s, the Russians had sent an expedition led by Vitus Bering, a Dane in their service. They liked what they saw here and sent Bering on a follow-up mission. With its abundance of sea otters and beavers, Bering had quickly realized the capital potential of the land; based upon his recommendations, the Russians rapidly erected a number of trading and hunting posts all along the coast, from Alaska as far south as what today is northern California. Bolstered by the prospects of a lucrative fur trade, the Russians were making their first bold move to annex the territory, either ignoring or just ignorant of Spain's outrageous claim.

> The American Indians supplied the potato to white settlers and taught them how to grow it successfully in this climate.

Arrival of the white explorers brought many changes to the generally peaceful tribes of this relatively well-off region. There is no documentation of the Americans Indians' early interactions with white men, but by the end of the 18th century, traders were beginning to swap guns and ammunition for furs. Unfortunately, smallpox came with the guns. As early as 1775, ships arriving on the Washington coast introduced Western diseases that decimated indigenous peoples who had no immunity.

Ironically, the Spanish and Russians were the first foreigners in the region, but they had started a diplomatic territorial battle that they were never to enter. Their sailing expeditions were nothing compared to England's imperialistic machine. The dominating force at the time, England flexed its financial muscle and sent Captain James Cook in 1778 to investigate the maritime fur trade. In 1792, the British commissioned George Vancouver to find the Northwest Passage and map the region, giving him extra leeway with supplies and money. He traveled the inland water routes and named every prominent geological feature after members of his crew. Puget Sound took the name of young Lieutenant Peter Puget.

THE FUR TRADERS About the same time, the young and independent United States started looking west. Robert Gray, an American fur trader sent by the Boston Company, explored the Washington coast in 1792 to verify its treasure trove of furry animals. The explorations took him to the mouth of the Columbia River, which he named for his ship, the *Columbia*; this discovery later became the basis for America's claim to the territory. Many American trade companies followed the Boston Company's example and sent hunting parties west. By 1812, the United States dominated the fur trade. The Russians slowly packed up many of their outposts, distracted by the Napoleonic Wars, while the Spanish also lost interest, deterred perhaps by the English presence.

The famous Lewis and Clark expedition of 1804–1806 spent the winter at the mouth of the Columbia River, never venturing north to Puget Sound. But on their coattails, a new generation of explorers—both English and American—headed west, convinced they could make a quick fortune in the fur trade. Permanent trading posts laid some of the foundations for later settlement.

Soon thereafter, missionaries came to "civilize" the American Indians with Western religion and medicine. However, the intentions of the missionaries often resulted in tension between the Indians and the new settlers. Eventually, skirmishes escalated into the various Indian Wars of the region, which started in the mid-1800s (mainly inland) and ended by the turn of the 20th century.

Following the War of 1812, the American and British governments signed a Treaty of Joint Occupation, giving both nations the right to trade and settle in the Northwest region—then known as the Oregon Country. The Hudson's Bay Company set up a base at Fort Vancouver, on the Columbia River opposite modern-day Portland, and ran a prosperous trading hub there between 1821 and 1848.

An 1846 treaty failed to properly define the border between American and British Canadian territory, instead naming an unspecified "main channel" as the boundary. While the two countries agreed to respect the 49th parallel as the dividing point, this

THE INFAMOUS PIG WAR

Tensions left over from the War of 1812 and the not-yet-forgotten American Revolution caused friction between the Americans and British in the Northwest. The American/British Treaty of 1846 failed to properly define the border of the British territory, instead naming an unspecified "main channel" as the boundary. The Americans and British agreed to use the 49th parallel. However, this latitude divided the San Juan Islands in two, leaving the British and American soldiers staring each other down across the makeshift border. The entente was preserved until a lone British pig wandered into an American settler's garden. The American shot and killed the pig—the only bullet fired during the whole 13-year dispute, a heated diplomatic struggle for control of the islands that came to be called the "Pig War." The "war" was finally resolved in 1872 when the islands were awarded to the United States by a German arbitrator.

latitude divided the San Juan Islands in two, leaving troops staring each other down across a makeshift border. A 13-year diplomatic struggle dubbed the Pig War (see "The Infamous Pig War" sidebar) was resolved in 1872, when the islands were awarded to the U.S. by a German arbiter.

THE FOUNDING OF SEATTLE The first white settlers—a half-dozen young Illinois families and their children, led by Arthur Denny—landed at Alki Point (modern West Seattle) in November 1851. A few months later, they moved across Elliott Bay in search of a sheltered harbor, and in 1853 the city was platted by Denny, Carson Boren and Dr. David Maynard near the location of modern Pioneer Square. It was named for the Suquamish Indian chief Sealth, whom Maynard had befriended.

The young town grew slowly around Henry Yesler's sawmill, but fishing and coal mining helped keep a flow of new settlers to Seattle. Stage routes were established and sea traffic increased steadily. The entire business district (65 square blocks) was razed by a disastrous fire in 1889—the same year Washington became the 42nd state, with Olympia as its capital—but within two years Seattle was rebuilt of iron, brick and stone.

When the Great Northern Railroad established a terminus in Seattle in 1893, the city was on its way to becoming a transportation hub. That role was cemented by the Yukon (Klondike) and Alaska (Nome) gold rushes of the late 1890s, as Seattle became the main supply depot for droves of prospectors who passed through the city en route north. (Klondike Gold Rush National Historical Park, in Seattle's Pioneer Square, today tells their story.) Seattle grew from 42,000 people in 1890 to 80,000 in 1900, and to 237,000 in 1910 as it annexed nearly a dozen adjoining towns.

Soon Seattle developed into one of the world's great seaports with more than 50 miles of wharves. Elliott Bay and the mouth of the Duwamish River were dredged and many of the downtown-area hills graded, with the fill used for harbor development. The completion in 1916 of the Lake Washington Ship Canal (linking inland waters to Puget Sound), on the heels of the 1914 opening of the Panama Canal, led to rapid economic growth in the 1920s.

After the stagnation of the Great Depression years, World War II brought another boom. William Boeing had established the Boeing Airplane Company in Seattle in 1916, and the government put it to work building warplanes in the 1940s. It grew to become one of the world's largest commercial aircraft companies. Shipbuilding and shipping provided huge economic boons during both world wars.

THE LATE 20TH CENTURY   Following the second World War, expansion in lumber, agriculture and fishing continued apace with the aircraft and war-era atomic energy industries. The 1962 Seattle World's Fair placed the city in the international spotlight. College dropout Bill Gates and friend Paul Allen set up Microsoft here in 1975 and within a decade rose to dominate the new software industry. Other companies settling in the Seattle area included Sega, Nordstrom, Eddie Bauer and Recreational Equipment, Inc. (REI). The rush of these young successful companies, combined with the backbone of Boeing, attracted a huge influx of young adults.

Boeing took some blows in the early 1990s, losing big contracts to McDonnell Douglas and Air Bus, and in 2002, corporate headquarters were relocated to Chicago. When Boeing hurts, so does Seattle. But despite mass layoffs, many of the aircraft production facilities remain in the Seattle area; at the end of 2003, Boeing's Everett plant was awarded a contract to manufacture the company's new 7E7 airliner. The regional economy is still very much on its feet, driven by the strong computer and biotechnology industries.

On a cultural level, many American Indian tribes have proudly reclaimed their heritage. A new generation of American Indians has gained prominence in business, education, the environmental movement and the arts. Tribal organizations are also reclaiming lands and fishing rights.

In the early '90s Seattle had its 15 minutes of cultural fame when unlikely members of its lively music scene gained national attention. The "grunge" phenomenon, associated with flannel shirts and a rough rock sound, was shunned by hardcore music fans as pure media hype. Seattle's thriving arts and music scene, however, is anything but hype—it is, after all, Jimi Hendrix's hometown. And bands like Nirvana and Pearl Jam established reputations as among the best in North America. The large number of students who live here ensure the town's status as a mecca for the young and talented. For alternative sounds, local and otherwise, tune in to KEXP 90.3 FM.

Seattle's current challenge is to reconcile its business opportunities with its natural resources, to strike a balance between expansion and preservation that will maintain its rich environmental and economic resources.

THREE

The Land &
Outdoor Adventures

 The northwest placeholder of the contiguous United States, Washington has enough different ecological zones to turn even the most jaded visitor into an amateur geographer. There's a wealth of dramatic scenery in this state: rugged coastline, dense forests and two large mountain ranges—one young and aspiring and the other part of a dominant and established volcanic chain. And the Seattle metropolitan area sits right in the heart of it all.

The young, low-lying Olympic Mountains, home (in their coastal valleys) to the only rainforest in the continental United States, reign over the Olympic Peninsula and dominate the west side of Puget Sound. From almost anywhere you stand in downtown Seattle, you'll see their sawtooth-like peaks rising beyond Elliott Bay. But the Olympics, named for the mythological home of the Greek gods, top out under 8000 feet elevation and are overshadowed by the Cascade Range, whose lower peaks surpass that height. This north–south chain of volcanic peaks starts in western Canada, runs down the middle of Washington and Oregon, and spills into northern California. The tallest of its summits, glacier-cloaked Mount Rainier, rises a dizzying 14,411 feet above the Sound not 60 miles southeast of downtown Seattle. So prominent is it on the southern horizon, longtime locals often describe sunny weather with the words, "The mountain is out today."

The monumental crests of the Cascade Range block the moisture-laden fronts moving eastward across the Pacific coastline, leaving the rains to fall on their western slopes and casting a semiarid rain shadow to the east. Along the coastal plain west of the Olympics, annual precipitation is among the heaviest in the United States—more than 150 inches—but in Seattle and central Puget Sound it is only 35 to 40 inches a year. (Communities east of the Cascades get 12 to 20 inches.)

Certainly, the heavy rainfall keeps Washington's vegetation lush. The drizzle and clouds that blanket the coastal region during much of the winter and spring nourish the incredibly green landscape that grows thick and fast. Numerous rivers fall from alpine wilderness and cut courses through pastoral valleys. Nearly half of the state is covered by evergreen forest; Seattle and other cities are surrounded by outdoor recreational opportunities, with mountains, lakes, streams and an ocean within easy reach. It's no surprise that residents and visitors have a hardy outdoorsy glow. After all, the proximity to nature is one of the things that draws people here.

GEOLOGY

The eruption of Mount St. Helens in 1980 was only the most recent reminder of the dramatic geological forces that have shaped Washington state. The Cascade Range began to rise just 20 million years ago. Volcanic eruptions reached a peak about two million years ago with the formation of the Northwest's long chain of "fire mountains," part of the Pacific Rim Ring of Fire.

While volcanoes may have built these mountains, glaciers carved them into their present form. For the last million years or so they have crept through the valleys and around the mountains, naturally sculpting the land—Puget Sound itself is a glacial trough. So, too, are 20-mile-long Lake Washington, the central city's Lake Union, and other bodies of water throughout the greater Seattle area, created with the retreat of the last Ice Age about 10,000 years ago. The vastly reduced remnants of some glaciers can still be seen on Cascade mountain slopes.

FLORA

The forests of Washington, even those in the greater Seattle area, contain some of the world's biggest trees. They hold records in height and circumference, with fir, pine, hemlock and cedar topping 300 feet. While everyone equates coniferous trees with Washington, there is much more to the flora of the region than its abundance of Douglas fir, white pine, red cedar and other evergreens. In fact, the pine-like Western hemlock with its irregular needles is the official state tree, populating the Olympic rainforest, as well as the low slopes of the Cascade mountains, and commonly growing to a height of 200 feet (some reach 300 feet).

Throughout western Washington, you will find bright displays of rhododendron, the state flower. Hundreds of varieties, with their mass of colorful blooms in shades of pink, red and purple, are found growing wild in meadows and parks, making this species a popular icon for photographers. They also have become a cornerstone of Washington backyard gardens.

In the lowland valleys, especially including Puget Sound, alder, oak, maple and other deciduous trees provide brilliant displays of color against an evergreen backdrop each spring and fall. Daffodils and tulips light up the fields, as do azaleas, red clover and other grasses grown by the many nurseries and seed companies prospering in the region. Wild berry bushes run rampant in this clime, offering blackberries, huckleberries, currants and strawberries for the picking. Indian paintbrush, columbine, foxglove, butter cups and numerous other wildflowers line the paths and brush the fields with color.

Along the Sound, lakes and tributary rivers, tall tufts of Douglas fir and hemlock pocketed with maple and alder sprout at water's edge and creep up the banks. In the spring, scores of violets poke out through the underbrush.

Thick groves of fir and cedar filter the sunlight, providing the perfect environment for mushrooms, lichens, ferns and mosses. As a result, mushrooming has become a favorite pastime of fungus-loving locals, as well as a tourist attraction for fine food lovers. Each spring, after a good rainfall, you can spy mushroomers sneaking off alone to their favorite gathering spot, always scanning the ground for the ultimate find: a crop of truffles, part of the mushroom family and an expensive delicacy in French and Northwest-regional restaurants. **Warning:** New gatherers should bring along an expert to decipher the poisonous mushrooms from the edible. While they will not show you their secret spots, they will steer you away from some serious health problems.

As the snow recedes, alpine wildflowers struggle to live on the rain-soaked meadows, yet a breathtaking array survive. The elegant tiger lily, beargrass, aster, fawnlily and sandwort with its small

THE ORIGINAL WOODY WOODPECKER

If you hear a rapid pounding noise, it's probably coming from the pileated woodpecker. Identified by its erect head feathers, it is the largest woodpecker in North America and the model for the cartoon character "Woody Woodpecker." Unlike its cartoon cousin, this bird lives primarily in old-growth forests, drilling for insects under tree bark.

pinwheel flowers above a mat of tough leaves, form a rainbow of colors that compliment the gray-green hillsides and decorate the rocky crevasses. Other hardy wildflowers peak through the short wiry grass and dwarf shrubs. Crowberry, red and white mountain heathers and tasty alpine huckleberries blossom and ripen in the early fall.

FAUNA

The low-lying woodlands in particular are home to an abundance of wildlife. It was this that first brought white settlers to Puget Sound, beginning with the trappers who came in droves searching for fur. Beaver and otter pelts, highly valued in China during the 19th century, were heavily hunted. Nearly decimated colonies, now protected by law, are coming back strong. Playful otters are often seen floating tummy up in coastal waters, while the bald eagle can be seen frequently on the Skagit River and other western Washington waterways.

Fish, especially salmon, were also a major factor in the economic development of the region, and remain so to this day, though numbers of spawning salmon are dropping drastically. Nonetheless, fishing fanatics are still drawn here in search of the five varieties of Pacific salmon along with flounder, lingcod, rockfish, trout, bass and many other varieties of sportfish. Angler or not, check out the fish ladders at the Hiram M. Chittenden Locks in Seattle's Ballard neighborhood to view huge salmon on their annual spawning migrations (June to November).

Among the more readily recognized creatures that reside in the Pacific Northwest's waters are orca (killer whales), porpoises and dolphins often spotted cavorting just offshore. When the orca show up, the playful seals and sea lions (orca's prey) disappear. Within the Sound, you're unlikely to spot any of the California gray whales that migrate twice a year (April–June and November–December) down the Washington coastline, but minke whales occasionally visit Puget Sound, as do Dall's porpoises, often mistaken for baby orca because of their similar coloration and markings.

Clamdiggers in Puget Sound are generally looking for the yellow-gray Japanese littleneck clam. An unusual species of clam that burrows two to three feet deep in these same mudflats is the geoduck (pronounced "gooey-duck"); the foot of this large clam, which weighs 10 pounds or more, does not fully retract into its six-to-eight-inch white oblong shell. Beachcombers may also find a shiny tan mollusk called the *cooperella subdiaphana* or a tiny white pear-shaped shell called carp. The brown or black *acmaea limatula* is a limpet found in rocks between tides. In shallow water you're likely to discover hairy triton, a large yellow white shell; the channeled dogwinkle, an inch-long mollusk with a yellow-brown dye shell; or the bluish-white barrel bubble.

In the Seattle urban area, especially in larger city parks that preserve plots of old-growth forest, there is a proliferation of such creatures as squirrels, raccoons, opossums, skunks, foxes and coyotes. Urban wetlands may also be home to muskrats and beavers. In the Cascade foothills just outside of the city are large numbers of mule deer and smaller numbers of black bears; weighing upwards of 300 pounds and reaching six feet tall, these bears usually feed on berries, nuts and fish, and avoid humans unless provoked by offers of food or danger to a cub. Cougars (mountain lions) are increasingly making their presence known as suburban housing projects encroach on their traditional hunting grounds. Bobcats, minks and even wolves may be found in these foothill forests. Watch for the Pacific giant salamander in fallen, rotting logs; it is the largest of its kind in the world—growing up to a foot in length and capable of eating small mice.

With a proliferation of protected refuges and preserves providing homes for great flocks of snow geese, great blue herons, kingfishers, cranes and other species, birdwatchers will be in seventh heaven in Washington, one of the fastest-growing birder destinations on the continent. In the central Puget Sound area, the Nisqually National Wildlife Refuge (off Route 5 between Tacoma and Olympia) provides safe haven for thousands of wintering waterfowl, as well as gulls, sandpipers and passerines. Over 300 species of birds live in the Pacific Northwest for at least a portion of the year. Easily accessible mudflats and estuaries

SLUG FEST

The banana slug thrives in Washington's moist climate. Not quite large enough to be mistaken for a speed bump, they leave telltale viscous trails. While it's the bane of gardeners, the slug is still regarded as a sort of mascot for the state. In many souvenir shops, you'll even find plush toy replicas and gag cans of slug soup.

throughout Washington provide refuge for egrets, cormorants, loons and migratory waterfowl making their way along the Pacific Flyway. Hundreds of pairs of bald eagles nest and hunt among the islands of Washington along with great blue herons and cormorants. You might see goshawks and spotted owls if you venture quietly into the state's old-growth forest zones.

The spotted owl has been the center of controversy in recent years, the focus of the recurring nature-versus-commerce debate. This bird is considered an "indicator species"—that is, because it is more easily seen than other, smaller species, biologists can safely assume that it is not alone in the threat it faces. As logging companies cut deeper into the old-growth forests, which have taken 150 years or more to grow, the habitat for this endangered owl grows smaller. (These nocturnal birds need thousands of acres per pair to support their indulgent eating habits.) The old-growth forests of the Pacific Northwest provide adequate nesting spots in the protected snags and broken branches of tall trees that shelter their flightless young. Recently, old-growth forest has become increasingly hard to come by and the owl's numbers are diminishing—only about 500 pairs survive in Washington today. Some scientists predict their extinction early in the 21st century if logging continues at its present rate. Environmental activists are fighting to keep Washington's forests free and clear of commercial logging roads to preserve their fragile ecosystems.

Outdoor Adventures

CAMPING

In the Seattle metropolitan area, camping options are generally limited to a few state parks; in most of those, campsites are open between April and October only. Between Seattle and Tacoma, not too far from Seattle-Tacoma International Airport, there's year-round camping at **Dash Point State Park** (near Federal Way) and **Saltwater State Park** (Des Moines). You can also travel by ferry to camp on Bainbridge Island at **Fay Bainbridge State Park** or to Port Orchard, on the Kitsap Peninsula, to camp at **Illahee State Park** or **Manchester State Park**. And Tillicum Village cruise boats will drop you at **Blake Island State Park**, a short hop from the Seattle waterfront. ~ 888-226-7688; www.parks.wa.gov.

In addition, you'll find a lone KOA **Kampground**, open year-round, in suburban Kent, southeast of Seattle. ~ 5801 South 212th Street, Kent, WA 98032; 253-872-8652, 800-562-1892.

Outside of the urban environment, you'll find that Washington parks rank among the top in North America as far as attendance goes. So plan ahead if you hope to do any camping during the busy summer months. Late spring and early fall present fewer crowds to deal with and the weather is still fine.

Much of Washington's scenic coastline is privately held, but there are a few scattered parks along the shore and even more inland, in the foothills and mountains. You can reserve campsites at several state parks from mid-May to mid-September by calling **Reservations Northwest**. ~ 800-452-5687. Or contact the **Washington State Parks and Recreation Commission** for more details. ~ P.O. Box 42650, Olympia, WA 98504; 360-902-8844 (general information), 888-226-7688 (reservations); www.parks. wa.gov. For camping in national parks and forests, including Mount Rainier National Park, contact the **Outdoor Recreation Information Center**. ~ REI Building, 222 Yale Avenue North, Seattle; 206-470-4060.

WATER SPORTS & SAFETY

Seattle is a paradise for water-sports lovers. Wedged as it is between fresh and salt water, where streams flow from pristine lakes into ocean bays, Seattle offers an incredible array of options to recreation lovers. Swimming, fishing, scuba diving, white-water rafting, kayaking and canoeing, sailing and windsurfing, scouring the shoreline in search of clams or just basking in the sun are only some of the choices.

Shallow lakes, rivers and bays tend to be the most popular spots since they warm up during the height of summer; otherwise, the waters of Washington are generally chilly. Whenever you swim, never do so alone, and never take your eyes off of children in or near the water.

With miles of coastline and island-dotted straits to explore, it's no wonder that boating is one of the most popular activities in Seattle. In fact, this city has a higher per-capita boat ownership than any other major city in the country—and that includes San Diego and Miami. Many memorable attractions, including numerous pristine marine parks, are accessible only by water and have facilities set aside for boaters. Write, call or visit the **Washington State Parks and Recreation Commission** for a boater's guide to Washington. ~ P.O. Box 42650, Olympia, WA 98504; 360-902-8844; www.parks.wa.gov.

A Salmon's
Odyssey

The life of a salmon is a long round-trip journey from a freshwater birth to the ocean, and back to birthplace. A salmon first enters the world in a small inland stream, where it grows for about a year before departing on its great journey.

There are five species of Pacific salmon—chinook (king), coho (silver), chum (dog), sockeye (red) and humpback (pink)—as well as steelhead, an ocean-run trout. Unlike most other fish, the anadromous salmon live part of their life in saltwater and another part in fresh. Salmon swim downstream to the open sea, changing their camouflage from dots for the river to smooth white for the ocean, where they flow with the currents for about two years. Then they head "home," finding the route back to their original streams by the smell of their home waters and by using the sun as a navigational reference.

These fish are driven to battle ferocious river rapids, swimming upstream against the current to spawn in the same placid pools where they were born. The journey can be as long as 900 miles (up Idaho's Salmon River) and the fish often have to jump up small waterfalls to get to their mating grounds. Ironically, after this long trip and their ritual spawning, the salmon die.

Now with many of the rivers dammed, salmon use manmade fish ladders (that look more like steps) to get back to their streams. Many salmon don't make it upstream past the huge dams, a fact that has prompted government authorities to actually truck some back to their spawning grounds to procreate and then perish.

FISHING   For information on fishing in Washington, contact the **Washington Department of Fish and Wildlife** concerning shellfish, bottomfish, salmon, saltwater sportfish and freshwater game fish. Ask for the Department of Fish Management. ~ 600 Capitol Way North, Olympia, WA 98501; 360-902-2200; www.wa.gov/wdfw.

Fees and regulations vary, but licenses are required for both salt- and freshwater fishing throughout the state. They may be purchased at sporting-goods stores, bait-and-tackle shops and fishing lodges. You can also find leads on guides and charter services in these locations if you are interested in trying a kind of fishing that's new to you. Charter fishing is the most expensive way to go; party boats take a crowd, but are less expensive and usually great fun. On rivers, lakes and streams, guides can show you the best place to throw a hook or skim a fly. But beware Seattle urban streams, such as the industrial Duwamish, which have exceedingly high mercury levels.

> Seattle was built on seven hills, though only six remain: the seventh hill, Denny, was scraped off and dumped into Puget Sound.

In downtown Seattle, you can drop your line right into Elliott Bay at **Waterfront Park** (Piers 57–61). But for the real deal, head to Ballard, where the city's commercial fishing fleet is based (at Fisherman's Terminal) and sportfishing tours can be chartered. **Adventure Charters** offers full-day guided salmon-fishing trips year-round. Afternoon tours are offered in the summer, and all gear is provided. ~ 7001 Seaview Avenue Northwest, Shilshole Bay Marina; 206-789-8245, 800-789-0448; www.seattlesalmon charters.com.

North of Seattle, **All Seasons Charter Service** operates two boats for salmon or bottomfish. ~ Port of Edmonds; 425-743-9590.

BOATING, KAYAKING & CANOEING   With miles of coastline and island-dotted straits to explore, it's no wonder that boating is one of the most popular activities in Washington. Many of the best attractions in the state, including numerous pristine marine parks, are accessible only by water and have facilities set aside for boaters. Write, call or visit the **Washington State Parks and Recreation Commission** for a boater's guide to Washington. ~ P.O. Box 42650, Olympia, WA 98504; 360-902-8844; www.parks.wa.gov.

Several waterways are suitable for extended canoeing and kayaking trips. Seattle-area boathouses, in fact, rent craft for

paddling on Lake Union and Lake Washington. Whitewater rafting is popular outside the city on rivers like the Skykomish and
Tieton.

To rent a single or double kayak in Seattle, call **Northwest
Outdoor Center** to reserve ahead. Kayaking on Lake Union is very
popular, and it's not unusual for all the center's 100-plus kayaks
to be rented on a nice day. Classes and guided trips from one day
to five days are available. ~ 2100 Westlake Avenue North; 206-
281-9694; www.nwoc.com.

At Lake Union's **Center for Wooden Boats,** not only can you
rent one of several different kinds of classic wooden rowboats,
you can also learn a bit about their history. There are also several small sailboats for rent, but only experienced boaters can
rent one. The center is a nonprofit, hands-on museum that also
offers sailing instruction and other heritage maritime skills such
as knot-tying, navigation and boat building. ~ 1010 Valley Street;
206-382-2628; www.cwb.org.

On Lake Washington—at Bellevue's Enatai Beach Park and
at the mouth of the Cedar River in Renton—**Cascade Canoe &
Kayak Centers** rent water craft and offer instruction. ~ 3519
108th Avenue Southeast, Bellevue, and 1060 Nishiwaki Lane,
Renton; 425-430-0111; www.canoe-kayak.com.

Over on Vashon Island, the owners of **Puget Sound Kayak
Company** both rent and sell kayaks. They offer instruction as
well, and in summer months lead kayak tours around the island's
shores, a day-long odyssey that almost always includes heron,
eagle, sea lion and seal sightings. The island's inner harbor is safe
for novices; tricky tidal currents can make a foray out into the
main channels more risky. ~ P.O. Box 2957, Vashon, WA 98070;
206-463-2957; www.pugetsoundkayak.com.

Serious windsurfers head south to the Columbia River Gorge—
when they have the time for a four-hour drive. When they don't,
Lake Washington, Elliott Bay and **Quartermaster Harbor** on
Vashon Island are prime spots for windsurfing—there's almost
always a breeze, often fairly stiff, and the air temperature is usually above 40°.

The water is another story: Puget Sound boarding requires a
dry suit, and it's a good idea on Lake Washington as well in spring
and fall. Prime put-ins are beach parks on the east side of Lake

**WIND-
SURFING**

Washington, especially Houghton Beach Park in Kirkland, Luther Burbank Park on Mercer Island and Gene Coulon Beach Park in Renton. On Lake Sammamish, Lake Sammamish State Park at the south end of the lake, in Issaquah, is popular. On Elliott Bay, Alki Beach in West Seattle is best, although some boarders put in at Myrtle Edwards park in downtown Seattle.

The top rental and general information place in the Seattle area is **Urban Surf**, near the University of Washington on the shores of the Lake Washington Ship Canal. ~ 2100 North Northlake Way; 206-545-9463; www.urbansurf.com.

SWIMMING   Do people swim in Puget Sound? Sure—most of the time on a dare. The area's salt waters don't warm much past 50°, even in August. But a few sheltered bays get considerably warmer than that, and on a sunny summer day a dip can be stimulating. Any other place, any other time, requires caution, not to mention fool-hardiness—hypothermia can arrive in less than two minutes if you're unprepared. Puget Sound's many freshwater lakes are another story; by midsummer they've usually warmed near 70° and attract hordes of bathers on sunny days.

FRESHWATER   The best swimming beaches on Lake Washington are at Juanita Beach Park and Houghton Beach Park in Kirkland; Gene Coulon Park in Renton; and Seattle's Seward Park, Colman Park, Madrona Park, Madison Park and Matthews Beach Park. Lake Sammamish State Park is the place to go on Lake Sammamish in Issaquah; many smaller outlying lakes offer public beaches.

SALTWATER   There aren't any truly warm bays in the immediate Seattle area; hardy souls hit the saltchuck at Alki Beach in West Seattle when the sun burns bright in August.

Better swimming is found west and south, at Ostrich Bay in Bremerton; Quartermaster Harbor on Vashon; and Penrose Point State Park on the Key Peninsula west of Tacoma. It's not for wimps; even Puget Sound natives are prone to ask if you really did go in that water. But if you truly want to immerse yourself in a visit to Puget Sound, immerse yourself.

SCUBA DIVING   Puget Sound's hundreds of miles of shoreline, scores of public beaches, extraordinary marine life and numerous underwater parks offer considerable opportunities for diving. But the Sound's av-

Hey! The Water's Fine

Even if you're a diehard landlubber, do not fail to go sightseeing here by boat at least once. Simply put, if you leave Seattle without plying its surrounding waters your trip will be incomplete. So don't hesitate: Head to the downtown central waterfront and make some waves.

On a clear day you can see forever, or so it would seem aboard one of the **Washington State Ferries**. Headquartered at Colman Dock, the ferries make frequent departures to Bremerton and to Bainbridge Island, both across Puget Sound to the west. From deck you'll be treated to grand views of Mount Rainier, Mount Baker and the Olympics Range, and you may even catch a glimpse of an orca (killer) whale. To Bremerton, you can ride the car-and-passenger ferry, the passenger-only boat or the high-speed ferry for pedestrians. At Pier 50 next door, you can board a passenger-only ferry to Vashon Island. ~ Pier 52; 206-464-6400.

This is your captain speaking. That's just part of the show on **Argosy Cruises**, which offer at least two tours every day year-round. On the harbor spin you'll get grand mountain views and see boat traffic like you won't believe: freighters, tugboats, sailboats, ferries, you name it. The narrator spices up the trip. ~ Pier 55; 206-623-4252, 800-642-7816.

Argosy and **Gray Line Water Sightseeing** join forces for their "locks tour." The tour goes north to Shilshole Bay, eastward through the Hiram M. Chittenden Locks into the Lake Washington Ship Canal and then on to the south tip of Lake Union. You return to the waterfront by bus. Going through the locks is an experience in itself. And along the way you might even see salmon jumping. ~ Pier 55; 800-426-7505.

A narrated harbor tour is included in the **Tillicum Village-Blake Island** four-hour excursion to 475-acre Blake Island Marine State Park, which has tons of things to see and do. ~ Pier 55; 206-933-8600.

S.S. Virginia V is the last authentic operating steamboat of the legendary "Mosquito Fleet," the motley flotilla of steamboats that once carried foot passengers and cargo around Puget Sound before the coming of highways and autos. Recently renovated, the *Virginia V* is available for charter cruises. ~ 206-624-9119, tickets 206-223-2060; www.virginiav.org.

A quieter, more peaceful way to see Elliott Bay is **Emerald City Charters**' sailboat tours. Pick a daytime or sunset tour and float gracefully past motorboats, ferries and tankers from May to mid-October. ~ Pier 54; 206-624-3931, 800-831-3274; www.sailingseattle.com.

erage temperature of around 55° means wetsuits are de rigueur, and full scuba gear is the frequent choice of divers. Of the many exciting dive spots in the area, one standout is **Brackett's Landing Underwater Park** in Edmonds. Numerous dive shops with equipment rentals and lessons are located around major population centers. With 11 locations between them, **Underwater Sports Inc.** (800-252-7177; www.underwatersports.com) and **Lighthouse Diving Centers** (800-777-3483; www.lighthousediving.com) are convenient to most Seattle-area locations. They offer lessons and trips, and they rent and repair equipment.

On the eastside, **Northwest Sports Divers Inc.** rents any equipment you might need. This full-service scuba shop also offers scuba certification classes. Closed Sunday. ~ 8030 Northeast Bothell Way, Kenmore; 425-487-0624; www.nwsportsdivers.com. In Bellevue, **Silent World** has classes, gear and rentals. There are beach dives on Sunday, as well as some one- and two-day trips to the San Juans. Closed Sunday. ~ 13600 Northeast 20th Street; 425-747-8842; www.silent-world.com.

JOGGING   In a generally cool climate, with pastoral back roads on the outskirts of much of Seattle and Tacoma, and an extensive network of public trails and greenbelts, runners will find innumerable routes. Some of the better-known trails, such as Seattle's Burke-Gilman and Green Lake, are often quite crowded, especially on weekends and after work in the summer.

Seattle's Washington Park Arboretum is an exceptionally beautiful mid-city forest enclave, landscaped with hundreds of native and exotic shrubs and trees. Trails are numerous; a typical loop would comprise a 5K.

INLINE SKATING & SKATEBOARDING

The Seattle area boasts dozens of outdoor and indoor venues catering to skateboarders and inline skaters. The **Seattle Center SkatePark** (305 Harrison Street; 206-684-7200) and **Ballard Skate Park** (Northwest 57th Street and 22nd Avenue Northwest; 206-684-4093), both open from dawn to dusk, are just two of them. Otherwise, it takes about an hour to skate around Seattle's **Green Lake** on the paved multi-use trail. You can rent inline skates at **Gregg's Greenlake Cycle**. ~ 7007 Woodlawn Avenue Northeast; 206-523-1822; www.greggscycles.com.

Except when the occasional snowstorm closes them down, golf courses in the area are open year-round.

Jackson Golf Club is a public 18-hole course with a par 3. Though the course has a few hills, it isn't very challenging. ~ 1000 Northeast 135th Street, Seattle; 206-363-4747. Golf pro Fred Couples grew up at the Jefferson Park Golf Club, which has 18 holes with an executive par 3. You can rent carts and clubs, and you can see the lake and the city at some points. ~ 4101 Beacon Avenue South, Seattle; 206-762-4513. Bellevue Municipal Golf Course is one of the most active courses in the state, probably because it's a good walking course with moderate hills. This public course has 18 holes and cart rentals. ~ 5500 140th Avenue Northeast; 425-452-7250.

GOLF

Northwest precipitation practically turns tennis into an indoor sport. You'll have to call a few days in advance to reserve an indoor court at one of these public facilities.

It helps to mention that you're an out-of-town visitor when you call—at least six days in advance—to reserve one of the ten hardtop indoor courts at the Amy Yee Tennis Center. The center also has four public outdoor courts. Tennis pros are available for lessons by appointment. ~ 2000 Martin Luther King Jr. Way South; 206-684-4764. The City of Bellevue operates the public courts at Robinswood Tennis Center. There are four indoor and four lighted outdoor courts; call six days in advance (start dialing at 8:30 a.m.). Pros are available for lessons. Fee. ~ 2400 151st Place Southeast at Southeast 22nd Street; 425-452-7690.

TENNIS

Take off on a guided ride to the top of a mountain east of Seattle. One of the best places for a ride is Bridle Trails State Park in Bellevue. Crisscrossed with 28 miles of trails the park is thickly forested with evergreens, firs and cedar. Used mainly by local riders, the park has no rental mounts. On a clear day, you can see more than 100 miles atop Tiger Mountain near Issaquah. Tiger Mountain Outfitters will get you there in a three-hour trail ride that will let you see Mt. Rainier 65 miles away in the distance and possibly black bear, deer and cougar within several yards. Call for reservations. ~ 24508 Southeast 133rd Street, Issaquah; 425-392-5090.

RIDING STABLES

It's no surprise to learn that Seattle has earned a nod from *Bicycling* magazine as one of the top bicycling cities in the country.

BIKING

Bicycle programs are administered by state, city and county transportation agencies, which has resulted in a network of bicycle lanes and trails throughout the region, many of them convenient for visitor recreational use.

Helpful information, including bicycle route maps, is available from several agencies. The Washington Department of Transportation operates the **Bicycle Hotline** to request a route map and informative brochure. ~ P.O. Box 47393, Olympia, WA 98504; 360-705-7277. **The Seattle Bicycling Guide Map** is available from the Seattle Transportation Department and can usually be found in bike stores and public libraries. ~ 600 4th Avenue, Room 708, Seattle, WA 98104; 206-684-7583. There's also a **King County Bicycling Guide Map** that may be downloaded online. ~ www.metrokc.gov/bike.htm. The **Cascade Bicycle Club** serves as an all-purpose club, for riders of all skill levels. The club operates a hotline, which provides general information about bicycling in the area and club-sponsored weekend rides. ~ 7400 Sandpoint Way Northeast; 206-522-2453.

The three-mile loop around **Green Lake**, north of the Ship Canal, is Seattle's most leisurely and rich in recreational detours. Although the central city is fairly hilly, especially if you're biking in an east– west direction, there are trails within Seattle that run near the water and on lower and flatter terrain that are ideal for recreational bicyclists. The most famous is the multi-use **Burke-Gilman Trail**, popular with bikers, walkers and joggers. It's flat, paved and, following an old railroad right of way, it extends from Gas Works Park on Lake Union, through the university campus, past lovely neighborhoods next to Lake Washington and on to Kenmore. In Kenmore, it links up with the **Sammamish River Trail**, which winds through Woodinville (and its wineries) and on to suburban Redmond. It's a lovely city-to-farmlands tour.

In West Seattle, the **Alki Bike Route** (6 miles) offers miles of shoreline pedaling—half on separated bike paths—from Seacrest Park to Lincoln Park. Besides changing views of the city and Puget Sound, you should have great views of the Olympic Peninsula mountains.

Bike Rentals   For bike rentals, repairs, new bikes and accessories in Seattle, try **Gregg's Greenlake Cycle**. ~ 7007 Woodlawn Avenue Northeast; 206-523-1822; www.greggscycles.com. **The Bicycle Center of Seattle,** near the Burke-Gilman Trail, has mountain bikes, hybrids and tandems. ~ 4529 Sand Point Way Northeast; 206-523-8300; www.bicyclecenterseattle.com. The place to buy and repair a bike on Alki Beach is the **Alki Bike & Board Company**. ~ 2606 California Avenue Southwest; 206-938-3322; www.alkibikeandboard.com.

Throughout the greater Seattle area, you'll find parks that offer at least a few miles of hiking trail through forest or along a stream or beach. One great park is Discovery Park in Seattle. All distances listed are one way unless otherwise noted.

HIKING

For short strolls in downtown Seattle, try **Freeway Park** and the grounds of the adjoining Washington State Convention Center (.5 mile) and **Myrtle Edwards** and **Elliott Bay parks** (1.25 miles) at the north end of the downtown waterfront. Within a few miles of downtown, the **Burke-Gilman Trail** (12 miles) extends from Gas Works Park in Seattle to Logboom Park in Kenmore and on to Redmond. And just across Elliott Bay, West Seattle offers about four miles of public shoreline to walk around Duwamish Head and Alki Point.

Further from the city center, the **Shell Creek Nature Trail** (.5 mile), in Edmonds' Yost Park at 96th Avenue West and Bowdoin Way, is an easy walk along a stream. Contact Edmonds Parks and Recreation for a guide to the area north of Seattle. ~ Edmonds Parks Department: 700 Main Street; 425-771-0227. In the southern suburbs, the trail along **Big Soos Creek** (4.5 miles), now protected in two parks, is an inviting ramble on a blacktop path next to one of the few wetland streams still in public ownership hereabouts. The trail winds from Kent-Kangley Road to Gary Grant Park. Follow signs off Route 516 in Kent at 150th Avenue Southeast.

In the Cascade foothills about 15 miles east of Seattle, three peaks nicknamed the "Issaquah Alps" (King County's Cougar

AUTHOR FAVORITE

At least once a month, regardless of season, I make time for a bike ride along the **Burke-Gilman Trail** (see above). Full of walkers, joggers, skaters and bike commuters, this well-used corridor offers both urban and wooded stretches, highlighting why the Emerald City is one of the nation's top cycling cities.

Mountain Regional Wildland Park, Squak Mountain State Park and Tiger Mountain State Forest) south of Issaquah include miles and miles of trail and road open to hikers year-round. **Cougar Mountain Regional Wildland Park** (206-296-4145) is the best bet for visitors with resident deer, porcupines, bobcats, coyotes, black bears and four square miles of untouched land with trails. Call for trail maps. Another good resource is the **Issaquah Alps Trails Club** (www.issaquahalps.org), which publishes several hiking guidebooks and offers excursions, group hikes and general hiking information. One representative hike is the **West Tiger 3, 2, 1 Trail** (8–10 miles), which meanders to an elevation of 3000 feet at the summit of West Tiger 3 for stunning aerial views. Leave Route 90 at the High Point exit (the first exit east of Issaquah) and you will see the small parking lot where the trailhead is located.

WINTER SPORTS

There's no skiing in Seattle itself, of course, except for spontaneous athleticism on the rare occasion of sufficient winter snow on city hills. But there are a half-dozen ski resorts within a two-hour drive of downtown, including the four mid-size areas that comprise **The Summit at Snoqualmie**, just 50 miles east on Route 90. ~ P.O. Box 1068, Snoqualmie Pass, WA 98068; 425-434-7669 or 206-236-1600; www.summit-at-snoqualmie.com. For full information on skiing in Washington, contact the **Pacific Northwest Ski Areas Association**. ~ P.O. Box 1720, Hood River, OR 97031; 541-386-9600; www.skiindustry.com/pnsaa.

Backcountry areas are popular among cross-country skiers, who purchase an annual U.S. Forest Service Sno-Park Permit ($21) and take off on national forest trails. For information, contact the **Outdoor Recreation Information Center**. ~ REI Building, 222 Yale Avenue North, Seattle; 206-470-4060.

Except during December, when the Seattle Center's Fisher Pavilion is converted to an ice-skating rink for Winterfest (see "Calendar of Events" in Chapter One), those who wear blades on their shoes have two options. North of Seattle, the **Highland Ice Arena** is open year-round. ~ 18005 Aurora Avenue North, Shoreline; 206-546-2431; www.highlandice.com. Southeast of Seattle, the **Kent Valley Ice Centre** has year-round skating, figure-skating instruction, and hockey leagues. ~ 6015 South 240th Street, Kent; 253-850-2400; www.familynightout.com.

FOUR

Downtown Seattle

Seattle looks irresistible from the air. You'll be captivated by deep bays, busy harbors, gleaming skyscrapers, parks stretching for miles and hillside neighborhoods where waterskiing begins from the backyard. Downtown Seattle, which reaches from the lofty heights of the Space Needle to the Pioneer Square underground and from the bustling waterfront to interstate Route 5, is compact enough for walkers to tour on foot, but is also readily explored by monorail, bus, boat and bike.

If you're energetic, you can see the highlights of downtown on one grand loop tour. Or you can sample smaller chunks on successive days. Since downtown is spread along a relatively narrow north–south axis, you can walk from one end to the other, then return by public transit via buses in the Metro Transit Tunnel or aboard the Waterfront Streetcar trolleys, each of which have stations in both Pioneer Square and the International District. The Monorail also runs north–south between Westlake Center and Seattle Center.

SIGHTS

A good place to orient yourself is the **Seattle-King County Visitor Information Center**. Closed Sunday. ~ Level 1, Galleria, 800 Convention Place; 206-461-5840, fax 206-461-8304; www.see seattle.org, e-mail visinfo@seeseattle.org.

But begin your city tour at **Pioneer Square** and its "old underground," which remains one of Seattle's major fascinations. It was at this location that Seattle's first business district began. In 1889, a fire burned the woodframe city to the ground. The story of how the city rebuilt out of the ashes of the Great Fire remains intriguing to visitors and locals alike.

To learn exactly how the underground was created after the new city arose, then was forgotten, then rediscovered, you really need to take the one-and-a-half-hour **Underground Tour**. Several of these subterranean pilgrimages are offered daily to the dark and cobwebby bowels of the underground—actually the street-level floors of buildings that were sealed off and fell into disuse when streets and sidewalks were elevated shortly after Pioneer Square was rebuilt (in fire-resistant brick instead of wood). Admission (reservations recommended). ~ 608 1st Avenue; 206-682-4646, fax 206-682-1511; www.undergroundtour.com.

Above ground, in sunshine and fresh air, you can stroll through 91 acres of mostly century-old architecture in the historic district (maps and directories to district businesses are available in most shops). Notable architecture includes gems like the **Grand Central Building** (1st Avenue South and South Main Street), **Merrill Place** (1st Avenue South and South Jackson Street), the **Maynard Building** (1st Avenue South and South Washington Street), and the **Mutual Life and Pioneer buildings** (1st Avenue and Yesler Way). The 1909 cast-iron **Pergola** in Pioneer Square Park was rebuilt after a 2001 semi-truck accident; other buildings were damaged by the Ash Wednesday earthquake that spring. More than 30 art galleries are located in the Pioneer Square area. Here you can shop for American Indian art, handicrafts, paintings and pottery.

The new city boomed during the Alaska Gold Rush. For a look back at those extraordinary times, stop by the Seattle branch of the **Klondike Gold Rush National Historical Park**, where you can see gold-panning demonstrations, a collection of artifacts, films and other memorabilia. ~ 117 South Main Street near Occidental Park; 206-553-7220, fax 206-553-0614; www.nps.gov/klse.

The main pedestrian artery is **Occidental Mall and Park**, a tree-lined, cobbled promenade running south from Yesler Way to South Jackson Street allowing pleasant ambling between rows of shops and galleries (don't miss the oasis of **Waterfall Park** off Occidental on South Main Street).

For an overview of the whole district, ride the rattling old manually operated elevator to the observation level of the 42-story **Smith Tower**, the tallest building west of the Mississippi River when it was built in 1914. (It remained Seattle's tallest until 1969.) Closed weekdays from November through March. ~ 2nd Avenue and Yesler Way; 206-682-9393, fax 206-622-9357.

Follow 1st Avenue south from the Pioneer Square neighborhood and you'll enter **LoDo**, or "Lower Downtown," a longstanding industrial zone now better known as home to Seattle's professional football and baseball franchises. The Seattle Sea-hawks of the National Football League play in **Seahawks Stadium,** which opened in 2002 on the ruins of the old concrete-dome Kingdome, razed in 2000. The Seattle Mariners of baseball's American League play at **Safeco Field,** notable for its retractable roof. Between the two is the **Stadium Exhibition Center,** a major venue for trade shows and exhibitions.

Sharp ethnic diversity has always marked the **International District,** next door to Pioneer Square to the southeast. Pass the 1906 **King Street Station** (2nd Avenue South and South Jackson

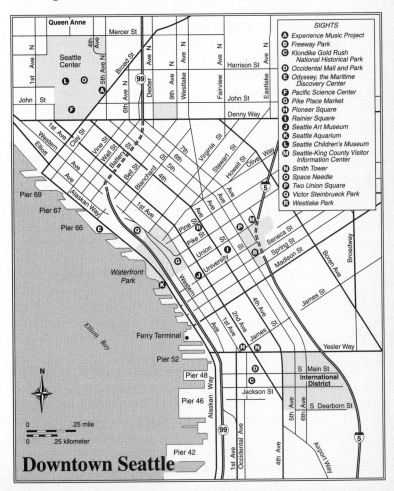

SIGHTS
- Ⓐ Experience Music Project
- Ⓑ Freeway Park
- Ⓒ Klondike Gold Rush National Historical Park
- Ⓓ Occidental Mall and Park
- Ⓔ Odyssey, the Maritime Discovery Center
- Ⓕ Pacific Science Center
- Ⓖ Pike Place Market
- Ⓗ Pioneer Square
- Ⓘ Rainier Square
- Ⓙ Seattle Art Museum
- Ⓚ Seattle Aquarium
- Ⓛ Seattle Children's Museum
- Ⓜ Seattle-King County Visitor Information Center
- Ⓝ Smith Tower
- Ⓞ Space Needle
- Ⓟ Two Union Square
- Ⓠ Victor Steinbrueck Park
- Ⓡ Westlake Park

Downtown Seattle

Street), whose striking clock tower still greets arriving passenger trains, to enter the polyglot community that emerged on the southern fringes of old Seattle. The International District has always mixed its Asian cultures and continues doing so today, setting it apart from the homogeneous Chinatowns of San Francisco and Vancouver. ~ Yesler Way to South Dearborn Street, 4th Avenue South to Route 5.

Chinese began settling here in the 1860s, Japanese in the 1890s, and today the "I.D.," as it's commonly known, is also home to Koreans, Filipinos, Thais, Vietnamese, Laotians and Cambodians. For all its diversity, the district clearly lacks the economic vitality, bustling street life and polished tourist appeal of other major Chinatowns. Yet some find the International District all the more genuine for its unhurried, even seedy, ambience.

A variety of mom-and-pop enterprises predominates in the I.D. —specialty-food and grocery stores, herbal-medicine shops, dim sum palaces and fortune-cookie factories. You're welcome to poke in for a look at how cookies, noodles, egg rolls and won ton wrappers are made at the **Tsue Chong Company**. Closed Sunday. ~ 801 South King Street; 206-623-0801, fax 206-382-2688.

The district's single major retail store is **Uwajimaya**; it's not only the largest Japanese grocery and gift store in the Northwest but also a worthwhile experience of Asian culture even if you're not shopping. ~ 600 5th Avenue South; 206-624-6248, fax 206-405-2996; www.uwajimaya.com.

Wing Luke Asian Museum offers a well-rounded look at the Northwest's Asian Pacific history and culture, representing ten groups of Asian Pacific immigrants. Presentations include historical photography and social commentary on the Asian-American experience. You may also see paintings, ceramics, prints, sculpture and other art. Closed Monday. Admission. ~ 407 7th Avenue South; 206-623-5124, fax 206-623-4559; www.wingluke.com, e-mail folks@wingluke.org.

The **Nippon Kan Theatre** is the centerpiece of the **Kobe Park Building National Historical Site** and hosts occasional dramas and other cultural presentations. The park and community gardens adjacent to it offer pleasant strolling. ~ 628 South Washington Street; 206-224-0181, fax 206-682-4348.

Hing Hay Park is the scene of frequent festivals—exhibitions of Japanese martial arts, Chinese folk dances, Vietnamese food fairs, Korean music and the like. ~ South King Street and May-nard Avenue South.

The old **waterfront**, which begins at the western edge of Pioneer Square, remains one of the most colorful quarters of the city and what many consider Seattle's liveliest "people place." On sunny summer days, it is the most popular tourist draw in the city. The waterfront grows more interesting by the year, a beguiling jumble of fish bars and excursion-boat docks, ferries and fire-boats, import emporiums and nautical shops, sway-backed old piers and barnacle-encrusted pilings that creak in the wash of wakes.

Hing Hay Park's colorful pavilion, built in 1975, was donated to the city by Taipei, Taiwan.

The action's concentrated between Piers 48 and 60, and again around Pier 70. Poking around by foot remains the favorite way to explore, but some folks prefer to hopscotch to specific sites aboard the **Waterfront Streetcar**, which runs from the International District to Pier 70. You also can climb into a horse-drawn carriage near Pier 60 for a narrated tour. Still another way to do it is via boat (see "Outdoor Adventures" in Chapter Two). Here's a sampler of attractions: As you stroll south to north, you'll encounter a harbor-watch facility, a dozen historical plaques that trace major events, a public boat landing, the state-ferry terminal at Colman Dock and the waterfront fire station whose fireboats occasionally put on impressive, fountainlike displays on summer weekends. Ye Olde Curiosity Shop houses a collection of odd goods from around the world, Ivar's (see Chapter Six) is the city's most famous fish bar, and cavernous shopping arcades include pier-end restaurants, outdoor picnic areas and public fishing. **Water-front Park** is a crescent-shaped retreat from commercialism pre-senting sweeping views over the harbor.

The **Seattle Aquarium** allows you to descend to an underwater viewing dome for up-close looks at scores of Puget Sound fish. Other exhibits include a sea otter pool, a coral reef tank teeming with sharks, and a giant Pacific octopus on an all-he-can-eat crab diet in an attempt to beat the size record set by the aquarium's last giant octopus, which reached 78 pounds before being released into the ocean in 2000 so he could mate. Salmon are born at the aquarium and allowed to migrate to the open sea, returning later to spawn. Admission. ~ Pier 59 at Pike Street; 206-386-4320, fax 206-386-4328; www.seattleaquarium.org.

Next to the aquarium is the **IMAX Dome**, whose highly recommended program features 70mm films such as the 1980 Academy Award–nominated *Eruption of Mt. St. Helens*. Admission. ~ Pier 59; 206-622-1868; www.seattleimaxdome.com, e-mail info @seattleimaxdome.com.

Pier 62/63 is a public park ten months of the year where you can often see anglers jigging for squid at high tide. During July and August, the pier becomes a world-class outdoor theater, with evening concerts b y pop, rock and blues music acts such as Lyle Lovett and Earth, Wind and Fire. The setting is unparalleled, with the Olympic Mountains across the sound lit pink by the summer sunset. Admission. ~ Summer Nights at the Pier, 206-281-8111; www.onereel.org.

Just a bit north is the Port of Seattle's **Pier 66**, the Bell Street Pier. With a small-craft marina, three restaurants, a museum, a conference center and a skybridge leading up to the booming Belltown shopping/restaurant district along 1st Avenue, this recent development has become a popular stop for travelers.

At Pier 66 on the waterfront, **Odyssey, the Maritime Discovery Center** contains four galleries of high-tech interactive exhibits for kids and adults that reveal how the industrial waterfront works, focusing on fishing, trade and boating. Children can steer a container ship into port, load a 20-ton cargo container onto a ship, and explore a scaled-down fishing boat. Other displays explain fishery management, the global economy, marine safety and environmental preservation. Closed Monday. Admission. ~ 2205

sights

AUTHOR FAVORITE

When I want to surprise and amaze my visitors, I take them to **Ye Olde Curiosity Shop**, a Seattle landmark that dates back to 1899. A combination souvenir shop and museum, it draws crowds with odd displays such as a Siamese twin calf, rare Eskimo walrus-tusk carvings, and one of the world's largest private collections of mummies (they all have names) and shrunken heads. You'll also find American Indian totem poles and masks, Russian stacking dolls, lacquerware and Ukrainian eggs, as well as antique coin-operated games that offer an easy way to get rid of pocket change. ~ 1001 Alaskan Way, Pier 54; 206-682-5844; www.ye oldecuriosityshop.com.

Alaskan Way; 206-374-4000, fax 206-374-4002; www.ody.org, e-mail education@ody.org.

If you continue north on the waterfront, past the handsome port headquarters building, you reach **Myrtle Edwards Park**, at the end of Alaskan Way, a greenbelt that offers downtown Seattle's best jogging route.

But you may instead want to backtrack toward Pier 59 and look for the Pike Hillclimb, on the east side of Alaskan Way. It leads up—almost straight up, 155 step's worth—past several decent restaurants and shops to the famed **Pike Place Market**. (There's an elevator for the walk-weary. You can also reach the north end of the Market from a stairway/elevator complex opposite the Pier 62/63 public wharf.) You'll also pass some piers whose sheds have been leveled to provide public access, the last vestiges of working waterfront on the central harbor—fish-company docks and such—as well as the Port of Seattle headquarters.

The venerable market, born in 1907, has proved itself one of the city's renewable treasures. Saved from the wrecking ball by citizen action in the early '70s, the market was later revitalized through long-term renovation. Today, the nine-acre **Pike Place Market National Historic District** and the surrounding neighborhood are in many respects better than ever. The main historic market now offers hundreds of different products in hundreds of categories, from alpaca clothing to different types of zucchini. In all, this is a public market experience unparalleled in the nation! To learn more, call for more information or stop at the Info Booth at 1st Avenue and Pike Street. ~ Virginia Street to just south of Pike Street, 1st to Western avenues; 206-682-7453, fax 206-625-0646; www.pikeplacemarket.org.

There are so many ways to enjoy the market that we can scarcely begin to list them. Come early for breakfast and wake up with the market (at least a dozen cafés open early). Come at noon for the ultimate experience of marketplace clamor amid legions of jostling shoppers, vendors hawking salmon and truck-farm produce, and street musicians vying for your contributions. Come to explore the market's lower level, often missed by tourists, a warrenlike collection of secondhand treasures, old books, magazines, posters and vintage clothing. Come to shop for the largest collection of handmade merchandise in the Northwest on hand-

WALKING TOUR
Seattle's Waterfront

Nowhere is the distinctive character of Seattle more visible than along the waterfront between Piers 52 and 70 and the adjacent Pike Place Market. (Of course, the waterfront contains many more piers south of this area, but they are used for industrial shipping and are inaccessible on foot. The best way to get a look is from a harbor tour boat.) This walking tour covers about two and a half miles. Although it can be completed in less than two hours, along the way you'll find enough points of interest to fill a whole day.

PIKE PLACE MARKET   Start at Pike Place Market, near the intersection of Pike Street and 1st Avenue on a steep hillside above the waterfront. (If you must park in this area, you're most likely to find a space beneath the Alaskan Way Viaduct downhill from the market. A better plan for drivers, though, is to park at one of the big lots around the Seattle Center and ride the monorail downtown. It lets you off just four blocks from the market.) On the street level are more than 100 food vendors' stalls where you'll find plenty of fresh fruits and veggies to snack on while you wander, free samples of tasty edible souvenirs, and fishmongers hawking fresh local seafood such as giant geoduck (pronounced "gooey duck") clams, along with arts-and-crafts stands. The lower level has small eateries and shops that sell exotica imported from such far-off lands as Egypt and India.

HARBOR STEPS PARK   From the south end of Pike Place Market, head south a short distance to Harbor Steps Park. (Here you're practically in front of the **Seattle Art Museum** (page 62); if time permits, it's well worth a visit either now or on the way back.) Walk down the broad 16,000-square-foot steps to Western Avenue. The waterfront promenade is just across the avenue. The steps take you down to Pier 59, site of the **Seattle Aquarium** (page 57) and the **IMAX Dome** (page 58). The aquarium is a must-see stop, where attractions include jellyfish, mi-

craft tables at the market's north end. Come to browse all the "nonproduce" merchandise surrounding the main market—wines, exotic imported foods, French kitchenware, jewelry and avant-garde fashions.

Among the market's many virtues, perhaps the best is that it is a real-life urban amenity popular with Seattleites every bit as much as visitors. What downtown workers do lends itself to travel itineraries equally well: Walk to the market late morning and enjoy gratory salmon and the largest octopus in captivity. The aquarium is in the middle of the public waterfront area.

PIERS 62–70   If you walk north, you'll pass **Pier 62/63**, a bare-wood park serving as a 4000-seat municipal concert venue that has hosted such performers as Lyle Lovett, Jonny Lang, Judy Collins and Los Lobos. Between Anthony's Pier 66 Restaurant and the Edgewater Inn on Pier 67 is **Odyssey, the Maritime Discovery Center** (page 58). Beyond the Edgewater Inn is the departure pier for the **Victoria Clipper** (high-speed ferry service to Victoria, B.C.; Pier 69). At the northern end of the waterfront is **Pier 70**, now home to offices and two restaurants but better known as the filming site for MTV's "The Real World: Seattle."

PIERS 55–57   If you walk south from the aquarium, you'll pass a large dining and shopping complex at **Pier 57**, where the central attraction for kids is a vintage carousel. **Pier 55** is the departure point for tour boats to **Tillicum Village** (206-933-8600, 800-426-1205), a replica Salish Indian village on a small island where trips include a traditional grilled salmon buffet. The pier is also home to **Argosy Cruises** (206-623-1445), offering daily boat tours of Seattle Harbor.

PIER 54   Pier 54 is the site of two venerable Seattle landmarks. **Ivar's Fish Bar** (206-467-8063), the original home of the clams and fish-and-chips restaurant that now has locations all over the Northwest, was started in 1938 by the late Ivar Haglund while he was director of Seattle's first aquarium next door. **Ye Olde Curiosity Shop** (page 58) is a combination souvenir shop and free museum.

PIER 52   Pier 52 is the terminal for the **Washington State Ferries** that run frequently to Bremerton, Bainbridge Island and Vashon Island. Taking any of these ferries as a foot passenger makes for a relaxing, low-cost scenic cruise and an introduction to the ferry system that will serve you well as you travel to other parts of the Puget Sound area.

PIONEER SQUARE   From the ferry terminal, you can either return the way you came, climbing back up the Harbor Steps, or go a few more blocks south to Pioneer Square, returning to central downtown along 2nd Avenue with its towering skyscrapers.

the atmosphere a few minutes. You could buy a coffee drink at Starbucks and listen to the street musicians invariably set up out front —perhaps the King Jesus Disciples, four excellent gospel singers who once prowled downtown streets as transients. Yes, this is the original **Starbucks** store, the very first of nearly 4000 around the world; it opened in 1971. ~ 1912 Pike Place; 206-448-8762.

After you've loaded up on coffee and tasty treats from the food vendors, wander down to **Victor Steinbrueck Park**, a small plaza   ◀ HIDDEN at the north end of Pike Place, overlooking Elliott Bay and the Olympics. On sunny days the crowd here ranges from backpacking European youths to bankers to religious proselytizers to Japanese schoolgirls on tour, holding hands. There's no better place to gain an appreciation of Seattle's cultural diversity. On your way back to your hotel, pick up some gifts to take home, or maybe just a loaf of bread for dinner. ~ Pike Place and Western Avenue.

Three blocks south of Pike Place Market is the **Seattle Art Museum,** designed by the husband/wife architectural team of Robert Venturi and Denise Scott. The five-story, limestone-faced building highlighted with terra-cotta and marble has quickly become a regional, postmodern landmark. You'll enter the museum via a grand staircase, but to see the collections, you'll have to ascend by elevator to the galleries. Known for its Northwest Coast American Indian, Asian and African art, the museum also features Meso-American, modern and contemporary art, photography and European masters. Do not miss the superb collection of African masks. Closed Monday. Admission. ~ 100 University Street; 206-654-3100, fax 206-654-3135; www.seattleartmuseum.org.

Located across the street from the Seattle Art Museum, the Seattle Symphony's massive **Benaroya Hall** gives the symphony its own dedicated concert facility after years of sharing space at Seattle Center with the opera and ballet. The grounds include a memorial garden dedicated to Washington residents who died in military conflicts from World War II to the present. ~ 200 University Street; 206-215-4700, fax 206-215-4701; www.seattle symphony.org, e-mail info@seattlesymphony.org.

If you walk east up Pine Street from the Market, you'll find yourself in the heart of Seattle's retail shopping district, which has undergone a remarkable rejuvenation. It's a delightful place to stroll whether you're intent on shopping or not. Major down-

SLIPPERY SLOPE

Yesler Way, located in the heart of the Pioneer Square area, originated as the steep "Skid Road" for logs cut on the hillsides above the harbor. They were skidded downhill to Henry Yesler's waterfront mill, then loaded onto boats and shipped to growing cities like San Francisco. Later, as the district declined, Yesler Way attracted a variety of derelicts and became the prototype for every big city's bowery, alias "skid row."

town hotels are clustered in the retail core, allowing easy walks in any direction. Here's one way to sightsee:

Westlake Center is an enormously popular, multilevel shopping arcade, a people place offering espresso bars, flower vendors, handicrafts and access to what's been heralded as downtown's "new underground." The marbled, well-lighted, below-street-level arcades were created as part of the city's new downtown transit tunnel. Metro buses (propelled electrically while underground) rumble by on the lowest level. Just above it are mezzanines full of public art, with vendors and shops, and underground access to a string of department stores. ~ 4th Avenue and Pine Street; 206-467-3044; www.westlakecenter.com. It faces upon triangular **Westlake Park,** which offers a "water wall" against street noise, a leafy copse of trees and an intriguing pattern of bricks that replicate a Salish Indian basket-weave design best observed from the terraces on the adjoining Westlake Center.

Walk south on 4th Avenue a few blocks to **Rainier Square,** between 4th and 5th avenues and University and Union streets, and discover a burgeoning underground of upscale enterprises. Follow its passageways eastward past a bakery, restaurants and access to the venerable and fabulously ornate **5th Avenue Theatre,** which opened in 1926 as a vaudeville theater. Today it hosts touring Broadway musicals. Continue east, up an escalator to the main plaza of the **Two Union Square** building and up to Freeway Park.

The nation's first major park to be built over a freeway, **Freeway Park** offers five-plus acres of lawns, gardens and fountains. Its many waterfalls and pools create a splashy, burbling sound barrier to city noise. Beds of summer-blooming flowers, tall evergreens and leafy deciduous trees create a genuine park feeling, inspiring picnics by office workers on their noon-hour break. Amble north through the park, and take a short detour beneath a street overpass toward University Street. (Steps next to more waterfalls zigzag up to Capitol Hill and dramatic views of city architecture.) ~ 6th Avenue and Seneca Street.

Continue north as the park merges with similarly landscaped grounds of the **Washington State Convention and Trade Center,** which offers occasional exhibits. Maps and information are on hand at the Visitor Information Center (206-461-5840, fax 206-461-8304), located on the first level of the Convention Center.

~ 800 Convention Place; 206-694-5000, fax 206-694-5399; www.wsctc.com, e-mail info@wsctc.com.

Head west through linking landscaping, back through Two Union Square. Cross 6th Avenue and enter the **US Bank Centre**, located on the corner of Union Street. This handsome building's lower levels contain the City Centre mall, featuring upscale shops and a theater complex, bold sculptures and stunning exhibits of colorful art glass. Wander and admire for a bit, stop for a meal or an espresso, then continue by leaving the building at the 5th Avenue and Pike Street exit. Cross 5th Avenue past what used to be the striking Coliseum Theater, now renovated and occupied by Banana Republic. Head west on Pike Street to 4th Avenue and turn right to enter Westlake Park, where you began this shopping district walk.

LODGING   Lodgings vary widely in style and price throughout the Seattle area. Downtown, there's a thick cluster of expensive luxury hotels interspersed with a few at moderate and even budget rates.

HIDDEN ►   The **Pioneer Square Hotel**, a Best Western property, combines a prime location with Four-Diamond historic charm. The essence of comfort is captured here by turn-of-the-20th-century decor and remarkably quiet rooms. Rates are quite reasonable by downtown standards. The Pioneer Square Historic District surrounding the hotel is a haven for fascinating restaurants, taverns, art galleries, shops and more. The ferry terminal and Seattle Art Museum are also within a few blocks. ~ 77 Yesler Way; 206-340-1234, 800-800-5514, fax 206-467-0707; www.pioneersquare.com, e-mail info@pioneersquare.com. DELUXE TO ULTRA-DELUXE.

Tucked into an office-and-apartment complex opposite the Seattle Art Museum is the **Inn at the Harbor Steps**, a charming 25-room boutique hotel. A quiet mid-town oasis, it offers garden views and contemporary furnishings, along with wet bars and fireplaces (in all but five rooms). Rates includes a full breakfast and evening wine. ~ 1221 1st Avenue; 206-748-0973, 888-728-8910, fax 206-748-0533; www.foursisters.com/inns/innatharborsteps. DELUXE.

Hostelling International—Seattle is a low-priced establishment on the edge of Pike Place Market. In addition to 204 beds—most of them bunk beds in dormitories, but including five private rooms for two—the bright, clean hostel has a kitchen, dining room, lounge, TV room and small library. Also available are bike storage and laundry facilities. ~ 84 Union Street; 206-622-5443, 888-622-5443, fax 206-682-2179; www.hiseattle.org, e-mail reserve@hiseattle.org. BUDGET.

The **Alexis Hotel** is an elegant little haven two blocks from the waterfront and close to downtown stores and business centers. The 109 rooms have soft colors and contemporary furnishings mixed with a few antiques, all done in good taste. Some of the roomy suites have fireplaces. The service in this renovated historic hotel is unmatched elsewhere. ~ 1007 1st Avenue; 206-624-4844, 800-426-7033, fax 206-621-9009; www.alexishotel. com. ULTRA-DELUXE.

The downtown location for the **Green Tortoise Hostel** is convenient to most central-Seattle attractions—among them Pike Place Market, just a block away. With functional private and dorm rooms, 24-hour check-in, a common room and a fully equipped kitchen, it's much like a traditional hostel, with one extra advantage: a free breakfast. Many guest services, such as tours and discounts at local clubs, pubs and restaurants, add value as well. ~ 1525 2nd Avenue; 206-340-1222, 888-424-6783, fax 206-623-3207; www.greentortoise.net, e-mail info@greentortoise. net. BUDGET.

◄ HIDDEN

Hotel Monaco offers stylish, upscale accommodations in 189 funky, plush rooms and suites. The grand high-ceilinged lobby has columns and pilasters and a white stucco fireplace spotlighted by azure hues. Make sure to take advantage of their in-room pet goldfish adoption program. ~ 1101 4th Avenue; 206-621-1770, 800-945-2240, fax 206-624-0060; www.monaco-seattle.com. ULTRA-DELUXE.

MARKETPLACE RETREAT

A retreat from the throngs in Pike Place Market is **Inn at the Market**. The hotel, several shops and a restaurant are centered by a brick courtyard with a 50-year-old cherry tree. Light and airy and furnished in French country style, the 70-room inn is one of Seattle's best. Rooms have views of the city, courtyard or water. ~ 86 Pine Street; 206-443-3600, 800-446-4484, fax 206-448-0631; www.innatthemarket.com, e-mail info@innatthe market.com. ULTRA-DELUXE.

Considered a luxury hotel in the 1930s, the **Pacific Plaza Hotel** is now a dignified, quiet downtown classic with 157 rooms. Though updated, it hasn't lost its old-fashioned flavor, with windows that open, ceiling fans and traditional furniture in rather small rooms. The concierge is very helpful. ~ 400 Spring Street; 206-623-3900, 800-426-1165, fax 206-623-2059; www.pacificplaza hotel.com, e-mail reservations@pacificplazahotel.com. MODERATE TO DELUXE.

If Seattle has a haven for the black-on-black dot-com set, the **W Seattle Hotel** is it. The chic hotel has an elegant nightclub ambience that extends from its cocktail lounge to the outstanding Earth and Ocean restaurant. Streamlined, ultramodern decor in the 417 guest rooms (on 26 stories) includes unique water sculptures, 27-inch TVs, and CD and video players. Depending upon your traveling companion, ask about the "pet amenity program" or look in the honor bar for an "intimacy kit." ~ 1112 4th Avenue; 206-264-6000, 877-946-8357, fax 206-264-6100; www. whotels.com. ULTRA-DELUXE.

One of Seattle's historic landmarks, **The Fairmont Four Seasons Olympic Hotel** is the epitome of elegance and style, worth a peek whether you stay here or not. When the hotel opened in 1924, it was the ultimate in fine lodgings of the day. The modified Italian Renaissance brick building, on a prime downtown site owned by the University of Washington, was filled with antique mirrors, marble, Italian and Spanish oil jars and bronze statuary. Terrazzo floors were laid by Italian work-

AUTHOR FAVORITE

When money's no object, my favorite Seattle lodging choice is the **Hotel Edgewater**. It has changed completely since the days when the Beatles used to fish for sand sharks from the windows, but the location—directly on the waterfront—is still hard to beat. The property began as a top-flight hotel on Pier 67, built in the 1960s for the World's Fair. It later slid into decay and was renovated in "mountain lodge" style—meaning stone fireplaces and natural-log furniture in the rooms. Half of the 238 rooms and suites have stunning views of Elliott Bay, West Seattle and the Olympic Peninsula. Rooms are comfortable, and the staff is accommodating. The restaurant has a fine water view. ~ 2411 Alaskan Way; 206-728-7000, 800-624-0670, fax 206-441-4119; www.edgewaterhotel.com, e-mail reserva tions@edgewaterhotel.com. ULTRA-DELUXE.

ers brought to Seattle for the project. The proud Washington State Hotel Association labeled its metropolitan member "a bit of New York transplanted to the Pacific Northwest." For years, the Olympic was the preferred site for social events, banquets, weddings and debutante balls. With time its elegance faded, but today the Four Seasons Olympic is again operating as the queen of hotels in the Pacific Northwest. ~ 411 University Street; 206-621-1700, 800-363-5022, fax 206-682-9633; www.fairmont. com. ULTRA-DELUXE.

The **Hotel Vintage Park** is a refurbished classic, with 126 upscale rooms and an excellent Italian restaurant. It offers luxury hotel amenities such as terry-cloth robes, fully stocked honor bars and soundproofed double-pane windows. The hotel provides a nightly hosted wine hour by the wood-burning fireplace in its lobby. ~ 1100 5th Avenue; 206-624-8000, 800-624-4433, fax 206-623-0568; www.hotelvintagepark.com. ULTRA-DELUXE.

The **Renaissance Seattle Hotel** offers luxury accommodations with views of Puget Sound, Lake Union and downtown. The 553 rooms are furnished in casual and contemporary earth-toned decor and guests enjoy access to the workout room, pool and whirlpool spa on the top floor. ~ 515 Madison Street; 206-583-0300, 800-278-4159, fax 206-624-8125; www.themadison.com, e-mail res@themadison.com. ULTRA-DELUXE.

The **Sorrento Hotel** is known for its personal service and attention to detail. A remodeled Italianate building that opened in 1909, the Sorrento is on a hilltop a few blocks above the downtown area. Beyond the quiet, plush lobby are a notable restaurant (the Hunt Club) and an inviting lounge. The Sorrento has been called one of the most romantic hotels in Seattle. All 76 rooms and suites have a warm, traditional, European atmosphere. ~ 900 Madison Street; 206-622-6400, 800-426-1265, fax 206-343-6155; www.hotelsorrento.com, e-mail mail@hotelsorrento.com. ULTRA-DELUXE.

The **Inn at Virginia Mason** is an attractive, nine-story brick building owned by the medical center next door. On the eastern edge of downtown, it caters to hospital visitors and others looking for a convenient location and pleasant accommodations at reasonable prices. The 79 rooms have dark-wood furnishings and teal and maroon decor. Two suites have a fireplace and whirlpool tub. There's a small restaurant by a brick terrace. ~ 1006 Spring

Street; 206-583-6453, 800-283-6453, fax 206-223-7545; www.
vmmc.org/dbaccommodations. MODERATE TO DELUXE.

The **Sheraton Seattle Hotel & Towers** manages to deftly combine the facilities of a large urban hotel with a personal touch. It has 840 rooms and suites, a cozy lobby with stunning displays of art, mostly glass. The pool and exercise room on the 35th floor have a grand view of the city with the Olympic Mountains as a backdrop. Stay in the Club Level (floors 31–33) and you'll have private breakfast, tea and evening hors d'oeuvres in the Club Lounge. The Towers (top floor) offer the same perks as the Club Level, but with even more luxuries and amenities including butler service. ~ 1400 6th Avenue; 206-621-9000, 800-325-3535, fax 206-621-8441; www.sheraton.com. ULTRA-DELUXE.

The Stranger, a free alternative rag, offers the most entertaining classified section in town, as well as down and dirty love-life columnist Dan Savage, a Seattle celebrity.

A Pacific Northwest theme runs through the **Grand Hyatt Seattle** and its 538 guest rooms and suites. Opened in the heart of the shopping district and next to the convention center in 2001, the Hyatt has brooked no expense in providing contemporary luxury lodging: marble showers, drapes that raise and lower from bedside switches, room doorbells that flash "do not disturb." The tri-level 727 Pine restaurant quickly earned raves upon opening. ~ 721 Pine Street; 206-774-1234, 800-233-1234, fax 206-774-6120; www.grandseattle.hyatt.com. ULTRA-DELUXE.

For Art Deco–era luxury at moderate prices, the **Roosevelt Hotel** is a good bet. A renovation of this 1930 hostelry has made the former skylit lobby a part of its restaurant, but a jazz piano still livens up the cozy space. Rooms are similarly small, but for heart-of-the-city location, this 20-story Coast Hotel satisfies most travelers. ~ 1531 7th Avenue; 206-621-1200, 800-426-0670, fax 206-233-0335; www.roosevelthotel.com. MODERATE TO DELUXE.

The **Camlin Hotel**, on the edge of downtown and a block from the convention center, was built in 1926. The 119-room hotel has a lovely lobby of marble with oriental carpets, a restaurant and lounge on the 11th floor and a conference room on the lobby level. Most of the oversized, classically furnished rooms have work areas, a popular feature for business travelers. ~ 1619 9th Avenue; 206-682-0100, 800-426-0670, fax 206-682-7415; www.camlinhotel.com, e-mail info@camlinhotel.com. DELUXE.

Pensione Nichols offers European-style lodging within a block   ◄ HIDDEN
of Pike Place Market. Eight rooms on the third floor of a historic
building share three baths and a large common space with a
stunning view of the bay, while two rooms share one bath on the
second floor. The rooms are painted a cheerful yellow; some have
windows, while others only have skylights. They are simply furnished with antiques. Two ultra-deluxe suites sleep four and have
fully equipped kitchens and private baths. A continental breakfast is served. ~ 1923 1st Avenue; 206-441-7125, 800-440-7125,
fax 206-448 -8906; www.seattle-bed-breakfast.com. MODERATE.

If its hip, minimalist luxury you want, Ace is the place. Lo-   ◄ HIDDEN
cated in the heart of Belltown's restaurant row, the **Ace Hotel's**
28 simply furnished rooms (hardwood floors, loft-like ceilings)
are split between standard European-style accommodations
(with shared washrooms) and more upscale deluxe rooms with
king-size beds and CD players. Avoid units overlooking 1st Avenue, especially on weekend nights, if you expect an early bed-
time. ~ 2423 1st Avenue; 206-448-4721, fax 206-374-0745;
www.theacehotel.com, e-mail info@theacehotel.com. MODERATE
TO DELUXE.

The **Mayflower Park Hotel** is connected to Westlake Center,
with further covered access to Nordstrom and Macy's/The Bon.
A handsome, renovated 1927 stone building whose thick walls
ensure quiet, the Mayflower's 171 rooms are furnished with
brass and Asian antiques. As was common in the '20s, the rooms
are somewhat small, but its location is hard to beat. ~ 405 Olive
Way; 206-623-8700, 800-426-5100, fax 206-382-6997; www.
mayflowerpark.com, e-mail mayflowerpark@mayflowerpark.
com. ULTRA-DELUXE.

The **Warwick**, on 4th Avenue a few blocks north of Westlake,
has some great views of Queen Anne Hill and downtown from
the upper floors. Rooms are in the Sheraton class, with queen-
size beds, cream and floral furnishings and balconies. It has a
swimming pool and exercise facilities, and an in-house dining
room. The Seattle Center is within easy walking distance. ~ 401
Lenora Street; 206-443-4300, 800-426-9280, fax 206-448-1662;
www.warwickhotels.com. MODERATE.

Located in a former 1920s apartment building, the **Claremont
Hotel** provides spacious guest rooms converted from studio apart-
ments. Decorated in soft tones of peach, green and blue, the rooms

retain some art deco architectural details and include sitting areas with love seats and large rooms with pedestal sinks and large bathtubs. ~ 2000 4th Avenue; 206-448-8600, 800-448-8601, fax 206-441-7140; www.claremonthotel.com, e-mail stay@claremonthotel.com. DELUXE TO ULTRA-DELUXE.

Between downtown and Seattle Center is the **Sixth Avenue Inn**, a five-story motor inn with 166 rooms. The rooms are a cut above those in most motels. They contain blond furniture and assorted plants and books. Those on the north and in back are the quietest. No pets. There's a restaurant overlooking a small garden. ~ 2000 6th Avenue; 206-441-8300, 888-627-8290, fax 206-441-9903; www.sixthavenueinn.com, e-mail sixth.avenue@starwoodhotels.com. DELUXE.

DINING

The fine **al Boccalino** serves some of the city's best Italian dinners. Located in a brick building in Pioneer Square, the restaurant's atmosphere is unpretentious and intimate, the antipasti imaginative, and the entrées cooked and sauced to perfection. Saddle of lamb with brandy, tarragon and mustard is a favorite choice. There are daily specials for every course. No lunch on Saturday or Sunday. ~ 1 Yesler Way; 206-622-7688, fax 206-622-1798; www.alboccalino.com, e-mail alboccalino@aol.com. MODERATE TO DELUXE.

For a romantic dinner, try **Il Terrazzo Carmine** in the Merrill Place Building. A cascading reflecting pool drowns out some of the freeway noise for patio diners. Entrées include roast duck with cherries or veal piccata with capers and lemon. The restaurant also features an extensive Italian wine list. No lunch on Saturday. Closed Sunday. ~ 411 1st Avenue South; 206-467-7797, fax 206-447-5716; www.ilterrazzocarmine.com. DELUXE.

HIDDEN ►

When aeronautical engineer Armandino Batali retired from Boeing, he went to culinary school, dug out old family recipes, and opened **Salumi** near the King Street Station. Now diners rush to his communal tables for home-cured Italian-style meats—prosciutto, salami and various sausages—sliced upon amazing sandwiches (or cut to order for takeout). Lunch Tuesday to Friday, dinner Saturday. ~ 309 3rd Avenue South; 206-621-8772; e-mail armo@rainsound.com. BUDGET TO MODERATE.

HIDDEN ►

It's impossible not to get thoroughly filled at **Zaina**, a friendly, low-key Greek eatery in the midst of the lower downtown business

Seattle's
Coffee Wars

*I*t doesn't take long for visitors to notice that Seattle's primary energy source is coffee. Coffee bars, the preferred business and social meeting spots, do a booming business, and it seems as if there's a drive-up espresso kiosk on every block. Conventional wisdom blames the weather for making the steamy, mood-lifting beverage more popular than Prozac, but on sunny summer days, you'll still see people waiting in line for iced lattes and granitas.

In 1971, "fresh coffee" still meant a new five-pound can of Folger's from the supermarket. Then Jim Stewart, with backing from his brother Dave, started Stewart Brothers Coffee, a small stand selling coffee beans in Pike Place Market. Jim first used a peanut roaster he'd bought from a vendor on a southern California beach but soon traveled to Italy to learn the art from master espresso roasters and purchased a real coffee-bean roaster. The unfamiliar smell of fresh roasted coffee wafted through the market and made his stand an instant hit. Later that same year, a second coffee-bean stand opened in Pike Place Market under the name Starbucks.

Soon the two rivals began buying coffee beans from different parts of the world, developing assorted distinctive blends and adding flavorings. In 1984 Starbucks started its first coffee bar at 4th and Spring streets in downtown Seattle. Meanwhile, Stewart Brothers began selling whole-bean coffee in bulk through supermarkets. Learning that there was another coffee wholesaler named Stewart, the brothers abbreviated the company's name to SBC Inc., which in turn inspired its trade name, Seattle's Best Coffee.

SBC grew to become the world's leading seller of specialty coffee beans, while Starbucks has expanded to nearly 4000 coffee bars, including locations in Tokyo, Beijing, Manila and Kuwait. Starbucks finally bought its in-city rival in 2003 but SBC retains an independent identity. The city now boasts 26 other retail and wholesale coffee-roasting companies as well as five green brokers (importers of unroasted coffee beans).

district. The place is packed with office workers at lunch, but the crowd thins out after 1 p.m. The food is filling and flavorful. ~ 108 Cherry Street; phone/fax 206-624-5687. BUDGET TO MODERATE.

On the outskirts of the International District you'll find **Chau's Chinese Restaurant**, a small, unpretentious restaurant that offers great seafood such as Dungeness crab with ginger and onion, clams in hot garlic sauce, bird's-nest scallops and rock-cod fillets with corn sauce. Choose the fresh seafood entrées over the standard Cantonese dishes. ~ 310 4th Avenue South; 206-621-0006. BUDGET TO DELUXE.

For great Vietnamese food at low prices, try **Saigon Gourmet**. After the green oilcloths and the white-lace curtains, there's no decor to speak of—just hungry patrons eager for a dish of shrimp, Cambodian noodle soup or papaya with beef jerky. Shrimp rolls here are some of the best in town. Closed Sunday. ~ 502 South King Street; phone/fax 206-624-2611. BUDGET.

White-linen tablecloths, black-rattan furnishings and loads of plants await you at **L.A. Seafood Restaurant & Lounge**, an upscale Cantonese restaurant in the International District. In the foyer, the specials—such as hot and smoky crab in a spicy sauce, red-pepper beef, fresh fish with vegetables or clams in black-bean sauce—are posted on the blackboard. ~ 424 7th Avenue South; 206-622-8181, fax 206-622-8186. MODERATE TO DELUXE.

Down on the waterfront, **Elliott's Oyster House** is the place to go for a selection of fresh, slurpy, massage-your-palate Northwest oysters on the half shell—as well as an impressive menu of fresh fish and other seafood. On crisp spring and summer days, you can dine outdoors and watch ferries pull out of their slip next door, bound for Bremerton or Bainbridge Island. Try the crab chowder, the mesquite-grilled ahi tacos, or the succulent swordfish steak. ~ 1201 Alaskan Way, Pier 56; 206-623-4340; www.elliottsoysterhouse.com. DELUXE.

There are several spots for casual waterfront dining, but our favorite is the **Bell Street Diner**. Sitting harborside beneath its more elegant upstairs parent, Anthony's Pier 66, the Diner has a nice selection of chowders, fish and chips, grilled salmon sandwiches, and other fare worthy of the location. But if you sit outside, beware of thieving seagulls. ~ 2201 Alaskan Way, Pier 66 at Bell Street; 206-448-6688, fax 206-728-2500; www.anthonys. com. BUDGET.

Hidden away in the Pike Place Market is **Place Pigalle**. Wind your way past a seafood vendor and Rachel, the bronze pig (a popular market mascot), to this restaurant with spectacular views of Elliott Bay. The dark-wood trim, handsome bar and other touches make for a European-bistro atmosphere. The restaurant makes the most of fresh ingredients from the market's produce tables. Dine on fresh Penn Cove mussels with bacon, celery and shallots in balsamic vinaigrette, calamari in a dijon-ginger cream sauce, or one of the daily fresh salmon specials. The dishes are artfully presented. Patio dining available in summer. Closed Sunday. ~ 81 Pike Street; 206-624-1756. DELUXE.

Tucked into a hillside in Pike Place Market, **Il Bistro** is a cozy cellar spot with wide archways and oriental rugs on wooden floors. Light jazz, candlelight and well-prepared Italian food make it an inviting spot on a rainy evening. Several pastas are served; the entrées include rack of lamb, veal scallopine, fresh salmon and roasted half-chicken served with garlic mashed potatoes. Dinner only. ~ 93-A Pike Street; 206-682-3049, fax 206-682-7880; www. ilbistro.net. DELUXE TO ULTRA-DELUXE.

Across the cobbled street, you can observe the eclectic mix of shoppers and artists in the Pike Place Market at **Three Girls Bakery**, a popular hangout. This tiny lunch counter and bakery with just a few seats serves good sandwiches—the meatloaf sandwich is popular—and hearty soups, including chili and clam chowder. You have more than 50 kinds of bread to choose from. The sourdough and rye breads are recommended. If you don't have room for pastries, buy some to take home. You won't regret it. ~ 1514 Pike Place; 206-622-1045, fax 206-622-0245. BUDGET.

The food at **Oriental Mart** is a combination of Filipino and   ◄ HIDDEN
Asian—and it's very good and very inexpensive. Try the pork

AUTHOR FAVORITE

When I'm craving authentic Mexican food, I head to **El Puerco Lloron**. Every meal served here includes wonderfully fresh tortillas, made by hand while hungry diners watch from the cafeteria line. The *chiles rellenos* compare with the best, and the tamales and taquitos are all authentic and of good quality. There's a fiesta atmosphere in the warm, steamy room. ~ Pike Place Market Hillclimb, 1501 Western Avenue; 206-624-0541. BUDGET.

adobo if they have it that day; otherwise, any of the chicken preparations are excellent. There's no better place for lunch at the Market. The lunch counter is in back of the food-and-novelties store. ~ 1506 Pike Place Market; 206-622-8488. BUDGET.

Nearly 300 businesses, more than 100 farmers, 150 craftspeople and a good 40 restaurants and eateries call Pike Place Market home.

A stone's throw away is **Chez Shea**, which shares the upper floor of a historic brick building. This intimate cubbyhole dining room offers superb Northwest regional cuisine with French influences, and enhancements such as excellent seafood. The prix-fixe menus include rich, inventive soups, salads and main dishes based on hearty ingredients such as roast chicken and lamb. Timing your dinner to coincide with sunset will produce an incomparably romantic experience. Dinner only. Closed Monday. ~ 94 Pike Street, third floor; 206-467-9990; www.chezshea.com. ULTRA-DELUXE.

HIDDEN ►

Off the same upstairs corridor is **Matt's in the Market**, packed into one of those unexpected closets that you'd miss if you blinked twice. You'll have to find a barstool if the small handful of tables at the back of the room are already packed, as they so often are. Warehouse-size windows look down upon the Pike Place food stalls where cooks shop twice a day . . . so you know the food is fresh. Opt for the wonderful and innovative seafood, like the smoked catfish salad or the seared albacore tuna. Closed Sunday and Monday. ~ 94 Pike Street, third floor; 206-467-7909. MODERATE.

HIDDEN ►

Also overlooking the market is **Copacabana**, Seattle's only Bolivian restaurant. But that isn't its greatest virtue. Tucked into the second floor of a lengthy, triangular historic brick building, its outdoor balcony tables offer mind-boggling views on sunny days. In the distance, the Olympic Mountains loom above the shimmering waters of Puget Sound. In the foreground below is the market's colorful bustle. Copacabana's food, typified by shrimp soup and *huminta*, a spicy corn pie, is decent; it's the view that causes local office workers to line up at the entrance, a curved wrought-iron stairway at the foot of Post Alley, before it opens at 11:30 for lunch. All the outside tables are gone by noon on clear days, so get there early. ~ 1520½ Pike Place; 206-622-6359. MODERATE.

In Post Alley, behind some of the market shops, you will find more than just a wee bit of Ireland at **Kells**. This traditional Irish restaurant and pub will lure you to the Emerald Isle with pictures and posters of splendid countryside. A limited menu includes Irish stew and meat pies. From the heavy, dark bar comes a host of domestic and imported beers. Irish musicians play live music seven days a week. ~ 1916 Post Alley; 206-728-1916, fax 206-441-9431; www.kellsirish.com/seattle. MODERATE

Talk about hidden—this place doesn't even have a sign. You enter through the pink door off of Post Alley. **The Pink Door**, with   ◄ HIDDEN
its Italian kitsch decor, is lively and robust at lunchtime. Especially good are the *lasagna della porta rosa* and a delicious cioppino. In the evening, the pace slows, the light dims and it's a perfect setting for a romantic dinner. In the summer, rooftop dining offers views of the Sound. Closed Monday. ~ 1919 Post Alley; 206-443-3241, fax 206-443-3341. DELUXE.

Off a brick courtyard above Pike Place Market, **Campagne** is one of the city's top restaurants. Diners enjoy French country cooking in an atmosphere both warm and elegant. The menu changes six times a year. Entrées may include rack of lamb brushed with puréed anchovy and garlic sauce or roasted sea bass with tarragon, lemon and tiny herb dumplings. The simply prepared dishes are usually the best: young chicken stuffed with ricotta, spinach and roasted herbs and served with sage-infused jus and rosemary roasted potatoes, for example. Dinner only. ~ 86 Pine Street; 206-728-2800, fax 206-448-7562; www.campagneseattle.com. DELUXE TO ULTRA-DELUXE.

Right below Campagne, off Pine Street, is **Cafe Campagne**, the   ◄ HIDDEN
larger restaurant's hugely popular, less expensive bistro. The café's food is even heartier than that upstairs, typified by sausages, roast meats, extravagant breakfasts and country-style desserts. The atmosphere is definitely more homey, with long tables and benches. ~ 1600 Post Alley; 206-728-2233; www.campagneseattle.com. MODERATE TO DELUXE.

The **Library Bistro** is a sleek 1940s-style eatery in the Alexis Hotel, featuring faux lizard-skin high-backed booths, copper and bronze checkerboard tiles and gleaming oak floors. Ten-foot-tall bookcases keep the place true to its name. The cuisine is American contemporary, with entrées such as coriander-braised short ribs and pork chops with pumpkin chutney. Wines hail from the Pacific Northwest. ~ 92 Madison Street; 206-624-3646, fax 206-340-8861; www.alexishotel.com. DELUXE.

Inside Hotel Monaco is the upscale **Sazerac,** named for a New Orleans cocktail of bourbon and peychaud bitters. The seasonal Southern-inspired menu may feature spicy gumbo, fried catfish with cole slaw or braised shortribs in red gravy. Mahogany booths and windows, velvet curtains and cushions, whimsical artwork and jazz playing in the background complete this trendy scene. ~ 1101 4th Avenue; 206-624-7755, fax 206-624-0050; www. monaco-seattle.com. DELUXE.

Padded white tablecloths, carpeting and an amber glow from the light fixtures give **Tulio** appealing warmth. Usually packed and festive, it's a place for great food and lively conversation rather than a quiet rendezvous. Go for the specials, such as pan-fried swordfish with fennel, and the desserts, which range from a rich tiramisu to delicate pistachio gelato. No lunch on Saturday and Sunday. ~ 1100 5th Avenue, 206-624-5500, fax 206-623-0568; www.hotelvintagepark.com. MODERATE TO DELUXE.

The decor is spare and clean in **Wild Ginger**, and the menu is pan–Southeast Asian. Mahogany booths fill the main dining room, and there's more seating on a wraparound mezzanine and in a second-story cocktail lounge. There's also a satay bar where skewered chicken, beef, fish and vegetables are grilled, then served with peanut and other sauces. The wondrous Seven Elements Soup, an exotic blend of flavors, is a meal in itself. No lunch on Sunday. ~ 1401 3rd Avenue; 206-623-4450, fax 206-623-8265. MODERATE TO DELUXE.

Another favorite among downtowners is the **Botticelli Café**. The small café is known for its *panini*—little sandwiches made

TAKE ME OUT TO THE BALL GAME

Seattleites are solid fans of their teams. The **Mariners** play baseball April through September at SAFECO Field. ~ 206-346-4001. Practically next door, at the Seahawks Stadium, the **Seahawks** football team kicks off August through December. ~ 206-628-0888, 888-635-4295. The **SuperSonics** basketball team shoots hoops from October through April at the Seattle Center's Key Arena. ~ 206-283-3865, 206-628-0888. Also in the Key Arena, women's basketball team the **Seattle Storm** plays May through August. ~ 206-217-9622. In the minor leagues, the **Thunderbirds** hockey team plays from September to March at Key Arena. ~ 206-448-7825. College football takes place in Husky Stadium on the University of Washington campus. ~ Montlake Boulevard; 206-543-2200.

of toasted focaccia bread and topped with olive oil, herbs, cheeses, meats and vegetables. The espresso and ices are good, too. Breakfast and lunch only. Closed Sunday in summer; closed Saturday and Sunday in winter. ~ 101 Stewart Street; 206-441-9235. BUDGET.

Contemporary, international cuisine prepared with imagination is served at the **Dahlia Lounge** near the shops of Westlake Center. Bright red walls, a neon sign and paper-fish lampshades create a celebratory atmosphere. Celebrity chef Tom Douglas draws upon numerous ethnic styles and uses Northwest products to develop such dishes as potstickers filled with lobster, shrimp and scallion served with sake sauce. His two other nearby restaurants focus on grilled meats (Palace Kitchen, 2030 5th Avenue; 206-448-2001) and fresh fins (Etta's Seafood, 2020 Western Avenue; 206-443-6000). ~ 2001 4th Avenue; 206-682-4142, fax 206-467-0568; www.tomdouglas.com, e-mail admin@tomdoug las.com. DELUXE TO ULTRA-DELUXE.

Just north of downtown, you'll find the thriving Belltown shopping, dining and nightlife scene. As you pass by, don't overlook **Le Pichet**, which offers Seattle's most authentic French ◀ HIDDEN bistro experience. It's a popular late-night spot for small plates of cheeses, pâtés, confits and other charcuterie, accompanied by glasses of surprisingly inexpensive imported French wines. Breakfast daily; no lunch or dinner on Tuesday and Wednesday. ~ 1933 1st Avenue; 206-256-1499. MODERATE.

Supported by Seattle Mariners' Latino baseball players, **Fandango** has made a splash with its gourmet take on the foods of Venezuela, Colombia, Peru, Brazil, Argentina and Mexico. Start with a *mojito* from the streetside bar, then sit near the open kitchen and watch the chefs spin out a variety of soups, salads and tapas. Or take a table in the elegant harborview dining room for marvelous beef, pork, duck and seafood preparations, as spicy as you like 'em. Dinner only. ~ 2313 1st Avenue; 206-441-1188; www.fandangoseattle.com, e-mail info@fandangoseattle. com. MODERATE TO DELUXE.

Named for the region between the Cascade Mountains and the Pacific Ocean, **Cascadia** specializes in haute cuisine crafted almost entirely from local ingredients. Rabbit and trout from Oregon, prawns from Alaska, mushrooms from British Columbia and fruit from Northern California all turn up in chef Kerry

Sear's elegant offerings, served against a backdrop of a nine-foot cascading waterfall. Prix-fixe meals invariably include an all-vegetarian offering. Dinner only. Closed Sunday. ~ 2328 1st Avenue; 206-448-8884, fax 206-448-2242; www.cascadiarestaurant.com. ULTRA-DELUXE.

Scarlet walls, high-backed booths and dim lighting help **Belltown Pizza** stand apart from your average pizza joint. It helps, too, that the pies here are damn tasty. Also on the menu is a small selection of pasta, salads and focaccia sandwiches. But after 10 p.m. on weekends, expect a hip, lively crowd that's more interested in the bar than the food. Dinner only. ~ 2422 1st Avenue; 206-441-2653. BUDGET TO MODERATE.

An elegant 1950s-style supperclub, **El Gaucho** does dramatic versions of American classics. Martinis are a specialty, and tableside performances include caesar salad tossings and aged-steak carvings. In the Pampas Room, below, there's live music (jazz and Latin) and dancing on weekends, while the cigar lounge offers more meditative relaxation. Dinner only. ~ 2505 1st Avenue; 206-728-1337, fax 206-728-4477; www.elgaucho.com. DELUXE TO ULTRA-DELUXE.

HIDDEN ► **Marco's Supperclub** is a little-known purveyor of fine, eclectic multiregional dishes in the creative Continental mode. The deep-fried sage leaves, an appetizer, are a true original. Quite filling meals are reasonable by Belltown standards. The mood here is decidedly bohemian, Paris-style jazz singers crooning softly from CD decks to diners who opt to sit at the long bar. In fine weather, there's sidewalk and garden seating. Dinner only. ~ 2510 1st Avenue; 206-441-7801. MODERATE TO DELUXE.

Arguably Seattle's best sushi bar is **Saito's**, where the fresh fish is sliced thick and the creations range from traditional Japanese to eclectic and contemporary. But there's more than raw seafood here: If the geoduck is fresh, ask for the butter *itamé*, a sauté of the giant clam with sugar snaps and shiitake mushrooms. Ichiro Suzuki is a regular here: If you don't know who he is, you know squat about Seattle. No lunch on Saturday. Closed Sunday and Monday. ~ 2120 2nd Avenue; 206-728-1333; www.saitos.net. MODERATE.

Anchoring the less glitzy side of Belltown is a restaurant/laundromat that's quintessentially Seattle but little known to visitors. Is **Sit & Spin** a '50s diner, with its chrome-edged formica

HIDDEN ►

tables, jukebox and retro-cafeteria menu? Is it just a utilitarian hangout where patrons scarf bargain meals while they wash their clothes? Is it a New Age shrine where herbal teas and vegetarian sandwiches tread lightly on the metabolism? Is it a hot spot of Seattle's arts and music culture, where the sharp-eyed visitor might spy a rock star in town to record at a famed nearby studio? It's all of these, a memorably unique establishment with live bands on weekends that's also a great place for lunch. ~ 2219 4th Avenue; 206-441-9484, fax 206-448-7210; www.sitandspin.net. BUDGET.

Artists and others without a lot of money for eats hang out at **The Two Bells Bar & Grill**. Local artwork on the walls changes every two months. This funky bar with 25 kinds of beer and a host of inexpensive good food is a busy place. You can always find good soups, sandwiches, burgers, salads and cold plates. Some favorites are an Italian-sausage soup and the hot beer-sausage sandwich. ~ 2313 4th Avenue; 206-441-3050, fax 206-448-9626. BUDGET.

SHOPPING

The oldest and loveliest structure in Pioneer Square is the Pioneer Building. In the basement, the **Pioneer Square Antique Mall** has more than 6000 square feet of space devoted to antiques and collectibles and maintained by some 60 dealers. ~ 602 1st Avenue; 206-624-1164.

The Pioneer Building, located in historic Pioneer Square, houses Seattle's first electric elevator.

The **Grand Central Building** houses 17 shops. Visitors can also enjoy drinks and baked goods at lobby tables adjacent to a brick fireplace. ~ 214 1st Avenue South; 206-623-7417.

Need a Morris Graves painting or a portrait of grunge legend Kurt Cobain? Several Pioneer Square galleries specialize in local artists, including **Linda Hodges Gallery** (316 1st Avenue South; 206-624-3034), **Davidson Galleries** (313 Occidental Avenue South; 206-624-7684) and **Greg Kucera Gallery** (212 3rd Avenue South; 206-624-0770).

In the heart of the Pioneer Square district is the **Elliott Bay Book Company,** featuring over 150,000 titles, including an outstanding stock of Northwest books. You're bound to enjoy browsing, snacking in the on-premises café or listening in on frequently scheduled readings by renowned authors. ~ 101 South Main Street; 206-624-6600, 800-962-5311; www.elliottbaybook.com.

Just a few blocks north, **Metsker Maps** is the perfect place to find a detailed map for your driving or hiking expedition, or to get hold of a specialized regional travel guide. ~ 701 1st Avenue; 206-623-8747, 800-727-4430; www.metskers.com.

Known as an "Oriental Woolworth's," **Higo Variety Store** has all kinds of small toys, bowls and sundries in the five-and-dime category. Also on hand are some more expensive articles such as hapi coats, kimonos and obi sashes. Closed Sunday. ~ 604 South Jackson Street; 206-622-7572.

Along the waterfront, the best shopping opportunities can be found on Piers 54 through 70.

Called the "Soul of Seattle," the **Pike Place Market** has been in business since 1907. Saved from the wrecking ball by citizen action in the early '70s, Pike Place is now a bustling bazaar with nearly 300 businesses (about 40 are eateries), 100 farmers (selling produce and flowers at tables and stalls) and 150 local artists and craftspeople. ~ 85 Pike Street; 206-682-7453; www.pike placemarket.org.

A notable establishment within the market is the **Pure Food Fish Market**, which ships fresh or smoked salmon anywhere in the U.S. ~ 1515 Pike Place; 206-622-5765. Also here is **Hands of the World**, where the specialty is ethnic jewelry, masks and home accessories such as carved picture frames and folkloric art from Asia and Africa. ~ 1501 Pike Place; 206-622-1696.

Just south of Pure Food Fish Market is **DeLaurenti Specialty Food and Wine**, a wondrously well-stocked gourmet store and

AUTHOR FAVORITE

I never tire of browsing the aisles of **Uwajimaya** in the International District. This vast store reflects Seattle's legendary connection with the Pacific Rim. It's one part grocery store, with fresh seafood, vegetables from local Oriental farms, and all manner of canned and frozen foods representing Japanese, Chinese, Korean, Thai, Vietnamese, Filipino and other East and Southeast Asian cultures. It's another part gift and housewares shop, featuring shoji screens and lamps, kanji clocks and watches, lacquerware music boxes, goldimari ceramic pieces, a wide range of books in several Asian languages, and much more. Plus it incorporates several fine little restaurants. Even when I'm not shopping, I wander through for a dose of traditional Asian culture. ~ 600 5th Avenue South; 206-624-6248, fax 206-405-2996; www.uwajimaya.com.

café with hundreds of cheeses, pâtés, canned goods, spices, breads, meats and, in season, fresh truffles that can go for $1500 a pound. ~ 1435 1st Avenue; 206-622-0141. Near Rachel, the market's famous bronze pig, is **MarketSpice**, which offers, among dozens of ◄ *HIDDEN* teas and spices, its own distinctive clove-tinged spiced tea blend; it makes a great Christmas gift. ~ 85-A Pike Place; 206-622-6340.

Across Pike Place from the main arcade is **Jack's Fish Spot**, ◄ *HIDDEN* where the fish is as good as that at the more famous fish stands, the prices are at least 50 cents a pound better—in some cases as much as $3 cheaper per pound—and the Dungeness crab, cooked on the spot, is the freshest in the market. They'll ship fresh salmon anywhere in the country, and Jack's smoked salmon, which comes from the only smokehouse in the market, is also the best. ~ 1514 Pike Place; 206-467-0514; www.jacksfishspot.com.

A few feet away, at the foot of Post Alley, **El Mercado Latino** carries Caribbean and Central American delights ranging from plantains to pasilla chiles to habañero sauces. ~ 1514 Pike Place; 206-623-3240.

On 1st Avenue just above the market, two stores across the street from one another offer uniquely Seattle wares. At **Dilettante Chocolates**, the family recipes, rich and dark, derive from the delights ancestor Julius Rudolph Franzen made as chocolatier for the last Romanov czar, Nicholas II. ~ 1603 1st Avenue; 206-728-9144; www.dilettante.com. Opposite, **Simply Seattle** is the best place downtown to get a gift or memento reflecting the city. It could be a Seattle Mariners T-shirt; it could be a carved wooden slug. ~ 1600 1st Avenue; 206-448-2207; www.simply seattle.com.

Close by is **Opus 204**, a small shop filled with a wondrous display of unusual and fine clothing, handicrafts, imports and gifts. ~ 2004 1st Avenue; 206-728-7707.

At the **Westlake Center** (4th Avenue and Pine Street), pushcarts loaded with jewelry, scarves and other small trappings lend a European flavor to the 80 retail establishments here. On the first floor, **Fireworks Gallery** (206-682-6462) takes its name from unusually fired sculptures. Also offered are a variety of intriguing home accessories, gifts and jewelry. **Millstream** (206-233-9719) sells Northwest sculpture, prints, pottery and jewelry by local artisans. ~ 400 Pine Street. Fast foods, available on the third floor, include teriyaki, pizza, enchiladas and yogurt.

Adjoining Westlake Center is the flagship store for **Nordstrom**, the department store chain that achieved prominence with its no-holds-barred customer service and chic goods. Located in the old Frederick & Nelson building, Nordstrom's has saltwater aquariums in the children's department as well as that classic Nordstrom touch, a grand piano played by a rotating roster of musicians. ~ 500 Pine Street; 206-628-2111; www.nordstrom.com. A few blocks away, **Nordstrom Rack** is a favorite haunt of Seattleites seeking elegant bargains. ~ 1601 2nd Avenue; 206-448-8522. Nearby **Alhambra** offers high-end women's clothing, Indonesian furniture and a variety of jewelry. ~ 101 Pine Street; 206-621-9571; www.alhambranet.com.

HIDDEN ▶

Fifth Avenue, Seattle's fashion street, is lined with shops displaying elegant finery and accessories. **Nancy Meyer** specializes in very fine European lingerie. ~ 1318 5th Avenue; 206-625-9200. **Rainier Square** houses several prestigious retail establishments. ~ 1333 5th Avenue. **Turgeon Raine** is an exceptionally good, locally owned jewelry store. ~ 1407 5th Avenue; 206-447-9488. Off 5th Avenue on Union is **Totally Michael's**, which has contemporary, upscale clothing. ~ 521 Union Street; 206-622-4920.

NIGHTLIFE

Seattle's nightlife, music and club scene is astounding for a city its size. More than 50 clubs, lounges, restaurants and taverns feature live or deejay-spun music, and dozens more have occasional performances. The offerings run the gamut from folk to punk/metal; dance venues range from all-night raves in port district warehouses to salsa nights at Latin bars. This is a city that has given the world Jimi Hendrix, Pearl Jam, Nirvana, Heart and Kenny G.

The best guide to the city's entertainment scene is *The Stranger*, an alternative weekly newspaper that carries a complete calendar of shows, dances, plays, cinema, performances, readings, art galleries and other goings-on. It's available free every Thursday at coffee shops, cafés, taverns, bookstores and newsstands throughout the Seattle area. A competing weekly, the *Seattle Weekly*, also provides comprehensive nightlife coverage; it's free every Wednesday. The *Seattle Times* and *Seattle Post-Intelligencer* also publish club guides in their Friday entertainment sections.

HIDDEN ▶

Half-price same-day tickets to many Seattle musical events, as well as most theater stagings, are available at **Ticket/Ticket**, which maintains booths at Pike Place Market, on Capitol Hill and in Bellevue. Call for directions, but they won't say over the phone what tickets they have that day. ~ 401 Broadway East (Broadway Market, Second Level); Pike Place Market, 1st Avenue and Pike Place; 206-324-2744; www.ticketwindowonline.com.

There are many low-key nightclubs in Pioneer Square, and on "joint-cover" nights, one charge admits you to nine places within a four-block radius. Among them is **Doc Maynard's**, heavy on rock-and-roll with live music on weekends. Cover. ~ 610 1st Avenue; 206-682-3705. The **New Orleans Creole Restaurant** offers live jazz and blues along with Cajun Creole food in an eclectic, laidback atmosphere. Cover on weekends. ~ 114 1st Avenue South; 206-622-2563. A mixed crowd enjoys deejay dance music and reggae at the **Bohemian**. Cover. ~ 111 Yesler Way; 206-447-1514.

At **Comedy Underground**, comics entertain nightly. Cover. ~ 222 South Main Street; 206-628-0303; www.comedyunderground. com. **Unexpected Productions** offers comedy performances and workshops in improvisational theater techniques. ~ The Market Theater, 1428 Post Alley, Pike Place Market; 206-781-9273; www.unexpectedproductions.org.

The Showbox nightclub, opposite Pike Place Market, features local, national and international live bands and all types of music, complete with restaurant and full bar. Cover. ~ 1426 1st Avenue; 206-628-3151; www.showboxonline.com.

The **Seattle Symphony**'s large performance space, **Benaroya Hall**, has enabled it to vastly expand its schedule and repertoire. Noted especially for its attention to American composers, the symphony, under the direction of Gerard Schwarz, is one of the top recording orchestras in the United States. ~ 200 University Street; 206-215-4700, tickets 206-215-4747; www.seattlesymphony.org.

AUTHOR FAVORITE

I'm a jazz lover, and there are two spots in Seattle that never disappoint. **Dimitriou's Jazz Alley** is a downtown dinner theater and premier jazz club that presents a regular schedule of top-name international acts like Maynard Ferguson, Shemekia Copeland and Spyro Gyra. Cover. ~ 6th Avenue and Lenora Street; 206-441-9729; www.jazzalley.com. Local jazz cats gather at venerable **Tula's**, which provides scat lovers with live music every night, plus a full menu and bar. Cover. ~ 2214 2nd Avenue; 206-443-4221; www.tulas.com.

For satirical/comical revues, try the **Cabaret de Paris** dinner theater. Closed Sunday. Cover. ~ Rainier Square, 1333 5th Avenue; 206-623-4111.

You may want to ask what's playing at two historic downtown venues: the **5th Avenue Theatre** (1308 5th Avenue; 206-625-1900; www.5thavenuetheatre.org), which specializes in Broadway shows and musicals, and the Paramount Theatre (911 Pine Street; 206-682-1414; www.theparamount.com), a popular concert location. Advance tickets for shows at both theaters are available from **Ticketmaster** (206-292-ARTS; www.ticketmaster.com).

Video games, beer and pub food—sounds like a classic video arcade. But **Gameworks** is much more than that. With the latest in electronic games, virtual-reality games and adventures, this has become the highly successful (and highly publicized) prototype for what is now a national chain. ~ 1511 7th Avenue; 206-521-0952; www.gameworks.com.

The **Paramount Theatre**, the elaborate movie palace of the 1920s, now offers Broadway shows and musicals. ~ 9th Avenue and Pine Street; 206-682-1414; www.theparamount.com.

Most of Seattle's best deejays spin at the **Bada Lounge**, an ultrasleek bar and club with inventive Asian-influenced cuisine and a pool room. ~ 2230 1st Avenue; 206-374-8717; www.badalounge.com. Many of the modern techno set head for **Club Medusa**, another cutting-edge nightclub just below the Market. ~ 2218 Western Avenue; 206-448-8887; www.clubmedusa.us.

Belltown, just north of Pike Place Market, has lots of activity after dark. **Crocodile Café**, one of Seattle's legendary spawning grounds for grunge, punk, rock and alternative bands, attracts a young crowd for live music. Closed Monday. Cover. ~ 2200 2nd Avenue; 206-441-5611; www.thecrocodile.com.

HIDDEN ▶   An after-dark stop made-to-order for travelers, **Sit & Spin** is a combination bar, restaurant, nightclub and laundromat where you can catch live music, poetry readings or live theater while your clothes whirl. Cover for shows. ~ 2219 4th Avenue; 206-441-9484; www.sitandspin.net.

For a special night out, **Teatro ZinZanni** offers Seattle's best dinner theater, a "place where the Moulin Rouge meets Cirque du Soleil." Chef Tom Douglas' five-course menu complements a three-hour European cabaret experience beneath a Belltown bigtop. ~ 2301 6th Avenue; 206-802-0015; dreams.zinzanni.org.

FIVE

Central Neighborhoods

The areas immediately north and east of downtown Seattle are the city's most accessible and frequently visited urban neighborhoods. Seattle Center bridges the span between Belltown and Lower Queen Anne; above it rises Queen Anne Hill, whose gentrified hilltop manses offer some of the finest views of the city skyline and Puget Sound. On its east side, the hill falls rapidly to Lake Union, a heart-shaped freshwater lake linked by channels and locks to both Lake Washington and Puget Sound. Beyond Lake Union rises cosmopolitan Capitol Hill, whose sizeable gay population rubs elbows with old-money Seattle families and alternative youth alike. It extends south to First Hill, home of Seattle University and many of the city's leading hospitals and medical clinics. Farther east, above and along the western shore of Lake Washington, impressive estates dot the charming residential communities of Montlake, Madison Park, Madrona and Leschi, each with its own dining and shopping district.

Seattle Center–Queen Anne

Seattle Center is, of course, dominated by a familiar landmark rising skyward—the Space Needle. This symbol of the city stands watch above the stunning Experience Music Project, nestling comfortably among museums, cultural centers and a sports arena, home of the Seattle SuperSonics professional basketball team. Just north of the arts and entertainment complex sits the stunning Queen Anne area, a hilly neighborhood of two parts. Lower Queen Anne, adjacent to the center, is rich with dining and entertainment options; Upper Queen Anne, a steep half-mile uphill, offers fanciful homes and great views, along with more shops and cafés. This is the part of Seattle where the downtown bustle starts to give way to more peaceful charms.

The visitor hub of Lake Union—at its south end, near downtown—is the Center for Wooden Boats, flanked by an upscale yacht harbor and a bevy of popular restaurants. A flurry of new hotels and businesses has added vitality to this neighborhood in recent years. More shops and restaurants, as well as a thriving houseboat community, extend up Eastlake Avenue; its counterpart, Westlake Avenue, is home primarily to a variety of maritime industries.

SIGHTS   **Seattle Center**, once the site of the 1962 World's Fair, is now a 74-acre campus with more than a dozen buildings housing a variety of offices, convention rooms and theaters. ~ 305 Harrison Street; 206-684-8582. Locals and visitors continue to flock to the **Space Needle** (admission; 206-905-2100, fax 206-905-2211; www.spaceneedle.com) for the view or a meal, to summer carnival rides at the **Fun Forest**, to the **Center House**'s short-order ethnic eateries and community-oriented festivals, and to wide-ranging exhibits and demonstrations at the **Pacific Science Center** (admission; 206-443-2001, fax 206-443-3631; www.pacsci.org).

The **Pacific Northwest Ballet** (tickets, 206-292-2787, fax 206-441-2440; information, 206-441-9411; www.pnb.org) has its offices and rehearsal space at the Phelps Center (where the public can watch the corps rehearse through a glass wall).

There is also a large skateboard park, which is open most of the year just in case you get the urge to hop on a slab of plywood with four wheels and "shred." And you can play ball at the **Nate McMillan Basketball Park** near the 5th Avenue parking lot. McMillan coaches the Sonics, who play home games in **Key Arena** on the west side of Seattle Center. ~ Seattle Center: Two miles north of the downtown core between Denny Way and Mercer Street; 206-684-7200, fax 206-684-7342; www.seattle center.com.

Beside the Pacific Science Center, the **Seattle Children's Theatre** (206-443-0807; www.sct.org) has jovial performances geared to a young audience. Kids will also enjoy visiting the center's **Seattle Children's Museum** on the ground floor of Center House. The collection features a kid's-size neighborhood and multicultural global village, a two-story walk-through re-creation of a mountain forest and mechanically oriented displays. There are also a giant Lego room, a small lagoon for children and a drop-in art

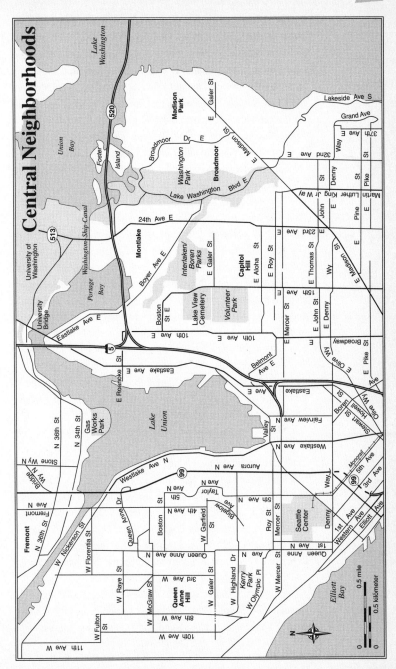

studio. ~ Seattle Center House; 206-441-1768, fax 206-448-0910; www.thechildrensmuseum.org.

The heart of Seattle Center is the **International Fountain**, where on warm summer days you'll see children (and some parents) dancing through the jets of water that shoot from a dome, often synchronized with music and lights. This was the site of an impromptu moving tribute following the 9/11 attack on New York. Nearby, the flags of all 50 states stand on individual poles in front of the **Flag Pavilion**, an exhibition hall.

For an interactive history lesson on Pacific Northwest rock-and-roll, stop by **Experience Music Project (EMP)**, a must for music lovers of all stripes. Conceived by Microsoft co-founder Paul Allen as a tribute to Seattle-born guitarist Jimi Hendrix, and designed by avant-garde architect Frank Gehry (who also built Los Angeles' Walt Disney Concert Hall), the garish structure, painted multiple metallic hues, sprawls like a smashed guitar at the foot of the Space Needle. A wander through music-history exhibits becomes an interactive experience with the help of wands and headsets: Visitors point and shoot to listen to a century's worth of music. Among the many other highlights at the 140,000-square-foot EMP are a vintage guitar collection, a rock fashion exhibit and the Hendrix Gallery. Those with rock-star fantasies will get a kick out of the Sound Lab, where they can perform on stage to their adoring fans. Allen is now financing an attached science-fiction museum, scheduled to open in 2006. Admission. ~ 325 5th Avenue North; 206-367-5483, 877-367-5483, fax 206-770-2727; www.emplive.com, e-mail experience@emplive.com.

For more highbrow musical offerings, Seattleites flock to the **Marion Oliver McCaw Hall for the Performing Arts**. Reopened in 2003 after a total refurbishment of the old Opera House, McCaw Hall is home to the Seattle Opera and Pacific Northwest Ballet. Two theaters—the **Bagley Wright Theatre** (155 Mercer Street; 206-443-2210; www.seattlerep.org), home to the Seattle Repertory Theatre, and the **Intiman Theatre** (201 Mercer Street; 206-269-1900; www.intiman.org)—stand nearby.

For a breathtaking view of Seattle's skyline and Elliott Bay, you can leave Seattle Center and go up Queen Anne Hill to **Kerry Park** at West Highland Drive and 2nd Avenue West. Or just walk east on Mercer Street to Lake Union.

The six miles or so of shoreline circling **Lake Union** present a varied mix of boat works and nautical specialty shops, street-end pocket parks, boat-in restaurants, seaplane docks, rental-boat concessions, ocean-research vessels, houseboats and flashy condos. You could spend a day exploring funky old warehouses and oddball enterprises. The lake's south end offers extensive public access to the shore behind a cluster of restaurants, a wooden-boat center and new park.

At the **Center for Wooden Boats**, dozens of vintage and replica vessels celebrate the maritime world before the days of fiberglass. A contingent of volunteers are nearly always on hand, handcrafting new boats, answering questions and offering lessons to onlookers who want to learn; students here can build a boat in a week. Many rowboats and sailboats are available for public rental. A gift shop helps support the enterprise. Closed Tuesday. ~ 1010 Valley Street; 206-382-2628, fax 206-382-2699; www.cwb.org. After viewing the historic vessels here, take a stroll down the docks of the adjacent yacht harbor to see luxury craft of the contemporary era.

LODGING   Conveniently located a block from Seattle Center, half of the **Best Western Executive Inn**'s 320 rooms (the west side) offer point-blank views of the Space Needle and Experience Music Project. Off the cozy lobby, guests may enjoy a fitness center with jacuzzi, a full-service restaurant and lounge. ~ 200 Taylor Avenue North; 206-448-9444, 800-351-9444, fax 206-441-7929; www.bwexec-inn.com, e-mail info@bwexec-inn.com. DELUXE.

The first seven decades of its life, the **MarQueen Hotel** was a residential apartment. Reopened after a renovation in 1998, it's now one of Seattle's most charming accommodations. Every room has modern kitchen facilities, including a refrigerator and microwave oven; some have full-service kitchens. The nearby Ten Mercer restaurant provides room service. Early-20th-century antiques furnish the mahogany-lined lobby. Request a west-facing room for a sunset view. ~ 600 Queen Anne Avenue North; 206-282-7407, 888-445-3076; www.marqueen.com, e-mail info@marqueen.com. DELUXE.

On Lower Queen Anne Hill is the **Hampton Inn & Suites**, a clean and comfortable if nondescript lodging. Standard rooms have either a king-size or two double beds, while studio, one- and two-room suites (with balconies) are also available. Full continental breakfast buffet included. ~ 700 5th Avenue North; 206-282-7700, 800-426-7866, fax 206-282-0899. DELUXE.

The lovely, Arts and Crafts–style **Inn of Twin Gables**, on the west slope of Queen Anne Hill, is best enjoyed at sunset, when you can watch the sun dip behind the Olympic Range from the enclosed front porch. Mother and daughter Fran and Katie Frame offer three antique-filled rooms, two of which share a bath. Gourmet breakfasts, served in a dining room with fir floor and box-beamed ceiling, are seasoned with herbs from the inn's own garden. ~ 3258 14th Avenue West; 206-284-3979, 866-466-3979, fax 206-284-3974; www.innoftwingables.com. MODERATE.

DREAMWORKS

For a rewarding, spur-of-the-moment visit, drop by Seattle Center on a summer evening for a contemplative quarter-hour of gazing at the **International Fountain**. The combination of changing lights and waterworks synchronized to music the first 15 minutes of every hour against a rose-tinted summer sunset can lull you into a dreamy state.

Request a lakeview suite on an upper floor if you book at the **Marriott Residence Inn Lake Union**. Around a lush atrium courtyard, filled with plants and a waterfall, rise 234 handsome rooms with full kitchens. The hotel provides continental breakfast and evening dessert, and a lap pool and exercise room to work off extra calories. ~ 800 Fairview Avenue North; 206-624-6000, 800-331-3131; www.residenceinn.com. DELUXE.

DINING

At the Space Needle's **Sky City Restaurant**, the entertainment—from 500 feet up—in either the restaurant or on the observation deck is seeing metropolitan Seattle, its environs, Puget Sound, the Olympic Mountains and Mt. Rainier, the Queen of the Cascade Range, as you rotate in a 360° orbit. The restaurant serves various seafood, beef, pasta and poultry dishes, such as salmon Wellington and beef medallions. No lunch on Saturday, but a great Sunday brunch. ~ 400 Broad Street; 206-905-2100, fax 206-905-2107; www.spaceneedle.com/restaurant.htm. ULTRA-DELUXE.

◀ HIDDEN

On the plaza at Five Point Square, next to the Chief Sealth statue, the **Five Point Cafe Chief's Lounge** is a distinctive Seattle landmark. With a sign on the door warning nonsmokers that smokers are welcome, and The Who's "Pinball Wizard" inevitably playing on the jukebox, it's a real joint. Why go? The food is good, no-nonsense and quite economical, and no one leaves hungry. Try the fish and chips or the meatloaf sandwich (yes, it's that kind of restaurant). ~ 415 Cedar Street; 206-448-9993. BUDGET.

For sublime breakfast pastries and delicious Mediterranean-inspired lunch items, head for **Macrina Bakery and Cafe,** a cozy European-style *patisserie* where the moss green walls are adorned with scrolls, ironwork, paintings and other work by local artists. Breakfast items include house-made coffee cakes, cereals and fruit pastries, while a changing lunch menu may offer such dishes as tartlet of roast chicken and goat cheese or cheese polenta with red chard. No dinner on weekends. ~ 2408 1st Avenue; 206-448-4032, fax 206-374-1782; www.macrinabakery.com. Also at 615 West McGraw Street (Queen Anne Hill); 206-283-5900. MODERATE.

When Kaspar Donier moved his acclaimed restaurant to the Seattle Center area, he lost the old location's view atop an office building, but gained a nicer home and a different dinner crowd. Now, symphony, opera and ballet patrons flock to **Kaspar's** to feast on his intriguing contemporary Northwest cuisine. Kaspar's braised lamb shanks, for instance, may be the Northwest's best; his scallops are sumptuous and plentiful. Dinner only. Closed Sunday and Monday. ~ 19 West Harrison Street; 206-298-0123, fax 206-298-0146; www.kaspars.com, e-mail info@kaspars.com. DELUXE.

Chutney's occupies a tidy, elegant space just a block from the Seattle Center. Its Indian menu is rich and varied, leaning heavily on hearty lentil and vegetable concoctions. The lunch buffet is unbelievably filling. Ask for the excellent garlic/chile chutney. No lunch on Sunday. ~ 519 1st Avenue North; 206-284-6799. MODERATE.

HIDDEN ► Three blocks away, but still within easy walking distance of Seattle Center, **Tup Tim Thai** is the Thai restaurant that locals favor over its better-known cousins north of the center. Tup Tim's soups and curries are the best in Seattle; it's advisable to arrive early for lunch, or for dinner on nights there are events at the center. No lunch on Saturday. Closed Sunday. ~ 118 West Mercer Street; 206-281-8833. BUDGET TO MODERATE.

While Lower Queen Anne hipsters congregate in the upscale bistro bar at **Ten Mercer**, those in the know head upstairs to a romantic candlelit restaurant. Cuisine is creative Continental, running the gamut from house-smoked tenderloin to vegetarian selections; the smoked sturgeon makes a wonderful appetizer. Service is friendly, and the wine list is well considered. Dinner only. ~ 10 Mercer Street; 206-691-3723, fax 206-691-1839; www.tenmercer.com, e-mail dinneranddrinks@tenmercer.com. MODERATE TO DELUXE.

At the eclectic, pan-Asian, hilltop **Chinoise Cafe**, you can find sushi and potstickers, *pad Thai* and Vietnamese salad roll—served

AUTHOR FAVORITE

I love the way charming **Sapphire Kitchen & Bar**—a touch of the western Mediterranean atop Queen Anne Hill—reflects the Spanish-Moroccan heritage of chef Leonard Ruiz Rede. The colorful, dimlit ambience may remind you of the *Arabian Nights* as you dig into a North African *meze* plate followed by delectable mussels Catalan (steamed with sherry and romescu sauce) or a seafood paella with scallops, prawns and chorizo sausage. Locals throng to this hidden delight for weekend brunch. ~ 1625 Queen Anne Avenue North; 206-281-1931. MODERATE.

at lightspeed to an appreciative Upper Queen Anne audience. The curries and the green papaya-shrimp salad draw raves. No lunch on weekends. ~ 12 Boston Street; 206-284-6671. MODERATE.

Hearty Northwest fare with a German accent is on the menu at **Szmania's**, a popular spot with an exhibition kitchen in the residential area of Magnolia, west of Queen Anne Hill. The specialties include seared ahi tuna over black rice with a red curry sauce; grilled venison with polenta and pears; and Alaskan halibut in a pinot noir sauce with lobster mashed potatoes. Dinner only. Closed Monday. ~ 3321 West McGraw Street; 206-284-7305, fax 206-283-7303; www.szmanias.com, e-mail ludger@ szmanias.com. MODERATE TO DELUXE.

On the south shore of Lake Union is **Chandler's Crabhouse and Fresh Fish Market**. The whiskey crab soup is good for starters before digging into a steamed crab, grilled salmon or other fresh seafood plate. During Crabby Hour (3 to 6:30 p.m. and 9:30 to closing), oyster shooters and other items are bargain-priced. Grab a table with a view of the water and enjoy. ~ 901 Fairview Avenue North; 206-223-2722, fax 206-223-9380; www. schwartzbros.com, e-mail chandlers@schwartzbros.com. DELUXE TO ULTRA-DELUXE.

Bicycles hang from the rafters. T-shirts are on sale in the lobby. **Cucina! Cucina!** is an open, spacious, noisy Italian restaurant with a large deck overlooking Lake Union where you can watch float planes land and take off or see kayakers gently paddling by. Diners can see into the open kitchen to watch the staff making pizzas large and small for baking in the woodburning ovens. One of the most interesting toppings is the barbecue chicken. You will find a variety of pasta dishes, such as linguine with roasted chicken and goat cheese, vegetarian or meat-filled calzones and good spinach and caesar salads. ~ 901 Fairview Avenue North; 206-447-2782, fax 206-223-9372. MODERATE.

Not only is the **BluWater Bistro** one of the most popular late-night bars on Lake Union, it's also an innovative restaurant serving ancho-chile salmon, jerk-chicken satay, tangy ribs in a chipotle-honey glaze, fresh-fish salads and steaks. Summer meals on the lakeside patio are replaced by fireside meals when the rain pours down. ~ 1001 Fairview Avenue North; 206-447-0769; www. bluwaterbistro.com, e-mail info@bluwaterbistro.com. MODERATE TO DELUXE.

Also on Lake Union's east shore is a sushi restaurant much loved by north downtown workers. **I Love Sushi** overlooks Lake Union and a small marina; a lunch repast is so reasonable—a large plate of expertly prepared sushi under $10—that you can dream of bidding on the boats for sale in the water next to the deck. ~ 1001 Fairview Avenue North; 206-625-9604; www.ilovesushi. com. MODERATE.

Siam on Lake Union serves authentic Thai cuisine in a friendly, comfortable setting. There are art objects from Thailand to look at while you wait for your order of Swimming Angel (chicken in a peanut-chili sauce over spinach) or another of the menu's 50-plus items. They vary in hotness and are rich with the flavors of coconut, curry, garlic, peanuts and peppers. No lunch on Saturday. Closed Sunday. ~ 1880 Fairview Avenue East; 206-323-8101. Two other locations: 101 John Street, Queen Anne, 206-285-9000; 616 Broadway East, Capitol Hill, 206-324-0892. BUDGET TO MODERATE.

The hillside overlooking Lake Union is a long way from Trinidad, but **Bandoleone** succeeds smashingly at its mix of Caribbean and Central American cuisine. Chile-seared fresh fish and roast lamb marinated in plum-pepper sauce typify the highly imaginative and seasonally changing offerings. The bar becomes a cigar smokers' haven late in the evening. Dinner only. ~ 2241 Eastlake Avenue East; 206-329-7559; www.bandoleone.net. MODERATE TO DELUXE.

SHOPPING   Outside of the kitschy souvenir shops on the Center grounds, there are a few interesting shops in Queen Anne, not generally considered one of Seattle's leading shopping districts. **GSS Jewelers** creates its own gold and silver designs in-house, with styles ranging from traditional to contemporary; diamonds, purchased directly from Israel, are good value. ~ 526 1st Avenue North; 206-284-2082.

The **Crane Gallery** deals in Asian antiques and artifacts of museum quality. Expect to pay top dollar for ceramics, bronzes, jade, furniture and other precious items. Closed Sunday and Monday. ~ 104 West Roy Street; 206-298-9425.

Along the banks of Lake Union in the south Lake Union district, refurbished warehouses house numerous stores selling outdoor and nautical gear. Also here is Seattle's largest antique dealer, **Antique Liquidators,** with 22,000 square feet of space selling the city's widest variety of used, practical furnishings. ~ 503 Westlake Avenue North; 206-623-2740.

Continue up the lakefront to the **Northwest Outdoor Center,** a full-service paddling shop whose helpful staff not only will sell you a seagoing or whitewater kayak, but will provide you with instruction ranging from beginning to advanced. Rentals are available, too. ~ 2100 Westlake Avenue North; 206-281-9694, 800-682-0637; www.nwoc.com.

Virtually next door is **Mariner Kayaks,** whose custom-crafted vessels are rated among the finest in the world. Brother owners Matt and Cam Broze are considered leaders in their sport, and Matt is the inventor of the modern paddle float used for rescues. Closed Sunday and Monday. ~ 2134 Westlake Avenue North; 206-284-8404; www.marinerkayaks.com.

Across the lake, **Patrick's Fly Shop** focuses on a different water sport: angling. Established in the 1950s, Washington's oldest fly-fishing shop offers classes in fishing techniques and fly tying, and will sell you all the gear you need to get started. ~ 2237 Eastlake Avenue East; 206-325-8988.

Got a hankering for Caspian osetra? Point your shoes toward the **Seattle Caviar Company,** the city's only importer of the treasured fish roe. If your budget won't allow you the stuff from central Asia, you'll also find Northwest sturgeon caviar . . . and a

---

FESTIVALS OF SUMMER

The Seattle Center grounds are the home of three popular and worthwhile annual events. The **Folklife Festival** on Memorial Day weekend attracts hundreds of thousands of fans for music of every possible description, especially ethnic. Folklife also features art and crafts, food, dance, mime, improv theater, juggling and acrobatics—all free, though a donation is suggested. ~ 206-684-7300. **Bumbershoot** occupies the other end of summer, Labor Day weekend, charging a modest admission but offering an equally kaleidoscopic lineup of music, food and arts, including national acts like B. B. King, Pearl Jam, Bonnie Raitt and George Thorogood. ~ 206-281-7788. The midsummer **Bite of Seattle** attracts dozens of the city's restaurants to the grounds, where patrons can try modestly priced samples of everything from ostrich to sautéed geoduck. ~ 206-684-7200.

variety of accoutrements. Closed Sunday and Monday. ~ 2833 Eastlake Avenue East; 206-323-3005; www.caviar.com.

Seattle-based **Recreational Equipment, Inc.,** is better known as **REI,** the largest consumer cooperative in the United States. Its flagship store offers an astonishing array of outdoor clothing and equipment—as well as a huge climbing wall, the tallest indoor freestanding climbing structure in the country. ~ 222 Yale Avenue North (Eastlake Avenue East and Denny Way); 206-223-1944, 888-873-1938.

NIGHTLIFE   Home of the 1962 World's Fair, the **Seattle Center** still offers innumerable nighttime diversions. ~ 305 Harrison Street; 206-684-8582; www.seattlecenter.com.

With the 2003 opening of the **Marion Oliver McCaw Hall for the Performing Arts,** the city's opera and ballet companies have traded in their World's Fair–era concert hall for a glamorous new venue, built on the same Seattle Center site. Founded in 1964, **Seattle Opera** is dedicated to producing theatrically compelling, musically accomplished opera. The leading Wagner company in America, Seattle Opera will bring back its acclaimed production of *The Ring of the Nibelung* in summer 2005. ~ 206-389-7676, 800-426-1619; www. seattleopera.org. **Pacific Northwest Ballet**'s annual production of Tchaikovsky's *Nutcracker*, with fanciful sets designed by famed children's illustrator Maurice Sendak, is a perennial favorite. ~ 206-441-2424, tickets 206-292-2787; www.pnb.org.

It costs just $1.50 to ride the Monorail, which zips between Seattle Center and Westlake Center in two minutes.

The **Seattle Repertory Theatre** plays an eclectic mix from musicals to classic dramas at the **Bagley Wright Theatre** and the **Leo K. Theatre**. ~ 155 Mercer Street between Warren Avenue and 2nd Avenue North; 206-443-2210; www.seattlerep.org. The nearby **Intiman Theatre** presents plays by the great dramatists, as well as new works. ~ 201 Mercer Street at 2nd Avenue North; 206-269-1900; www.intiman.org.

Sky Church is the Experience Music Project's performance hall at the foot of the Space Needle. As befits its name, it's a modern, cathedral-like space where music lovers come to worship tunesmiths of all genres, from alt and indie rock to classic blues. Cover. ~ Seattle Center; 206-292-2787; www.emplive.com.

Around the corner a few blocks, the little bar with the big reputation is called **Tini Bigs**. This Scotch and martini bar draws visitors from far beyond its immediate neighborhood for its stiff pours and dim-lit ambience. ~ 100 Denny Way; 206-284-0931; www.fujipub.com/tinibigs.

Atop Queen Anne Hill, the **Paragon Bar and Grill** is a mecca for live music lovers. Blues and old-fashioned rock bands play most nights. But it's often more crowded around the 30-foot-long bar during daily happy hour. ~ 2125 Queen Anne Avenue North; 206-283-4548.

Alternative rock bands perform seven nights a week at **Graceland**: a dimly lit, low-ceilinged club, it's not a Memphis mansion, but the King would be proud. Cover. ~ 198 Eastlake Avenue East; 206-381-3094.

A 30-plus crowd packs the lounge at **Daniel's Broiler** nightly to hear hours of popular standards from the lively piano bar. ~ 809 Fairview Avenue North; 206-621-8262; www.schwartz bros.com.

Jillian's Billiard Club has dozens of tables—rack 'em!—and a deejay spinning tunes Friday through Sunday nights. ~ 731 Westlake Avenue North; 206-223-0300; www.jillians.com. Just up the lakeshore, karaoke holds center court in the lounge at **China Harbor** Sunday through Wednesday nights. ~ 2040 Westlake Avenue North; 206-286-1688.

▼▼▼▼▼▼▼▼▼▼▼▼

Capitol Hill and East of Lake Union

Take a walk down Broadway, in Capitol Hill, and you'll see one of the most vibrant gay communities in the country. Seattle's diverse array of gay inns, clubs and meeting places is one of the many reasons travelers are increasingly flocking to the city. While gay activities and nightlife are found throughout the city, the highest concentration is in this neighborhood. There are many fascinating alternative shops and friendly restaurants here, and lovely Volunteer Park is home to the Seattle Asian Art Museum. Madison Avenue, which skims the south end of Capitol Hill, runs diagonally northeast from downtown; stretching along its last few blocks, before it comes to an end at Lake Washington, is the upscale, lakeside Madison Park neighborhood. Montlake, on the south side of the Ship Canal opposite the University of Washington, is just north of here; quiet Madrona is hidden among side streets to the south.

SIGHTS On the east side of Lake Union, **Capitol Hill** is a mixed neighborhood that is a fun place to browse. Within a block or two you can toss back an exotic wheatgrass drink at a vegetarian bar, slowly sip a double espresso at a sidewalk café, shop for radical literature at a leftist bookstore or hit a straight or gay nightclub. If you can't find it on Capitol Hill, Seattle probably doesn't have it. Broadway Avenue is the heart of this district known for its boutiques, yuppie appliance stores and bead shops. Gay clubs and stores are also concentrated on Broadway, as well as on nearby streets like 15th Avenue East and East Olive Way.

Home of some of the city's finest Victorians, this neighborhood also includes **Volunteer Park**. Here you'll find the **Seattle Asian Art Museum**. This Art Moderne building was a gift to the city in the 1930s by Dr. Richard Fuller, who was the museum's director for the next 40 years. The Japanese, Chinese and Korean collections are the largest, but the museum also has south and southeast Asian collections. Japanese folk textiles, Thai ceramics and Korean screen paintings are some of the highlights. One admission fee will get you into here and the Seattle Art Museum if you visit within the same week. Admission. ~ Volunteer Park, 1400 East Prospect Street; 206-654-3100, fax 206-654-3135; www.seattleartmuseum.org.

Not far away, **St. Mark's Episcopal Cathedral** is an imposing Romanesque edifice from the outside; an austere, cavernous space inside whose unusual shape (more a square than a long rectangle) was dictated by its location on a bluff overlooking downtown. The cathedral's superb acoustics and massive Flentrop organ make it a frequent site for recitals, as well as the city's most renowned performance of Handel's *Messiah* each Christmas. The gift shop offers books, CDs and knickknacks. ~ 1245 10th Avenue East; 206-323-0300, fax 206-323-4018; www.saintmarks.org.

Northeast of Capitol Hill and on the south side of Union Bay, 230-acre **Washington Park** presents enough diversions indoors and out to fill a rich day of exploring in all sorts of weather. Most famous is the **Washington Park Arboretum** (which occupies most of the park with 10,000 plants), at its best in the spring when rhododendrons and azaleas—some 10 to 15 feet tall—and groves of spreading chestnuts, dogwoods, magnolias and other flowering trees leap into bloom. It also boasts one of the largest holly collections in the country. Short footpaths beckon from the Visitors Center. But two in particular deserve mention—Azalea Way and Loderi Valley—which wend their way down avenues of pink, cream, yellow, crimson and white blooms. The arboretum's renowned **Japanese Garden** (admission) is especially rewarding in the spring months, and both arboretum and garden present splendid fall colors in October and early November. In the Winter Garden, everything is fragrant, and the Woodland Garden highlights the arboretum's acclaimed collection of Japanese maples. ~ Lake Washington Boulevard East and East Madison Street; Visitors Center: 2300 Arboretum Drive East; 206-543-8800, fax 206-325-8893; www.wparboretum.org. Japanese Garden: 1502 Lake Washington Boulevard East; 206-684-4725.

Miles of duff-covered footpaths lace the park. For naturalists, the premier experience will be found along the one-and-a-half-

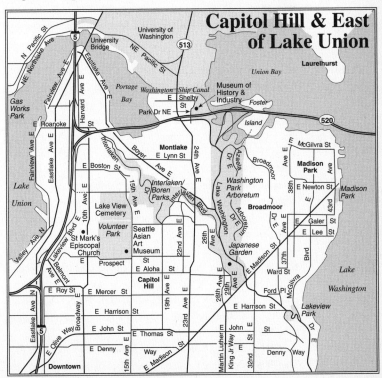

mile (each way) **Foster Island Trail** at the north end of the park on Foster Island behind the Museum of History and Industry (see below). This footpath takes you on an intriguing bog-walk over low bridges and along boardwalks through marshy wetlands teeming with ducks and wildfowl, fish and frogs and aquatic flora growing rank at the edge of Lake Washington, across the Montlake Cut.

On Broadway, the public art will give you a free dance lesson—just follow the bronze "Dancing Steps" imbedded in the sidewalk.

In summer, you can join the canoeists paddling the labyrinth of waterways around **Foster Island**, sunbathers and picnickers sprawling on lawns, anglers casting for catfish and trout and the swimmers cooling off on hot August afternoons. Canoes are for rent through the University of Washington.

On rainy days the **Museum of History and Industry** is a fitting retreat. It's the city's best early-day collection and pays special tribute to Puget Sound's rich maritime history, as befits any museum located next door to this vital waterway. Closed Monday. Admission. ~ 2700 24th Avenue East; 206-324-1125, fax 206-324-1346; www.seattlehistory.org, e-mail information@seattle history.org.

LODGING   Just one block north of the Harvard Exit Theater sits **Bed & Breakfast on Broadway**, a 1906 home with four bedrooms, all with private baths. Breakfast is continental (pastries, fruit, coffee) but with Broadway literally at your feet, you won't go hungry for food or entertainment. ~ 722 Broadway Avenue East; 206-329-8933, fax 206-726-0918; www.bbonbroadway.com. MODERATE TO DELUXE.

A mother-daughter team runs the **Salisbury House**, a quiet, dignified, gracious Capitol Hill home two blocks from Volunteer Park. Cathryn and Mary Wiese offer five crisp, clean rooms (all have private baths) furnished with antiques and wicker. Fresh flowers, duvets on the beds, a full (meatless) breakfast and thoughtful innkeepers make this a well-done bed and breakfast. There are fireplaces in the living room and library and a refrigerator guests may use. ~ 750 16th Avenue East; 206-328-8682, fax 206-720-1019; www.salisburyhouse.com, e-mail sleep@salisburyhouse.com. DELUXE.

Gaslight Inn is a bed and breakfast brimming with urban flair. The 1906 four-square house is furnished with oak, maple and glass antiques. Various period styles have been effectively combined with modern amenities in the 16 guest rooms. Most have private baths, and six boast fireplaces. Gaslight has a heated, outdoor pool (closed in winter) and an outdoor deck that overlooks the city. The inn serves a continental buffet breakfast. ~ 1727 15th Avenue East; 206-325-3654, fax 206-328-4803; www.gaslight-inn. com, e-mail innkeepr@gaslight-inn.com. MODERATE TO DELUXE.

Located on Millionaire's Row, the **Shafer-Baillie Mansion** is a turreted and gabled reminder of an earlier era with its wide porches, library, formal dining room and ballroom with a copper fireplace. Built in 1914, the grand 15,000-square-foot mansion is the largest on Capitol Hill. This bed-and-breakfast inn has 11 suites, all with refrigerators and televisions and most with private baths. ~ 907 14th Avenue East; 206-322-4654, 800-922-4654, fax 206-329-4654; www.shaferbaillie.com. MODERATE TO ULTRA-DELUXE.

Near Volunteer Park in the Harvard-Belmont Historic District is the **Bacon Mansion**, a historic 1909 Tudor stucco home. In addition to the two-story carriage house, which has a living room, dining room and two guest rooms with a private bath in each, there are nine guest rooms in the main house, seven with private bath. The Capitol suite has a sun room with wet bar, fireplace, queen-size bed, view of the Space Needle and a big bathtub. ~ 959 Broadway East; 206-329-1864, 800-240-1864, fax 206-860-9025; www.baconmansion.com, e-mail info@baconmansion.com. MODERATE TO ULTRA-DELUXE.

DINING

West of Broadway, on Pike and Pine streets, is a collection of bars and restaurants catering to the hipster population. **611 Supreme** is a cheery, comfy café specializing in crêpes both sweet and savory. Try the ham-and-cheese crêpe, or the carmelized apple version. No lunch on weekdays. Closed Monday. ~ 611 East Pine Street; 206-328-0292. BUDGET.

Ayutthaya is a corner restaurant renowned for its Thai cookery. Small, clean-lined and pleasant in blue and lavender, Ayutthaya features plenty of chicken and seafood dishes along with soups and noodles. Flavors blend deliciously in the curried shrimp with green beans, coconut milk and basil. Or try the chicken sautéed in peanut-chili sauce. No lunch on Sunday. ~ 727 East Pike Street; 206-324-8833, fax 206-324-3135. BUDGET TO MODERATE.

At **Osteria La Spiga**, the fare is down-home Italian, the decor rustic tile, and the crowded tables lively. Soups, salads, panini and pastas are done with flair, and when the lights go down, the atmosphere is about as charmingly romantic as Broadway dining gets. No lunch Saturday through Tuesday; no dinner on Sunday. ~ 1401 Broadway Avenue; 206-323-8881. BUDGET TO MODERATE.

HIDDEN ► The newest venture of James Beard Award–winning chef Johnathan Sundstrom is **Lark**, an intimate restaurant that opened not far from the University of Seattle in late 2003. In a distinctively Northwest ambience of open beams, ceiling fans and draped room dividers, diners share multiple small plates ranging from artisan cheeses to braised short ribs, sautéed chanterelles to smoked prosciutto with fig chutney. Dinner only. Closed Monday. ~ 926 12th Avenue; 206-323-5275. DELUXE.

Café Septième is Kurt Timmermeister's re-creation of small Parisian cafés that cater to the literati and students. This full-service restaurant carries plenty of reading material and turns out cups of good coffee, lattes and light fare. Sandwiches and salads are standard, but the real treat is the mouth-watering display table, loaded with cakes, pies and cookies. Breakfast, lunch and dinner. ~ 214 Broadway East; 206-860-8858, fax 206-860-0760. BUDGET TO MODERATE.

The **Broadway Grill** is a famed mainstay of the Capitol Hill scene. Its food is mainstream-grill breakfast and burger fare, moderately priced and dependable if unimaginative. But it's better known as a place to hang out and watch the passing parade on Broadway. ~ 314 Broadway East; 206-328-7000, fax 206-325-4734. BUDGET TO MODERATE.

More health-conscious nibblers head for the **Gravity Bar**, a full-service vegetarian restaurant with white woodwork and modern cone-shaped glass-topped tables. The extensive menu includes tofu avocado rollups, tempeh burgers, brown rice salad and a selection of vegetable and fruit juices. ~ 415 Broadway East; 206-325-7186. BUDGET.

Since Capitol Hill never truly closes, its two dessert emporia are integral to the area's atmosphere. You can buy a box of chocolate truffles at **Café Dilettante**, but you'd be missing a divine late-evening experience—a midnight table in a crowded, mirrored room. Try the Coupe Dilettante, the restaurant's exceptional ice cream sundae swimming in Dilettante's dark Ephemere sauce, or

Where Are
They Now?

Nearly 30,000 visitors each year make pilgrimages to Seattle to visit the gravesites of deceased superstars. The headstone of martial arts film hero **Bruce Lee** (1940–1973), engraved in English and Chinese, is found in Lake View Cemetery on Capitol Hill, just north of Volunteer Park. Alongside, another headstone marks the final resting place of his son, **Brandon Lee** (1965–1993), who died in a freak gunshot accident while filming *The Crow*. ~ 1554 15th Avenue East, Seattle; 206-322-1582.

Lake View Cemetery is also the final resting place of several Seattle historical figures—among them founding fathers Henry L. Yesler (1830–1892) and David "Doc" Maynard (1808–1873), and Chief Seattle's daughter Princess Angeline (1820?–1896).

Legendary guitarist **Jimi Hendrix** (1942–1970), who reigned as Seattle's most famous rock musician until his fatal drug overdose a year after his landmark appearance at Woodstock, is interred at Greenwood Memorial Park in suburban Renton. Because of the large number of fans who still visit the grave, a large open-air family mausoleum has been built on the site. ~ 350 Monroe Avenue Northeast, Renton; 425-255-1511.

Incidentally, Jimi Hendrix attended central Seattle's Garfield High School, where Bruce Lee met his future wife Linda Emery (class of '63) while he was giving a guest lecture on Chinese philosophy at Garfield High. Jimi and Bruce also shared the same birthday, November 27.

Don't look for the grave of Seattle's other deceased rock superstar, **Kurt Cobain** (1967–1994), lead singer and guitarist of the grunge group Nirvana. His remains were cremated and the ashes scattered in the Wishkah River near the south boundary of Olympic National Park. The river provides the water supply for the city of Aberdeen, Washington—Cobain's hometown. If you can't make the pilgrimage out to Aberdeen, head for Seattle's Viretta Park instead. This tiny park, due south of Cobain's former Madrona home, has become an informal memorial site, complete with flowers, candles and graffiti left by fans. ~ 151 Lake Washington Boulevard East.

any of dozens of other desserts. This is among the best chocolate in the country. ~ Dilettante Chocolates, 416 Broadway East; 206-329-6463, fax 206-329-0782; www.dilettante.com. BUDGET.

HIDDEN ► At **B & O Espresso**, the emphasis is less on chocolate, the atmosphere is a bit more cozy than glitzy and the late-night crowds are large. Like the Dilettante, the B & O offers a limited menu of soups, salads and sandwiches. But dessert is the main course. Diners can choose from more than two dozen different pies, cakes and European-style tortes. ~ 204 Belmont Avenue East; 206-322-5028, fax 206-322-5707. BUDGET.

HIDDEN ► You know any restaurant that celebrates Bastille Day *must* be authentically French. That's the case with **Cassis**, a delightful, off-the-beaten-track bistro on the route north from Capitol Hill toward Montlake. Come here to assuage your Gallic inclinations for *boeuf bourguignon* and *coq au vin*, *cassoulet* and steak *frites*, and, of course, fine wines and cheeses. Dinner only. ~ 2359 10th Avenue East; 206-329-0580. www.cassisbistro.com, e-mail reservations@cassisbistro.com. DELUXE.

HIDDEN ► Almost across the street from Kingfish, **Monsoon** is a family-operated Vietnamese café with an open kitchen and a sleek, elegant appeal. The tamarind prawn soup is a local favorite, and fresh seafood entrées—halibut steamed with shiitake mushrooms in a banana leaf, for instance—draw raves. Vegetarians find much to like on a menu notable for items prepared in chile oil or coconut milk. No lunch on weekends. Closed Monday. ~ 615 19th Avenue East; 206-325-2111; www.monsoonseattle.com. MODERATE.

In a small house surrounded by gardens in the Madison Park–Montlake area is **Rover's**, which specializes in five-course meals of Northwest cuisine with a French accent and is just the place for those romantic occasions. Chef Thierry Rautureau creates the ever-changing menu based on locally available, fresh produce. In addition to seafood in imaginative sauces, entrées might include rabbit, venison, pheasant and quail. A good selection of Northwest and French wines is available. Service is friendly and helpful, and there is patio seating in summer. Dinner only. Closed Sunday and Monday. ~ 2808 East Madison Street; 206-325-7442, fax 206-325-1092; www.rovers-seattle.com. ULTRA-DELUXE.

It's standing-room only every night at tiny **Harvest Vine**, Seattle's best spot to enjoy the small savory plates the Spanish know as *tapas*. Locals come to graze on chef Joseph Jiménez de

Jiménez's crab-stuffed *piquillo* peppers, venison on black-trumpet mushrooms, smoked sturgeon with trout caviar and *pulpo de feira* (Galician-style octopus), and to enjoy bottles of Spanish wine in the lower-level Basque *txoco*. Dinner only. Closed Sunday and Monday. ~ 2701 East Madison Street; 206-320-9771. MODERATE TO DELUXE.

One of the city's premier all-vegetarian restaurants is **Cafe Flora**, where it's no sin to enjoy a glass of wine or beer with your lentil-pecan pâté or eggplant *envoltini*. Sage polenta is crafted with roasted butternut squash and crimini mushrooms; the cashew-apple salad and pear-gorgonzola pizza are big sellers. Of the two spacious dining rooms, opt for the covered garden patio. Closed Monday. ~ 2901 East Madison Street; 206-325-9100; www.cafe flora.com, e-mail cafeflora@mindspring.com. MODERATE.

A colorful and lively Spanish-eclectic restaurant in the Madison Park area, **Cactus** serves a cuisine representative of many different cultures, but mostly influenced by Southwestern food. Start with one of the most unusual items on the menu—a salad of baby field greens topped with beer-battered goat cheese, candied hazelnuts and a roasted-jalapeño-and-apple vinaigrette. The ancho-cinnamon chicken is marinated in ancho chile, cinnamon and Mexican chocolate and glazed with honey. No lunch on Sunday. ~ 4220 East Madison Street; 206-324-4140; www.cactusrestau rants.com. MODERATE.

At unpretentious **Cafe Lago**, in the Montlake area, Italian rules the roost. Huge antipasto plates come laden with bruschetta, eggplant-and-olive caponata, roasted garlic, prosciutto ham and various cheeses. Lasagna, layered with ricotta and béchamel, sells

AUTHOR FAVORITE

I don't have to travel to the Deep South to get a taste of gourmet soul cookin', but I must expect to wait in line at the stylish **Kingfish Café**, where sepia-tinted family-album photos (including one of cousin Langston Hughes, the great African-American writer) adorn the walls. Big Daddy's Pickapeppa Steak is a menu favorite, along with the buttermilk fried chicken, the barbecued pork, and the crab and catfish cakes (served Benedict style at Sunday brunch). Closed Tuesday and Saturday for lunch, Sunday for dinner. ~ 602 19th Avenue East; 206-320-8757; e-mail kingfishcafe@aol.com. MODERATE.

out early every night; wood-fired, thin-crust pizzas and gorgonzola steaks are also crowd pleasers. Dinner only. Closed Monday. ~ 2305 24th Avenue East; 206-329-8005. MODERATE.

HIDDEN ►
Two reasons to go to **Dulces Latin Bistro**: sweets (*dulces* in
Spanish) and cigars. A romantic hideaway in the Madrona neighborhood, the restaurant offers a delightful fusion of contemporary
Mediterranean and Mexican cuisine: paella Valenciana, chorizo-
stuffed ravioli, Guadalajara-style *carne asada*. Leave room for a
marvelous dessert, like the *cajeta* (Mexican caramel) or chocolate
tart, and an after-dinner drink in author Tom Robbins' favorite
cigar-and-martini bar. When Havanas become legal in the U.S.,
you'll get 'em here. Dinner only. Closed Sunday and Monday. ~
1430 34th Avenue; 206-322-5453, fax 206-322-5275; www.dul
ceslatinbistro.com. MODERATE TO DELUXE.

HIDDEN ►
Owned by former schoolteachers and named for the orphan-
age in John Irving's *The Cider House Rules*, **St. Clouds** takes social responsibility seriously: Once a month, patrons join its chefs
in cooking for the homeless. Irving's sense of "home and family"
is likewise pursued in the menu of this Madrona eatery, split between "Home for Dinner" options—herb-roasted chicken,
cheeseburger and fries—and gourmet "Out for Dinner" choices:
parmesan-crusted pork tenderloin, saffron-fennel seafood stew,
seared ahi tuna. Sweet potato-bourbon-pecan pie is to die for. A
rotating and eclectic roster of musicians enlivens the bar most
nights. Closed Tuesday. ~ 1129 34th Avenue; 206-726-1522;
www.stclouds.com. MODERATE TO DELUXE.

SHOPPING
The trendy boutiques of Capitol Hill draw shoppers looking for
the unusual, though there are many standard stores, too. You'll
see dozens of shops with new and vintage clothing, pop culture
items, and ethnic wear and artifacts, all interspersed with myr-
iad cafés and coffeehouses.

No one might blame you for thinking **Area 51** is run by aliens.
The '60s/'70s decor at this retro furniture store is unusual, to say
the least: neon-colored rotary phones, for instance, and gym
lockers-turned-wardrobes. ~ 401 East Pine Street; 206-568-4782.

Any alternative sexual community needs a literary center, and
the **Beyond the Closet Bookstore** fits the bill to a tee. The range
of books and magazines runs the gamut from political to erotic,
and includes both mainstream media and small presses. ~ 518
East Pike Street; 206-322-4609; www.beyondthecloset.com.

Yes, it's a sex shop. But **Toys in Babeland** isn't what you'd expect. Plate-glass front windows, plenty of lighting and comfy benches have turned this purveyor of toys, books and body products into a neighborhood hangout. Come here to feel empowered, admire the tasteful-albeit-pornographic glass art and meet more locals than at the corner café. ~ 707 East Pike Street; 206-328-2914; www.babeland.com.

If you're into music you won't hear on Top-40 radio, take a wander down East Olive Way. The **Fillipi Book and Record Shop** has an inventory of old sheet music and 78- and 45-rpm records, including hard-to-find jazz. Closed Sunday and Monday. ~ 1351 East Olive Way; 206-682-4266.

Broadway Market is filled with popular shops like **Urban Outfitters**. Featuring casual urban wares, this shop offers new and vintage clothing, jewelry, housewares and shoes for the hip crowd. ~ 401 Broadway East; 206-322-1800.

There's no shortage of reading material on Broadway. From the racks at **Broadway News,** you can pick up the latest edition of *Der Spiegel, Le Figaro* or *The New York Times.* ~ 204 Broadway Avenue East; 206-324-7323. **Bailey/Coy Books** is well-stocked with fiction and philosophy, as well as gay and lesbian literature. ~ 414 Broadway East; 206-323-8842. **Marco Polo** carries an extensive collection of travel literature and guides (like this one), plus globes and travel gear. ~ 713 Broadway Avenue East; 206-860-3736; www.marcopolos.com.

At the **Washington Park Arboretum Visitor Center Gift Shop** are gardening books, cards, china, earrings, necklaces, serving trays and sweatshirts. You can also buy plants from the arboretum greenhouse. ~ 2300 Arboretum Drive East; 206-543-8800; www.wparboretum.org.

STARGAZING

Robert Redford's Sundance Festival may be more famous, but the **Seattle International Film Festival** is actually the largest independent film event in the country. Each spring, SIFF draws hundreds of thousands of cinema lovers for its 25-day run in Capitol Hill and downtown theaters, and each year at least one of the SIFF favorites goes on to national acclaim. Screenings, lectures and receptions abound at this large, well-attended film festival. Admission. ~ 206-464-5830.

NIGHTLIFE In the "Pike-Pine corridor," west of Broadway, a string of stylish (and stylized) bars stretches toward downtown. East of Broadway, the clubs along Pike and Pine drop down a notch on the scene scale and gain in loungeability.

Hit the wooden dancefloor at the **Century Ballroom** for swing and salsa with live bands. Lessons are free with cover. Closed Monday and Tuesday. ~ 915 East Pine Street, 2nd floor; 206-324-7263; www.centuryballroom.com.

With its mohair booths and starry ceiling, the **Baltic Room** is a glamourous retro cocktail lounge. Music (both live and deejayed) ranges from jazz to hip-hop to Bollywood. Cover on weekends. ~ 1207 East Pine Street; 206-625-4444; www.thebalticroom.com.

The Garage offers an unusual coupling of restaurant and up-scale cocktail lounge with billiards parlor and double-deck bowling alley. Its spaciousness—it does, in fact, occupy a former automobile garage—makes it an inviting venue for Halloween, New Year's and other special-occasion parties. ~ 1130-34 Broadway Avenue; 206-322-2296; www.garagebilliards.com.

Barça is a slinky lounge popular with the pierced and tattooed set. There's no live music, but deejays perform on weekends. Prime viewing is from the balcony. ~ 1510 11th Avenue; 206-325-8263; www.barcaseattle.com.

Nostalgia reigns at the **Harvard Exit Theater**. Once the elegant home of a women's club, it still has the parlor with a fireplace and piano. This is the place to see award-winning foreign and art films. Auditoriums are wheelchair accessible. ~ 807 East Roy Street; 206-323-8986.

Gay Scene Capitol Hill offers a number of popular gay and lesbian clubs and bars, including the following:

Not your ordinary Seattle café, **Coffee Messiah** beckons with a large pink neon cross perched on the rooftop. The interior is painted a deep purple, with red velvet curtains and religious images. A pilgrimage to this coffee shrine would not be complete without a trip to its coin-operated discotheque bathroom, decorated to simulate Hell with pictures of the devil surrounding a black sink and toilet. Open mic Tuesday, experimental music Wednesday and Thursday. ~ 1554 East Olive Way; 206-861-8233; www.coffeemessiah.com.

One of the biggest clubs in the area is **R Place Bar & Grill**. Depending on your mood, you can plunk down at the sports bar, throw darts, enjoy a music video, shoot pool, enjoy tunes from the jukebox or feast on quesadillas and taco salad. ~ 619 East Pine Street; 206-322-8828; www.rplaceseattle.com.

Founded in 1985, the **Wild Rose** claims to be the oldest women's bar on the West Coast, offering food and drink as well as camaraderie. Occasional live music. ~ 1021 East Pike Street; 206-324-9210.

Also popular is **Neighbours**, offering deejay dance music seven nights a week, including retro disco and Latin nights. Cover. ~ 1509 Broadway Avenue; 206-324-5358; www.neighboursonline.com.

There's a piano bar and dinner service at **Thumper's**, which is also a lunch and Sunday brunch place. Cabaret on weekends. Cover. ~ 1500 East Madison Street; 206-328-3800.

Vogue is the mecca of Seattle's leather/lace/latex enthusiasts. Partly gay and partly not, it features industrial and new-wave deejay music most nights. Themes vary—for instance, Wednesday is gothic night while Sunday is fetish night. Cover. ~ 1516 11th Avenue; 206-324-5778. The leather crowd also favors **The Cuff** (1533 13th Avenue; 206-323-1525) and **Seattle Eagle** (314 East Pike Street; 206-621-7591).

For a round of beers in a classic bar, head to the **Elite Tavern** for its busy pub atmosphere. ~ 622 Broadway Avenue East; 206-324-4470.

VOLUNTEER PARK   Many of Seattle's finest Victorians flank this 48-acre park, designed by the famed Olmsted brothers in the early 20th century. A conservatory at 15th and Galer has three large (and free!) greenhouses filled with tropical plants, flowering plants and cacti. The park contains the Seattle Asian Art Museum (see "Sights" earlier in this chapter). Be sure to head up to the top of the water tower for a great view of the region. ~ 15th Avenue East from East Prospect Street to East Galer Street.   **PARKS**

BOREN/INTERLAKEN PARKS   A secret greenway close to downtown is preserved by these neighboring parks on Capitol Hill; it's just right for an afternoon or evening stroll. ~ Entry points are on 15th Avenue East across from the Lakeview cemetery and at East Galer Street and East Interlaken Boulevard.   ◄ *HIDDEN*

SIX

Northern Neighborhoods

Few guidebooks look at the Lake Washington Ship Canal as a single unit. Yet a west-to-east traverse of Seattle, loosely tracing the northern shoreline of this important eight-mile transportation route, opens visitors' eyes to a wondrous diversity of working waterfront and recreational shoreline. Construction of the locks and canal began in 1911 and created a shipping channel from Puget Sound to Lake Washington via Lake Union. Along its banks today you can see perhaps the liveliest continuous boat parade in the West: tugs gingerly inching four-story-tall, Alaska-bound barges through narrow locks; rowboats, kayaks, sailboards and luxury yachts; gill-netters and trawlers in dry dock; government-research vessels; aging houseboats listing at their moorings; and seaplanes roaring overhead.

All in all, the ship canal presents a splendid overview of Seattle's rich maritime traditions. But you'll also discover plenty that's new: the rejuvenated neighborhood of Fremont, a renovated Fishermen's Terminal and a handful of trendy, waterside restaurants. Amid the hubbub of boat traffic and ship chandlers, you'll also encounter quiet, street-end parks for birdwatching, foot and bike paths, and a great university with its surrounding campus community.

A mile or so north of the ship canal, another body of water—charming Green Lake—is the focal point of several neighborhoods. Adjacent Woodland Park and Green Lake Park straddle Aurora Avenue North (Route 99) and together offer more than 400 acres of park, lake and zoo attractions. And to the south and southeast of the lake is Wallingford, a hip neighborhood of edgy shops and ethnic restaurants that stretches along North 45th Street, all the way from Route 99 to the University of Washington campus area.

Heading north from Green Lake, you'll cut through the Northgate and Shoreline neighborhoods and finally cross from King into Snohomish County. Here, less urban and more maritime cities and villages line Northern Puget Sound. Edmonds is of most interest to visitors. You won't have to travel far to catch a glimpse of the region's past, before Seattlemania lured businesses and families to relocate here.

BALLARD–FREMONT AREA   Ballard is one of Seattle's most dis-   **SIGHTS**
tinctive neighborhoods, exemplified by the wry slogan, "Ya, sure, y'betcha," a nod to its Nordic heritage. Ever tried lutefisk? If you want to attempt this lye-soaked cod dish (few do), this is the place. Ballard shut down to greet Norway's royal family on a state visit to the United States in 1975; and each year, Ballardites parade down Northwest Market Street to observe Norwegian Independence Day on May 17. The parade ends at Bergen Place, a triangle of urban parkland (bounded by Northwest Market and Leary streets and 22nd Avenue Northwest) named for its Norwegian sister city and dedicated by King Olav V.

For the casual visitor, the best place to learn about Ballard's Scandinavian roots is the **Nordic Heritage Museum**, the only facility of its kind in the country. In five separate ethnic galleries, artifacts such as antique boats and furnishings, textiles and household goods, books and photographs tell the story of immigrants from Norway, Sweden, Denmark, Iceland and Finland, and demonstrate how timber and fisheries drew them here more than a century ago. The museum also maintains an extensive research library and sponsors a variety of community events—music, film, art—with a Nordic theme. Closed Monday. Admission. ~ 3014 67th Street Northwest; 206-789-5707, fax 206-789-3271; www.nordicmuseum.com, e-mail nordic@intelistep.com.

Hiram M. Chittenden Locks is where all boats heading east or west in the ship canal must pass and thus presents the quintessential floating boat show; it's one of the most-visited attractions in the city. Visitors crowd railings and jam footbridges to watch as harried lock-keepers scurry to get boats tied up properly before locks are either raised or lowered, depending on the boat's direction of passage. Terraced parks flanking the canal provide splendid picnic overlooks. An underwater fish-viewing window gives you astonishing looks at several species of salmon, steelhead and sea-going cutthroat trout on their spawning migrations (June to November). Lovely botanical gardens in a parklike setting offer yet more diversion. ~ 206-783-7059, fax 206-782-3192.

Fishermen's Terminal is home port to one of the world's biggest fishing fleets, some 700 vessels, most of which chug north into Alaskan waters for summer salmon fishing. But you'll always be able to see boats here—gill-netters, purse-seiners, trollers, factory ships—and working fishermen repairing nets, painting boats and the like. Interpretive signage describes the various vessels and the nuances of the fishing industry. Here, too, are net-drying sheds, nautical stores and shops selling marine hardware and commercial fishing tackle. One café opens at 6:30 a.m. for working fishermen; there's a pub, a fish-and-chips window, a fresh seafood market and one good seafood restaurant (Chinook's) overlooking the waterway. You may shed a tear at the Seattle Fishermen's Memorial, where family members leave flowers and birthday cards beside the names of loved ones who have perished in the seas. ~ 1900 West Nickerson Street, on the south side of Salmon Bay about a mile east of the locks; 206-728-3395, fax 206-728-3393.

The **Fremont** neighborhood is locally famous for the sculpture *Waiting for the Interurban*, whose collection of lifelike commuters is frequently adorned in funny hats, scarves and other cast-off clothing. Centered around Fremont Avenue North and North 34th Street at the northwest corner of Lake Union, the district is top-heavy with shops proffering the offbeat (handmade dulcimers, antiques and junk).

HIDDEN ► Perhaps most offbeat of all is the **Fremont Troll**, another famous sculpture found beneath the north footings of the Aurora Bridge. When the nearby Magnolia Bridge was damaged by mudslides, Fremont residents archly averred that their bridge escaped harm because it was under a troll's guardianship. ~ 35th Street North, under the Aurora Bridge.

GREEN LAKE AREA   The star of the parks in Seattle's northern neighborhoods, and due north of Fremont via Fremont Avenue, is **Woodland Park Zoo**, which has won praise for its program of converting static exhibits into more natural, often outdoor environments. Most notable are the African Savannah, Gorilla Exhibit, the Marsh and Swamp and the Elephant Forest where you can see Thai elephants working at traditional tasks. There's also a Tropical Rain Forest, heralded as a "journey through different levels of forest," and a seasonal contact yard and family farm. The Trail of Vines is an Asian rainforest where Indian pythons,

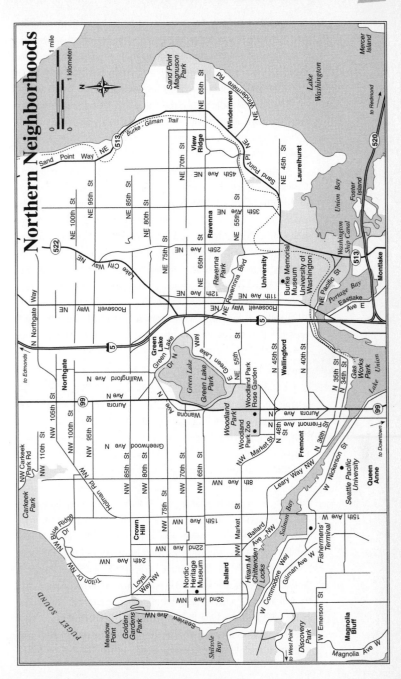

Northern Neighborhoods

1 mile

1 kilometer

N

PUGET SOUND

Meadow Point

Golden Gardens Park

Shilshole Bay

Triton Dr NW

NW Blue Ridge Dr

Carkeek Park

NW Carkeek Park Rd

NW 110th St

NW 105th St

NW 100th St

NW 95th St

Holman Rd NW

Crown Hill

NW 85th St

NW 80th St

NW 75th St

NW 70th St

NW 65th St

24th Ave NW

22nd Ave NW

15th Ave NW

8th Ave NW

Seaview Ave NW

Loyal Way NW

32nd Ave NW

Nordic Heritage Museum

Ballard

NW Market St

Ballard Ave NW

Hiram M Chittenden Locks

Salmon Bay

W Commodore Way

Gilman Ave W

Fishermens' Terminal

15th Ave W

Seattle Pacific University

Queen Anne

W Nickerson St

Lake Union

Gas Works Park

N 34th St

N 35th St

Magnolia Bluff

W Emerson St

Discovery Park

to West Point

Magnolia Ave W

Greenwood Ave N

Aurora Ave N

99

N 105th St

N 100th St

N 95th St

N 85th St

N 80th St

N 70th St

N 65th St

Wanona

Woodland Park

Woodland Park Zoo

Woodland Park Rose Garden

Green Lake

Green Lake Park

Green Lake Way N

Green Lake Dr N

Wallingford Ave N

NW Market St

N 46th St

Fremont Ave N

Fremont

N 45th St

N 40th St

Wallingford

Leary Way NW

Aurora Ave N

99

to Downtown

N Northgate Way

Northgate

5

to Edmonds

Roosevelt Way NE

NE Northgate Way

NE 100th St

NE 95th St

NE 85th St

NE 80th St

NE 75th St

NE 65th St

Lake City Way NE

522

NE 70th St

View Ridge

Sand Point Way NE

513

Burke - Gilman Trail

Sand Point Magnuson Park

NE 65th St

Windermere

NE Windermere Rd

Lake Washington

Mercer Island

Ravenna

Ravenna Park

Ravenna Blvd

25th Ave NE

35th Ave NE

45th Ave NE

NE 55th St

55th St

NE 45th St

Laurelhurst

Sand Point Pl

University

University of Washington

Burke Memorial Museum

NE Pacific St

11th Ave NE

12th Ave NE

15th Ave NE

Union Bay

Foster Island

Washington Ship Canal

Montlake

513

520

to Redmond

Portage Bay

Eastlake Ave E

5

lion-tailed macaques, orangutans, Malayan tapirs and siamangs live. Published daily is a public feeding schedule: that is, when the public can watch certain animals being fed, not when the public is fed to the animals. Admission. ~ 5500 Phinney Avenue North; 206-684-4800, fax 206-615-1070; www.zoo.org.

Immediately adjacent to the zoo is the **Woodland Park Rose Garden**, with more than 5000 seasonal plants—some modern hybrids, some old-time favorites. ~ 5500 Phinney Avenue North; 206-684-4863.

At its northeast edge, Woodland Park nudges up against **Green Lake Park**. Enormously popular with all ages and classes of Seattleites, this is simply the best outdoor people-watching place in the city. Two loop trails circle the shore (the inner trail is 2.8 miles long, the outer 3.2 miles) and welcome all comers. On summer days, both paths are filled with strollers and race-walkers, joggers and skaters, bikers and nannies pushing prams. On the lake you will see anglers, canoeists, sailboarders, swimmers, bird-watchers and folks floating in inner tubes. Rentals of all manner of land and water craft are available near the park center. ~ East Green Lake Drive North at Northeast 65th Street; 206-684-4075.

UNIVERSITY DISTRICT   It's a short jaunt east and south from Green Lake to the U District. Exceptional architecture, a garden setting and easy access make a campus tour of the **University of Washington** (or U-dub, as locals call it) a highlight of a Seattle visit. The university began downtown in 1861; in 1895, it was moved to its present site. The campus borders the canal north of Montlake Cut (part of the waterway) and is a haven for anyone who enjoys the simple pleasure of strolling across a college campus. There's plenty to boggle the mind on its 693 acres: handsome old buildings in architectural styles from Romanesque to modern; Frosh Pond; red-brick quads and expanses of lawn and colorful summer gardens; canal-side trails on both sides of the Montlake Cut; access to the Burke-Gilman Trail; and a lakeside **Waterfront Activity Center** (206-543-9433) with canoe and rowboat rentals, as well as an adjacent rock-climbing practice facility. ~ Southeast Husky Stadium parking lot, off Montlake Boulevard.

The **Burke Memorial Museum of Natural History and Culture** is the oldest university museum in the West. Established in 1885, it has a notable collection of more than three million American Indian and Pacific Rim artifacts. Two permanent exhibits attract attention: "The Life and Times of Washington State" offers children a lesson in 500 million years of natural history, while "Pacific Voices" is a rich adult-oriented look at Asian and Pacific cultures, complete with video storytelling from members of those communities. There's a well-stocked gift shop and a popular coffeehouse, the **Burke Museum Café** (206-543-9854), in the basement. ~ Northeast 45th Street and 17th Avenue Northeast; 206-543-5590, fax 206-685-3039; www.washington.edu/burkemuseum.

The Alaska-Yukon-Pacific Exposition of 1909 was held on the University of Washington campus, and several of its fine buildings date from that event.

The **Henry Art Gallery** focuses on modern and contemporary art, with an emphasis on cutting-edge installations. Don't miss the excellent photography collection on display here. You'll also find an outdoor sculpture garden, auditorium and children's education center. Closed Monday. Admission. ~ 15th Avenue Northeast and Northeast 41st Street; 206-543-2280, fax 206-685-3123; www.henryart.org.

At the **Visitors Information Center,** you can pick up a useful (and free) walking tour map. The map describes quirky bits of UW history as the hour-plus walk meanders under tall trees and past stately brick buildings. The Henry Suzzallo Library resembles a Gothic cathedral. The Medicinal Herb Garden may be the largest of its kind in the United States. The tree-enclosed Sylvan Grove Theater is the site of numerous trysts, plays and weddings. Fountains, ponds, a rose garden and views of Lake Washington and Mount Rainier add texture to the lovely campus. The visitors center is closed weekends. ~ 4014 University Way Northeast; 206-543-9198, fax 206-616-6294; www.washington.edu.

EDMONDS AND NORTHERN SUBURBS   North of Seattle, the long-time (former) mill town of **Edmonds** has a lively charm and provides a link to the Olympic Peninsula. Ferries leave hourly from the Edmonds ferry landing, on a waterfront that has a recently redone beach park, a long fishing pier and an underwater park that is popular with divers. The park teems with marine life that swims around sunken structures: boats, a dock, a bridge model and others. On shore, the **Edmonds Beach Rangers** host summer beach walks. ~ 425-771-0230, fax 425-771-0253.

The **Edmonds Chamber of Commerce** wins the prize for quaintness. Its information center is housed in a pioneer log cabin that looks like a storybook house. ~ 121 5th Avenue North, Edmonds; 425-670-1496, fax 425-712-1808; www.edmondswa. com, e-mail hidden@edmondswa.com.

A visit to the **Edmonds Historical Museum** with its working shingle-mill model, maritime heritage exhibits and collections of logging tools and household furnishings gives a better understanding of the pioneer heritage and industrial history of Edmonds. A walking tour takes you past the old shingle mills, Brackett's Landing (where the earliest pioneers settled), and numerous buildings constructed in the late 1800s and early 1900s. Closed Monday and Tuesday. ~ 118 5th Avenue North, Edmonds; 425-774-0900; www.historicedmonds.org.

LODGING

HIDDEN ►

Located across the street from the Woodland Park Zoo, the Phinney Ridge neighborhood's **Chelsea Station on the Park** is one of Seattle's most charming bed-and-breakfast inns. Occupying two adjoining Federal Colonial–style brick homes of 1929 vintage, Chelsea Station has nine rooms of varying size with Craftsman furnishings, private baths and phones (the Morning Glory Suite even boasts a piano). Breakfast is gourmet indeed: Ask about the smoked salmon hash. Three-night minimum stay between April and October. ~ 4915 Linden Avenue North; 206-547-6077, 800-400-6077; www.bandbseattle.com. MODERATE.

It makes sense that a European-style lodge would be steps from the worldly University of Washington campus. The **College Inn Guest House** has 27 private guest rooms in a historic (1909) three-story Tudor with shared bathrooms and gender-segregated shower facilities. Every room has a sink, a desk, a phone and a

JUST LIKE HOME

Seattle's neighborhoods offer a handful of hotels and numerous bed-and-breakfast options. A B&B can be a great value, offering a casual atmosphere, home-cooked food included in the room rate and personal contact with an innkeeper who usually knows the city well. Contact **A Pacific Reservation Service**. Closed weekends. ~ 206-784-0539, fax 206-431-0932; www.seattlebedandbreakfast.com, e-mail pacificb@nwlink.com.

single or double bed, but no television. Continental breakfast is included; many guests take dinner downstairs in the Cafe Allegro or have a late-night beer in the College Inn pub. ~ 4000 University Way Northeast; 206-633-4441, fax 206-547-1335; www.collegeinnseattle.com. BUDGET TO MODERATE.

Only a few blocks away is hip **Watertown**, a sleek and artsy, nautically themed 100-room hotel with state-of-the-art amenities. A unique service in the nonsmoking property is its "a la cart" program: there's a games cart, a surf cart (with computer and printer), a spa cart (for relaxing bathing) and a goodnight cart (for restful sleep). All rooms have microwaves and refrigerators. Continental breakfast and shuttle service to downtown attractions are included in the room rate, as are loaner bicycles great for exploring the U District. ~ 4242 Roosevelt Way Northeast; 206-826-4242, 800-944-4242, fax 206-315-4242; www.watertownseattle.com. DELUXE.

Next door, under the same ownership, is the older **University Inn**, whose heated outdoor pool, spa and café welcome Watertown guests along with its own. Rooms in the south wing of this bright, cheery, nonsmoking hotel are more spacious; north-wing rooms have showers but no bathtubs. If you're a workout addict, you may prefer Watertown's modern fitness center to this hotel's "closet." Breakfast is included. ~ 4140 Roosevelt Way Northeast; 206-632-5055, 800-733-3855, fax 206-547-4937; www.universityinnseattle.com. MODERATE.

Also in the University District is the **Best Western University Tower Hotel**, a 16-story tower with 155 corner rooms. All units have views of the mountains or the lake and cityscape. Standard hotel furnishings adorn the spacious rooms, decorated in art deco style. A handsome restaurant and lounge are on the floor below the lobby; breakfast is included. ~ 4507 Brooklyn Avenue Northeast; 206-634-2000, 800-899-0251, fax 206-545-2103; www.meany.com. MODERATE TO DELUXE.

A favorite of visitors to the University of Washington, both gay and straight, the **Chambered Nautilus Bed and Breakfast Inn** ◄ HIDDEN is only four blocks from the campus—down the hill on the east side overlooking University Village. Breezily casual, the spacious home has a family atmosphere. Games and books, soft chairs by the fireplace and all-day tea and cookies add to the homeyness. Ten guest rooms on the second and third floors have antique furnishings. All have private baths and four feature private porches; two have gas fireplaces, and four offer kitchens. A full gourmet breakfast is served, sometimes on the sun porch. ~ 5005 22nd Avenue Northeast; 206-522-2536, 800-545-8459, fax 206-528-0898; www.chamberednautilus.com, e-mail stay@chamberednau tilus.com. MODERATE TO ULTRA-DELUXE.

The **Maple Tree B&B**, a renovated 1923 vintage home, offers charming accommodations for up to three people, complete with private bath and balcony. A light breakfast is included. No smoking. ~ 18313 Olympic View Drive, Edmonds; 425-774-8420; themapletreeb_b.home.comcast.net, e-mail themapletree b_b@attbi.com. MODERATE.

Hidden away in a little business complex full of shops and restaurants, the **Edmonds Harbor Inn** provides basic motel-style accommodations with updated pastel decor and light wood furnishings, a breakfast area and a meeting space. Sadly, none of the rooms has a view of the harbor. ~ 130 West Dayton Street, Edmonds; 425-771-5021, 800-441-8033, fax 425-672-2880; www.nwcountryinns.com/edmonds.html. MODERATE TO DELUXE.

Rooms in the three-story **TraveLodge** are comfortably decorated and clean, with dark blue carpets, curtains and bedspreads and cable television. There are even a few kitchenette and jacuzzi units. Other amenities include hot tubs and continental breakfast. ~ 23825 Route 99 North, Edmonds; 425-771-8008, 800-578-7878, fax 425-771-0080; www.travelodge.com. BUDGET TO MODERATE.

DINING   **BALLARD–FREMONT AREA**   Is it sacrilege to have a Cajun-Creole barbecue restaurant in oh-so-Scandinavian Ballard? Not when the Norwegians are first in line! For more than two decades, **Burk's Cafe** has been blending fresh seafood and home-made sausages in exquisite New Orleans–style dishes like jambalaya and filé gumbo, as well as barbecue ribs, rockfish court-bouillon and fried-oyster sandwiches. ~ 5411 Ballard Avenue Northwest; 206-782-0091. BUDGET.

Many are those who say **Bad Albert's Tap & Grill** has Seattle's best burger. It's hard to argue with this juicy sandwich, packed high with condiments. But the eggs Benedict served for weekend brunches at this neighborhood hole-in-the-wall are superb as well, and occasional live music completes a lively scene. ~ 5100 Ballard Avenue Northwest; 206-782-9623. BUDGET.

On a drab, busy street, the unprepossessing **Le Gourmand** is one of Ballard's best-kept secrets. Since 1985, this intimate restaurant has offered classic French food prepared with fresh local ingredients, including shrimp mouseseline and a crackly crème brûlée. Its tiny European-style bar, Sambar, serves light fare nightly except Sunday. Dinner only. Closed Sunday through Tuesday. ~ 425 Northwest Market Street; 206-784-3463. ULTRA-DELUXE.

Ponti Seafood Grill is near the Fremont Bridge on the Lake Washington ship canal. The Mediterranean-style restaurant offers spectacular views of the canal from flower-filled patios. The menu has mostly seafood, though there are good pasta and chicken dishes as well. No lunch on Saturday or Sunday. ~ 3014 3rd Avenue North; 206-284-3000, fax 206-284-4768; www. pontiseafoodgrill.com. DELUXE TO ULTRA-DELUXE.

In hip Fremont, **El Camino** is a pretty pastel venue famous for its delicious margaritas, gourmet Mexican menu and rubbernecking clientele. Black cod is served with a black-bean purée, mussels in an ancho-chile cream sauce, cumin-rubbed pork loin with a tomatillo mole. The loosely Spanish Colonial decor extends to the rear bar, with an outside deck that's packed all summer. Dinner only. ~ 607 North 35th Street; 206-632-7303. MODERATE.

When you're nostalgic for an old coffeehouse with an upbeat, neighborhood flair, head for **Still Life in Fremont Coffeehouse**. It has high windows, a friendly atmosphere, music, great soups and generous sandwiches. ~ 709 North 35th Street; 206-547-9850. BUDGET.

It's easy to drive past **Brad's Swingside Cafe** and not even realize you've missed it. By all means, backtrack. From a small,   ◄ HIDDEN

AUTHOR FAVORITE

Touristy though it may be, the great view, alder-grilled fish and historic photos of native Salish people in old-time Seattle combine to make **Ivar's Salmon House** one of my favorite Seattle restaurants. The restaurant, done in Northwest American Indian longhouse–style architecture and decor, also features views of the kayak, canoe, tugboat, windsurfer and yacht activity on Lake Union. The menu includes prime rib, alder-smoked salmon and black cod, and Northwest American Indian–style. ~ 401 Northeast Northlake Way; 206-632-0767, fax 206-632-0715; www.ivars.net. DELUXE.

one-man kitchen, chef-owner Brad Inserra turns out his innovative take on pan-Italian classics—veal, seafood, and linguine *aglio e olio* in an elaborately garnished garlic-and-olive oil sauce. Service in the dining room is as homespun as the cuisine. Dinner only. Closed Sunday and Monday. ~ 4212 Fremont Avenue North; 206-633-4057. MODERATE.

HIDDEN ▶

GREEN LAKE AREA The decor may be more-than-slightly off kilter at the **Bizzarro Italian Café**, but the food most decidedly is not. A block off Wallingford's main drag, this cluttered and kitschy little restaurant is packed *from* the rafters with all manner of unusual furnishings. The madness extends to the Forest Floor Frenzy, seasonal wild mushrooms tossed with roasted garlic and walnuts and served with rigatoni, a vegetarian's delight. Or opt for any of the marvelous tuna or lamb dishes. No lunch weekdays. ~ 1307 North 46th Street; 206-545-7327. MODERATE.

Seattle is not known for great Mexican food. One happy exception is the **Chile Pepper**, an unpretentious Wallingford café where the kitchen knows what pasillas, moles and poblanos are. The *chiles rellenos* are quite good. Closed Sunday. ~ 1427 North 45th Street; 206-545-1790. BUDGET TO MODERATE.

After a show at the Guild 45th Street Theatre, make a beeline across the street for **Jitterbug**. Upbeat and lively, this is the place to go for generous portions of well-prepared Northwest regional food with Southwestern and Asian influences. The everchanging menu may include *huevos rancheros* or grilled fresh fish. Breakfast is the most popular meal of the day. ~ 2114 North 45th Street; 206-547-6313, fax 206-548-1069. MODERATE.

SOUTHERN SPECIALTIES

There aren't many places to find *feijoada* in the Northwest, and maybe even fewer to get *caipirinha*. So Seattle's South American contingency is dedicated to **Tempero do Brasil**, a U District oasis of traditional Bahían-Brazilian cuisine and often-live Latin pop-jazz. *Feijoada*, Brazil's national dish, is a slow-cooked stew of black beans with ham, sausage and garlic, served with collard greens. *Caipirinha* is made from distilled sugar-cane juice, with lime and ice, and is not for the weak of heart. If you sit at the bar, wash down your salt cod cakes with a cold Brazilian beer. No lunch weekdays. Closed Sunday. ~ 5628 University Way Northeast; 206-523-6299. BUDGET.

At **Kabul,** immigrants Sultan Malikyar and Wali Khairzada give you the only thing you're missing by not traveling to their native Afghanistan: great Afghani food. Like Middle Eastern cuisine with a North Indian flair, the fare ranges from *samosa*-like dumplings with a tangy dipping sauce to lamb kebabs with garlic-yogurt sauce on basmati rice. Live sitar music plays Tuesdays and Thursdays. Dinner only. ~ 2301 North 45th Street; 206-545-9000. BUDGET.

The emerging Tangletown neighborhood between Wallingford and Green Lake is home to **Eva,** a charming bistro where ◄ HIDDEN acclaimed chef Amy McCray holds center court. Her highly original menu may employ south-of-the-border, or even south Asian, elements in the preparation of meat, fish and poultry. A vegetarian favorite is the light and creamy *cabrales* flan, made of blue cheese with a pear relish and served on a walnut cracker. Eva's marvelous adjoining wine bar has become a popular gathering place. Dinner only. Closed Monday. ~ 2227 North 56th Street; 206-633-3538. MODERATE TO DELUXE.

The **Santa Fe Café** offers a fussy version of Southwestern cuisine, more avocados and cilantro than beans and tortillas. Chile-flavored beer, anyone? Wags might call it Northwest/Southwest Contemporary cuisine; it's worth a visit after a trip to the Woodland Park Zoo. ~ 5910 Phinney Avenue North; 206-783-9755. MODERATE.

You've got to love the name of the **Stumbling Goat,** eight blocks farther north. The charming and popular café presents an eclectic menu ranging from standard bistro fare (roasted chicken, pan-fried trout) to a vegetarian barley-mushroom risotto. Dinner only. Closed Sunday and Monday. ~ 6722 Greenwood Avenue North; 206-784-3535. MODERATE.

One of Seattle's best Greek restaurants is just up the road at **Yanni's.** Locals pack the *taverna* for spanakopita, moussaka, dolmathes and other Balkan specialties, like deep-fried calamari and *horiatiki* salad. Greek wines and beers share the menu. The baklava dessert is especially tempting. ~ 7419 Greenwood Avenue North; 206-783-6945. BUDGET.

UNIVERSITY DISTRICT   Named for the lovely green waters of Portage Bay, which it overlooks, the hard-to-find **Agua Verde** ◄ HIDDEN **Cafe & Paddle Club** offers a unique twist: You can rent a kayak and work up an appetite on Lake Union before returning for the café's creative tacos (halibut-avocado, for instance, and flank steak with onions and peppers) and other *muy picante* Mexican food. Margaritas and Mexican beers lend a festive feel to this colorful, casual corner of the U District. Closed Sunday. ~ 1303 Northeast Boat Street; 206-545-8570; www.aguaverde.com. BUDGET.

The traditional food of alpine regions is inevitably hearty, stick-to-your-ribs fare. The offerings of the **Himalayan Sherpa Restaurant** are no exception. From the "rooftop of the world" come dishes like *momos*, steamed meat or vegetable-filled dumplings with a tangy sauce, and Sherpa stew, a savory soup of beef, onions, carrots and potatoes. Photos of the Dalai Lama and famous Sherpa mountain guides share wall space with Tibetan prayer flags. Closed Monday. ~ 4214 University Way Northeast; 206-633-2100; www.himalayansherpa.com. BUDGET.

Over in University Village is **Atlas Foods,** where late risers can get breakfast all day long. Despite its shopping-mall location, Atlas has a neighborhood-café vibe with a hip and reasonably priced bar. The wide-ranging menu runs from home cookin' favorites, like Southern fried chicken, to fish tacos and squash ravioli. Open daily for breakfast, lunch and dinner. ~ 2820 Northeast University Village Place; 206-522-6025. MODERATE.

Union Bay Café serves Northwest regional foods with an Asian and Italian influence. The seasonal entrées might include grilled sturgeon with roasted garlic, tomato and dill and hazelnut chicken on sautéed spinach with lemon butter. More unusual is the filet of ostrich grilled and served with Walla Walla sweet onions and a sauce of port wine, green peppercorn and sage. Lighter entrées are available in the simple, classic café. The appetizer list is almost as long as the regular menu. Dinner only. Closed Monday. ~ 3515 Northeast 45th Street; 206-527-8364, fax 206-527-0436. DELUXE.

North of the university is the Maple Leaf district, where locals flock in droves to the **Maple Leaf Grill**. Oyster stew (with red onions, artichoke hearts, ham, spinach and cream) is a longtime house favorite, and the marinated flank steak sandwich is tender and tasty. But regulars swear by the nightly fresh sheet of five specials. Ambience is casual, and conversation flows as easily as the beer at the convivial bar. No lunch on Sunday. ~ 8929 Roosevelt Way Northeast; 206-523-8449. MODERATE.

EDMONDS AND NORTHERN SUBURBS If you venture up to Edmonds, try **Ciao Italia**. This small restaurant on the main drag doesn't look like much from the outside—thankfully the lace curtains block out most of the traffic view. But the traditional Italian fare is good; best choices include spaghetti *mirechiaro* (a garlicky seafood pasta in white-wine sauce) and veal piccata. Dinner only. ~ 546 5th Avenue South, Edmonds; 425-771-7950. MODERATE.

> The Edmonds Art Walk map points out the public artworks on display: bronze and copper sculptures, tile murals, stained glass and others.

A café and bakery, **Brusseau's Sidewalk Café** features country-style breakfasts, homemade meatloaf sandwiches, homemade soups and a wide variety of desserts. The restaurant has a pleasant courtyard with planters and picnic tables. Try their quiche Lorraine or omelette special. Breakfast and lunch only. ~ 117 5th Avenue South, Edmonds; 425-774-4166. BUDGET TO MODERATE.

Every table at **Arnies at the Landing** has a dandy second-floor view of Puget Sound and the Edmonds harbor. Chicken, steak and pasta are on the regular menu, but your best bet is to order from the fresh daily seafood list. There's a variety of fresh broiled fish, and the clam chowder has won awards. The three-course early dinner (until 6 p.m.), available Sunday through Friday, is a bargain. Sunday brunch. ~ 300 Admiral Way, Edmonds; 425-771-5688, fax 425-771-7624. MODERATE TO DELUXE.

Located a block from the ferry landing, **Café de Paris** is known for its authentic French cuisine, served in a small dining room or on the glass-enclosed sunporch. No lunch on weekends. ~ 109 Main Street, Edmonds; 425-771-2350. MODERATE TO DELUXE.

Chanterelle has a rustic atmosphere, with wooden floors and American cuisine. It's bright, cheerful and busy at mealtimes with patrons ordering salads and sandwiches. Open daily for breakfast, lunch and dinner. ~ 316 Main Street, Edmonds; 425-774-0650, fax 425-771-5783. MODERATE.

BALLARD–FREMONT AREA As Seattle's Nordic enclave, you might expect that Ballard would have shops catering to those of the fair hair-itage. The **Scandinavian Gift Shop** offers embroidered wool sweaters, kitchenware, music and a variety of knickknacks. ~ 2016 Northwest Market Street; 206-784-9370. **Kristy's Scandinavian Gifts** is smaller but features colorful craftwork and the requisite miniature trolls. ~ 2205 Northwest Market Street;

SHOPPING

206-789-3010. The gift shop of the **Nordic Heritage Museum** has more upscale art and a fine book selection. ~ 3014 67th Street Northwest; 206-789-5707.

If you're in the market for a potato gun, would like to snack on Pez, crave a glow-in-the-dark slug or are searching for a popping Martian, head on over to **Archie McPhee's** in Ballard. This novelty-and-toy store offers more than 10,000 exotic items from all over the world. ~ 2428 Northwest Market Street; 206-297-0240; www.mcphee.com.

Seattle's first all-children's bookstore, the **Secret Garden Bookshop,** has books for parents, too. Its frequent kids-oriented events—music, classes, readings—set this store apart from others of its ilk. ~ 2214 Northwest Market Street; 206-789-5006; www.secretgardenbooks.com.

For the *feng shui*–conscious home-decor buyer, **Greener Lifestyles** is a treasure trove of furniture and fabrics made from nontoxic natural materials including hemp, and reclaimed or sustainably harvested woods: no clear-cut lumber here. You can also get a private consultation on how to create a home with lifestyle-enhancing qualities. ~ 5317 Ballard Avenue Northwest; 206-545-4405; www.greenerlifestyles.com.

So big that the British rock band Radiohead once spent seven hours browsing its collection of vintage vinyl (a half-million old albums and 45s), **Bop Street Records** is in a class of its own. Jazz, blues and rock dominate the inventory, which includes used CDs and cassette tapes. ~ 5219 Ballard Avenue Northwest; 206-297-2232; www.bopstreet.com.

Almost next door, **Second Ascent** responds to customers' desire for quality, new and used equipment for (primarily) backcountry adventure sports. If you're a backpacker and camper, a climber, a cyclist or an off-piste skier (you'll find telemark gear

AUTHOR FAVORITE

Being of Swedish-Finnish heritage, I was raised in a home where *köttbullar* (Swedish meatballs), *limpa* bread and *lutefisk* were a way of life. When my mother is in town, I always take her to Ballard to shop at **Olsen's Scandinavian Foods.** This is the place to go for lingonberries, *fiskbullar* (fish cake) and other distinctly northern European culinary imports. ~ 2248 Northwest Market Street; 206-783-8288.

here, but no alpine equipment), you may find what you want at a bargain price. ~ 5209 Ballard Avenue Northwest; 206-545-8810; www.secondascent.com.

The **Afishionado Gallery** at Fishermen's Terminal is chock full of art, T-shirts and various kitsch of a distinctly marine, um, flavor. Nothing fishy about that. ~ 1900 West Nickerson Street; 206-283-5078.

Funky Fremont is a destination for those in search of whimsical antiques, particularly '50s and '60s vintage clothing. **Deluxe Junk** has campy housewares and mid-century furnishings, as well as movie-worthy props in an old funeral parlor. Closed Tuesday and Thursday. ~ 3518 Fremont Place North; 206-634-2733. **Private Screening** specializes in offbeat garb, including embroidered shirts and skirts of the Gene Autry era. ~ 3504 Fremont Place North; 206-548-0751. **Fritzi Ritz** will take you back to the days when you were Rockin' Around the Clock. Closed Sunday and Monday. ~ 3425 Fremont Place North; 206-633-0929. At the **Fremont Antique Mall**, on the other hand, you'll find just about everything you never desired. ~ 3419 Fremont Place North; 206-548-9140.

One of the city's more unusual stores is **Dusty Strings**, which specializes in acoustic stringed instruments such as hammered dulcimers and lever harps, hand-crafted on site. Heaven for serious folk musicians, it also has guitars, banjos and mandolins; volumes of sheet music and CDs; and frequent workshops, some of them on rarely seen ethnic instruments. ~ 3406 Fremont Avenue North; 206-634-1662; www.dustystrings.com.

GREEN LAKE AREA   A wooden school building has been converted into a charming little shopping complex known as **Wallingford Center**, and it's become the spiritual heart of this neighborhood. Among its shops are **Zanadia** (206-547-0844), for exotic gifts and furnishings; **Yazdi** (206-547-6008), for women's wear imported from the tropics; **Boston Street** (206-634-0580), for children's clothing; and **Imagination Toys** (206-547-2356), where those same kids will find sturdy educational playthings. Also in Wallingford Center is the **Second Story Bookstore** (206-547-4605), which even features a books-on-tape rental library. ~ 1815 North 45th Street.

Down the street a few blocks, **Open Books—A Poem Emporium** carries nothing but poetry . . . and a wine bar to enjoy the words of the great and the obscure. Closed Sunday and Monday. ~ 2414 North 45th Street; 206-633-0811; www.openpoetry books.com.

For travel books, greater Seattle residents inevitably head for **Wide World Books** before they leave town. The city's longest established globetrotters' bookshop, in business for decades, has virtually any title you might seek as well as a range of accessories, from language tapes to a passport-photo service. ~ 4411 Wallingford Avenue North; 206-634-3453; www.travelbooksandmaps.com.

Up on activity-oriented Green Lake, **Gregg's Greenlake Cycle** will send you off on your three-mile circumvention of the lake by renting you a bike, roller skates or inline skates. (Snowboards are also rented, but that won't do you much good here.) Gregg's sells a high volume of touring bikes, and stocks all manner of two-wheel transport. ~ 7007 Woodlawn Avenue North; 206-523-1822; www.greggscycles.com.

Runners ambulate a few steps further to **Super Jock 'n Jill**, where podiatrists and staff schooled in body mechanics will put you in the right shoes for your foot type and activity level. This is Jogger Central for race information, training and route information. ~ 7210 East Green Lake Drive North; 206-522-7711; www.jocknjill.com.

UNIVERSITY DISTRICT Dominated by the UW campus is the University District, a commercial neighborhood overflowing with a vast array of retail shops. One that attracts many tourists is **La Tienda/Folk Art Gallery**. Here you'll find handpicked craft items from all over the world, including those made by 200 selected American artisans. ~ 4318 University Way Northeast, 206-632-1796; and 2050 Northwest Market Street (Ballard), 206-297-3605; www.latienda-folkart.com.

HIDDEN ►   A retired anthropology professor owns and operates **Between Cultures**, which presents a museum-quality collection of tribal, folk and ethnographic art primarily from Latin America and the Pacific Rim region. ~ 8809 Roosevelt Way Northeast; 206-523-0053; e-mail betweencultures@earthlink.net.

EDMONDS AND NORTHERN SUBURBS **American Eagles** is, simply, the largest hobby shop in the United States, with an inventory of more than 87,000 different items—fully one-fourth of them miniature soldiers. The specialty is model transportation:

Browsing
for Books

It should come as no surprise that residents of a rainy-day city such as Seattle would be voracious readers. And what better place to seek out special tomes than the student-populated University District?

The largest bookseller in Washington is **University Book Store**, where addicted readers can browse happily for hours. There's a huge selection of literature, technical books and college texts, as well as music and camera sections, some clothing and stationery. ~ 4326 University Way Northeast; 206-634-3400, 800-335-7323, fax 206-634-0810; www.bookstore.washington.edu.

Of course, with a campus so close, there are plenty of other places to find reading material. Many a student starts his or her day with a stop at **Bulldog News and Fast Espresso** for its vast selection of foreign newspapers and magazines. ~ 4208 University Way Northeast; 206-632-6397; www.bulldognews.com. Nearby, the **Magus Bookstore** has a huge inventory of used books. ~ 1408 Northeast 42nd Street; 206-633-1800; www.magusbks.com. **The Globe Books** specializes in new and used books in the humanities and natural sciences, and boasts an excellent collection of antique maps. Closed Wednesday and every other Friday. ~ 5220 University Way Northeast; 206-527-2480.

Cinema Books—downstairs from the Seven Gables Theatre—carries everything on film and theater, from biographies and fanzines to screenplays and technical literature. Closed Sunday. ~ 4753 Roosevelt Way Northeast; 206-547-7667. **East West Bookshop of Seattle** specializes in books on Asian religions and metaphysical thought, and hosts frequent forums. ~ 6500 Roosevelt Way Northeast; 206-523-3726; www.ewbookshop.com. **All For Kids Books and Music**, near University Village, provides just what it promises ... in spades. ~ 2900 Northeast Blakely Street; 206-526-2768; www.allforkids.com. Seattle's largest **Barnes & Noble Booksellers** is just around the corner. ~ University Village; 206-517-4107.

model trains, model planes, model automobiles. ~ 12537 Lake City Way Northeast; 206-440-8448; www.americaneagleshobbies.com.

There are a number of good shops in Edmonds' renovated Old Mill Town. Within it, check out the **Old Mill Town Antiques**, where you can find dolls, glasses and antique furniture. ~ 201 5th Avenue South, Edmonds; 425-771-9466.

More than 150 dealers sell their wares at the **Aurora Antique Pavilion**. ~ 24111 Route 99, Edmonds; 425-744-0566.

NIGHTLIFE　Despite the passing of the popular Ballard Firehouse, this district remains one of Seattle's most active for live music—albeit in often rustic settings. Case in point: the **Tractor Tavern** offers a mix of live rock, country, Cajun, Latin, Celtic and alternative music. Cover. ~ 5213 Ballard Avenue Northwest; 206-789-3599; www.tractortavern.com. The nearby **Sunset Tavern** has primarily alternative and indie rock acts. Closed Monday. Cover. ~ 5433 Ballard Avenue Northwest; 206-784-4880.

Elsewhere in Ballard, **Conor Byrne's Public House** has live music five nights a week, specializing in Irish, folk, bluegrass and blues. Saturday is Celtic Night, and every other Sunday features Irish set dancing. The Old World building has exposed bricks, high ceilings and low light. Weekend cover. ~ 5140 Ballard Avenue Northwest; 206-784-3640; www.conorbyrnepub.com.

Next door, **Lock & Keel** is a maritime-flavored pub with frequent live blues and acoustic performers. ~ 5144 Ballard Avenue Northwest; 206-781-9092. And around the corner, **Mr. Spot's**

DINNER AND A FOREIGN FILM

Seattle's most active small **cinema district** is near the University of Washington in a cultural mecca along and near 45th Street. These theaters are all operated by Landmark Theatres and specialize in foreign, art and independent films. ~ **The Guild 45th Street Theatre**, 2115 North 45th Street (Wallingford), 206-633-3353; **Metro Cinemas**, 4500 9th Avenue Northeast, 206-633-0055; **Neptune Theatre**, 1301 Northeast 45th Street, 206-633-5545; **Seven Gables Theatre**, 911 Northeast 50th Street, 206-632-8820; and **Varsity Theatre**, 4329 University Way Northeast, 206-632-3131. This neighborhood is also home to a profusion of small cafés and restaurants catering to the evening before- and after-show crowd.

Chai House serves up an eclectic mix of world musicians along with—what else?—international teas. ~ 2133 Northwest Market Street; 206-297-2424.

There are plenty of options in this neighborhood for beer drinkers. The **Old Town Alehouse** has dozens of options on tap or by the bottle. ~ 5233 Ballard Avenue Northwest; 206-782-8323. **The Old Pequliar** welcomes a rowdy lot to its quaint English pub-style ambience. ~ 1722 Northwest Market Street; 206-782-8886.

In Fremont, the longstanding **Buckaroo Tavern** is a big draw for the Harley crowd. ~ 4201 Fremont Avenue North; 206-634-3161. To enjoy a beer in more modern (and moderate) surroundings, dive into **Hale's Brewery & Pub.** ~ 4301 Leary Way Northwest; 206-782-0737. Or climb the steps to the popular **Red Door Alehouse**, identifiable only by its red door. ~ 3401   ◄ HIDDEN
Evanston Avenue North; 206-547-7521.

For a good game of pool, **The Ballroom** in Fremont is the place to be. The dancing here is less ballroom than rump-shaking. ~ 456 North 36th Street; 206-634-2575.

Looking for more highbrow entertainment? Look no further than **The Empty Space Theatre**, which specializes in works by new playwrights. ~ 3509 Fremont Avenue North; 206-547-7500; www.emptyspace.org.

The **Mostly Nordic Chamber Music Series and Smorgasbord** brings strings to the Nordic Heritage Museum each winter and spring. ~ 3014 Northwest 67th Street; 206-789-5707; www.nordicmuseum.com.

Your best bet for nightlife in the Wallingford–Green Lake area is to visit a local watering hole and soak in the local ambience. A great place to do just that is **Murphy's Pub**, which guarantees a good supply of Guinness, Hale's and Irish conviviality. ~ 1928 North 45th Street; 206-634-2110.

Latona by Green Lake is a smoke-free tavern that hosts jazz and folk musicians on weekends. ~ 6423 Latona Avenue Northeast; 206-525-2238. The **74th Street Ale House** is a delightful neighborhood tavern in the Greenwood area. ~ 7401 Greenwood Avenue North; 206-784-2955.

For a little tropical flavor, you may want to check out the **Luau**   ◄ HIDDEN
Polynesian Lounge. With its funky tiki-bar decor, it's a poor

man's Trader Vic's—and the mai tais are great. ~ 2253 North
56th Street; 206-633-5828.

Near the University of Washington, you will find an array of
clubs and places to park yourself at night. The "cultured" stuff
is all on campus, mostly at the **Meany Hall for the Performing
Arts**. Here's where you'll find the UW World Series of music,
dance and theater; the International Chamber Music series; and
a schedule of presentations by the campus music, drama and
dance programs. Most series run during the school year, October
through May. ~ Memorial Way, near 15th Avenue Northeast and
Northeast 41st Street; 206-543-4880, 800-859-5342; www.
meany.org. Also here, in July, is the Northwest Mahler Festival
(206-667-6567; www.nwmahlerfestival.org).

Located just barely off campus, the happening student hangout in the U District is the **Big Time Brewery & Alehouse**, which
offers beer, pizza and a rowdy young crowd. Seattle's oldest
brewpub (c.1988), it has an antique bar, shuffleboard in the back
room and a museum-like collection of beer bottles, cans, signs
and memorabilia. ~ 4133 University Way Northeast; 206-545-
4509; www.bigtimebrewery.com.

Nearby, **Tommy's Nightclub & Grill** features deejay dance
music and live reggae and rock on alternating nights and some
of the cheapest beer in town. ~ 4552 University Way Northeast;
206-634-3144; www.tommysnightclub.com.

If the walls could talk at the **Blue Moon Tavern**, what stories
they'd have to tell! This survivor of the Beat era, with its aged,
graffiti-covered booths, was saved from the wrecking ball by
public outcry; a favorite hangout of author Tom Robbins, the
tavern funds a literary journal and sponsors annual writing contests. ~ 712 Northeast 45th Street; 206-633-6267. Next door,
The Rainbow stages weekend alternative rock and metal. ~ 722
Northeast 45th Street; 206-634-1761.

There are cocktail service, full dinner and comedy shows
Thursday through Sunday at **Giggles Comedy Club**. Cover on
Friday and Saturday. ~ 5220 Roosevelt Way Northeast; 206-
526-5347.

BEACHES & PARKS

DISCOVERY PARK 🚶 🚲 With two miles of beach trail and
nine miles of footpaths winding through mixed forest and across
open meadows, this bluff-top preserve (Seattle's largest at 534

acres) protects a remarkable "urban wilderness." Here are sweeping vistas, chances to watch birds (including nesting bald eagles) and study nature, the **Daybreak Star Indian Cultural Center** (206-285-4425, fax 206-282-3640) featuring art and cultural exhibits from various tribes, an interpretive center with environmental displays and educational programs, four miles of road for bicycling and an 1881 lighthouse (oldest in the area). Fort Lawton Historic District includes Officers' Row and military buildings surviving from the park's days as an Army fort. There are areas suitable for picnics; restrooms and a visitor center are at the park's east gate. ~ Located a quarter-hour drive north of downtown in the Magnolia district. The main entrance is at 3801 West Government Way and 36th Avenue West; 206-386-4236, fax 206-684-0195.

CARKEEK PARK 🚶 🚲 Tucked into a woodsy canyon reaching toward Puget Sound, this 216-acre wildland protects Piper's Creek and its resurrected runs of salmon and sea-going trout. Signs explain how citizens helped clean up the stream and bring the salmon back. Trails lead past spawning waters, to the top of the canyon and through a native-plant garden. You will find picnic areas, restrooms, play areas and beachcombing (as long as you take nothing home with you) and a pioneer orchard. ~ Take 3rd Avenue Northwest to 110th Street Northwest, turn and follow the signs; 206-684-0877, fax 206-364-4685.

Adjacent to Sand Point Magnuson Park is the National Oceanic & Atmospheric Administration's Sound Garden. The park that gave the Seattle rock band its name is full of sculptures that move and chime when the wind blows.

GOLDEN GARDENS 🚶 🏖 🚤 🛥 ⚓ North of Ballard on Shilshole Bay, this 88-acre park has waterfront, woods, a creek and a sandy beach that swarms with young picnickers and sunbathers in summer. You can watch glorious sunsets from here. There are fire pits, a boat ramp, basketball hoops, wheelchair accessible soccer and football fields and trails, and a public fishing pier. On the slope east of the beach, the park has numerous walking paths under the trees. ~ 206-684-4075, fax 206-684-4853; e-mail parksinfo@seattle.gov.

GAS WORKS PARK occupies property that dangles like a giant green tonsil from Lake Union's north shore. Until 1956, the park's namesake "gas works" produced synthetic natural gas from coal and crude oil. Some of the rusting congeries of pipes, airy catwalks, spiraling ladders, tall towers and stubby tanks were torn down during park construction, but enough remains (repainted in snappy colors) to fascinate youngsters and old-timers alike. ~ 2101 North Northlake Way.

SAND POINT MAGNUSON PARK This 350-acre site carved from the Sand Point Naval Air Station presents generous access to Lake Washington and wide views across the lake. It's a favorite place to launch a boat, swim or toss a frisbee. You'll find picnic areas, restrooms, softball fields, tennis courts, swimming beaches with summer lifeguards and a wheelchair-accessible wading pool. ~ Located on Lake Washington, northeast of downtown Seattle, at Sand Point Way Northeast and 65th Avenue Northeast; 206-684-4075, fax 206-684-4853; e-mail parksinfo@ seattle.gov.

SEVEN

Southern Neighborhoods

South of interstate Route 90, Seattle sprawls into an amalgam of seemingly endless residential neighborhoods and vast industrial zones. These may not be the most postcard picturesque sections of Seattle, but for those who search a little, there's plenty to satisfy.

About ten miles south of downtown, interstate Route 5 passes Boeing Field, Seattle's original international airport and still an arrival and departure point for many charter and freight flights. Numerous Boeing corporation hangars are located at this airfield, and at any time of day or night you are likely to see test aircraft take off and land. The industrial neighborhood of Georgetown abuts Boeing Field to its north. The long ridge of Beacon Hill rises above Route 5 to its east; beyond, extending from the International District to the foot of Lake Washington, Rainier Avenue South runs through a series of neighborhoods with substantial Asian immigrant and African-American populations. Among them is Columbia City, a recently gentrified strip whose historic buildings now are home to several fine restaurants.

West Seattle is one of the city's neighborhood treasures. The enclave, south and west of downtown, is linked to the rest of the city by a long highway bridge that passes over the mouth of the Duwamish River—where container ships from across the Pacific unload their cargo on manmade Harbor Island. West Seattle offers the city's finest aggregation of seaside parks and paths, along with stupendous views of the downtown skyline shining across the waters of Elliott Bay. Some seven miles of roads follow the water's edge around Alki Beach—the nearest thing Seattle has to Southern California's Venice Beach—and along the shore of Puget Sound to Lincoln Park and beyond. At low tide, there are miles of sandy strands, tide flats and a sprinkling of tidepools. Ferries depart West Seattle's Fauntleroy Dock for pastoral Vashon Island, a 37-square-mile mecca for artists, writers and bed-and-breakfast operators.

133

Below West Seattle, the suburb of Burien gives way to the community of Sea-Tac, home to the vast Seattle-Tacoma International Airport. Here, a wide range of hotels, motels and other amenities serve short-term—or newly arrived or departing—Puget Sound visitors. The nearby Westfield's Southcenter shopping mall is the hallmark of industrial Tukwila, a transportation hub at the meeting of Routes 5 and 405. Immediately east and south, Renton and Kent are sprawling cities in their own right, Boeing towns still recovering from the severe sting of lay-offs that preceded and followed the aerospace giant's corporate move to Chicago. Des Moines, extending west below Route 5 to the shores of Puget Sound, attracts mariners to its marvelous marina; south along the shoreline to Federal Way are popular saltwater parks. Federal Way abuts Tacoma's Pierce County, as does Auburn, to the east; the latter is home to a giant shopping mall and the Muckle-shoot Indian Reservation, which boasts the region's largest gambling casino and a new outdoor concert venue, the White River Amphitheatre, already drawing top-name national acts.

SIGHTS   The **Museum of Flight**, centered in a traffic-stopping piece of ar-chitecture called the Great Gallery on the west side of Boeing Field, is a must. In the glass-and-steel gallery, 22 aircraft hang suspended from the ceiling, almost as if in flight. In all, more than 135 air- and spacecraft (many rare) trace the history of a century of aviation. You'll see the world's first fighter airplane, the first airliner to carry stewardesses, the first presidential jet Air Force One and the only existing M-21 Blackbird spyplane.

The 1909 **Red Barn** houses one wing of the museum. The so-called barn was originally a boat-building factory on the banks of the nearby Duwamish River. Later, Bill Boeing bought it and turned it into the original headquarters for the Boeing Corporation. Relocated several times, the Red Barn now houses exhibits on Boeing's early days in the airplane business, a far cry from today's mammoth factories. Visitors can also tour the op-erating air traffic control tower. Admission. ~ 9404 East Mar-ginal Way South; 206-764-5720, fax 206-764-5707; www.museum offlight.org, e-mail info@museumofflight.org.

HIDDEN ▶   Truly a hidden treasure are the **Kubota Gardens**, an exotic oasis of Japanese horticulture in the Rainier Beach neighbor-hood. Paths wind through areas of traditionally pruned pine trees, around the Necklace of Ponds with its series of waterfalls, and past broad lawns that cry out for picnickers. Annual May and September plant sales help to keep admission free. ~ 55th

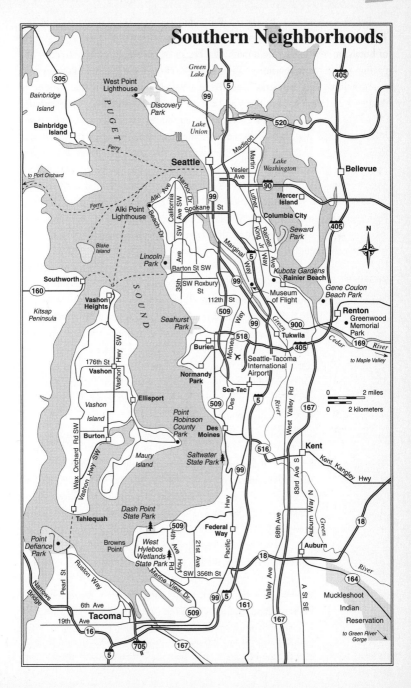

Southern Neighborhoods

Avenue South and Renton Avenue South, Rainier Beach; 206-725-4400.

Two-mile-long **Alki Beach** is the place to find Seattle's approximation of a beach scene. Though the waters of Puget Sound are chilly, to say the least, the summer sun beckons hordes of bikini-clad teens and twenty-somethings to gather for barbecues and volleyball games. A long, double-wide sidewalk is ideal for joggers, bicyclists and in-line skaters (rentals available); a strand of casual cafés follows the northwest-facing beach for several blocks. Look for a monument to the Denny party, Seattle's first white settlers who established landfall here, and a three-foot-high replica of New York's Statue of Liberty. At the beach's west end, the 1913 **Alki Point Lighthouse** (3201 Alki Avenue Southwest), operated by the Coast Guard, invites visitors for half-hour guided tours of the 37-foot-tall facility.

Look offshore from Alki Point and you'll spot forested Blake Island. Here is **Tillicum Village**, built around a huge cedar longhouse (styled after the dwellings of the Northwest Coast American Indians) situated on the edge of a 475-acre marine state park. The village presents traditional salmon bakes and performances by the Tillicum Village Dancers. Tillicum Village charters Argosy vessels from Pier 55 on Seattle's central waterfront year-round. ~ 206-933-8600, fax 206-933-9377; www.tillicumvillage.com. **Kitsap Harbor Tours** depart for Blake Island from the Bremerton waterfront in summer. ~ 360-377-8924.

The hub of West Seattle is an area known simply as **The Junction** (California Avenue Southwest and Southwest Alaska Street). Handsome historical murals adorn the sides of many buildings; summer street festivals frequently close the main thoroughfare, and from June through October, a popular farmers' market operates Sundays in an adjacent parking lot. Farther south, Fauntleroy Way Southwest passes sprawling **Lincoln Park** (see "Beaches & Parks" below) and leads to the Fauntleroy dock, from which state ferries make the 15-minute crossing to Vashon Island.

No shopping malls, no fast-food restaurants—just natural beauty and a hometown feel. That's the draw to 14-mile-long **Vashon Island**. In addition to the Fauntleroy crossing, Vashon is accessible by another 15-minute ferry from Tahlequah, near Tacoma's Point Defiance Park, creating a lovely Seattle-to-Tacoma country-road alternative to Route 5.

Since Vashon is also served by a passenger-only ferry that leaves from downtown Seattle's main ferry dock, it's a popular destination for bicyclists and backpackers heading for the island's youth hostel or one of its many B&Bs. The island's little-traveled back roads offer long, leisurely rides through deep second-growth forests and pastoral farmland, with a smattering of U-pick berry and fruit farms. Vashon is home to a thriving community of artists, potters, weavers and other craftspeople—many of whose studios are periodically open to passersby, especially during holiday weekends—as well as writers and musicians. It's also home to a growing gay and lesbian community.

Vashon Highway runs the length of the island, passing through the town of Vashon, with its smattering of small shops and restaurants, and on south past the original home of **Seattle's Best Coffee**. Housed in a turn-of-the-20th-century freighthouse, this roastery is a great place to stop and fill your cup with fresh-brewed Guatemala or Costa Rican estate coffee, a great bargain at 50 cents. You can also buy gift packages to take home. ~ 19529 Vashon Highway; 206-463-3932, fax 206-463-5051.

Burton, a small community halfway down the island, has a few small galleries and stores, a restaurant and two inns. It's also the turnoff for a secluded, lovely beach park, **Burton Acres Park**, ◄ HIDDEN an excellent place to go for a picnic or a beach stroll, to launch canoes or kayaks, or even to swim in the cool salt water of Quartermaster Harbor. On July Fourth, a local anonymous benefactor pays for a fireworks show on a barge in the middle of the harbor; it's one of the best displays on the West Coast. ~ Burton Acres Park, Bayview Drive Southwest, outer loop.

Side roads beckon from the highway to a handful of poorly marked state beaches and county parks. **Point Robinson County**

AERONAUTIC ACROBATICS

In 1955, when Boeing's first commercial jet prototype was about to be unveiled, public skepticism about its ability to fly was widespread. So Chief Pilot Tex Johnston took the plane up for a flight on Seattle's Seafair Sunday, when hundreds of thousands of fans would be lining the shores of Lake Washington to watch the hydroplane races. Johnston not only did a fly-by, he barrel-rolled the plane barely 2000 feet overhead—a performance captured by news cameras to forever dispel rumors the plane couldn't fly.

Park on Maury Island (linked to Vashon via an isthmus at the hamlet of Portage) is easier to find and particularly interesting since it's next door to the Coast Guard's picturesque Point Robinson Lighthouse (not open to the public).

Back on the mainland, historical museums in the adjacent Boeing communities of **Renton** and **Kent** showcase that area's 19th-century roots. The **Renton Historical Museum**, near the Cedar River, exhibits reminders of an era when this town at the south end of Lake Washington was an important coal-shipping port. Closed Sunday and Monday. Admission. ~ 235 Mill Avenue South, Renton; 425-255-2330. And the **Greater Kent Historical Society Museum** displays original pioneer furnishings in the historic Meeker House. Closed Sunday through Tuesday. Admission. ~ 855 East Smith Street, Kent; 253-856-5185.

Seattle's rock legend Jimi Hendrix is buried in Renton. A caretaker can show you the guitarist's grave at **Greenwood Memorial Park**. ~ 350 Monroe Avenue Northeast, Renton; 425-255-1511.

The attraction of maritime **Des Moines** is its waterfront. Hundreds of yachts and sportfishing craft make their home at the **Des Moines Marina**, centered around a historic harbormaster's home. Anthony's Homeport restaurant, at the south end of the marina, offers a gull's-eye view from its upper-floor lounge. Wander out the long pier at the north end of the marina after dark and you'll find dozens of anglers "jigging" for small squid beneath the lights.

The Weyerhauser Company, largest forest-products company in the United States, has its corporate headquarters just off Route

BLACK DIAMOND—COAL AND BREAD

Black Diamond (about 35 miles southeast of Seattle on Route 169) is an old coal-mining town with the odds and ends of its mining, logging and railroading history on display at the **Black Diamond Historical Society Museum**. This intriguing museum is housed in an 1884 railroad depot. Open Thursday and weekends or by appointment. ~ Baker Street and Railroad Avenue; 360-886-2142. But the real reason most folks stop here—on their way to Mt. Rainier, the Green River Gorge or winter ski slopes—is the famous **Black Diamond Bakery**. At last count, the bakery and its wood-fired ovens produced some 30 varieties of bread. ~ 32805 Railroad Avenue; 360-886-2741.

5 in Federal Way, a town over halfway from Seattle to Tacoma. Here are a pair of horticultural highlights open year-round to the public. The **Rhododendron Species Botanical Garden** is the largest of its kind in the world, showcasing more than 500 rhododendron species and hybrids on 22 acres. Spring is the best time to visit, although some plants may bloom in summer or even winter. Closed Thursday (March to May) and Friday (June to February). Admission March through October. ~ Weyerhaueser Way South, Federal Way; 253-661-9377; www.rhody garden.org.

At the **Pacific Rim Bonsai Collection**, visitors may see gardeners trained in bonsai-stunting techniques pruning and propagating these diminutive plants—among them a 1000-year-old dwarf Sierra juniper. Tours at noon on Sunday, or by appointment. Closed Thursday (March to May) and Thursday to Saturday (June to February). ~ Weyerhaueser Way South, Federal Way; 253-924-5206; www.weyerhauser.com/bonsai.

LODGING

Villa Heidelberg is a bed and breakfast in a Craftsman-style home on a corner hillside. The German-flavored inn has a wide wraparound porch that overlooks gardens of roses and rhododendrons. Inside, the atmosphere is comfortable and relaxed. The house features leaded glass windows, beamed ceilings and the original 1909 gaslight fixtures and embossed wall coverings. The six guest rooms are decorated in pastel florals and feature brass or oak beds and oak dressers. A full breakfast is served. ~ 4845 45th Avenue Southwest, West Seattle; 206-938-3658, 800-671-2942, fax 206-935-7077; www.villaheidelberg.com, e-mail info@villaheidelberg.com. MODERATE TO DELUXE.

Vashon Island abounds with bed-and-breakfast inns, some of them in quaint old farmhouses surrounded by meadows and orchards. One is the **Betty MacDonald Farm**, the former home of Betty MacDonald who authored *The Egg and I*, *Onions in the Stew*, and all the Mrs. Piggle Wiggle children's books. The first two books wryly chronicle life on the Olympic Peninsula and Vashon Island. The six-acre farm overlooks Puget Sound and Mt. Rainier and offers two guest accommodations, a cedar-paneled loft and a private cottage, both furnished with oriental carpets, Northwest Indian print fabrics, antiques, full kitchens stocked with breakfast supplies and wood-burning stoves. Guests also enjoy beach access, trail bikes, private decks and gardens. For nighttime reading, there are books by MacDonald. ~ 12000 99th Avenue Southwest; 206-567-4227, 888-328-6753, fax 206-567-4555; www.bettymacdonaldfarm.com. MODERATE TO DELUXE.

Situated in the tiny town of Burton, the **Back Bay Inn** is a New England–style lodging with an airy, open dining room downstairs and four spare, elegant bedrooms up. A brick entryway is edged with bright flowers six months of the year, and a brick patio is open for dining in warm weather. Breakfasts, especially weekend brunch, are excellent. It's also open for dinner Tuesday through Saturday, serving Northwest cuisine. ~ 24007 Vashon Highway Southwest, Burton; 206-463-5355, fax 206-463-6663; www.thebackbayinn.com. MODERATE.

"Alki," the state motto, is an Indian word that means "bye and bye."

The AYH **Ranch/Hostel**, about a mile outside the town of Vashon, caters to bicycle and foot travelers; free pickup is provided from the Thriftway Grocery in town. Hostel lodgings range from campsites and tepees (May through October only) to seven private rooms with bath. Extensive grounds allow room for roaming. In summer, when the dorm facilities are open, there are free pancakes for all. ~ 12119 Cove Road Southwest; 206-463-2592, fax 206-463-6157; www.vashonhostel.com. BUDGET TO MODERATE.

Also in a pastoral setting with resident deer, **Artist's Studio Loft** offers a carriage house cottage with a beamed ceiling, skylights, ceiling fan, kitchenette and outdoor hot tub. Other accommodations include a suite with a private entrance, French doors, cathedral ceilings, and potted palms, a smaller room decorated with Mexican tiles and wicker furnishings, and a cottage. The rate includes a continental breakfast. ~ 16529 91st Avenue Southwest; 206-463-2583, fax 206-463-3881; www.asl-bnb.com, e-mail meadowart@asl-bnb.com. MODERATE TO DELUXE.

A stone's throw from Sea-Tac Airport, the **Seattle Marriott** is a wonderfully luxurious hotel featuring a 20,000-square-foot tropical atrium five stories high. Around it are 459 guest rooms. A restaurant, lounge, whirlpool, health club with massage therapy (by appointment) and game room round out the amenities. Airport shuttle is provided. ~ 3201 South 176th Street, Sea-Tac; 206-241-2000, 800-643-5479, fax 206-248-0789; www.marriott.com. DELUXE.

Just outside the airport entrance, the **Coast Sea-Tac Hotel** offers a less pricey but marvelously convenient lodging option for those in transit. All 146 rooms are standard edition but include such amenities as hair dryers and coffeemakers; 32 suites also have refrigerators, and every guest has access to a pool, sauna, jacuzzi and exercise room. Pets are welcomed, and there's airport shuttle service 24 hours a day. ~ 18220 International Boulevard, Sea-Tac; 206-246-5535, 800-325-4000; www.coasthotels.com. MODERATE.

In a quiet wooded area southeast of Seattle is the **Maple Valley**   ◄ *HIDDEN*
Bed and Breakfast. The two-story contemporary home has open-beamed ceilings, peeled-pole railings, cedar walls and detailed wood trim. Guests like to relax on the antique furniture on the front porch. The two guest rooms are individually decorated and color coordinated with French doors that open onto a large deck. Both have log beds. On cool nights, heated, sand-filled pads ("hot babies") are used to warm the beds. A full breakfast is served on country-stencil pottery in a dining area that overlooks trees, wandering birds and ponds with ducks. ~ 20020 Southeast 228th Street, Maple Valley; 425-432-1409, 888-432-1409, fax 425-413-1459; www.seattlebestbandb.com/maplevalley, e-mail wildlife pond@hotmail.com. MODERATE.

The mixed language in **Deux Tamales**' name is intentional: What   **DINING**
this casual Columbia City restaurant calls "Franco-Latino cuisine" is more like Mexican food in the hands of a French-trained chef. Here's the place to come for gourmet meat and chicken dishes or tamales in a rich sauce, served in a mildly bohemian ambience with one of Seattle's best margaritas. Dinner only. Closed Monday. ~ 4868 Rainier Avenue South, Columbia City; 206-725-1418; www.deuxtamales.com. MODERATE.

"Sicilian soul food" is the byword of **La Medusa**, a block down and across the street. Sit before the big windows on the street and pretend you're in Palermo as you dine on spaghetti *con le sarde* (with sardines, fennel, raisins and pine nuts). There's also a kids' menu. For dessert, don't miss the homemade cannoli, a ricotta-stuffed pastry. Dinner only. Closed Sunday and Monday. ~ 4857 Rainier Avenue South, Columbia City; 206-723-2192. MODERATE.

Nearby, **Tutta Bella** serves authentic Naples-style pizzas from the stove of its open kitchen. A favorite is the Quattro Stagioni, or "Four Seasons": artichokes, fennel, roasted red pepper, yellow squash and herb mushrooms, plus Cotto ham for non-vegetarians. You can also get salads and panini sandwiches, but leave room for desserts like gelato and tiramisu. ~ 4918 Rainier Avenue South, Columbia City; 206-721-3501; www.tuttabellapizza.com. BUDGET.

HIDDEN ▶ Great Chinese-style seafood in an out-of-the-way location is what you'll find at the family-owned **Hong Kong Seafood Restaurant** in Rainier Beach. Choose your fish from the tanks on the wall, or opt for the delectable prawns with walnuts in a white cream sauce, accompanied by fresh steamed pea sprouts. There's also a fine selection of other Cantonese dishes. ~ 9400 Rainier Avenue South, Rainier Beach; 206-723-1718. MODERATE.

The only vestige left standing of an early-20th-century West Seattle amusement park is the **Luna Park Cafe**, but it's done with flair. Photos and memorabilia, including old neon signs and tableside jukeboxes packed with hits from the 1950s, complement a menu of burgers, shakes and generous blue-plate specials. Three meals daily. ~ 2918 Avalon Way Southwest, West Seattle; 206-935-7250. BUDGET.

Spend a perfect summer day at Alki Beach, then take in dinner at the **Alki Café**, where a well-rounded menu that changes four times a year includes great salads, seafood, meat, chicken and pasta dishes. Specials of the evening are listed in the two dining areas. Be sure to leave room for the delicious fruit tortes and cheesecakes. Breakfast is a big affair, featuring do-it-yourself omelettes, gingerbread grillcakes and chicken-fried steak. ~ 2726 Alki Avenue Southwest, West Seattle; 206-935-0616. BUDGET TO MODERATE.

The Alki Strip is not the Gaza Strip, but it seems the perfect waterfront location for **Phoenicia at Alki**, a long-established eastern Mediterranean restaurant. Its Lebanese owner, Hussein, serves up a variety of delectable dishes at his intimate eatery, ranging from the commonplace to the innovative. Try "Pearls of the Sea," an olio of various seafoods, from fish and shellfish to tentacled squid. Dinner only. Closed Monday. ~ 2716 Alki Avenue Southwest, West Seattle; 206-935-6550. MODERATE.

HIDDEN ▶ Keep your eyes peeled as you head south along Beach Drive from Alki Point for **La Rustica**, a family-owned and -operated Italian restaurant. This streetcorner oasis in an otherwise residential district offers some of the freshest homemade pastas in the city, complemented by outstanding Tuscan-style sauces and a fine and affordable wine list. Dinner only. Closed Monday. ~ 4100 Beach Drive Southwest, West Seattle; 206-932-3020. MODERATE.

In a neighborhood without a lot of upscale restaurants, **Ovio Bistro** wins kudos. From seared ahi tuna to tender pork medallions and vegetarian dishes, this low-lit café, with seasonal sidewalk seating, offers a lovely romantic retreat. The wine bar is small but offers the best choice of vintages to be found south of downtown Seattle. Closed Monday. ~ 3247 California Avenue Southwest; 206-935-1774. MODERATE TO DELUXE.

Also in West Seattle, the **Cat's Eye Cafe** has great coffee, excellent muffins and super sandwiches . . . not to mention plenty of feline pictures and paraphernalia. Soup and sandwich for lunch is an excellent choice. Breakfast and lunch only. ~ 7301 Bainbridge Place Southwest, West Seattle; 206-935-2229. BUDGET.

Just uphill from the Fauntleroy ferry terminal, near a one-time trolley turnabout (long since consumed by residential growth), **Endolyne Joe's** is a whimsical treat that promises a new menu ◄ *HIDDEN* and a facelift in its decor every three months. One season it may be an Italian restaurant, another a New Orleans–style café, yet another a Route 66 truck stop. At any time, food is universally hearty, service steady, and the bar a great place to strike up a conversation with a Fauntleroy local. Three meals daily. ~ 9261 45th Avenue Southwest, West Seattle; 206-937-5637. MODERATE.

Vashon Island is one of the least likely places to find decent Mexican food, but there it is at **Casa Bonita**, a small family-run enclave in the town of Vashon. Here are such unusual (for the Northwest) delights as chicken *en mole* and *molcajete*, a hearty

AUTHOR FAVORITE

Like generations of West Seattleites before us, my family and I flock to the **Husky Deli**, in the heart of the Alaska Junction district, whenever we need a homemade ice-cream fix—it's a phenomenally tasty treat on hot summer days. Any time of year, we can find hard-to-get imported ingredients for home cooking, or nosh at the deli and sandwich counter. ~ 4721 California Avenue Southwest, West Seattle; 206-937-2810. BUDGET.

stew. Meals are filling and economical. ~ 17623 100th Avenue Southwest; 206-463-6452. MODERATE.

HIDDEN ▶ If you want to act like a real islander on Vashon, breakfast consists of a visit to **Bob's Bakery**, a tiny storefront on the main highway in town. Each morning Bob bakes up more than three dozen different delights, ranging from lemon-rosemary pound cake to cranberry-orange muffins. Grab a goodie, a cup of coffee and the newspaper, have a seat on the bench out front and watch the world go by for a half hour or so. Closed Sunday and Monday. ~ 17506 Vashon Highway; 206-463-5666. BUDGET.

The old island hangout is **Sound Food Restaurant**. The restaurant is known for its casual atmosphere—windows overlooking the gardens and lots of wood inside. Breakfast, served seven days a week, consists of hearty, traditional fare. But at lunch and dinner the restaurant converts to a bistro-dining theme, serving such eclectic dishes as grilled shrimp with polenta and *pad Thai* with fennel and ham. Breads, pastries and desserts come fresh from the in-house bakery. Breakfast daily; lunch and dinner Monday through Saturday. ~ 20312 Vashon Highway Southwest; 206-463-0888. BUDGET TO MODERATE.

In the largely immigrant community of White Center, wedged between West Seattle and Burien, you'll find **Taqueria del Rio**, one of the most authentic Mexican outposts this side of the Rio Grande. Order at the counter of the open kitchen, but pay in the adjoining gift shop, where you can browse the wide selection of Latin CDs, colorful piñatas and Virgin de Guadalupe votive can-

ALL ABOARD FOR DINNER

Dining cars built in the 1930s and 1950s, refurbished in style, offer unusual views of the Seattle area to passengers who book a ride on the **Spirit of Washington**. The train travels from Renton north for 22 miles along the east shore of Lake Washington to Woodinville. Top-quality meals at ultra-deluxe prices are served during the journey—dinners daily, and lunch and brunch on weekends. In Woodinville, passengers disembark for a tour of the beautifully landscaped Columbia winery. On the return journey, they enjoy dessert and coffee and watch the scenery go by. The train crosses Wilburton Trestle, the longest (975 feet) wooden trestle in the Northwest. Closed Monday in winter. ~ 625 South 4th Street, Renton; 800-876-7245; www.spiritofwashingtondinnertrain.com. ULTRA-DELUXE.

dles as you wait for your *tacos al carbon* to be grilled. ~ 10230 16th Avenue Southwest, White Center; 206-767-9102. BUDGET.

For an unusual experience in low-priced dining, head to the increasingly Latino suburb of Burien, where you'll find **El Trapiche Pupusería & Restaurant**. This homespun, unpretentious little restaurant serves authentic Salvadoran specialties such as *pollo asado* (a skinless, boneless chicken breast chargrilled in annatto-seed marinade), *pescado frito* (whole deep-fried tilapia), *pupusa de chicharrón* (cornmeal rounds stuffed with shredded pork and served with spicy slaw) and beef hoof soup (an acquired taste, to be sure). El Trapiche's novelty draws a growing clientele from all parts of the city. ~ 127 Southwest 153rd Street, Burien; 206-244-5564, fax 206-242-2120. BUDGET TO MODERATE.

An excellent Thai restaurant convenient to Sea-Tac Airport is **Bai Tong**. Located in a former A&W drive-in, this eatery is known for its steamed curry salmon, grilled beef with Thai sauce and marinated chicken. The carpeted dining room is lush with potted plants, and the walls are adorned with photos of mouthwatering dishes. ~ 15859 Pacific Highway South, Sea-Tac; phone/fax 206-431-0893. BUDGET TO MODERATE.

In the Southcenter area, heavy with franchise restaurants, **Grazie Caffe Italiano** is a welcome find. A charming, plant-filled   ◀ HIDDEN
Italian café sequestered in a strip mall, this little restaurant has a fresh salad bar and a menu of fine pastas and Northern Italian entrées. Service is friendly and attentive. ~ 16943 Southcenter Parkway South, Tukwila; 206-575-1606. MODERATE.

If you dine at only one restaurant in Renton, make it the **Melrose Grill**. It is said that boxer Jack Dempsey was once the bouncer at the former bar of this renovated, early-20th-century building. Today it's an elegant steakhouse with rows of private booths for intimate dining. Fine wines are available by the glass and bottle. ~ 819 Houser Way South, Renton; 425-254-0759. MODERATE TO DELUXE.

Just south of the city line between Renton and Kent is a wonderfully atmospheric Asian shopping center called the Great Wall Mall. Perhaps the best reason to visit, besides browsing the grocery and gift shops, is to enjoy a meal at the **Imperial Garden Seafood Restaurant**. From Peking duck two ways to weekend dim sum every way, this is the place where southside Chinese families come for fine dining on white linen—surrounded by tank after tank of the fish and lobsters they're preparing to consume. Three meals daily. ~ 18230 East Valley Highway, Kent; 425-656-0999. MODERATE TO DELUXE.

In downtown Kent, **Spiro's Greek Island** offers spanakopita to souvlaki, *avgolemono* soup to honey-rich baklava, plus weekend belly dancing. Murals decorate the walls of this family operation, which draws diners from all directions. Try the Athenian platter: moussaka, dolmades, marinated lamb with orzo and vegetables, Greek salad and pita bread. ~ 215 1st Avenue South, Kent; 253-854-1030. BUDGET TO MODERATE.

Des Moines has several fine seafood restaurants near its marina, but you'll get more bang for your buck if you step back a couple of blocks to **Wally's Chowder House**. After your requisite helping of creamy Puget Sound clam chowder, order a generous piece of grilled seafood—what other restaurant will offer you King salmon at only slightly over market cost? ~ 22531 Marine View Drive, Des Moines; 206-878-4140. MODERATE.

SHOPPING   With the exception of its handful of major shopping malls, the southside of Seattle is no shoppers' mecca. **Westfield's Southcenter Mall** (Southcenter Parkway off Route 5, Tukwila; 206-246-7400) and Auburn's **SuperMall of the Great Northwest** (1101 Supermall Way, Auburn; 253-833-9500) are the best of the bunch, but you won't find many stores that you don't already know from your own hometown.

For music lovers, a good stop in West Seattle is **Easy Street Records**, where many of the area's bands and deejays shop for their own tunes. The newest indie-rock CDs share shelf space with historic vinyl and rare imports; astute staff will direct you to listening stations before you make your purchase. There's even a bar and budget-priced café here. ~ 4559 California Avenue Southwest, West Seattle; 206-938-3279.

Two miles down the highway from Vashon Island's north ferry terminal, near Seattle's Best Coffee, **Owen's Antiques** has 11 rooms of 19th-century antique furniture and accessories, a quilt room, an Asian room and a country room. Closed Monday through Wednesday. ~ Vashon Highway and Cemetery Road; 206-463-5193.

A mile farther down the highway is the **Country Store**, an eclectic collection of clothing, garden supplies, food products, gifts and nursery plants. Spring is a great time to stroll the grounds and experience the vast array of flowers. ~ 20211 Vashon Highway Southwest; 206-463-3655; www.tcsag.com.

Across the street, **Minglement** has handicrafts from around the world, including pottery and jewelry, plus a selection of natural foods, teas and herbs. ~ Vashon Highway and Ellisport Road Southwest; 206-463-9672.

Perhaps the single most popular store on the south side of downtown is the North American flagship warehouse of **IKEA**, the Swedish home-furnishings giant. You can spend hours wandering the maze of corridors through this charming store, and even if you had no intention of doing so, the prices are so low as to convince you to buy. There's also a wonderful cafeteria at the heart of the store, where you can get Swedish meatballs or indulge in a real Scandinavian-style smorgasbord for lunch or dinner. ~ 600 Southwest 43rd Street, Renton; 425-656-2980.

Vashon's annual Strawberry Festival, the weekend after July Fourth, is highlighted by a Saturday parade that features the Antique Tractor Society, the Vashon Island Marching Kazoo Band and the local grocery store's precision grocery cart drill team.

In downtown Kent, the selection of literature and art at **New Woman Books & Wild Women Gallery** ranges from self-help to novels to greeting cards. Plush sofas provide a relaxed reading area at the rear of the little shop. Closed Sunday and Monday. ~ 213 West Meeker Street, Kent; 253-854-4311; www.newwoman books.com.

NIGHTLIFE

For theater, West Seattle's **ArtsWest Theater and Gallery** offers community theater to jazz concerts. Call for a schedule. ~ 4711 California Avenue Southwest, West Seattle; 206-938-0339.

Salty's on Alki is a marvelous spot for a quiet drink with a sunset view across Elliott Bay toward the downtown Seattle skyline. On Friday nights, the bar is packed with rhythm-and-blues lovers who come for the weekly show. Seafood dinners here are special-occasion pricey, but there's a great Sunday brunch. ~ 1936 Harbor Drive Southwest, West Seattle; 206-937-1600.

West Seattle's younger crowd frequents **Rocksport**, a sports bar that books local rock bands for dancing on weekend nights. ~ 4209 Southwest Alaska Street, West Seattle; 206-935-5838. And nestled almost beneath the West Seattle bridge is the **Steel Sky Pub**, which provides a showcase for emerging singer-song-

◀ *HIDDEN*

writers of light, folk-oriented rock music. ~ 3803 Delridge Way Southwest, West Seattle; 206-935-2412.

Incongruously located in conservative downtown Kent, **Trax Bar & Grill**, which backs up to the railroad tracks, has a resident macaw and a Friday- and Saturday-night "Retro Diva Revue": male dragsters impersonate Madonna, Cher, Dolly Parton and other famous female singers. ~ 226 1st Avenue South, Kent; 253-854-8729.

> Like Boeing, Seattle's other economic giant, Microsoft, also has its own museum, but it only exists in cyberspace. Look it up at www.microsoft.com/museum.

There are plenty of small casinos in south Seattle, especially along International Boulevard in Tukwila, but none compares to the **Muckleshoot Casino** on the Indian reservation just southeast of Auburn. The showroom has nightly live entertainment, and there are poker tables and slot machines galore. ~ 2402 Auburn Way South, Auburn; 253-939-7484.

Just down the road, the open-air **White River Amphitheatre** has become a major venue for touring rock acts, from Jimmy Buffett to the heavy-metal Ozzfest bands. ~ 40601 Auburn-Enumclaw Road Southeast, Auburn; 360-825-6200.

BEACHES & PARKS

SEWARD PARK 🏃🚲⚓🛥️🚤⛵ On Bailey Peninsula, this 300-acre park jutting into Lake Washington encompasses Seattle's largest virgin forest. Walking through it on one of several footpaths is the prime attractions, but many come to swim and sunbathe, launch a small boat, fish or visit a fish hatchery. Seward Park offers a rare opportunity to see nesting bald eagles in an urban setting. The best introductory walk is the two-and-one-half-mile shoreline loop stroll; to see the large Douglas firs, add another mile along the center of the peninsula. The swimming beaches' gentle surf is ideal for children, and there are lifeguards in summer. You can fish from the pier for crappie and trout. There are tennis courts, picnic areas, restrooms and play areas. ~ Located on the west shore of Lake Washington, southeast of downtown, at Lake Washington Boulevard South and South Orcas Street; 206-684-4075, fax 206-684-4853; e-mail parksinfo@seattle.gov.

LINCOLN PARK 🏃🚲⚓ This major multipurpose park in southwest Seattle is situated on a nose-shaped bluff just south of the Fauntleroy Ferry Terminal. There are rocky beaches strewn with tidepools and a network of quiet paths winding through groves of madrona, Douglas fir, cedar and redwoods. The park also offers play and picnic areas, an outdoor heated saltwater pool, tennis courts, a horseshoe pit, a football field and several miles of bike paths. ~ Off Fauntleroy Avenue Southwest, south of West Seattle; 206-684-8021, fax 206-233-7023.

SEAHURST PARK 🏃 🏊 🚣 ⛴ ⚓ A well-designed, 152-acre site where landscaping divides 4000 feet of saltwater shore-line into individual chunks just right for private picnics and sun-bathing. A nature trail and some three miles of primitive foot-path explore woodsy uplands and the headwaters of two creeks. Other facilities include picnic areas, restrooms, and a marine lab-oratory with a viewable fish ladder. A complete renovation of the shoreline, removing the seawall and restoring the beach to a na-tive condition, is underway. ~ Located at Southwest 144th Street and 13th Avenue Southwest, via Exit 154B from Route 5, Burien; 206-988-3700.

GENE COULON BEACH PARK 🏊 🚣 ⛴ ⚓ At the south tip of Lake Washington in Renton, this handsomely landscaped site is most notable for the loads of attractions within its 55 acres: one and a half miles of lakeside path, the wildfowl-rich estuary of John's Creek and a "nature islet," a lagoon enclosed by the thousand-foot floating boardwalk of "Picnic Gallery," a seafood restaurant, a fast-food restaurant, and interesting architecture rem-iniscent of old-time amusement parks. A logboom-protected shore-line includes a fishing pier. There's a boat harbor with an eight-lane boat launch, and good fishing from the pier for trout and salmon. The bathing beach is protected by a concrete walkabout with summer lifeguard. There are picnic grounds and floats, restrooms, play areas, and volleyball and tennis courts; there's a restaurant on park grounds and others nearby. ~ Bordered by Lake Wash-ington Boulevard North in Renton, north of Route 405 via Exit 5 and Park Avenue North; 425-430-6600, fax 425-430-6603.

SALTWATER STATE PARK 🏃 🚣 ⚓ You'll share this busy park with lots of locals, nearly 800,000 visitors a year, so don't expect solitude. But among the 88 acres, do revel in the fine views, some 1500 feet of shoreline and quiet woods with two miles of hiking trails. A sunken barge about 150 yards offshore from a prominent sandspit attracts a variety of perch and seasonal fish and divers.

There are picnic areas, restrooms, showers, play areas and a concession stand. ~ Located on Marine View Drive (Route 509) about halfway between Seattle and Tacoma, west of Route 5 via Exit 149; 253-661-4956, fax 206-870-4294.

▲ There are 51 campsites ($15 per night), of which 22 can accommodate RVs. Closed in winter.

HIDDEN ►   **WEST HYLEBOS WETLANDS STATE PARK** 🚶 A rare chunk of urban wetland tucked between industrialization and subdivisions, the 68-acre park offers examples of all sorts of wetland formations along a one-mile boardwalk trail—springs, streams, marshes, lakes, floating logs and sinks. You'll also see remnants of ancient forest, plentiful waterfowl, more than a hundred species of birds and many mammals. Facilities are limited to portable toilets. Day-use fee, $5. ~ On South 348th Street at 4th Avenue South, just west of Route 99 and Exit 142.

DASH POINT STATE PARK 🚶 🚲 ⛵ 🏖 🎣 🛶 Nearly 500 acres of forested wildland with 3300 feet of saltwater shoreline preserve a bit of solitude just barely outside the Tacoma city limits. Seven and a half miles of trail ramble through mixed forest of second-growth fir, maple and alder. The park's beach is onen of the few places on Puget Sound where you'll find enjoyable saltwater swimming—shallow waters in tide flats are warmed by the summer sun. Tides retreat to expose a beachfront nearly a half-mile deep. There's fishing from the pier at Brown's Point Park south of Dash Point State Park, and swimming in tide flat shallows (no lifeguard). Facilities include picnic areas, restrooms and showers. Day-use fee, $5. ~ Located just northeast of Tacoma on Southwest Dash Point (Route 509); 253-661-4955, fax 253-661-4995.

▲ There are 100 developed sites ($15 per night) and 38 sites with hookups ($21 per night). Reservations: 888-226-7688.

GREEN RIVER GORGE The Green River Gorge is less than an hour from downtown Seattle but is worlds away from the big city. The heart of the gorge covers only some six miles on the map but is so twisted into oxbows that it takes kayakers 14 river miles to paddle through it. Just 300 feet deep, the steep-walled gorge nevertheless slices through solid rock (shale and sandstone) to reveal coal seams and fossil imprints and inspire a fine sense of remoteness. State and county parks flank the gorge.

The **Green River Gorge Conservation Area** includes three state parks. Here we pick the two developed parks at the entrance and exit of the gorge and one nearby state park on a lake. ~ 253-931-3930, fax 253-931-6379.

Flaming Geyser State Park 🏃 🚴 🛶 ⛵ Once a resort, this 667-acre park downstream from the exit of Green River Gorge offers four miles of hiking trails and nearly five miles of riverbank. Originally, the flaming geyser area was a test site for coal samples, but miners found natural gas instead, which, when lit, produced a 20-foot flame. The "flaming geyser" is only eight inches high now, and can be seen off one of the trails. Pick up a trail map and brochure at the main office. Fish for rainbow trout and steelhead in season (check the posted regulations). There are picnic areas, restrooms, play areas, volleyball courts, a horseback riding area (but no stables) and horseshoe pits. Day-use fee, $5. ~ Green Valley Road, three miles west of Route 169, south of Black Diamond; 253-931-3930, fax 253-931-6379.

Kanaskat–Palmer State Park 🏃 🚴 🛶 ⛵ Lovely walking on riverside paths, especially in summer is the hallmark of this 310-acre park upstream from the entrance to Green River Gorge. During fishing season, try for steelhead and trout (check posted regulations). Picnic areas, restrooms, showers, volleyball courts and horseshoe pits are the facilities here. Day-use fee, $5. ~ On Cumberland-Kanaskat Road off Southeast 308th Street, 11 miles north of Enumclaw and Route 410; 360-886-0148, fax 360-886-1715.

▲ There are 31 standard sites ($16 per night) and 19 with partial hookups ($22 per night). Reservations: 888-226-7688.

Nolte State Park 🏃 🚴 🏊 🎣 🛶 ⛵ Surrounding Deep Lake, 117-acre Nolte Park is famous for its huge Douglas firs, cedars and cottonwoods. A one-and-a-quarter-mile path circles the lake taking you around nearly 7200 feet of shoreline and past the big trees; a separate nature trail interprets the forest. You can swim at the lake (no lifeguards); motorboats are prohibited. The lake is open for fishing year round, offering trout, bass, crappie, catfish and silvers. There's a minimal picnic area. Closed October to mid-April. Day-use fee, $5. ~ On Veazie-Cumberland Road just south of Southeast 352nd Street, six miles north of Enumclaw and Route 410; 360-825-4646, fax 360-802-9960.

EIGHT

Eastside Neighborhoods

The eastside of Seattle, extending from Lake Washington to the Cascade foothills, blends the urban and rural assets of this metropolitan region. Here you'll find wineries and archaeological sites, prime birdwatching areas and homey bed and breakfast inns.

The biggest city is Bellevue, whose skyline of office buildings and hotel towers belies its lack of strong community identity. Although it is Washington's fifth largest city (with about 115,000 people), to Seattle residents Bellevue is all about upscale shopping centers. Indeed, its downtown Bellevue Place and Bellevue Square complexes are all that many non-Bellevueites know about the city. But there are lovely parks and charming lakeside residential districts and a growing number of fine restaurants.

Kirkland, on the other hand, wins hands-down praise for its quaint lakeside charm. More accessible to the water than any other community hugging the shores of Lake Washington, it has a wealth of parkland, numerous charming cafés and art galleries, and an inviting marina on Moss Bay—projected in the late 19th century to be an iron-and-steel-intensive "Pittsburgh of the West." Area residents are glad that effort failed.

A generation ago, Woodinville was a timber town at the foot of the foothills. Today it's a growing tourist center, the sawmills replaced by western Washington's biggest concentration of boutique wineries, fine dining and lodging, and a downtown that hasn't forgotten the community's woodland heritage.

Redmond is best known as the home of Bill Gates' Microsoft Corporation, as well as video-game giant Nintendo. But those who venture east from Bellevue and Kirkland to the northern edge of Lake Sammamish will also find one of the Seattle area's finest centers for outdoor recreation in Marymoor Park.

Bellevue is the fifth-largest city in Washington, its suburban sprawl broken by high-rise complexes of office buildings, shops and department stores. Crossing Lake Washington between Seattle and Bellevue is the **Evergreen Point Floating Bridge**, the world's longest floating bridge (1.4 miles).

SIGHTS

Bellevue Square, with some 200 stores, is one of the largest malls in the state. ~ Northeast 8th Street and Bellevue Way Northeast, Bellevue; 425-454-2431; www.bellevuesquare.com.

At Bellevue Square is the **Bellevue Art Museum**, which is scheduled to reopen in fall 2004. Exhibits and public programs emphasize the work of Northwest contemporary artists, craftspeople and designers. Admission. ~ 510 Bellevue Way Northeast at Northeast 6th Street, Bellevue; 425-519-0770; www.bellevueart.org.

To see what Bellevue used to be like before freeways, commuters and office towers, stroll the short stretch of shops along Main Street westward from Bellevue Way Northeast in **Old Bellevue**.

Adults and children alike are enchanted with the **Rosalie Whyel Museum of Doll Art**. Hundreds of antique and modern dolls are on display in a building that is patterned after a brick Victorian mansion. Admission. ~ 1116 108th Avenue Northeast, Bellevue; 425-455-1116, fax 425-455-4793; www.dollart.com, e-mail dollart@dollart.com.

Bellevue boasts a surprisingly diverse network of parks embedded within its neighborhoods. Adjacent to Bellevue Square is **Downtown Park**, whose 19 acres include a broad waterfall and a five-acre meadow enclosed by a canal. **Mercer Slough Nature Park** boasts 320 acres of natural wetland habitat and six miles of trails, as well as a blueberry farm, an environmental education center and a canoeing and kayaking center. ~ 2102 Bellevue Way Southeast; 425-452-6881.

Wilburton Hill Park is centered around the Bellevue Botanical Garden, filled with native and ornamental Northwest plants. The park covers over 100 acres and has more than three miles of hiking trails as well as softball and soccer fields. ~ 12001 Main Street off 116th Avenue Northeast; 425-452-2750.

North of Bellevue, hugging the Lake Washington shore, is **Kirkland**, with remnants of small-town charm. Pedestrian traffic is encouraged, with easy access to the lake and a one-and-a-half-mile walking/biking path. At Moss Bay, there's a public boat ramp and marina, shops, cafés and a brewery. The **Arthur Foss**, a 112-foot tugboat built in 1889, is open for tours in the summer. Originally steam-powered, the tug was given a diesel engine in 1934.

Woodinville's wineries are on the southwest corner of town. Chief among them is **Château Ste. Michelle**, the state's largest winery with daily tasting and tours. Situated on a turn-of-the-20th-century estate, it also has duck and trout ponds, experimental vineyards and outdoor concerts on summer weekends. ~ 14111 Northeast 145th Street, Woodinville; 425-415-3300, fax 425-415-3657; www.ste-michelle.com, e-mail info@ste-michelle.com.

Nearby are the **Columbia Winery** (14030 Northeast 145th Street, Woodinville; 425-888-2776; www.columbiawinery.com) and the **Redhook Brewery** (14300 Northeast 145th Street, Woodinville; 425-483-3232; www.redhook.com), both of which offer tours.

Heading down Route 202, you'll come to **Redmond**. At the north end of Lake Sammamish is **Marymoor County Park**, a delightful 640-acre mix of archaeology and history, river and lake, meadows and marshes, plus an assortment of athletic fields. A one-mile footpath leads to a lakeside observation deck, and there's access to the ten-mile Sammamish River Trail, which connects to Seattle's Burke-Gilman Trail at the north Lake Washington community of Bothell. The circa-1904 **Clise Mansion**, near a pioneer windmill, was built as a hunting lodge; today it holds the Marymoor Museum (425-885-3684) of regional history. Facilities include picnic areas, restrooms, play areas, horseback-riding trails, tennis courts, a model-airplane airport, a climbing wall and an archaeological site. Also here is the **Marymoor Velodrome** (2400 Lake Sammamish Parkway Northeast; 206-675-1424), one of the nation's premier tracks for world-class bicycle racers. ~ 6046 West Lake Sammamish Parkway Northeast off Route 520; 206-296-2964, fax 206-296-2968.

LODGING

HIDDEN ►

If you've ever wanted to stay at your own private athletic club, the **Bellevue Club Hotel** is the place. The 67 luxurious rooms feature sunken tubs, cherrywood furnishings, original art and French doors that open onto private patios. What's more, hotel guests are automatic members in a club that offers indoor and outdoor tennis, racquetball and squash, an Olympic-size swimming pool, aerobics classes and extensive workout facilities. There also are fine-dining and casual restaurants. ~ 11200 Southeast 6th Street, Bellevue; 425-454-4424, 800-579-1110, fax 425-688-3101; www. bellevueclub.com. ULTRA-DELUXE.

Big and broad-shouldered, the **Hyatt Regency Bellevue** is the classiest place to stay in Bellevue. The mood is corporate, quality's high and access is convenient. The 382 rooms are painted in

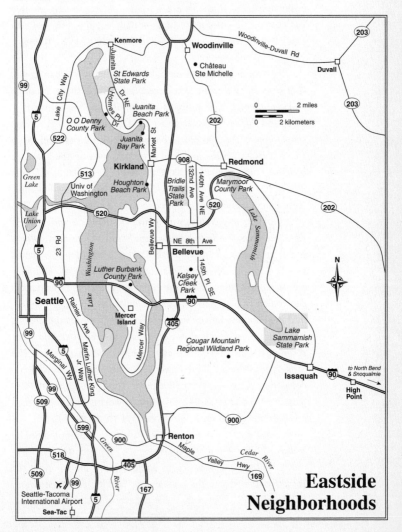

Eastside Neighborhoods

earth tones, and have soft lighting, contemporary furnishings and all the amenities, including room service. For a fee, guests may use the adjoining health club. ~ 900 Bellevue Way Northeast, Bellevue; 425-462-1234, 800-233-1234, fax 425-646-7567; www. bellevuehyatt.com. DELUXE TO ULTRA-DELUXE.

The neon candy cane that stands in front of **Kanes Motel** has been a longtime landmark off Route 90 in southeast Bellevue. This simple but clean and comfortable motel has phones, TVs, desks and mini-fridges in every room, and guests can get free passes to use facilities at the adjacent Bally's gym. ~ 14644 Southeast Eastgate Way, Bellevue; 425-746-8201, 800-746-8201; www. kanesmotel.com. BUDGET.

The **Woodmark Hotel on Lake Washington** is a handsome, four-story brick structure on Lake Washington's shore. Its small scale, residential-style lobby, and comfortable bar with a fireplace and shelves of books create the ambience of a welcoming, stylish home. The 100 rooms have all the amenities: mini-bars, two televisions, robes and hair dryers. Rooms on the lake side have panoramic views. ~ 1200 Carillon Point, Kirkland; 425-822-3700, 800-822-3700, fax 425-822-3699; www.thewoodmark. com, e-mail mail@thewoodmark.com. ULTRA-DELUXE.

The **Shumway Mansion** is a historic mansion with a New England flavor. To save it from demolition, the present owners had it moved to a knoll in north Kirkland, where it now stands as a bed-and-breakfast inn and accommodates guests, weddings and social functions. When a group takes over, overnight visitors can retreat to a tiny reading alcove on a second floor. The formal inn contains European furnishings, rugs out of the Orient, lace curtains and silk floral arrangements. Each of the eight rooms has a queen-size bed and antiques and easy chairs. The innkeepers serve a full breakfast in the morning and homemade cookies at night. ~ 11410 99th Place Northeast, Kirkland; 425-823-2303, fax 425-822-0421; www.shumwaymansion.com, e-mail info@shumwaymansion.com. MODERATE TO DELUXE.

A posh wilderness resort in a near-urban setting: that's **The Willows Lodge**. From its giant river-rock fireplace to the century-old Douglas fir beams in its cathedral-like lobby, from the Japanese-style spa to the outstanding Barking Frog restaurant, this hotel is all about rustic luxury. Each of the 88 rooms has a CD stereo and DVD system, high-speed internet, a fireplace and a

East into
the Cascades

Down the interstate Route 90 corridor at the south end of Lake Sammamish, **Issaquah** marks the point where metropolis gives way to Cascade forests. A charming town in its own right, it boasts a community theater that is reckoned among the best in the region.

As Route 90 rises into the foothills, two smaller towns are worthy of special note. **North Bend**—over which daunting Mount Si, a day-hiker's dream, forever looms—is best known as the town of "Twin Peaks" from the television series of the early 1990s. It's adopted an alpine theme for its downtown buildings, but it hasn't caught on with the vigor of some others. This hamlet sits snugly in the shadow of looming Mt. Si. The **North Bend Ranger District Forest Service Station** offers maps, books and other outdoor-recreation information. Closed Saturday and Sunday. ~ 42404 Southeast North Bend Way, North Bend; 425-888-1421.

Snoqualmie preserves its heritage as an old rail town with an ornate, old railroad depot that is home to the **Snoqualmie Valley Railroad**; it makes a five-mile trip through the Snoqualmie Valley on weekends (April through October) and runs a special Christmas train. Inside the depot, the **Northwest Railway Museum** displays old railroad equipment and sleeper and dining car paraphernalia. Admission. ~ 38625 Southeast King Street, Snoqualmie; 425-888-3030; www.trainmuseum.org.

Nearby is **Snoqualmie Falls**, a thundering cataract with a small park, observation platform and trails leading to the river below the 270-foot falls. Atop the cataract is the luxurious **Salish Lodge**, considerably renovated since it served as the model for Piper Laurie's sawmill in David Lynch's "Twin Peaks."

jetted tub. Balconies or patios open onto luxuriant gardens and the Château Ste. Michelle winery. Besides the hotel restaurant, the renowned Herbfarm (see "Dining" below) is on site. ~ 14580 Northeast 145th Street, Woodinville; 425-424-3900, 877-424-3930; www.willowslodge.com. ULTRA-DELUXE.

The **Bear Creek Inn** is a Cape Cod house set among trees on an acre of land. There's a large rock fireplace in the sitting room, a patio and a deck with a hot tub. The three rooms feature wood furniture with oak and pine trim painted with flowered designs. ~ 19520 Northeast 144th Place, Woodinville; 425-881-2978. MODERATE TO DELUXE.

Set on three-plus acres, **A Cottage Creek Inn** has its own creek, pond and gazebo on the grounds. The English Tudor house features four rooms, one with a brass bed, one with an antique bed, all with their own bathrooms. There are full jacuzzis in the two larger rooms and a communal outdoor hut tub. There's a pleasant sitting room with a piano, which guests are encouraged to play. Full breakfast included. ~ 12525 Avondale Road Northeast, Redmond; phone/fax 425-881-5606; www.cottagecreekinn.com, e-mail innkeepers@cottagecreekinn.com. MODERATE TO DELUXE.

The **Edgewick Inn** in North Bend is a straight-forward motel with 42 clean and quiet units and two suites with jacuzzis. Three rooms are wheelchair accessible. ~ 14600 468th Avenue Southeast, North Bend; 425-888-9000, fax 425-888-9400. MODERATE.

DINING

Bis on Main features a blend of American and European cuisine, offering specialties such as the *vol au vent,* a puff-pastry ring

AUTHOR FAVORITE

When I want to spend a pricey night in the lap of luxury, I can't think of a more dramatic setting to do it than the clifftop **Salish Lodge at Snoqualmie Falls**, perched on the cliff overlooking the spectacular falls. The 91 rooms and suites are decorated in an upscale-country motif with down comforters, wicker furniture, woodburning fireplaces and jacuzzis. Only a few rooms have views of the falls, but the interiors are so well cone that most visitors console themselves by watching the falls from the lounge or observation deck. There is also a full-service spa. ~ 6501 Railroad Avenue Southeast, Snoqualmie; 425-888-2556, 800-826-6124, fax 425-888-2533; www.salishlodge.com, e-mail salish@salishlodge. com. ULTRA-DELUXE.

filled with crab and lobster. Reservations encouraged. ~ 10213 Main Street, Bellevue; 425-455-2033, 877-207-5301, fax 425-455-2720. MODERATE.

The Eastside's most highly acclaimed new eatery in recent years is the **Seastar Restaurant and Raw Bar**, a spacious and elegant spot in a sleek downtown office complex. Owner-chef John Howie's constantly changing, seafood-focused menu has strong Northwest regional and Pacific Rim accents, while the raw bar features Northwest oysters on the half-shell and other chilled delights. More than 50 wines are offered by the glass. No lunch weekends. ~ 205 108th Avenue Northeast, Bellevue; 425-456-0010, fax 425-456-0020; www.seastarrestaurant.com. DELUXE.

The open kitchen at **Andre's Eurasian Bistro** is as entertaining as the food. This restaurant offers a menu with Vietnamese specialties like spring rolls or chicken with lemongrass, as well as Continental selections, such as lamb with garlic. Vietnamese chef Andre Nguyen comes with experience from some of Seattle's best restaurants. No dinner on Monday; no lunch on Saturday. Closed Sunday. ~ 14125 Northeast 20th Street, Bellevue; 425-747-6551, fax 425-747-4304. MODERATE.

Plunk down $22 at **Sushi-Ten Hama** and you'll get all the fresh-made sushi you can eat—and when they say "all," that's exactly what they mean. Sit at the sushi bar and order 'til you drop; the yellowtail, ahi and salmon are especially good, but don't overlook more exotic delights such as octopus and roe. ~ 2217 140th Avenue Northeast, Bellevue; phone/fax 425-643-6637. MODERATE.

◀ HIDDEN

South Asian families throng to **Raga**, which should leave no doubt that this is one of greater Seattle's best Indian restaurants. The exotic decor—silk hanging from the ceiling, sitar and sarod on the walls, a firepit in the center of the room—complements the food. Try the Malai chicken kebab, marinated with cashews and cream then grilled in a tandoori oven. ~ 212 Central Way, Kirkland; 425-827-3300. BUDGET TO MODERATE.

In downtown Kirkland—hidden out of easy view in a shopping mall—is the **Purple Café and Wine Bar**. A long curving bar welcomes oenophiles, who can dine there while enjoying dozens of wines by the glass, or move into the spacious dining room. The menu features salads, sandwiches, pizzas and pasta, as well as yummy entrées: salmon medallions in a wasabi-soy reduction sauce, for instance, or pork tenderloin with a mango-basil glaze.

◀ HIDDEN

~ 323 Park Place Center, Kirkland; 425-828-3372, fax 425-828-3769; www.thepurplecafe.com. Also at 14459 Woodinville-Redmond Road, Woodinville (425-483-7129). MODERATE TO DELUXE.

The best spot for a view of Lake Washington while you dine is **Yarrow Bay Grill and Beach Café**. In the upper-level Yarrow Bay Grill, booths and tables are set against windows that extend in a wide semi-circle overlooking the lake. The Northwest cuisine emphasizes fresh seafood; salmon and chicken are smoked in-house, and the flavorful clam chowder is excellent. Downstairs, the more casual Yarrow Beach Café offers an interesting menu with specials that travel to different ports-of-call and a bar with Northwest wines and microbrewed beers. The bargain here at the café is happy hour on weeknights when, with a drink purchase, you can choose from generous portions of appetizers such as Cajun popcorn shrimp, steamed mussels and smoked salmon for half-price. No lunch at the Yarrow Bay Grill. ~ 1270 Carillon Point, Kirkland; 425-889-0303 or 425-889-9052, fax 425-803-2982; www.ybgrill.com, e-mail info@ybgrill.com. MODERATE TO ULTRA-DELUXE.

HIDDEN ► Overlooking Juanita Creek north of Kirkland, **Cafe Juanita** is a pricey but dependably excellent restaurant. Intimate and quiet, the creekside atmosphere is romantic. Owner-chef Holly Smith's Northern Italian menu centers on game, poultry and pasta; the wine list is superlative. Dinner only. Closed Monday. ~ 9702 120th Place Northeast, Kirkland; 425-823-1505; www.cafejuanita.com, e-mail info@cafejuanita.com. DELUXE TO ULTRA-DELUXE.

A couple of local residents who grew up in Pakistan and Bangladesh have opened **Shamiana**. The food is cooled to an American palate but can be spiced to a full-blown, multistar *hot*. A buffet of four curries, salad, *nan* and *dal* is offered at lunch. Dinners are à la carte, and include entrées such as lamb curry with rice *pulao* or chicken *tikka*. No lunch on Saturday and Sunday. ~ 10724 Northeast 68th Street, Kirkland; 425-827-4902, fax 425-828-2765. MODERATE.

HIDDEN ► One of the best Japanese restaurants in all of Puget Sound is hidden in the Totem Lake West shopping center in suburbia. **Izumi** features an excellent sushi bar. Entrées are fairly standard—beef, chicken sukiyaki and teriyaki and tempura—but the ingredients are especially fresh and carefully prepared. Service is friendly. No lunch on weekends. Closed Monday. ~ 12539 116th Avenue Northeast, Kirkland; 425-821-1959. MODERATE TO DELUXE.

Reservations are hard to come by, and it's a bit of a challenge getting there, but **The Herbfarm** is the Seattle area's equivalent to the Napa Valley's French Laundry: the ultimate in exquisite meals prepared from locally grown ingredients. Each week, the restaurant picks a theme (e.g., "Chambers of the Sea") and builds a nine-course tasting menu with paired wines to illustrate it. Never tried miner's lettuce or ice cream flavored with maple blossoms? You will at The Herbfarm. Dinner only. Closed Monday through Wednesday; closed Monday through Thursday in winter. ~ Willows Lodge, 14590 Northeast 145th Street, Woodinville; 425-485-5300; www.theherbfarm.com. ULTRA-DELUXE.

Sophistication is definitely not the attraction at the **Armadillo**, Woodinville's outpost of Texas-style barbecue. Service is accompanied by wisecracks; the menu is one big collection of bad puns; the decor has been described as "road kill." But the food—hearty ribs, brisket and chicken—is as close to decent barbecue as you will get in the land of salmon. And the hot sauce is actually hot. ~ 13109 175th Street Northeast, Woodinville; 425-481-1417, fax 425-485-8525. BUDGET TO MODERATE.

At **Pogacha**, a Croatian version of pizza is the mainstay. The pizzas, crisp on the outside but moist inside, are baked in a brick oven. Because the saucing is nonexistent or very light, the flavor of the toppings—pesto and various cheeses, alone or over vegetables or meat—is more apparent. Other entrées include Adriatic-inspired grilled meats and seafood, salads and pastas. ~ 120 North-

AUTHOR FAVORITE

Even in Bangkok, I have a hard time finding a Thai restaurant as good as **Typhoon!** Chef/owner Bo Lohasawat Kline is a culinary wizard, making everyday Thai cuisine unique and adding some rare dishes of her own, like *miang kum*—an appealing finger food that invites you to wrap baby spinach leaves around various minced condiments and season them with a dipping sauce. No lunch on weekends. ~ 8936 161st Avenue Northeast in Bella Bottega Center, Redmond; 425-558-7666; www.typhoonrestaurants.com. MODERATE.

west Gilman Boulevard, Issaquah; 425-392-5550; www.pogacha. com. Also at 119 106th Avenue Northeast, Bellevue; 425-455-5670. MODERATE.

Twede's Café, which served as the model for the diner in television's "Twin Peaks," has faux gas lamps, wood paneling and neon across the ceiling. Rebuilt after a fire, it still offers what Agent Cooper called "a damn fine cup of coffee," best enjoyed with a slice of the infamous cherry pie. ~ 137 West North Bend Way, North Bend; 425-831-5511. BUDGET.

The **Salish Lodge at Snoqualmie Falls** offers spectacular views over the falls and canyon below, and the food is first rate. The menu leans toward what has become known as Northwest cuisine: lots of seafood, fresh fruits and vegetables, and fame. The restaurant boasts the largest wine list in the state and a dessert list almost as long. ~ 6501 Railroad Avenue Southeast, Snoqualmie; 800-826-6124; www.salishlodge.com, e-mail salish@salish lodge.com. ULTRA-DELUXE.

SHOPPING   In Bellevue, **Bellevue Square** has 200 of the nation's finest shops, department stores and restaurants. ~ Northeast 8th Street and Bellevue Way Northeast, Bellevue; 425-454-8096; www.bellevue square.com.

Just down the street, **Bellevue Place** has another 20 upscale stores—among them **Elements Gallery** (425-454-8242), which features Northwest craftspeople's work (including woodwork, glass and pottery) as well as fashion jewelry. Closed Sunday. ~ 10500 Northeast 8th Street, Bellevue; 425-453-5634.

One of the most elegant shops in Bellevue is **Alvin Goldfarb Jeweler.** Specializing in 18-carat platinum and gold pieces crafted by an in-house goldsmith who also works with precious and semiprecious gems, this is a mecca for discriminating people who desire a one-of-a-kind item. Closed Sunday. ~ 305 Bellevue Way Northeast, Bellevue; 425-454-9393; www.alvingoldfarbjeweler.com.

Eastside alpine sports lovers make **Marmot Mountain Works** a regular stop, regardless of season. This is the place to be outfitted for backpacking, climbing or backcountry skiing. Seattle visitors can also arrange rentals of such items as tents, packs, boots and Nordic skis, as well as crampons and ice axes. ~ 827 Bellevue Way Northeast, Bellevue; 425-453-1515; www.marmot mountain.com.

If you're looking for the unusual, browse through **Ming's Asian Gallery**, two stories full of Asian antiques and art from China, Korea, Japan and Southeast Asia. ~ 10217 Main Street, Bellevue; 425-462-4008.

Collectors of marine antiques can pick up old brass lights, wooden wheels, telescopes or diving equipment of days gone by on two floors at **Cuttysark**. The shop also has a large collection of old U.S. and foreign flags. Closed Sunday and Monday. ~ 10235 Main Street, Bellevue; 425-453-1265; www.cuttysark.net.

Northwest Fine Woodworking is owned by woodworkers and is stocked with fine hand-crafted furniture, boxes and screens. Closed Sunday. ~ 601 108th Avenue, Plaza 100, Bellevue; 425-462-5382.

Hunters of antiques appreciate the **Kirkland Antique Gallery**. The mall has more than 80 dealers selling antiques and collectibles. ~ 151 3rd Street, Kirkland; 425-827-7443.

Excellent Northwest ceramics, jewelry and blown glass make **Lakeshore Gallery** a fine place to stop even if you have no intention of buying. The carved woodwork is especially well done. ~ 15 Lake Street, Kirkland; 425-827-0606.

The **Kirkland Arts Center**, representing a bevy of local artists in a variety of media, is housed in the beautifully refurbished, historic Peter Kirk Building, which dates from the late 19th century. ~ 620 Market Street, Kirkland; 425-822-7161.

The long-abandoned Kirkland rail depot is now home to **Eastside Trains**, which stocks everything a model-train enthusiast could possibly want—and probably more. ~ 217 Central Way, Kirkland; 425-828-4098.

Refurbished farmhouses, a barn and a feed store are stocked with handicrafts and artful, designer clothing at Issaquah's **Gilman Village**. Among the 40-plus shops clustered in these historic

GREENERY GALORE

Its 50th anniversary in business fast approaching (in 2006), **Molbak's Greenhouse and Nursery** may be greater Seattle's favorite garden shop. Need a new house plant? A maple sapling? Maybe just some verbena for ground covering? Molbak's will take care of you. Christmas-season displays draw visitors from miles around. ~ 13625 Northeast 175th Street, Woodinville; 425-483-5000; www.molbaks.com.

structures is **Made in Washington** (425-392-4819), which handles pottery, specialty foods and wine, dinnerware and wood carvings. ~ 317 Northwest Gilman Boulevard, Issaquah; 425-392-6802; www.gilmanvillage.com.

Hedges Cellars is a Yakima Valley winery that has opened a full-fledged tasting room on the west side of the Cascades; some aging is done here. Hedges is known for its reds, especially cabernets and merlots. ~ 195 Northeast Gilman Boulevard, Issaquah; 425-391-6056; www.hedgescellars.com.

You can always take a self-guided "window tour" at Boehms Candies. The best time? Monday through Friday from 10 a.m. to 3 p.m. when the factory is filled with workers.

Satisfy your sweet tooth at **Boehms Candies**, where hundreds of chocolates are hand-dipped every day. From mid-June to September, you can take a guided factory tour (reservations are required; this is a popular spot) and watch the skilled workmanship that goes into making candies of this quality. ~ 255 Northeast Gilman Boulevard, Issaquah; 425-392-6652; www.boehmscandies.com.

In North Bend, 31 miles east of Seattle, the **Factory Stores at North Bend** is a mall with 50 stores selling well-known brands—Nike, the Gap, Van Heusen, Big Dog, Bass, Hanes—at discount prices. ~ 461 South Fork Avenue Southwest, North Bend; 425-888-4505.

NIGHTLIFE **Daniel's Broiler** has a live pianist playing contemporary hit seven nights a week. ~ Bellevue Place, 10500 Northeast 8th Avenue, 21st floor, Bellevue; 425-462-4662.

Live sports events via satellite plus an extensive bar menu are on tap at **Chadfield's Sports Pub** located in the Hyatt Regency Bellevue. ~ 900 Bellevue Way Northeast, Bellevue; 425-462-1234.

For highbrow offerings, check out the annual **Belle Arte Concert Series** at the Kirkland Performance Center. Between October and April, five internationally reputed chamber-music groups—trios, quartets, quintets—perform to sellout audiences. ~ 350 Kirkland Avenue, Kirkland; 425-893-9900; www.belle arte.org.

The **Shark Billiards Club** presents live bands on Friday and Saturday nights, special events like bikini contests midweek—and free pool every night. Music is mainly dance-oriented '70s and '80s retro. Cover for bands and events. ~ 52 Lakeshore Plaza, Kirkland; 425-803-3003; www.thesharkclub.com.

For microbrew lovers, the **Kirkland Roaster & Alehouse** is the place to go. Everything here is about the beer, including the decor. Even the walls are covered with beer labels. ~ 111 Central Way, Kirkland; 425-827-4400.

Enjoy live blues tunes on Friday and Saturday at **Forecasters Public House at the Redhook Brewery**. ~ 14300 Northeast 145th Street, Woodinville; 425-483-3232; www.redhook.com.

A third popular brewpub is owned by Oregon-based Rogue Ales. The **Issaquah Brewhouse** welcomes children to its non-smoking streetside café, but allows cigarettes at the back bar with crafty house beers like Brutal Bitter and Dead Guy Ale. ~ 35 West Sunset Way, Issaquah; 425-557-1911; www.rogue.com.

Good things come in small packages, and the **Village Theatre** proves it. The local casts here will tackle anything, be it Broadway musicals, dramas or comedy. ~ 303 Front Street North, Issaquah; 425-392-2202; www.villagetheatre.org.

KELSEY CREEK PARK 🚶 This unique park is a 150-acre farm with an old homestead and farm animals in the barnyard. There are hiking trails, jogging paths, wooded glens, a creek and an 1888 log cabin. ~ 13204 Southeast 8th Place, Bellevue; 425-452-7688, fax 425-452-2804.

BEACHES & PARKS

JUANITA BEACH PARK 🚶 🏊 🚤 Juanita Beach Park draws big crowds of area residents from late June through September, with good reason. Its sandy beach is one of the best on Lake Washington; the roped-off swimming area is vast; and the water warms up fairly early in the shallow bay. There's a concession building and adequate changing facilities, a picnic area and plenty of room for anglers to ply their craft without interfering with swimmers. ~ Access from Juanita Drive Northeast, five minutes north of downtown Kirkland. Across the bay, **Juanita Bay Park** is basically undeveloped, offering wildlife watchers a huge wetland area that attracts waterfowl, blackbirds and the occasional eagle or osprey. ~ Access is from Market Street North, five minutes north of downtown Kirkland; 425-828-1217.

◀ HIDDEN

O.O. DENNY COUNTY PARK 🚶 🏊 🚤 Also located on Lake Washington, just north of Kirkland, O.O. Denny offers miles of heavily wooded hiking trails and a sheltered picnic area on the lake. While there are no lifeguards, people do swim and fish. Restrooms are available. ~ From Route 405 take Northeast 116th Street

◀ HIDDEN

Exit, head west on Juanita Drive Northeast, and turn left on Holmes Point Drive Northeast; 206-296-8687, fax 206-296-8686.

SAINT EDWARDS STATE PARK 🏃 🚴 ⛵ 🏊 This former Catholic seminary still exudes the peace and quiet of a theological retreat across its 316 heavily wooded acres and 3000 feet of Lake Washington shoreline. Except for a handful of former seminary buildings, the park is mostly natural, laced by miles of informal trails. To reach the beach (no lifeguard), take the wide path just west of the main seminary building. It winds a half mile down to the shore, where you can wander left or right. Side trails climb up the bluff for the return loop. There's also a year-round indoor pool (fee), plus picnic areas, restrooms, a tennis court, a horseshoe pit, soccer and baseball fields, basketball, volleyball, badminton and a gymnasium (fee). ~ Located on Lake Washington's eastern shore, between Kenmore and Kirkland on Juanita Drive Northeast; 425-823-2992.

LUTHER BURBANK COUNTY PARK 🏃 🏊 🏖 At the northeast corner of Mercer Island in Lake Washington, this little jewel presents some 3000 feet of shoreline to explore along with marshes, meadows and woods. The entire 77-acre site is encircled by a loop walk. You can fish from the pier for salmon, steelhead, trout and bass, and in summer swim at the beach. Among the facilities are picnic areas, restrooms, a play area, tennis courts and an amphitheater with summer concerts. ~ Entrance is at 84th Avenue Southeast and Southeast 24th Street, via the Island Crest Way exit from Route 90 on Mercer Island, east of Seattle; 206-236-3545.

LAKE SAMMAMISH STATE PARK 🏃 🚴 🏊 🚣 🏖 🛶 🚤 A popular, 431-acre park at the southern tip of Lake Sammamish near Issaquah, it offers plenty to do, including swimming (no lifeguard), boating, picnicking, hiking and birdwatching along 6858 feet of lake shore and around the mouth of Issaquah Creek. Look for eagles, hawks, great-blue heron, red-wing blackbirds, northern flickers, grebes, kingfishers, killdeer, buffleheads, widgeon and Canada geese. Picnic areas, restrooms, showers, soccer fields and a jogging trail are the facilities here. ~ Located at East Lake Sammamish Parkway Southeast and Southeast 56th Street, two miles north of Route 90 in Issaquah (15 miles east of Seattle) via Exit 17; 360-902-8844.

NINE

Tacoma & Southern Puget Sound

First-time visitors to southern Puget Sound may find that it's the constantly changing geography that's the region's most memorable and striking feature. On a map, Southern Puget Sound looks like a fistful of bony fingers clawing at the earth. This maze of inlets, peninsulas and islands presents plentiful saltwater access and invites days of poking around.

What nature created here, partly by the grinding and gouging of massive lowland glaciers, is a complex mosaic. From the air, arriving visitors see a green-blue tapestry of meandering river valleys weaving between forested ridges, the rolling uplands dotted by lakes giving way to Cascade foothills and distant volcanoes, the intricate maze-way of Southern Puget Sound's island-studded inland sea.

From on high it seems almost pristine, but a closer look reveals a sobering overlay of manmade changes. Even as Seattle's downtown becomes "Manhattanized," the region is being "Los Angelesized" with the birth of a freeway commuter culture stretching south through Tacoma to Olympia. Farmlands and wetlands, forests and meadows are giving way to often poorly planned, hastily built housing tracts, roads and shopping centers.

For the traveler, such rapid growth means more traffic and longer lines for the ferry; more-crowded campgrounds, parks and public beaches; busier bikeways and foot trails; more folks fishing and boating and clam-digging. Downtown parking can be hard to find and expensive. But don't despair. South of the heart of Seattle you'll still find a wealth of parks and wilderness, waterways and beaches. With an ample array of outdoor activities, southern Puget Sound serves as Seattle's back door to the wilderness—including spectacular Mount Rainier National Park.

The Tacoma/Olympia region is rich in history, parks, waterfalls and cultural landmarks. Tacoma features numerous architectural gems; nearby villages like Gig

Harbor are ideal for daytrippers. One of the nation's prettier capital cities (and here you may have thought Seattle was the capital of Washington!), Olympia is convenient to the wildlife refuges of southern Puget Sound, as well as to American Indian monuments and petroglyphs.

SIGHTS   Despite a lingering mill-town reputation, **Tacoma**, the city on Commencement Bay, has experienced a lively rejuvenation in recent years and offers visitors some first-rate attractions. Charles Wright, president of the Great Northern Railroad, chose it as the western terminus of his railroad, and he wanted more than a mill town at the end of his line. Some of the best architects of the day were commissioned to build hotels, theaters, schools and office buildings.

Today, Tacoma is the state's "second city" with a population of 179,000. The city jealously protects its treasure trove of turn-of-the-20th-century architecture in a pair of historic districts overlooking the bay on both sides of Division Avenue. The 1893 **Old City Hall** at South 7th and Commerce streets was modeled after Renaissance Italian hill castles. The 1889 **Bostwick Hotel** at South 9th Street and Broadway is a classic triangular Victorian "flatiron."

The **Pantages Theater**, an exquisitely restored 1918 masterpiece of the vaudeville circuit designed by Marcus Priteca, is the centerpiece of Tacoma's thriving theater district, and one of the finest of its kind in the nation. The 1800-seat Pantages is home to symphony, opera, ballet and major national touring acts. (And it outstrips in sheer opulence, Tacomans like to point out, anything Seattle has to offer.) The Pantages is worth visiting simply to gawk at its glittering grandeur. It's joined in the Broadway Center for the Performing Arts by the **Rialto Theater**, another restored 1918 belle, and the **Theatre on the Square**, devoted to its resident drama company, Tacoma Actors Guild. ~ Broadway Center, 901 Broadway, Tacoma; tickets, 253-591-5894; tours and general information, 253-591-5890, fax 253-591-2013.

Nearby, the **Tacoma Art Museum** hosts international-class shows, such as an exhibit featuring Picasso's ceramics and works on paper. The permanent collection focuses on the early works of Dale Chihuly. Closed Monday. Admission. ~ 1701 Pacific Avenue, Tacoma; 253-272-4258, fax 253-627-1898; www.tacoma artmuseum.org, e-mail info@tacomaartmuseum.org.

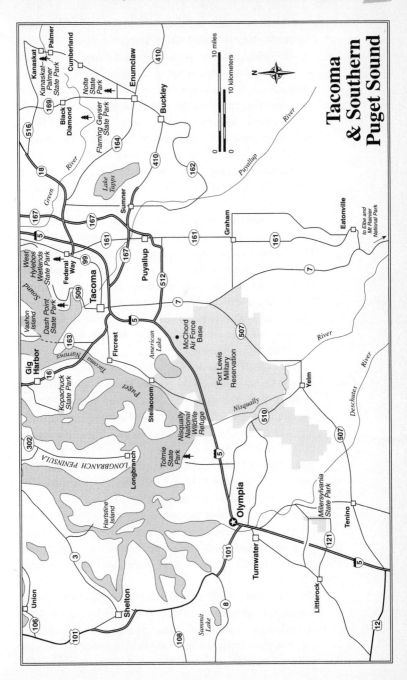

Tacoma
& Southern
Puget Sound

History adds more depth to Tacoma's appeal at the **Union Station/Washington State History Museum** complex. The side-by-side buildings not only are aesthetically appealing—the restored copper-domed Union Station is now the federal courthouse, the history museum is a sweeping, arched modern counterpart—they also offer cultural wealth inside. **Union Station**'s 70-foot diameter rotunda dome rises 60 feet above ground level; the Beaux Arts neoclassical–style building dates from 1911. The rotunda holds one of the world's finest exhibits of glass art made entirely by Tacoma native Chihuly, the renowned founder of the Pilchuck School of blown-glass art. ~ 1717 Pacific Avenue, Tacoma; 253-572-9310.

The **Washington State History Museum** next door offers a comprehensive view of the state's human cultures, from the original inhabitants dependent on salmon to the logging, fishing and farming that first brought settlers to the Northwest. Interactive exhibits allow visitors to sit in the driver's seat of a covered wagon, take a stab at separating wheat from chaff and experience a coal mine cave-in. Closed Monday. Admission. ~ 1911 Pacific Avenue, Tacoma; 253-272-3500, 888-238-4373, fax 253-272-9518; www.wshs.org.

The **Chihuly Bridge of Glass**, a tunnel of light and color created by Chihuly, connects the History Museum to the **Museum of Glass**. Dedicated to showcasing glass art from around the world, the museum also features contemporary painting, sculpture and mixed media pieces. Most exciting is the Hot Shop, a glass workshop where a resident team of glass blowers plies its trade. Closed Monday and Tuesday. Admission. ~ 1801 East Dock Street; 253-284-4750, fax 253-396-1769; www.museum ofglass.org, e-mail info@museumofglass.org.

The **Job Carr Cabin Museum** is a reconstruction of the first permanent settlers' log cabin that commemorates Tacoma's founding with original artifacts, photos and historical displays. Closed Sunday through Tuesday. ~ 2350 North 30th Street, Tacoma; 253-627-5405.

A treat for both kids and adults is **Point Defiance Park**, set on a sloping peninsula above the south Puget Sound shore. This 700-acre urban park has an outstanding zoo and aquarium with a Pacific Rim theme. You can watch the fish from above or through underwater viewing windows. The **zoo** (253-591-5337, fax 253-

591-5448) has penguins, beluga whales, polar bears, an elephant barn and a farm where city children can pet goats and sheep. In Point Defiance, you can also see Camp 6 Logging Museum; Fort Nisqually, a reconstruction of the original 1850 Hudson's Bay Company post (closed Monday and Tuesday except in summer); NeverNeverLand, a picnic and playground area (open Memorial Day through Labor Day); rhododendron, rose, Japanese and na-

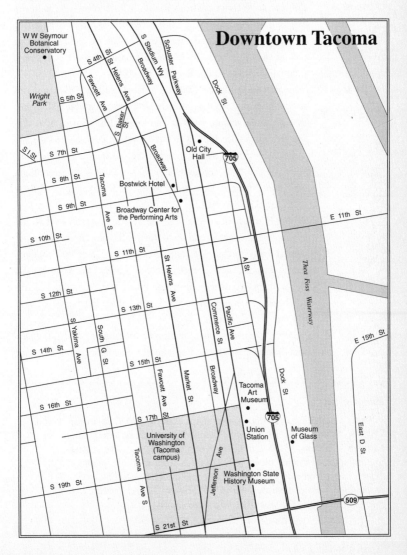

Downtown Tacoma

tive Northwest gardens; and numerous scenic overlooks. A good beach walk is at the base of the bluff edging the park, heading west from Owen Beach. Since the water is swift here, it's best to walk at low tide. The **Boathouse Marina** offers boat rentals and fishing (253-591-5325, fax 253-305-1085). ~ North 54th and Pearl streets, Tacoma; 253-305-1000; www.metroparkstacoma.org.

HIDDEN ▶   Halfway between Point Defiance and downtown, tucked along Foss Waterway, **Thea's Park** is a little-known oasis in the city. Not only is this idyllic three-acre enclave rarely crowded, it is exceptionally well landscaped, with a walking path, footbridge and meandering creek. ~ On South 4th Street and Dock Street, Tacoma; 253-305-1000, fax 253-305-1098.

HIDDEN ▶   A half hour east of Tacoma, in the **Puyallup Valley**, a series of river-bottom flower farms blaze with daffodil and tulip blooms. One of the largest growers is **Van Lierop Bulb Farm**, a family-operated farm since 1934. Van Lierop welcomes visitors to its shop and gardens during the height of the bloom season in March and April. Closed May through January. ~ 13407 80th Street East, off Pioneer Avenue East, from Route 512, Puyallup; 253-848-7272, fax 253-848-9142.

Gig Harbor, situated across the Tacoma Narrows off Route 16, is a classic Puget Sound small town. The community that arose around the harbor was founded as a fishing village by Croatians and Austrians, and named for the small, low-draft vessels ("gigs") capable of maneuvering into its waters. Today, charming shops, galleries, inns and cafés wind along Harborview Drive and intersecting streets.

You'll see every sort of pleasure craft here; it's one of the best boat-watching locales on Puget Sound. The tight harbor entrance

URBAN OASIS

Without a doubt, Tacoma's prettiest garden spot is the **W. W. Seymour Botanical Conservatory**, a graceful Victorian domed conservatory constructed at the turn of the 20th century with over 12,000 panes of glass. Inside are exotic tropical plants, including birds of paradise, ornamental figs, cacti and bromeliads; seasonal displays of flowers; a collection of orchids; and a fish pond with waterfall. ~ 316 South G Street, Tacoma; phone/fax 253-591-5330; www.metroparkstacoma.org.

funnels boats single-file past dockside taverns and cafés where you can watch the nautical parade. Or, rent a boat from Gig Harbor Rent-A-Boat and join the flotilla. ~ 8829 North Harborview Drive; 253-858-7341; www.gigharborrentaboat.com, e-mail gig harborrentaboat@centurytel.net.

Steilacoom about five miles south of Tacoma is a quiet counter-   ◄ HIDDEN
point to Gig Harbor's bustle. Founded by Yankee sea captains in the 1850s, it exudes a museum-like peacefulness and preserves a New England look among its fine collection of clapboard houses. Get a self-guiding brochure at **Steilacoom Historical Museum**. Open Friday through Sunday in February, November and December; open Wednesday through Sunday from March through October. Closed Monday and the month of January. ~ 112 Main Street, Steilacoom; 253-584-4133.

At the 1895 **Bair Drugstore** you can order an old-fashioned float from the 1906 soda fountain. ~ On Lafayette Street near Wilkes Street, Steilacoom; 253-588-9668, fax 253-588-0737.

Fort Lewis, astride Route 5 south of Tacoma, is one of the most important Army posts in the United States, having gained strength during the Pentagon consolidation. Nearby **McChord Air Force Base** has grown in stature as well. Both posts offer museums open to the public. The **McChord Air Museum** has historic air-craft, flight simulators for visitor use, and other artifacts covering the base's history from World War II on. Closed Sunday and Monday. ~ On the base near the main entrance, Route 5, Exit 125; 253-982-2485; www.mcchordairmuseum.org. The **Fort Lewis Military Museum** covers the history of the post from 1917 to the present. Open Wednesday through Sunday afternoon. ~ Building 4320, on Post, right off Route 5, Exit 120; 253-967-7206; www.lewis.army.mil.

At the southern tip of Puget Sound, **Olympia**'s state capitol dome rises boldly as you approach on Route 5, a tempting land-mark for travelers and an easy detour from the busy freeway. But this community of some 39,000 offers visitors more to peruse than government buildings and monuments. Nevertheless, the capitol campus may be the best place to begin your explorations.

You can take a daily guided tour seven days a week through the marbled halls of the Romanesque **Legislative Building** and see other buildings on the grounds—**Temple of Justice, Executive Mansion** and **State Library**.

Mt. Rainier National Park

Mt. Rainier, the huge landmark mountain visible (on clear days) from everywhere in the Puget Sound area, makes for a spectacularly scenic all-day trip from Tacoma, although you could spend weeks in this area and only sample a small portion of its recreational possibilities. Heading south from the city on Route 167, go seven miles to Puyallup, turn off on Route 161, and suddenly you're off the freeway and on your way through the forests and farmlands of Pierce County. As you approach from the north and west, the forest gets thicker and thicker as you draw nearer, and the roadsided rivers get swifter and swifter. The national park is almost surrounded with national-forest wilderness areas as buffer zones against clear-cut logging.

NORTHWEST TREK WILDLIFE PARK   Located about 17 miles south of Puyallup is Northwest Trek Wildlife Park, Washington's premier animal park. Where you can take an hour-long tram tour for an up-close look at large animals native to the Pacific Northwest (bison, caribou, moose) roaming in a 435-acre natural habitat. There's usually a wait, so expect to spend two to three hours here. Closed Monday through Thursday from November to mid-February. Admission. ~ 11610 Trek Drive East (off Route 161), Eatonville; 360-832-6122, fax 360-832-6118; www.nwtrek.org.

MT. RAINIER NATIONAL PARK   If you arrive via Route 706 you will have to go through Elbe on Route 7, which has the **Mt. Rainier Scenic Railroad**, a steam-powered train that makes a 14-mile trip through the lush forest and across high bridges to Mineral Lake. It runs daily in July and August and on Saturday and Sunday in June, September and December. A four-hour dinner train is offered Friday through Sunday in the summer. ~ P.O. Box 921, Elbe, WA 98330; 360-569-2588, 888-783-2611, 888-773-4637 (for dinner train only); www.mrsr.com. Once inside

The nearby **State Capitol Museum** includes a fine collection of Northwest Coast Indian artifacts. Closed Sunday and Monday. Admission. ~ 211 West 21st Avenue, Olympia; 360-753-2580, fax 360-586-8322; www.wshs.wa.gov.

Downtown, the handsomely restored **Old Capitol**, at 7th Avenue and Washington Street across from stately Sylvester Park, will catch your eye with its fanciful architecture. But most the park, you may be almost overwhelmed by the scenery. **Mt. Rainier** is so monstrous (14,411 feet) that it makes everything around it seem trivial. In fact, Mt. Rainier is the tallest mountain in the Northwest and has more glaciers—26—than any other mountain in the contiguous 48 states. Mt. Rainier National Park has numerous visitor centers and interpretive exhibits along winding roads. For park information, call the National Park Service at 360-569-2211 ext. 3314; www.nps.gov/mora.

LONGMIRE   The **Longmire Museum** emphasizes the park's natural history with rock, flora and fauna exhibits as well as displays on the human history of the area. Its old historic buildings have stood since the 1880s when the Longmire family lived there. ~ Longmire, WA; 360-569-2211 ext. 3314.

PARADISE   About 15 miles into the park, a turnoff on the left takes you up to timberline at Paradise, one of the most beautiful places in the park. Head to the busy **Henry M. Jackson Visitor Center**, which has several exhibits and audiovisual shows; it has a snack bar and gift shop. Closed weekdays (except holidays) between October and April. ~ Paradise, WA; 360-569-2211 ext. 2328.

SUNRISE   Beyond the Paradise turnoff, Route 706 is closed in the winter but stunning in the summer as it traverses Backbone Ridge, offering panoramic views of the jagged Catamount Range to the southeast. In about 15 miles you'll join Route 123 northbound. Another ten miles brings you to the summit of 4675-foot Cayuse Pass. Four miles farther on is the turnoff on the left that winds by switchbacks up the east slope of the mountain to **Sunrise Visitor Center**, a 16-mile climb to the highest point in the park that you can reach by car. Numerous trails fan out from the center for day hikes, but be aware that even in July, there is often snow on the trails. ~ 360-663-2574.

HOMEWARD   When you descend from Sunrise, turn north (left) on Route 123 and you're on your way out of the park. The highway takes you 38 miles through Mt. Baker–Snoqualmie National Forest. Route 410 will take you back to Tacoma.

of downtown is a potpourri of disparate attractions—the **Washington Center for the Performing Arts** at 512 Washington Street Southeast, galleries, the **Capitol Theater** at 5th Avenue and Washington Street with its old films and local theater, and a bit of Bohemia along 4th Avenue West.

Percival Landing is an inviting, harborside park with observation tower, kiosks with historical displays, picnic tables, cafés   ◄ HIDDEN and boardwalks next to acres of pleasure craft. ~ At the foot of State Avenue at Water Street, Olympia.

For a longer walk, head south on Water Street, cross 4th and 5th avenues, then turn west and follow the sidewalk next to the Deschutes Parkway (or get in your car and drive) around the park-dotted shores of manmade **Capitol Lake**, which is two and a half miles from the town of Tumwater.

Tumwater marks the true end of Puget Sound. Before Capitol Lake was created, the sound was navigable all the way to the Deschutes River. **Tumwater Historical Park**, at the meeting of river and lake, is rich in both history and recreation. One of two pioneer houses here was built in 1860 by Nathaniel Crosby III (Bing Crosby's grandfather). Down by the river you can fish, have a picnic, explore fitness and hiking trails, watch birds in reedy marshes and see more historical exhibits. Across the river, a handsome, six-story, brick brew house built in 1906 marks an early enterprise that lives on in a 1933 brewery a few hundred yards south. ~ 777 Simmons Avenue, Tumwater; 360-754-4160, fax 360-754-4166.

Follow Deschutes Parkway south to **Tumwater Falls Park** (not to be confused with Tumwater Historical Park), a small park that's a nice spot for a picnic lunch and whose main attraction is the namesake "falls," twisting and churning through a rocky defile. Feel the throb of water reverberating through streamside foot-paths. Listen to its sound, which the Indians called "Tumtum." You'll find plenty of history in the headquarters exhibit, includ-ing an American Indian petroglyph and a monument recounting the travails of the first permanent settlement north of the Colum-bia River here in 1845. ~ Deschutes Way and C Street, Tumwater; phone/fax 360-943-2550.

Ten miles south of Olympia are **Mima Mounds**, an unusual group of several hundred hillocks spread across 450 acres. Scien-tists think they could have been created by glacial deposits or, be-lieve it or not, busy gophers. There is a self-guided interpretive trail offering a close look at this geologic oddity, as well as several miles of hiking trails. Wildflowers paint the mounds yellow, pink and blue from April through June. ~ Wadell Creek Road, Little-rock; 360-748-2383, fax 360-748-2387.

Howl with the wolves at **Wolf Haven International** southeast of Olympia. The 80-acre refuge shelters about 30 gray wolves. Guides give tours daily from April through October and on weekends in other months. On summer weekends, visitors gather for singing, storytelling and joining in the wolves' howls. Closed Tuesday and the month of February. Admission. ~ 3111 Offut Lake Road, Tenino; 360-264-4695, fax 360-264-4639; www.wolfhaven.org, e-mail info@wolfhaven.org.

LODGING

Many of Tacoma's historic residences have been transformed into small inns and B&Bs. The **Greater Tacoma Bed & Breakfast Reservations Service** can help arrange lodging. ~ 253-627-6916, 800-406-4088, fax 253-272-9116; www.tacomainns.org, e-mail info@tacomainns.org.

The **Villa** is a 1925 Italianate mansion also on the National Historic Register. Six sizable guest rooms have jacuzzis or soaking tubs, fireplaces and views. The verandas, patio with fountain, and landscaped gardens add to the Mediterranean allure. Guests will also enjoy a hot tub, and complimentary wine and hors d'oeuvres. ~ 705 North 5th Street, Tacoma; 253-572-1157, 888-572-1157, fax 253-572-1805; www.villabb.com, e-mail villabb@aol.com. DELUXE TO ULTRA-DELUXE.

The **Sheraton Tacoma Hotel** is an elegant hotel next to the Tacoma Convention Center. The 319 rooms have a contemporary decor and most have views of Mt. Rainier or Commencement Bay. The concierge levels (24th and 25th floors) serve complimentary continental breakfast and late-afternoon hors d'oeuvres. ~ 1320 Broadway Plaza, Tacoma; 253-572-3200, 800-845-9466, fax 253-591-4105; www.sheratontacoma.com. ULTRA-DELUXE.

AUTHOR FAVORITE

Chocolates left on my pillow is but one of the reasons I have sweet dreams when I stay at **Chinaberry Hill**. This luxurious 1889 Victorian bed and breakfast offers three spacious romance suites with bay windows, double jacuzzis, private baths with showers and harbor views or a fireplace. The adjacent two-story carriage house, with its cabin atmosphere, is ideal for families featuring a queen-sized curved iron canopy bed, a double bed loft and a jacuzzi alcove. Appointed with period antiques and surrounded by gardens, the inn is an inviting retreat. ~ 302 Tacoma Avenue North, Tacoma; 253-272-1282, fax 253-272-1335; www.china berryhill.com, e-mail chinaberry@wa.net. DELUXE TO ULTRA-DELUXE.

No Cabbages Bed and Breakfast is a lovely home with a view of the water and access to the beach. It has three guest rooms with both private and shared bathrooms, and a suite with its own private entrance. The house is laden with eclectic, primitive folk art and interesting conversation. The grounds feature deer, fox, woodpeckers and a prayer labyrinth for introspection and walking meditation. The innkeeper serves an outstanding breakfast. ~ 10319 Sunrise Beach Drive Northwest, Gig Harbor; 253-858-7797; www.gigharbor.com/nocabbages, e-mail trout@harbor.com. MODERATE TO DELUXE.

For modern comfort, consider the friendly **Best Western Wesley Inn**, just off Route 16 near the main turnoff to downtown Gig Harbor. Guest rooms come with wet bars, microwave ovens and mini-refrigerators, as well as TVs, phones with data ports, hairdryers, ironing boards and coffeemakers. Pay a bit more for a fireplace or jacuzzi tub. A heated outdoor pool and spa are open seasonally, and a deluxe continental breakfast is served each morning, compliments of management. ~ 6575 Kimball Drive, Gig Harbor; 253-858-9690, 888-462-0002; www.wesleyinn.com, e-mail wesleyinn@wesleyinn.com. MODERATE TO DELUXE.

High above Capitol Lake, on a grassy bluff with a view of the manmade lake and capitol dome, is the **Red Lion Hotel Olympia**. Popular with business and government travelers, it has 190 commodious rooms with practical furnishings, a lounge, a restaurant overlooking the lawns and water, and an outdoor swimming pool. Waterside rooms have the best views and are the quietest. ~ 2300 Evergreen Park Drive, Olympia; 360-943-4000, fax 360-357-6604; www.redlion.com. MODERATE.

The **Lighthouse Bungalow** is a beautifully restored 1920s-era beachfront property with waterfront access to Bud Inlet on Puget Sound. The four-bedroom, four-bath upstairs unit sleeps ten and

LET'S MAKE A DEAL

Midwestern timber baron George Weyerhaeuser arrived in Tacoma in September 1900 ready to do a deal. He wound up buying 900,000 acres of wilderness timberland for $1 million. Not only was that the start of the Northwest's giant timber companies, it was the largest single check ever written to that point.

is furnished with mission-style antiques, hardwood floors, a full kitchen, a jacuzzi bath and views of the Sound and Olympic Mountains from its deck. The cozy one-bedroom, lower-level unit includes a sitting room and sleeps up to three. The owners lend bicycles, kayaks and a canoe. ~ 1215 East Bay Drive, Olympia; 360-754-0389, fax 360-754-7499; www.lighthousebunga low.com, e-mail info@lighthousebungalow.com. DELUXE TO ULTRA-DELUXE.

Eight blocks from the Capitol, the **Ramada Governor House** is the latest version of a vintage downtown hotel. Its 122 rooms —some with views of the lake, harbor and Capitol building—are spread over eight floors. The hotel has above-standard furnishings, though most rooms are small, and a seasonal pool, indoor jacuzzi, exercise room and sauna. A number of packages and discounts are available. ~ 621 South Capitol Way, Olympia; 360-352-7700, 800-228-2828, fax 360-943-9349. DELUXE.

The **Tyee Hotel**, three miles south of Olympia, is just off Route 5, but traffic noise is muted by walls. The 145-room, two-story Tyee has some resort amenities: 17 acres of grounds, a pool, a spacious lobby with a fireplace. The restaurant serves three meals a day, and the pastel rooms are well-furnished and comfortable. ~ 500 Tyee Drive, Tumwater; 360-352-0511, 800-386-8933, fax 360-943-6448; e-mail tyeehotel@aol.com. MODERATE.

DINING

Sophistication and elegance describe the ambience at **Altezzo** in the Sheraton Tacoma Hotel. There are superb views of Commencement Bay and Mt. Rainier from this gourmet Italian restaurant, located several stories above the city. The menu changes daily; entrées include grilled pork loin chop stuffed with fontina cheese and artichoke hearts and *cioppino*, a hearty tomato-based stew of Dungeness crab, prawns, calamari, clams and other fresh seafood. Reservations recommended. Dinner only. Closed during summer holidays. ~ 1320 Broadway Plaza, Tacoma; 253-572-3200, fax 253-591-4105. MODERATE TO DELUXE.

For great Mediterranean-style bistro fare, look no further than **The Primo Grill**. Belfast-born chef Charlie McManus has created a charming restaurant that perfectly suits the new arts–oriented thrust of downtown Tacoma: There's vibrant art not only on the walls, but in the kitchen. Consider the saffron risotto with grilled scallops, prawns and asparagus, or the slow-roasted pork shoulder with caper-mint salsa verde. Wine is half-price on Wednesday; Thursday is *tapas* night. Reservations recommended. No lunch on weekends. ~ 601 South Pine Street, Tacoma; 253-383-7000; www.primogrilltacoma.com. MODERATE TO DELUXE.

Mandarin and Szechuan fare is the specialty at **Charlie Chan's**, a family-run establishment where pictures of the owner with such celebrities as Jeff Smith (TV's Frugal Gourmet and a fellow Tacoman) are proudly displayed. Especially good are the Mongolian beef, vegetable dishes and sizzling rice soup. ~ 10009 Bridgeway Southwest, Tacoma; 253-435-4466, fax 253-581-9591. BUDGET TO MODERATE.

If you've a hankering for barbecued ribs, fried chicken or catfish, try **Southern Kitchen**. This is no antebellum mansion, just a plain, well-lighted café with good food. Just as good as the entrées are the greens, grits, yams, fried okra, biscuits, homemade strawberry lemonade and melt-in-your-mouth corncakes served up alongside. The cooks are Southern stock themselves, so you can count on this fare being authentic. Breakfast is served all day. ~ 1716 6th Avenue, Tacoma; 253-627-4282. BUDGET.

HIDDEN ► The storefront setting is equally unprepossessing, but ethnic food of an entirely different sort is the fare at **May's Vietnamese Restaurant**, where curries and sautés reflect the slightly European spin Vietnamese cuisine applies to Southeast Asian food. May's chicken curry, dark and rich, is divine. ~ 2514 Proctor Street North, Tacoma; 253-756-5092, fax 253-761-8547. BUDGET.

HIDDEN ► At **The Spar** in Old Town (Tacoma's original settlement site, two miles north of downtown), pub food reaches unaccustomed heights. The Spar is famous for "chicken & jos," deep-fried chicken and potato pieces not recommended for health enhancement. You can also get a remarkably good caesar salad, along with crab sandwiches in season. Breakfast served on weekends. ~ 2121 30th Street North, Tacoma; 253-627-8215, fax 253-627-0895; www.the-spar.com, e-mail info@the-spar.com. BUDGET.

HIDDEN ► Boasting one of the finest views of any harbor, **The Green Turtle** is hidden away in an unlikely but fantastic waterfront location. Diners, who sit inside a room quaintly painted to resemble an aquarium, are treated to views of Mt. Rainier, Puget Sound and the entrance to Gig Harbor. The food is excellent, served by friendly and competent waitstaff. Pacific Rim inspired, the menu weighs heavily on seafood (blackened yellowfin tuna, Hawaiian *ono*), but roast duck, chicken and Angus beef are also featured; vegetarian dishes are available upon request. No lunch on Saturday and Sunday. ~ 2905 Harborview Drive, Gig Harbor; 253-851-3167; www.thegreenturtle.com. DELUXE TO ULTRA-DELUXE.

If you've never been visited by a seal or a sea otter while dining, **The Beach House at Purdy** will give you that opportunity. Chef Gordon Naccarato's delightfully low-key restaurant, on Henderson Bay just south of the Route 302 bridge to the Key Peninsula, offers outdoor patio seating along with cozy indoor dining. Come early for Beach House oysters, roasted on the half-shell with creamed spinach, apple-smoked bacon and walnuts, and stay for saké salmon, duck-leg confit or pork chili verde. Reservations recommended. Dinner only. ~ 13802 Purdy Drive Northwest, Gig Harbor; 253-858-9900, fax 253-858-9901; www. beachhouserestaurant.com, e-mail goodeats@beachhouserestau rant.com. MODERATE TO DELUXE.

One of the best views in Olympia is from **Falls Terrace**, through huge windows overlooking Tumwater Falls on the Deschutes River. A good way to start your meal is with some Olympia oysters. The menu features pasta dishes, an excellent bouillabaisse and an array of chicken and beef entrées. Desserts are more ice-cream theatrics than tasty morsels. Reservations recommended. ~ 106 South Deschutes Way, Olympia; 360-943-7830, fax 360-943-6899; www. fallsterracerestaurant.com. MODERATE TO DELUXE.

Gardner's Seafood and Pasta is no secret to locals, who flock   ◄ HIDDEN
to this small restaurant. While seafood is the specialty here, there are several pastas that are very good, too. Try the pasta primavera. The Dungeness crab casserole is rich with cream, chablis and several cheeses. Homemade ice cream and other desserts fill out the meal. Dinner only. Closed Sunday and Monday. ~ 111 West Thurston Street, Olympia; 360-786-8466. DELUXE.

AUTHOR FAVORITE

Do you enjoy good tempura? Then don't walk, run to **Fujiya** in downtown Tacoma. Masahiro Endo, owner and chef, is a great entertainer with his knife at the sushi bar. In addition, the chicken sukiyaki is delicious. Closed Sunday. ~ 1125 Court C, Tacoma; phone/fax 253-627-5319. MODERATE.

Patrons don't usually go to a restaurant for the water, but at **The Spar Cafe and Bar** it truly is exceptional because it comes from the eatery's own artesian well. Once a blue-collar café, the

restaurant features large photographs of loggers felling giant Douglas firs. On the menu are thick milkshakes, giant sandwiches, prime rib and Willapa Bay oysters. ~ 114 East 4th Avenue, Olympia; 360-357-6444, fax 360-352-2969. BUDGET TO MODERATE.

Before the Alaska Gold Rush thrust Seattle into prominence at the turn of the 20th century, Tacoma was Puget Sound's leading city.

Boaters, legislators, lobbyists, tourists and waterfront strollers congregate at the **Budd Bay Cafe** at Percival Landing. You can sit outside on the big deck and watch the boats come and go while you enjoy some of the specialties: fresh pasta and seafood, homemade soups, micro beers (including their own Budd Bay Ale), Northwest wines and desserts from the in-house bakery. An elaborate champagne brunch is served Sunday. ~ 525 North Columbia Street, Olympia; 360-357-6963, fax 360-786-8474; www.buddbaycafe.com, e-mail contactus@budd baycafe.com. MODERATE.

The **Whale's Tail Dockside Deli and Espresso Bar** is a bright little café on the boardwalk at Olympia's Percival Landing. Fast and friendly service, tasty homemade soups and sandwiches, deep-dish quiche and a fine view of Budd Bay have made this spot a favorite. Try the muffins, hand-dipped ice creams and espresso. ~ 501 North Columbia Street, Olympia; 360-956-1928, fax 360-956-0110. BUDGET.

In a neighborhood less frequented by tourists, **Portafino Restaurante** is a charming restaurant in a turn-of the-20th-century home. Seven tables fill the former living and dining rooms, with more tables on the enclosed porch. Classical music plays softly in a subdued atmosphere. Fresh Northwest foods are served, often under mild sauces. Dinner only. Closed Monday and Tuesday. ~ 101 Division Street, Olympia; 360-352-2803, fax 360-943-8812. MODERATE.

In downtown Olympia, the **Urban Onion** serves sizable breakfasts, good sandwiches and hamburgers and a hearty lentil soup. Dinners include chicken, seafood and *gado gado*—a spicy Indonesian dish of sautéed vegetables in tahini and peanut sauce, along with Mexican entrées. They also offer several vegetarian specials. The restaurant is part of a complex of shops in the former Olympian Hotel. ~ 116 Legion Way, Olympia; 360-943-9242, fax 360-754-2378; www.caterforme.com. MODERATE.

The Olympia area isn't the place you'd expect gourmet French-Northwest cuisine, but chef Jean-Pierre Simon exceeds expectations at **Jean-Pierre's**. Located in a historic old home near the Olympia Brewery, Simon serves up luscious crêpes, pastas and fish entrées that meld French provincial influences with local ingredients—such as Dungeness crab. Closed Sunday. ~ 316 Schmidt Place, Tumwater; 360-754-3702, fax 360-754-1352. ULTRA-DELUXE.

In the Proctor District in north Tacoma you can find Northwest foods, gifts and clothing at the **Pacific Northwest Shop**. ~ 2702 North Proctor Street, Tacoma; 253-752-2242. Fine Irish imports are in stock at **The Harp & Shamrock**. ~ 2704 North Proctor Street, Tacoma; 253-752-5012. The **Old House Mercantile** offers gifts for the kitchen and garden as well as a selection of teapots and jewelry. ~ 2717-A North Proctor Street, Tacoma; 253-759-8850. Educational toys are found at **Teaching Toys**. ~ 2624 North Proctor Street, Tacoma; 253-759-9853. The **Northwest Museum Store** at the Washington State History Museum features American Indian gifts, jewelry and pottery. ~ 1911 Pacific Avenue, Tacoma; 253-798-5880.

SHOPPING

Near the Tacoma Dome downtown, **Freighthouse Square** is a thriving collection of shops and eateries in an old railroad warehouse. A dozen restaurants comprise an often-crowded food court; dozens of shops offer local crafts, jewelry, ethnic gifts, flowers and food items. ~ 25th and East D streets, Tacoma; 253-305-0678.

O'Leary's Bookstore carries comic books as well as some used titles. ~ 3828 100th Street Southwest, Tacoma; 253-588-2503.

For sportswear and outdoor gear in Tacoma, try **Sportco**. Shop warehouse-style for hunting, fishing, camping gear and guns. ~ 4602 East 20th Street, Tacoma; 253-922-2222; www.sportco.com. Or visit **Duffle Bag Army Navy Inc.** for camping, hunting and workwear. ~ 8207 South Tacoma Way, Tacoma; 253-588-4433; www.thedufflebag.com.

In Gig Harbor, **The Beach Basket** features, of course, baskets and other gifts. ~ 4102 Harborview Drive, Gig Harbor; 253-858-3008. Scandinavian utensils, books and gifts can be found at **Strictly Scandinavian**. ~ 7803 Pioneer Way, Gig Harbor; 253-851-5959. **Mostly Books** stocks books (you're kidding), book-marks and postcards. ~ 3126 Harborview Drive, Gig Harbor; 253-851-3219.

Downtown Puyallup has several fine antique stores within walking distance of each other on Stuart Street and Meridien Way. Check out **Antique City**'s furniture and small collection of '50s cowboy toys, dolls, furniture, books and cookie jars. ~ 105 South Meridien, Puyallup; 253-840-4324.

In Olympia, contemporary women's clothing and accessories are found at **Juicy Fruits**. ~ 111 Market Street, Suite 103; 360-943-0572. **Olympic Outfitters** is housed in a restored, brick-and-metal building and is stocked with everything from bicycles to backpacking and cross-country ski gear. ~ 407 East 4th Avenue; 360-943-1114.

NIGHTLIFE   **Drake's Downtown Café & Cabaret** offers happy-hour specials and deejay dancing on weekends. Cover. ~ 734 Pacific Avenue, Tacoma; 253-572-4144. **Katie Downs Tavern** is an adults-only pub overlooking Commencement Bay with a menu featuring local microbrews, seafood and pizza. ~ 3211 Ruston Way, Tacoma; 253-756-0771. Boasting one of the largest selections of draught beer in the state is the **Ale House Pub**. ~ 2122 Mildred Street West, Tacoma; 253-565-9367.

The **Tacoma Little Theatre** is a community theater producing five plays a year. ~ 210 North I Street, Tacoma; 253-272-2281; www.tacomalittletheatre.com.

South of Tacoma is **Happy Days Diner and Time Tunnel Lounge**, where deejays spin Top-40 nightly. Cover on Friday and Saturday. ~ 11521 Bridgeport Way Southwest, Lakewood; 253-582-1531.

The **Tides Tavern** in Gig Harbor features live bands on select weekends playing '50s and '60s rock and some rhythm-and-blues. Cover for live shows. ~ 2925 Harborview Drive, Gig Harbor; 253-858-3982.

BEACHES & PARKS   **POINT DEFIANCE PARK** 🏃 🚴 🛶 ⛵ 🚤 ⚓ Jutting dramatically into Puget Sound, this 700-acre treasure is hailed by some as the finest saltwater park in the state, by others as the best city park in the Northwest. Here are primeval forests, some

50 miles of hiking trails, over three miles of public shoreline and enough other attractions to match almost any visitor's interests. Five Mile Drive loops around the park perimeter with access to trails, forest, beach, views, attractions and grand overlooks of Puget Sound. The park is also known for its zoo and aquarium, particularly the shark tank (fee). Popular with boaters, there's a fully equipped marina with boat rentals, a boathouse (253-591-5325) and a restaurant. You can fish from the pier or in a rented boat. You'll find picnic areas, restrooms, play areas, tennis courts and a snack bar at the boathouse. Day-use fee, $5. ~ The entrance is on North 54th and Pearl streets; 253-305-1000, fax 253-305-1098.

KOPACHUCK STATE PARK
Spectacular views across Carr Inlet toward the Olympic Mountains from a half-mile of shoreline gives Kopachuck much to boast about. Many car-top boaters launch from the beach near the park to fish for bottomfish and salmon or paddle out to Cutts Island Marine State Park a half-mile away. No lifeguard is on duty. There are picnic areas, restrooms and showers. Day-use fee, $5. ~ Located on Kopachuck Drive Northwest at Northwest 56th Street, about seven miles west of Gig Harbor and Route 16; 253-265-3606, fax 360-644-8112.

▲ There are 41 sites for tents and RVs ($15 per night); no hookups are available. Closed October through April.

NISQUALLY NATIONAL WILDLIFE REFUGE   This 3000-acre refuge's ecosystem is a diverse mix of conifer forest, deciduous woodlands, marshlands, grasslands and mud flats and the meandering Nisqually River (born in Mt. Rainier National Park). Here, the river mixes its fresh waters with the salt chuck of Puget Sound. The refuge is home to mink, otter, coyote and some 50 other species of mammals, over 200 kinds of birds and 125 species of fish. Trails thread the refuge; longest is the five-and-a-half-mile dike-top loop that circles a pioneer homestead long since abandoned. Fishing yields salmon, steelhead and cutthroat. Facilities include an education center and restrooms. Day-use fee, $3 per family. ~ Route 5 Exit 114, about 25 miles south of downtown Tacoma; 360-753-9467, fax 360-534-9302; nisqually.fws.gov.

> The Nisqually National Wildlife Refuge is an important stop for migratory shorebirds and waterbirds on the Pacific Flyway.

TOLMIE STATE PARK 🚶 🚐 ⛵ ⚓ 🎣 🏊 🚤 ⛴ A salt marsh with interpretive signs separates 1800 feet of tide flats from forested uplands overlooking Nisqually Reach. The sandy beach is fine for wading or swimming; at low tide you may find clams. A two-and-a-half-mile wheelchair-accessible perimeter hiking trail loops through the park's 106 acres. An artificial reef and three sunken barges 500 yards offshore and almost-nonexistent current make the underwater park here popular for divers. Fishing yields salmon and cod. You'll find picnic areas, restrooms and showers. Day-use fee, $5. ~ Hill Road Northeast, northeast of Olympia via Exit 111 from Route 5; phone/fax 360-456-6464.

MILLERSYLVANIA STATE PARK 🚶 🚴 🚐 ⛵ 🎣 🏊 🚤 Some 840 acres of primeval conifer forest and miles of foot trail are this park's big appeals. But visitors also come to enjoy its 3300 feet of shoreline along Deep Lake, where you can swim, launch a small boat (no wake) or fish for trout, bass, perch and crappie. Facilities include picnic areas and restrooms. Day-use fee, $5. ~ Exit 95 just east of Route 5, ten miles south of Olympia; 360-753-1519, fax 360-664-2180.

▲ There are 120 standard sites ($15 per night) and 48 sites with hookups ($21 per night). No reservations necessary October to May. Reservations: 888-226-7688.

Outdoor Adventures

FISHING

Salmon, of course, is the big draw for anglers on Puget Sound. State hatchery programs see to it that the anadromous fish are available year-round, but the months from midsummer to mid-fall bring the bulk of salmon—and anglers—to these waters. From mid-July to late August, chinook salmon are king; by Labor Day coho take over, until October. Then chum arrive, but since they tend to be plankton eaters they don't bite. Pink salmon return in odd numbered years, in August, and are most plentiful in the Sound north of Seattle, near Everett. Sockeye can be found in Lake Washington from late June to August.

Several charter companies operate fishing trips on the Sound. The cost, which can range from $35 to $80 and up, usually includes everything except lunch and the fishing license (which you can purchase through the charter company).

If you're in Tacoma, you can fish from a dinghy in Puget Sound off Point Defiance Park.

KAYAKING & BOATING

Located near the tip of the peninsula in Point Defiance Park, the **Boathouse Marina** has 20 14-foot dinghies for rent. Most of the time they're rented by anglers, but you can take them out to explore the Sound if you prefer. Also for rent are motors to power the boats. ~ 253-591-5325.

A wide range of rentals including sea kayaks and single kayaks, powerboats, sailboats and sportfishing boats are available from **Rent-a-Boat & Charters**. Nonsailors can charter a sailboat. ~ 8829 North Harborview Drive, Gig Harbor; phone/fax 253-858-7341; www.gigharborrentaboat.com.

Although the water temperature in Puget Sound averages a cool 45° to 55°, diving is quite popular, especially from October through April, when there's no plankton bloom because of reduced sunlight during those months. With several dive clubs in the Seattle–Tacoma area, there are usually many dives scheduled each weekend: a wall dive off Fox Island perhaps, or a shore dive at Three Tree Point (near Federal Way) or Sunrise Beach (near Gig Harbor). Southern Puget Sound and the area around Vashon Island are considered the best places to dive—you'll see starfish, crabs, ling cod, scallops and many more species. Be prepared, however: Currents are extremely strong south of Seattle so you'll need to check the tides and currents carefully before diving. The dive shops listed below can provide details about these hazards as well as information on local dive spots. If you're not an experienced diver, you can arrange lessons with these shops, although it takes several days to complete training for certification. The outfits listed all rent and sell gear and accessories as well as offer a variety of instruction.

SCUBA DIVING

Washington State fishers catch more than 1.3 billion pounds of fish and seafood annually, more than half the nation's total edible catch.

In Tacoma, **Lighthouse Diving** takes divers to Canada, the Cayman Islands and other destinations for trips that range from one day to a week. Night dives are available. Lighthouse pros meet divers at designated locations. They use one tank per dive. ~ 2502 Pacific Avenue, Tacoma; 253-627-7617, fax 253-627-1877; www.lighthousediving.com. In Port Orchard, contact **Tagert's**

Dive Locker for diving, camping trips and holiday dives, such as an Easter egg hunt underwater. Night dives are available. Trips are no more than a half day and use two to three tanks per dive. ~ 205 Bethel Avenue; 360-895-7860. **Aquaquest Divers Inc.** has local boat trips and night dives. Trips last from one day to a week. ~ 7824 East River Road, Puyallup; 253-845-5350.

Underwater Sports Inc. offers shore and boat dives as well as dives abroad—both tropical and night dives. They repair gear. Dives are a day long and use two or three tanks. ~ Tacoma: 9606 40th Avenue Southwest; 253-588-6634. Olympia: 3330 Pacific Avenue Southeast; 360-493-0322; www.underwatersports.com.

JOGGING

In Tacoma, the main road through Point Defiance Park, Five Mile Loop, is a spectacular hilly passage through deep old-growth forest, with occasional breakouts offering lovely views of Puget Sound. This is the route used by the Sound-to-Narrows, an early summer 12K that's one of the country's most popular road races.

Olympia's Capitol Lake greenbelt trails pass through pretty woods, and offer great views of the State Capitol Building and the lake itself. A loop would encompass five kilometers or more.

SKIING

Crystal Mountain Resort, on a ridge off the northeast flank of Mount Rainier, is one of Washington's most popular ski areas and has been rated No. 12 in the United States by Skiing magazine. Nine chair lifts serve a 3100-foot vertical, climaxing atop 7012-foot Silver King Peak–from which unparalleled views of Rainier itself may be had. The resort has numerous lodging and dining options, as well as a full rental shop. ~ 33914 Crystal Mountain Boulevard, Crystal Mountain; 360-663-2265, 888-754-6199, fax 360-663-3001; www.skicrystal.com.

GOLF

Just south of Tacoma is the **Lake Spanaway Golf Course** in Pierce County Park. The 18-hole public course was cut out of a forest, so it's treelined but fairly open. It has a putting green and a pro shop and rents power and pull carts. ~ 15602 Pacific Avenue, Spanaway; 253-531-3660.

TENNIS

Call two or three days in advance to reserve one of the four public hardtop indoor courts (or five racquetball courts) at **Sprinker Recreation Center**. Professionals are available for lessons. Fee. ~ 14824 South C Street at Military Road, Tacoma; 253-798-4000.

Su Dara Riding offers a "tranquil, peaceful"one-hour ride for up to seven people through woodland thick with firs and maples. On a clear day there are views of Mt. Rainier. Su herself says, "We ride rain or shine." ~ Puyallup; 253-531-1569; www.sudara.com.

RIDING STABLES

When it comes to bicycling in Tacoma and Pierce County, "things are just getting going," according to one of the city's public works planners. The area does not yet have the extensive network of lanes and trails that they have up in Seattle, but continues to develop its bicycle and pedestrian plan. Meanwhile, the **Pierce County Department of Public Works** puts out a bike route map. ~ 2401 South 35th Street, Tacoma; 253-798-7250. The **Tacoma Wheelmen's Bicycle Club** operates a recorded Ride Line. ~ 253-759-2800.

BIKING

For a pleasant bike ride sans cars, head to Point Defiance Park's Five Mile Drive, which is closed to vehicular traffic every Saturday morning until 1 p.m.

Among the more popular and convenient places to ride in the city is a two-mile lane along the **downtown waterfront**. Beginning at Schuster Parkway and McCarver Street, this multi-use lane (it's separated from traffic, however) extends to Waterview Street along Ruston Way and Point Defiance Park. Within **Point Defiance Park**, a shoulder lane of Five Mile Drive loops around the peninsula. Call the Metropolitan Park District for more information. ~ 253-305-1000; www.metroparkstacoma.org.

Nisqually National Wildlife Refuge and Point Defiance Park in Tacoma are a hiker's haven. All distances listed for hiking trails are one way unless otherwise noted.

HIKING

A wonderful river-delta walk, **Brown Farm Dike Trail** (5.5 miles), which starts on the Brown Farm Road, loops through the Nisqually National Wildlife Refuge. You may see bald eagles, coyotes, great blue heron, red-tail hawks and a variety of waterfowl such as wood, canvasback and greater scaup ducks, as well as mallards and pintails. Views stretch from Mt. Rainier to the Olympics. You'll also see many of the islands in the south, Steilacoom and the Tacoma Narrows Bridge.

Route 5 is the main north–south highway connecting Seattle, Tacoma and Olympia. **Route 16** leads north from Tacoma, across the Tacoma Narrows Bridge toward Gig Harbor and farther north toward Bremerton. The two main ac-

Transportation

CAR

cess roads to Mount Rainier are **Route 7,** which runs south then east (as **Route 706**), and **Route 410,** which travels east then south.

AIR

Situated ten miles north of Tacoma and 20 miles south of downtown Seattle is **Seattle-Tacoma International Airport,** also known as Sea-Tac. For detailed information, see "Transportation" in Chapter Two.

CAR RENTALS

Rental agencies at Seattle-Tacoma International Airport include **Avis Rent A Car** (800-331-1212), **Budget Rent A Car** (800-527-0700), **Dollar Rent A Car** (800-800-4000), **Hertz Rent A Car** (800-654-3131) and **Thrifty Car Rental** (800-367-2277). **Ace Xtra-Car Rentals** (800-227-5397) offers low rates and shuttle service to the airport.

TEN

Olympic Peninsula & Western Puget Sound

 One of the most spectacular sights for many Seattle visitors is sitting on the dock of the bay—Elliott Bay, that is—watching the sun set behind the stark profile of the Olympic Mountains. The area is even more memorable looking from the inside out.

The Olympic Peninsula is a vast promontory bounded on the east by Puget Sound, the west by the Pacific Ocean and the north by the Strait of Juan de Fuca. With no major city, it retains a feeling of country living on the edge of wilderness, which indeed it is.

The shortest way to get to the peninsula is by marine highway—that is, the Washington State Ferry system—to Bainbridge Island and/or the Kitsap Peninsula. Bainbridge has, in many ways, become a bedroom community for Seattle workers, but it has maintained a strong rural charm popular among weekend adventurers, particularly bicyclists. The arrowroot-shaped Kitsap Peninsula, framed by Puget Sound on the east and long, natural Hood Canal on the west, is home to the big naval port of Bremerton, the delightful Norwegian enclave of Poulsbo, the historic Indian settlement of Suquamish, and the well-preserved old company town of Port Gamble.

But the reason most visitors travel to the Olympic Peninsula is to spend time in Olympic National Park, which dominates the peninsula. This is a primeval place where eternal glaciers drop suddenly off sheer rock faces into nearly impenetrable rainforest, where America's largest herd of Roosevelt elk roams unseen by all but the most intrepid human eyes, where an impossibly rocky coastline cradles primitive marine life forms as it has done for millions of years. No fewer than five Indian reservations speckle sections of a coast famed as much for its shipwrecks as for its salmon fishing.

The Washington coast is known for its heavy rainfall, and justifiably so. Although the Olympics are not high by many standards—its tallest peaks are under 8000 feet—they catch huge amounts of precipitation blowing in from the Pacific Ocean. So much snow falls that more than 60 glaciers survive at elevations as low as 4500 feet. Even greater amounts fall on the windward slopes: 140 inches a year and more in the Forks area. Not only does this foster the rapid growth of mushrooms and slugs, but it has also led to the creation of North America's greatest rainforest in the soggy Hoh River valley. Yet a mere 40 miles away as the raven flies, Sequim—in the Olympic rain shadow—is a comparative desert with only about 15 inches of rain per year.

Today, typical Olympic Peninsula visitors travel first from Seattle to Port Townsend and use Route 101 as their artery of exploration. Port Townsend is considered the most authentic Victorian seacoast town in the United States north of San Francisco, and its plethora of well-preserved 19th-century buildings, many of them now bed and breakfasts, charms all visitors. Less than an hour's drive west, the seven-mile Dungeness Spit (a national wildlife refuge) is the largest natural sand hook in the United States and is famed for the delectable crabs that share its name. Port Angeles, in the center of the north coast, is home to the headquarters of Olympic National Park and is its primary gateway—and the peninsula's largest town with 19,000 people. The bustling international port town also has a direct ferry link to Victoria, Canada, across the Strait of Juan de Fuca.

Neah Bay, the northwesternmost community in the continental United States, is the home of the Makah Indian Museum and Cultural Center and an important marina for deep-sea fishing charters. Clallam Bay, to its east, and La Push, south down the coast, are other sportfishing centers. The logging town of Forks is the portal for visitors to the national park's Hoh Rainforest.

Bainbridge Island

The main town of picturesque Bainbridge Island is—surprise!—Bainbridge Island. Located just a 35-minute ferry ride from Seattle's Colman Dock (pick up a self-guiding brochure with map, *A Downtown Guide to Bainbridge Island*, before boarding), you can see it on foot.

SIGHTS To see more than obvious attractions on **Bainbridge Island**, head for the mile-long waterfront footpath called **Walkabout** to the left of the ferry landing. Follow it along the shoreline, past shipyards and hauled-out sailboats under repair, to **Eagle Harbor Waterfront Park** and its fishing pier and low-tide beach. Carry on to a ship chandler and pair of marinas. Return as you came or make it a loop trip by walking up to **Winslow Way**, where you can stop for

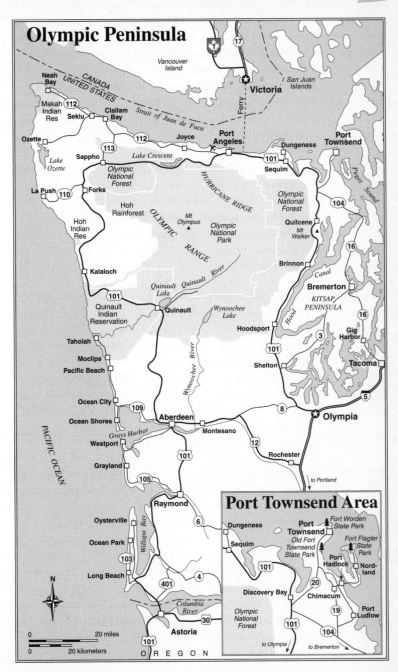

Olympic Peninsula

Vancouver
Island

CANADA
UNITED STATES

Neah
Bay

Makah
Indian
Res

112

Sekiu

Clallam
Bay

Ozette

112

Strait of Juan de Fuca

Joyce

Sappho

113

Lake Crescent

Lake
Ozette

La Push

110

Forks

Hoh
Rainforest

Olympic
National
Forest

OLYMPIC

Mt
Olympus

HURRICANE RIDGE

Hoh
Indian
Res

RANGE

River

Kalaloch

Quinault
Lake

Quinault River

Quinault

101

Quinault
Indian
Reservation

Wynoochee
Lake

Taholah

Moclips

Pacific Beach

Wynoochee River

Ocean City

109

Aberdeen

Ocean Shores

Grays Harbor

Montesano

PACIFIC OCEAN

Westport

101

Grayland

105

Raymond

6

Oysterville

Willapa Bay

Ocean Park

103

Long Beach

401

4

N

Columbia River

0   20 miles

0   20 kilometers

Astoria

101

O R E G O N

30

17

Victoria

Ferry

San Juan
Islands

Port
Angeles

Dungeness

101

Sequim

Port
Townsend

Puget Sound

104

Olympic
National
Forest

Quilcene

Mt
Walker

16

Brinnon

Canal

Bremerton

KITSAP
PENINSULA

Hood

Hoodsport

3

16

Gig
Harbor

101

Shelton

Tacoma

8

Olympia

5

12

Rochester

to Portland

Port Townsend Area

Dungeness

Port
Townsend

Fort Worden
State Park

Sequim

Old Fort
Townsend
State Park

Fort Flagler
State Park

Port
Hadlock

Nord-
land

101

Discovery Bay

20

Chimacum

19

Port
Ludlow

Olympic
National
Forest

101

104

to Olympia

to Bremerton

espresso or shop. If you tire of boutiques, step into **Winslow Hardware**, where the local folk come to chat and buy essential tools.

Bainbridge Island Vineyards and Winery is the only winery in the Seattle area that grows its grapes on-site. There is a tasting room, gardens, a wine museum of antiques and a picnic area on this family farm estate winery. The Ferryboat White label is popular with visitors. Open afternoons Wednesday through Sunday; open only on weekends in January and February. ~ 682 Route 305; 206-842-9463.

If you enjoy gardens, don't miss a tour of the famous **Bloedel Reserve** (though you'll have to drive here). Once a private estate, the reserve has 150 acres of forest, meadows, ponds and a series of beautifully landscaped gardens. Reservations are required for a tour. Closed Monday and Tuesday. Admission. ~ 7571 Northeast Dolphin Drive; 206-842-7631, fax 206-842-8970; www.bloedelreserve.org.

LODGING
Serenity and comfort in the countryside characterize **The Buchanan Inn**, a fully remodeled 1912 New England barn that now operates as a bed and breakfast also serving afternoon wine. Located on the south end of Bainbridge Island, the inn has four spacious rooms, some with gas fireplaces and whirlpool tubs. On its one and a half acres of gardens also sit private cottages with cedar hot tubs available by reservation. No children under 16 allowed. ~ 8494 Northeast Odd Fellows Road; 206-780-9258, 800-598-3926, fax 206-842-9458; www.buchananinn.com, e-mail jgiibs@buchananinn.com. DELUXE.

DINING
Specializing in mesquite-grilled steaks and seafood, the **Island Grill** provides casual fine dining amid a dark green and burgundy color scheme with hardwood floors. Dishes include fresh Northwest seafood, prime steaks, pastas and salads. Weekend brunch. ~ 321 High School Road Northeast; 206-842-9037. MODERATE TO DELUXE.

The white-linen tablecloths and low lighting at the **Bistro Pleasant Beach** bespeak a comfortable island elegance. The chef specializes in eastern Mediterranean seafood but includes a couple of succulent chicken dishes, pastas and aged beef entrées. The leg of lamb, served with roasted garlic, fresh herbs and shallot–rose cabernet sauce, comes recommended. Made-to-order pizzas are baked in the wood-fired oven. When the weather's nice, patio seating is available. Closed Monday. ~ 241 Winslow Way West; 206-842-4347, fax 206-842-6997. MODERATE TO DELUXE.

Exotic flavors and innovative sauces are what you'll find at the **Four Swallows**, an upscale Italian restaurant located in a spacious 1880s farmhouse. The kitchen staff, utilizing fresh Northwest ingredients, whips up gourmet, thin-crust pizzas and zesty pastas. The entrées show the chef's creativity, and include grilled veal chops with porcini-mushroom sauce and *brodetto*, a fresh fish-and-shellfish stew in a rustic saffron-tomato-fennel broth. Dinner only. Closed Sunday and Monday. ~ 481 Madison Avenue; 206-842-3397; www.fourswallows.com, e-mail gkf424@aol.com. MODERATE TO DELUXE.

> The town that used to be called Winslow is now known just as Bainbridge Island.

A pleasant spot to relax with a beer and a sandwich or fish and chips is the deck at the **Madrona Waterfront Cafe**. The view from the deck above the water is always a delight, and it's only about five blocks from the ferry dock. The food, which includes salmon sandwiches, Northwest seafood stew and gorgonzola chicken fettuccine, is reasonably priced, but high for what you get—stick with something simple and enjoy the view. Madrona serves Saturday and Sunday brunch. ~ 403 Madison Avenue South; 206-842-8339. MODERATE.

The cozy **Pegasus** is a traditional coffeehouse with lots of reading material, conversation, freshly baked pastries and assorted coffees. ~ 131 Parfitt Way; 206-842-6725; www.pegasuscoffee house.com. BUDGET.

Walk into the **Streamliner Diner** and it's like stepping back into a Midwestern diner. There are eight tables, a small bar and an open kitchen that serves up breakfast burritos, fried egg sandwiches, scrumptious omelettes and buttermilk waffles. Lunches include soups, salads and quiches. Breakfast and lunch only. ~ 397 Winslow Way; 206-842-8595. BUDGET.

FAY BAINBRIDGE STATE PARK A small park (17 acres), it nevertheless curls itself around a long sandspit to present some 1400 feet of shoreline. The only campground on Bainbridge Island is here. Facilities include picnic areas, restrooms, showers, a play area, horseshoe pits and volleyball courts. Day-use fee, $5. ~ At Sunrise Drive Northeast and Lafayette Road

BEACHES & PARKS

about six miles north of the town of Bainbridge Island at the island's northeast tip; 206-842-3931, fax 360-753-1594.

▲ There are 10 standard sites ($15 per night), 26 RV hookups ($21 per night) and 13 primitive walk-in sites ($10 per night). Closed mid-October to mid-April.

FORT WARD STATE PARK 🏃🚴 🛶 ⚓ ⛵ 🚤 🚣 Located at the south end of Bainbridge Island, this park offers 137 acres of paths, forest and picnic sites, as well as a mile-long beach, complete with salmon and lingcod fishing for day-use visitors. Locked service road is accessible by walking. Day-use fee, $5. ~ 206-842-4041, fax 360-385-7248.

Kitsap Peninsula

Only an hour from the heart of Seattle, the Kitsap Peninsula makes a fine retreat from the city. In June and July, Kitsap and Olympic Peninsula visitors should watch the roadsides for the delicate pink blossoms of native rhododendron bushes, which thrive in the understory of the Douglas fir forests.

SIGHTS   If you take the ferry or drive to the Navy town of Bremerton, you'll pass by the **Puget Sound Naval Shipyard**. The best way to get here is the Washington State Ferry (cars and walk-ons; one hour) or state foot-ferry (50 minutes) or the passenger-only fast ferry (40 minutes) from Seattle's Colman Dock (Pier 52) through Rich Passage to Bremerton. Although the shipyard is not open for public tours, it's an amazing sight even from a distance. ~ Burwell Street and Pacific Avenue, near the ferry dock, Bremerton; 360-476-7111, fax 360-476-0937; www.psns.navy.mil.

Bremerton Naval Museum, a half-block north of the ferry dock, looks back to the days of Jack Tar and square-riggers and includes a wood cannon from 1377. ~ 402 Pacific Avenue, Bremerton; 360-479-7447, fax 360-377-4186; e-mail bremnavmuseum@aol.com.

Docked along the waterfront by the Navy shipyard is the **USS Turner Joy**, a former Navy destroyer where the bridge, engine room and berth areas can be explored on self-guided tours. Admission. ~ 360-792-2457, fax 360-377-1020.

In the small town of Keyport, located off Route 308 between Poulsbo and Silverdale, you'll find the **Naval Undersea Museum**. Historical exhibits here focus on the Navy's undersea activities from the Revolutionary War to the present. Diving and defense displays explore such subjects as nautical archaeology and the history of the submarine. There's also an interactive installation on the ocean environment. ~ 1 Garnett Way, Keyport; 360-396-4148; num.kpt.nuwc.navy.mil, e-mail underseainfo@kpt.nuwc.navy.mil.

From Bremerton, Route 3 runs up the eastern side of the Kitsap Peninsula. Turn down Route 305 past Liberty Bay and you'll

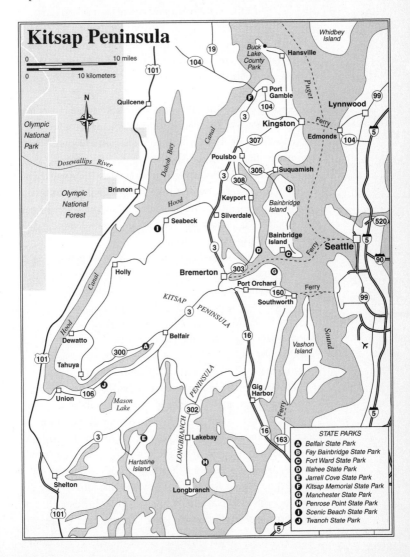

Kitsap Peninsula

0   10 miles
0   10 kilometers

Whidbey Island

Buck Lake County Park

Hansville

Puget

101

104

19

Quilcene

N

Olympic National Park

Dosewallips River

Port Gamble

104

3

Kingston

Lynnwood

99

Edmonds

104

5

307

Poulsbo

305

Suquamish

308

Keyport

B

Bainbridge Island

Silverdale

Olympic National Forest

Brinnon

Hood

Dabob Bay

Canal

Seabeck

I

Bainbridge Island

D

C

Seattle

520

5

Holly

3

Bremerton

303

G

Port Orchard

160

Southworth

Ferry

99

90

KITSAP PENINSULA

3

Dewatto

300

A

Belfair

16

Vashon Island

Sound

Tahuya

106

J

Union

Mason Lake

LONGBRANCH PENINSULA

302

Lakebay

Gig Harbor

16

163

Hood Canal

101

3

E

Hartstine Island

H

5

Shelton

Longbranch

101

5

STATE PARKS
- **A** Belfair State Park
- **B** Fay Bainbridge State Park
- **C** Fort Ward State Park
- **D** Illahee State Park
- **E** Jarrell Cove State Park
- **F** Kitsap Memorial State Park
- **G** Manchester State Park
- **H** Penrose Point State Park
- **I** Scenic Beach State Park
- **J** Twanoh State Park

come to the charming town of **Poulsbo**. "Velkommen til Poulsbo" is an oft-repeated phrase in "Washington's Little Norway." There are some wonderful samples of historic architecture on a **walking tour** of town; the **Greater Poulsbo Chamber of Commerce** can provide a guide map. ~ 19168 Jensen Way, Poulsbo; 360-779-4848, fax 360-799-3115; www.poulsbo.net/gpcc.

Looking like a lane in far-away Scandinavia, the main street of Poulsbo is lined with wonderful galleries and boutiques.

At the **Poulsbo Marine Science Center**, you can learn about the various forms of marine life that inhabit the waters of Southern Puget Sound; they even have touch tanks of friendly sea creatures. Admission. ~ 18743 Front Street Northeast, Poulsbo; 360-779-5549, fax 360-779-8960; www.poulsbomsc.org.

A good place to learn about the region's American Indian heritage is the town of **Suquamish**. Chief Sealth and the allied tribes he represented are showcased at the **Suquamish Museum**. There's an outstanding collection of photographs and artifacts, along with mock-ups of a typical American Indian dwelling and the interior of a longhouse. Two award-winning video presentations are shown in a small theater. Admission. ~ 15838 Sandy Hook Road off Route 305, Suquamish; 360-598-3311, fax 360-598-6295; www.suquamish.nsn.us/museum.

HIDDEN ▶

Chief Seattle's Grave, set under a canopy of dugout canoes in a hillside graveyard overlooking Seattle (his namesake, with a slight adjustment in spelling; he was known as Sealth), is just a few miles down Suquamish Way. Follow the road signs.

One of the West's last company towns, **Port Gamble** is a favored visitor stop. Situated on a bluff at the intersection of Admiralty Inlet and Gamble Bay, this century-old community was once owned by the Pope and Talbot lumber firm.

HIDDEN ▶

The oldest running lumber mill in the U.S. (operating since 1853) was closed in 1995. Although all the sawmill workers were laid off, the town is still owned by Pope Resources. The town had long been home to about 150 sawmill workers and their families, who rented homes from the company. Picturesque frame houses, towering elms and a church with Gothic windows and a needle spire give the community a New England look. Don't miss the mock-ups of Captain Talbot's cabin and A. J. Pope's office at the **Port Gamble Historic Museum**. The museum is open by

appointment only from November through April. Admission. ~
Route 3, Port Gamble; 360-297-8074, fax 360-297-7455; www.
portgamble.org.

Also worth seeing is the **Sea and Shore Museum** on the second floor of the quaint, 1853 **Port Gamble General Store**. Other
historic homes and buildings are occupied by former Pope and
Talbot employees but can be seen from the outside; a walking-
tour guide can be obtained at the General Store. ~ 3 Rainier Avenue, Port Gamble; phone/fax 360-297-2426; www.ofseaandshore.
com, e-mail ofseashr@sinclair.net.

Visitors driving to Port Townsend typically cross the one-and-
a-half-mile **Hood Canal Floating Bridge** on Route 104 from the
Kitsap Peninsula. Located 30 miles southeast of Port Townsend,
it is the world's only floating bridge erected over tidal waters and
one of the longest of its kind anywhere. Constructed in 1961, the
bridge was washed away during a fierce storm in February 1979,
but was rebuilt in 1982.

The eastern shore of **Hood Canal** is located a mere mile or two   ◄ HIDDEN
from the western side of the channel, but in character it's worlds
apart. Beach access is limited, but views across the canal to the
Olympic Mountains are splendid, settlements few and quiet and
back roads genuine byways—few tourists ever get here. This is
also where the canal bends like a fishhook to the east, which has
been nicknamed the "Great Bend."

To see the east shore in its entirety, begin at Belfair, leaving
Route 3 for Route 300. At three miles, watch for Belfair State Park
on the left. The road now narrows and traffic thins on the way
to the modest resort town of Tahuya; shortly beyond, the canal
makes its great bend. The road dives into dense forest, bringing
you in about 11 miles to a T-junction; bear left, then left again to
the ghost town of Dewatto. Take Dewatto Bay Road eastward out
of town, then turn north and follow signs 12 miles to a left turn
into the little town of **Holly**, or continue north 15 miles more to
Seabeck, founded in 1856 as a sawmill town and popular today
with anglers, scuba divers and boaters.

Rooms at Poulsbo's **Holiday Inn Express** are modern and com-   **LODGING**
fortably furnished with big beds, satellite television, microwaves
and other basic amenities. There is an outdoor jacuzzi and con-

tinental breakfast is included. ~ 19801 7th Avenue Northeast, Poulsbo; 360-697-4400, 800-465-4329, fax 360-697-2707; www. hiexpress.com/poulsbowa, e-mail psbwa@silverlink.net. DELUXE.

DINING

The family-run **Benson's** offers eclectic Northwest cuisine in a large but intimate dining room. The seasonal menu may include assorted seafoods with a garlic cream sauce served over angel hair pasta or rack of New Zealand lamb *au jus* roasted with *herbes de* Provence. Save room for the macadamia nut torte! No dinner on Sunday. Closed Monday. ~ 18820 Front Street, Poulsbo; 360-697-3449, fax 360-697-9904. DELUXE.

Casa De Luna features fast and cheap traditional Mexican or Mexican-American fare. Diners are treated to colorful murals and sweet ballads while munching on tacos and burritos and sipping Negra Modelo. ~18830 Front Street Northeast, Poulsbo; 306-779-7676. BUDGET.

Those with a sweet tooth should head to **Sluys Poulsbo Bakery** for sticky sweet Scandinavian pastries and stick-to-your-ribs traditional breads. ~ 18924 Front Street Northeast, Poulsbo; 360-697-2253. BUDGET.

SHOPPING

You'll find paintings, pottery, weavings, cards, rosemaling, baskets, woodturnings, and even food products created by local artists at the **Verksted Co-operative Gallery**. ~ 18937 Front Street Northeast, Poulsbo; 360-697-4470; www.verkstedgallery.com. The **Potlatch Gallery** carries a fine selection of prints, glasswork, pottery and jewelry by Northwest artists. ~ 18830-B Front Street Northeast, Poulsbo; 360-779-3377; www.potlatchgallery.com.

Head to **Boehm's Chocolates** for Swiss-European chocolates, truffles and fudge. ~ 18864 Front Street Northeast, Poulsbo; 360-697-3318.

BEACHES & PARKS

MANCHESTER STATE PARK This one-time fort overlooking Rich Passage includes abandoned torpedo warehouses and some interpretive displays explaining its role in guarding Bremerton Navy Base at the turn of the 20th century. The park is infamous for its poison oak—stay on the two miles of hiking trails, or try the 3400 feet of beach. The rocks off Middle Point attract divers. Fishing yields salmon and bottomfish. There are picnic areas, restrooms and showers. Day-use fee, $5.

~ Located at the east foot of East Hilldale Road off Beach Drive, east of Bremerton; 360-871-4065, fax 503-378-6308.

▲ There are 35 standard sites ($15 per night), 3 primitive walk-in sites ($10 per night), 15 RV hookup sites ($21 per night) and one group camp with 12 hookups ($21 apiece, $2 per head for tent campers). Reservations: 888-226-7688.

BUCK LAKE COUNTY PARK 🏃🐎🚣🚣🛶 Near Hansville on the northern tip of the Kitsap Peninsula, picturesque Buck Lake is a good spot for quiet, contemplative fishing or a relaxing summer swim. Trout fishing is excellent on the lake or from the shore. Facilities include restrooms, picnic tables, a baseball diamond, a volleyball court, barbecue pits and a playground. ~ Buck Lake Road; take Route 104 from Kingston to Hansville Road and follow it north; 360-337-5350, fax 360-337-5385.

SALISBURY POINT 🚣🏄🚣🚤🛶 This tiny, six-acre park with a small stretch of saltwater beach is next to Hood Canal Floating Bridge and gives views of the Olympic Mountains across the canal. Shrimping is popular here. There are restrooms, picnic shelters and a playground. ~ North of Hood Canal Floating Bridge, turn left on Wheeler Road and follow the signs; 360-337-5350, fax 360-337-5385.

KITSAP MEMORIAL STATE PARK 🏃🐟🚣🚤🛶 This 58-acre park four miles south of Hood Canal Floating Bridge has a quiet beach well suited for collecting oysters and clams. Between the canal, beach and playground facilities there's plenty to keep the troops entertained, making this a good choice for family camping. Restrooms, showers, a shelter, tables and stoves, boat moorage buoys, a playground and a volleyball court are available; some facilities are wheelchair accessible. Day-use fee, $5. ~

OLD MAN HOUSE STATE PARK

A day-use-only facility, **Old Man House State Park** was once the site of a longhouse. Check out the interpretive and historical displays. A small, sandy beach overlooks the heavy marine traffic that cruises through Agate Passage. You'll find pit toilet and picnic tables. Closed in winter. ~ On the Kitsap Peninsula north of Agate Pass off Route 305; 206-842-3931, fax 206-385-7248.

From Kingston take Route 104 (which turns into Bond Road) to Route 3, then follow it north until you reach the park; 360-779-3205, fax 360-779-3161.

▲ There are 20 standard sites ($15 per night); 18 sites with hookups ($21 per night); and a trailer dump ($5). A blufftop log cabin with full bedding, bath towels and a kitchenette (no stove) is also available; $135 per night in peak season.

ILLAHEE STATE PARK 🚶 🚴 ⛵ 🎣 🏕 🛥 🏊 🚤 Wooded uplands and 1700 feet of saltwater shoreline are separated by a 250-foot bluff at this site. A steep hiking trail connects the two park units. On the beach is a wheelchair-accessible fishing pier where anglers can cast for perch, bullhead and salmon; at the south end are tide flats for wading. Facilities include a picnic area, restrooms, showers, a baseball field, a play area and horseshoe pits. Day-use fee, $5. ~ Located at the east foot of Sylvan Way (Route 306) two miles east of Route 303 northeast of Bremerton; 360-478-6460, fax 360-792-6067.

▲ There are 24 standard sites (no hookups); $15 per night. Reservations: 888-226-7688.

BELFAIR STATE PARK 🚶 🚴 ⛵ 🏕 Two creeks flow through this 63-acre park en route to Hood Canal, affording both fresh and saltwater shorelines. Along its 3700 feet of beachfront the saltwater warms quickly across shallow tide flats, but pollution makes swimming here risky; many instead swim in a lagoon with a bathhouse nearby. Shellfish are usually posted off-limits. There are picnic areas, restrooms and showers. Day-use fee, $5. ~ Route 300, three miles west of Belfair; 360-275-0668.

Every year in May, 88 acres of native rhododendrons burst into bloom at Scenic Beach State Park.

▲ There are 137 tent sites ($15 per night) and 47 full hookup sites ($21 per night); dump station ($5). Reservations: 888-226-7688.

SCENIC BEACH STATE PARK 🚶 ⛵ 🎣 🏕 🛥 🚤 Well named it is, with glorious views across Hood Canal to the Olympics and north up Dabob Bay. Nearly 1500 feet of cobblestone beach invites strolls; scuba divers also push off from here. Anglers try for salmon and bottom fish at the nearby artificial reef, and there's a boat launch less than a mile from the park. There are picnic areas, restrooms, showers, a play area, a horseshoe pit, a volleyball area and a community center. Day-use fee, $5. ~ Located just west of Seabeck on Miami Beach Road North- west, about nine miles northwest of Bremerton; 360-830-5079, fax 360-830-2970.

▲ There are 52 standard sites, no hookups ($15 per night); and two primitive sites ($10 per night). Closed in winter. Reser- vations: 888-226-7688.

Before either Seattle or Tacoma were so much as a tug on a fisherman's line, Port Townsend was a thriving lumber port. Founded in 1851,

Port Townsend Area

it has retained its Victorian seacoast ambience better than any other community north of San Francisco. Much of the city has been designated a National Historic Landmark district, with more than 70 Victorian houses, buildings, forts, parks and monuments. Many of the handsomely gabled homes are open for tours and/or offer bed-and-breakfast accommodations.

The best way to see **Port Townsend** is on foot. When you drive into town on Route 20, you'll first want to stop at the **Port Town- send Chamber of Commerce** visitors center. Then continue east on Route 20 as it becomes Water Street. ~ 2437 East Sims Way, Port Townsend; 360-385-2722; www.ptguide.com, e-mail info@ ptchamber.org.

SIGHTS

At the corner of Water and Madison streets, you'll find the **Jefferson County Historical Society Museum** in City Hall, fea- turing Victorian antiques, artifacts and thousands of photos of Port Townsend's early days. Admission. ~ 540 Water Street, Port Townsend; 360-385-1003, fax 360-385-1042; www.jchsmu seum.org, e-mail jchsmuseum@olympus.net.

Heading west on Water Street by foot, note the elegant stone and wood-frame buildings on either side of the street, most of them dating from the 1880s and 1890s. Turn right on Adams Street; halfway up the block on the right is the **Enoch S. Fowler Building,** built in 1874, the oldest two-story stone structure in Washington. A former county courthouse, it now houses the weekly newspaper.

Turn left at Washington Street and five blocks farther, on your right, you'll see **The James House,** built in 1889. It has five chim- neys and a commanding view of the harbor—and in 1973 became the Northwest's first bed and breakfast. ~ 1238 Washington

Street, Port Townsend; 360-385-1238, 800-385-1238, fax 360-379-5551; www.jameshouse.com, e-mail info@jameshouse.com.

Turn right up Harrison Street, then right again at Franklin Street. Two blocks farther, at Franklin and Polk streets, the **Captain Enoch S. Fowler Home**, built in 1860, is the oldest surviving house in Port Townsend and is typical of New England–style homes.

Two more blocks ahead, you will encounter the **Rothschild House**, built in 1868 by an early Port Townsend merchant. Notable for its outstanding interior woodwork, it's maintained by the State Parks Commission for public tours. Closed October through April. Admission. ~ Franklin and Taylor streets, Port Townsend; 360-397-8076, fax 360-385-1042; www.parks.wa.gov/roths child.htm.

A block north, **Trinity Methodist Church** (1871) is the state's oldest standing Methodist church. Its small museum contains the Bible of the church's first minister. ~ Jefferson and Clay streets, Port Townsend.

A block east, the 1889 **Ann Starrett Mansion**, now a bed-and-breakfast inn, offers public tours from noon until three. Admission. ~ 744 Clay Street, Port Townsend; 360-385-3205; www.starrettmansion.com, e-mail info@starrettmansion.com.

The **Lucinda Hastings Home** was the most expensive house ever built in Port Townsend when it was erected in 1889 at a cost of $14,000. ~ Clay and Monroe streets, Port Townsend.

Turn right here, and return down Monroe to Water Street and your starting point at City Hall. Get back in your car and drive north on Monroe Street. (The arterial staggers a half-block right at Roosevelt Street onto Jackson Street, then turns right onto Walnut Street.) All roads flow into W Street, the south boundary of **Fort Worden Conference Center**. Authorized in 1896, it includes officers' row and a refurbished **Commanding Officer's House** (admission), the **248th Coast Artillery Museum** (admission), gun emplacements, a concert pavilion, marine interpretive center and **Point Wilson Lighthouse**. Fort Worden offers stretches of beach that command impressive views of the Cascades and nearby islands. ~ Port Townsend; 360-344-4400; www.fortworden.org.

On the dock at Fort Worden is the **Port Townsend Marine Science Center**. Of special interest are its four large touch tanks, representing different intertidal habitats, where creatures like starfish, anemones and sea cucumbers can be handled by curious visitors. Hours vary seasonally; call ahead. Admission. ~ Port Townsend; 360-385-5582; www.ptmsc.org, e-mail info@ptmsc.org.

The James House claims to have been the Pacific Northwest's first **LODGING** bed and breakfast. Just a few steps from shops and restaurants at the foot of the bluff that stands behind lower downtown, it dates from 1889, though it's only been a bed and breakfast since 1973. The house is unmistakable for its five chimneys; inside, the floors are all parquet. All rooms have private baths. There are a fireplace and a library, and a full breakfast is served. Save a few moments to enjoy the English gardens with an impressive view of the water. Kids over 12 are welcome. ~ 1238 Washington Street, Port Townsend; 360-385-1238, 800-385-1238, fax 360-379-5551; www.jameshouse.com, e-mail info@jameshouse.com. DELUXE TO ULTRA-DELUXE.

For those less than enthralled with bed and breakfasts, the **Palace Hotel** provides historic accommodation in a former seafarers' bordello. Though nicely renovated, this is a bit rustic: After checking in at the main lobby you must climb a long flight of stairs (or two) to your room. There are 15 guest chambers, each with antiques recalling the red-light flavor of the past. Three of the rooms, including the madam's former room, even have kitchenettes. ~ 1004 Water Street, Port Townsend; 360-385-0773, 800-962-0741, fax 360-385-0780; www.palacehotelpt.com, e-mail palace@olympus.net. DELUXE TO ULTRA-DELUXE.

The renowned **Ann Starrett Victorian Mansion Bed and Breakfast Inn**, a National Historic Landmark built in 1889, is a classic mansion in Victorian style. High on a bluff overlooking downtown Port Townsend and Puget Sound, it combines diverse archi-

---

CHEAP SLEEPS

For students and backpackers, there are two youth hostels in eastern Jefferson County. The first is at **Fort Worden State Park**, open year-round. ~ Port Townsend; 360-385-0655; www.olympus.net/ftworden. BUDGET. The other hostel is at **Fort Flagler State Park**, open June 1st through September. ~ Located three miles north of Nordland; 360-385-1288. BUDGET.

tectural elements—frescoed ceilings, a free-hung spiral staircase, an eight-sided dome painted as a solar calendar, the requisite gables and dormer window—into a charming whole. The 11 guest rooms all have private baths and are furnished with antiques, of course. The gourmet breakfast menu changes daily. ~ 744 Clay Street, Port Townsend; 360-385-3205, 800-321-0644, fax 360-385-2976; www.starrettmansion.com. DELUXE TO ULTRA-DELUXE.

With so many heritage choices, few visitors actually opt for a motel stay. If you do, check out **The Tides Inn**, along the waterfront at the south end of town. Among the 21 units are five efficiencies and nine with hot tubs; most units have balconies overlooking the bay. ~ 1807 Water Street, Port Townsend; 360-385-0595, 800-822-8696, fax 360-379-1115; www.tides-inn.com. MODERATE TO ULTRA-DELUXE.

South of town about 20 miles, **Port Ludlow Resort and Conference Center** is one of the Northwest's premier family resorts. It boasts a championship golf course, tennis courts, swimming pools, a marina, hiking and biking trails and 1500 acres of land. There are 38 guest rooms with fireplaces, oversized jetted tubs, kitchens and decks and a restaurant with marvelous views of water and mountains. ~ 1 Heron Road, Port Ludlow; 360-437-0310, 800-732-1239, fax 360-437-0411; www.portludlowresort.com. ULTRA-DELUXE.

DINING

For an evening of fine dining, it would be hard to top the **Manresa Castle**. Located in an 1892 hilltop inn that overlooks the town and bay like a German castle on the Rhine River, it combines an elegant restaurant and an Edwardian pub. The menu offers regional and seasonal specialties, everything from curry chicken

AUTHOR FAVORITE

Ask locals where to eat, and chances are they'll recommend the **Fountain Café**. You'll probably have to stand in line for a seat, but the wait will be worth it. Occupying the ground floor of a historic building (is there anything else in downtown Port Townsend?), the Fountain serves outstanding seafood and pasta dishes, including oysters as you like 'em. Soups and desserts are homemade. The decor is in keeping with the eclectic penchant of many young local artists. ~ 920 Washington Street, Port Townsend; 360-385-1364. MODERATE.

and bouillabaisse to tiger prawns. Sunday brunch is also served. Closed Sunday through Tuesday in winter. ~ 7th and Sheridan streets, Port Townsend; 360-385-5750, fax 360-385-5883; www. manresacastle.com. DELUXE.

With a great location offering spectacular views, the **Surf Waterfront Café** complements its surroundings with pleasant blue-and-white decor and marine artwork. Fresh, simply prepared local seafood, particularly salmon, clams, mussels and oysters, is the specialty. ~ 106 Taylor Street, Port Townsend; 360-385-2992, fax 360-385-7106. MODERATE.

Breakfasts draw full houses at the **Salal Cafe**. Huge omelettes and various seafood and vegetarian recipes get *oohs* and *ahs*, as do the burgers and meat dishes. Lunch features gourmet home-style cooking, along with pastas and sandwiches. No dinner. ~ 634 Water Street, Port Townsend; 360-385-6532. BUDGET.

It's on a back street in Port Townsend. On Friday and Saturday nights a vibes player in the corner provides soft jazz and Caribbean rhythms. Not much makes sense about **Khu Larb Thai**; ◄ HIDDEN nonetheless, its fare is probably the best Thai food in Washington State. Curries are rich and flavorful; *pad Thai*, usually mundane, is interesting; mussel hot pots are divine. The rich soups, especially the seafood concoctions, are practically enough for a meal by themselves. And the black rice pudding is an unusual treat. Come early for a table on weekend nights. Closed Monday. ~ 225 Adams Street, Port Townsend; 360-385-5023. BUDGET TO MODERATE.

Some say the **Shanghai Restaurant** serves the best Chinese food this side of Vancouver's Chinatown. Forget the view of the RV park across the street, and enjoy the spicy Szechuan and northern Chinese cuisine. ~ Point Hudson, Port Townsend; 360-385-4810, fax 360-385-0660. BUDGET.

The **Chimacum Café**, nine miles south of Port Townsend, is ◄ HIDDEN a local institution. This is food like grandma should have made—country-fried chicken dinners, baked ham and so forth, followed, of course, by homemade pies brimming with fresh fruit. Breakfast, lunch and dinner are served. ~ 9253 Rhody Drive, Chimacum; 360-732-4631. BUDGET TO MODERATE.

Port Townsend offers the most interesting shopping on the peninsula with its array of galleries, antique and gift shops, book-   **SHOPPING** stores, gourmet dining and all-purpose emporiums. Proprietors have paid particular attention to historical accuracy in restoring commercial buildings. Many of the shops feature the work of talented local painters, sculptors, weavers, potters, poets and writers.

If you're looking for antiques, try the **Port Townsend Antique Mall** or any of the many other shops along the 600 through 1200 blocks of Water or Washington streets. ~ Antique Mall: 802 Washington Street, Port Townsend; 360-379-8069.

Among the many fine galleries for contemporary arts and crafts are **Ancestral Spirits Gallery**, which features Inuit and Northwest Coast tribal artwork. ~ 701 Water Street, Port Townsend; 360-385-0078. **Artisans on Taylor** specializes in local Northwestern crafts and hand-formed glass beads. ~ 236 Taylor Street, Port Townsend; 360-379-8098.

BEACHES & PARKS

FORT WORDEN STATE PARK A 433-acre estate right in Port Townsend, this turn-of-the-20th-century fort includes restored Victorian officers houses, barracks, theater, parade grounds and artillery bunkers. A beach and a boat launch are on Admiralty Inlet, at the head of Puget Sound. Try the dock or beach for salmon fishing. Restrooms, picnic areas, tennis courts and lodging are found here. Day-use fee, $5. ~ The entrance is located on W Street at Cherry Street, at the northern city limits of Port Townsend; 360-385-4370 ext. 4421, fax 360-385-7248; www.olympus.net/fortworden.

If Fort Worden looks familiar, it could be because it was used in the filming of the Richard Gere–Debra Winger classic, *An Officer and a Gentleman.*

▲ There are 80 RV hookup sites ($21 per night). Reservations are strongly recommended year-round: 200 Battery Way, Port Townsend, WA 98368.

KAH TAI LAGOON NATURE PARK This midtown park, which features 50 acres of wetlands and 35 acres of grasslands and woodlands, is a great place for birdwatching: more than 50 species have been identified here. There are two and a half miles of trails, a play area for kids, interpretive displays, restrooms and picnic areas. ~ 12th Street near Sims Way, Port Townsend; 360-385-2722, fax 360-379-3804.

OLD FORT TOWNSEND STATE PARK Decommissioned in 1895 when Indian attacks on Port Townsend (the town) were no longer a threat, the fort site has seven miles of trails and a beach on Port Townsend (the inlet). You can fish from the shore.

You'll find restrooms and picnic areas. Closed October through May. Day-use fee, $5. ~ Old Fort Townsend Road, three miles south of the town of Port Townsend off Route 20; 360-385-3595, fax 360-385-7248.

▲ There are 40 standard sites ($15 per night) and 3 primitive sites ($10 per night).

FORT FLAGLER STATE PARK 🚶 🚲 🚣 🎣 🚤 ⛵ 🛥️ 🎣
The long-abandoned fort building, which dates from 1898, is a minor attraction here: bigger is the saltwater beach on Admiralty Inlet, popular for clamming, beachcombing and fishing for salmon, halibut, sole, crab and shellfish. There are also a boat launch, hiking trails, restrooms, picnic areas and lodging. Day-use fee, $5. ~ Off Route 116, on the north tip of Marrowstone Island, eight miles northeast of Hadlock; 360-385-1259, fax 360-379-1746.

▲ There are 137 standard sites ($15 per night) and 10 RV hookup sites ($21 per night). No camping November through February. Reservations: 888-226-7688.

DOSEWALLIPS STATE PARK 🚶 🚲 🚣 🎣 At the mouth of the Dosewallips River on the Hood Canal, a long, serpentine arm of Puget Sound, this 425-acre park is especially popular among clam diggers and oyster hunters during shellfish season. There are a mudflat beach, hiking trails, restrooms, showers and picnic areas. Day-use fee, $5. ~ Route 101, in Brinnon, 37 miles south of Port Townsend; 360-796-4415, fax 360-796-3242.

▲ There are 100 standard sites ($15 per night) and 40 RV hookup sites ($21 per night). Reservations: 888-226-7688.

OLYMPIC NATIONAL FOREST 🚶 🚲 🏇 🚣 🎣 🚤 🛥️ 🎣
Surrounding Olympic National Park on its east, south and northwest sides, this national forest provides ample recreational opportunities, including good fishing for trout and, in some areas, for rock cod and salmon in the forest's many lakes and rivers. It includes five wilderness areas on the fringe of the park. There are restrooms and picnic areas. Dogs and hunting are allowed in the national forest, but not in Olympic National Park. Some areas of the park and some campgrounds close seasonally due to weather. ~ Numerous access roads branch off Route 101, especially south of Sequim, and between Quilcene and Hoodsport, on the east side of the Olympic Peninsula; 360-956-2400, fax 360-956-2330.

▲ There are 23 campgrounds throughout the forest. Camping costs range from free to $15 per night. Three cabins, sleeping four to six people, rent for $30 to $40 per night.

▼▼▼▼▼▼▼▼▼▼▼▼▼▼
Port Angeles Area

The northern gateway to Olympic National Park as well as a major terminal for ferries to British Columbia, the Port Angeles area is one of northwest Washington's main crossroads. Sequim on Route 101, 31 miles west of Port Townsend, and nearby Port Angeles are two of the peninsula's more intriguing towns. On the Strait of Juan de Fuca at the foot of the Olympic Mountains, this region often may be dry when it's pouring rain just a few miles south.

SIGHTS

The town of **Sequim** (pronounced "Squim") is graced with a climate that's unusually dry and mild for the Northwest: it sits in the Olympic rain shadow. A major attraction just north of town is the **Olympic Game Farm**, whose animals—lions, tigers, bears, buffalo and many others—are trained for film roles. Driving tours of the farm are available year-round; walking tours, including a studio barn, are offered during the summer. Admission. ~ 1423 Ward Road, Sequim; 360-683-4295, fax 360-681-4443; www.olygamefarm.com, e-mail gamefarm@olympus.net.

In the Sequim–Dungeness Valley area, the **Museum and Art Center** preserves the native and pioneer farming heritage of Sequim and showcases the work of local artists. ~ 175 West Cedar Street, Sequim; 360-683-8110.

For visitor information, contact the **Sequim–Dungeness Valley Chamber of Commerce Visitors Center**. ~ 1192 East Washington Street, Sequim; 360-683-6197; www.cityofsequim.com.

North off Route 101, the Dungeness Valley is dotted with strawberry and raspberry fields. Weathered barns left over from the area's dairy farming days are still visible. Pay a visit to the **Cedarbrook Herb Farm**, where 300 different varieties of herbs and spices fill the air with a marvelous (but undefinable!) aroma and inspire many a gourmet chef to go on a culinary buying spree. ~ 1345 Sequim Avenue South, Sequim; 360-683-7733, fax 360-681-3040; www.cedarbrook.com, e-mail cedbrook@olypen.com.

Opposite the mouth of the Dungeness River is one of the Olympic Peninsula's most remarkable natural features: the **Dungeness Spit**, almost seven miles long and the largest natural sand hook in the United States. A short trail within the adjacent **Dungeness Recreation Area** provides access to this national wildlife refuge. At the end of the spit, the **New Dungeness Lighthouse** rises 63 feet above the sea. Established in 1857, the lighthouse is now on the National Register of Historic Places. Visitors who brave the five-and-a-half mile walk out along the spit will be rewarded with an in-depth tour of the facilities.

The Dungeness Spit and the surrounding bay and estuary are teeming with wildlife, including seabirds, seals, fish, crabs and clams.

Seventeen miles west of Sequim on Route 101 is the fishing and logging port of **Port Angeles**, the Olympic Peninsula's largest town. A major attraction here is the **City Pier**. Adjacent to the ferry terminal, it boasts an observation tower, promenade decks and a picnic area. ~ Port Angeles; 360-417-6254.

The **Arthur D. Feiro Marine Life Center**, where visitors can observe and even touch samples of local marine life, is also found at the City Pier. Call for hours. Admission. ~ Port Angeles; 360-417-6254.

As the gateway to Olympic National Park, Port Angeles is home to national park headquarters. At the **Olympic National Park Visitor Center**, you'll find an excellent slide show and exhibits on the natural and human history of the park. ~ 3002 Mt. Angeles Road, Port Angeles; 360-565-3132; www.nps.gov/olym/home.htm.

The **Museum of Clallam County** divides its contents between the federal building at 1st and Oak streets (exhibits) and the Lincoln School at 8th and C streets (genealogical information and county archival research information). Closed Saturday and Sunday. ~ Port Angeles; 360-452-2662.

For tourist information, contact the **North Olympic Peninsula Visitor & Convention Bureau**. ~ 338 West 1st Street, Port Angeles; 360-452-8552; www.olympicpeninsula.org.

LODGING

You'll feel good right down to your cockles—as well as your steamer clams, butter clams and horse clams—after shellfishing on the saltwater beach outside the **Sequim Bay Resort**. The eight fully equipped housekeeping cottages here are suitable for vacationing families and shoreline lovers. There are no pets allowed in the cottages. There are also guest laundry facilities and hookups for RVs. Two-night minimum stay required. ~ 2634 West Sequim Bay Road, Sequim; 360-681-3853, fax 360-681-3854. BUDGET.

HIDDEN ►   Just a spit from the Spit—Dungeness, that is—is the **Groveland Cottage**, by the coast north of Sequim. The early-20th-century building has four carpeted rooms with art, antique decor and private baths. There is also a private cottage with a queen-size bed and private bath. The rooms may be simple, but service is not: coffee is delivered to your room in anticipation of the gourmet breakfast. The accent overall is on comfort. They also rent 32 vacation cottages in the area. ~ 4861 Sequim-Dungeness Way, Dungeness; 360-683-3565, 800-879-8859, fax 360-683-5181; www. sequimvalley.com/groveland.html, e-mail simone@olypen.com. MODERATE.

Perhaps the nicest motel-style accommodation in these port communities is the **Red Lion Hotel**. A modern building that extends along the Strait of Juan de Fuca opposite the ferry dock, it offers rooms with private balconies overlooking the water. A strand of beach and swimming pool beckon bathers. ~ 221 North Lincoln Street, Port Angeles; 360-452-9215, 800-733-5466, fax 360-452-4734; www.redlionportangeles.com. DELUXE.

Victoria, across the strait on Vancouver Island, is said to be "more British than the British"—but the same slogan could almost apply to **The Tudor Inn**. The host serves a traditional English breakfast and afternoon refreshment in the restored Tudor-style home. Most of their antique collection is Old English, and the well-stocked library will steer you to books on a wide variety of

AUTHOR FAVORITE

Situated on the water with spectacular views of the San Juan Islands, the **Domaine Madeleine Bed and Breakfast** excels in both comfort and hospitality. There are five rooms at this charming inn, including a honeymoon cottage. There's the Renoir Suite, with a 14-foot-high basalt fireplace, impressionist art and feather beds, and the Ming Room, with 19th-century antiques, a jacuzzi and a large private balcony. All rooms have fireplaces and collections of French perfumes. Four rooms have jacuzzis for two. Relax in the cozy coffee nook or try your hand at the antique organ. The full gourmet breakfast is elegantly presented—don't miss it. Gay-friendly. ~ 146 Wildflower Lane, Port Angeles; 360-457-4174, 888-811 8376, fax 360-457-3037; www.domainemadeleine.com, e-mail romance@domainemadeleine.com. ULTRA-DELUXE.

subjects. All five bedrooms have private baths; one has a gas fire-place and small balcony. ~ 1108 South Oak Street, Port Angeles; 360-452-3138, 888-286-2224, fax 360-457-9360; www.tudor inn.com, e-mail info@tudorinn.com. MODERATE TO DELUXE.

DINING

El Cazador is a casual, family-run restaurant with red and green table linens, whitewashed walls and Mexican artwork. What sets it apart is its use of fresh seafood in traditional Mexican dishes that consistently win local "best of" awards. The burrito Veracruz stuffed with baby shrimp is a standout. ~ 531 West Washington Street, Sequim; 360-683-4788, fax 360-683-2203; www.el-ca zador.com. BUDGET.

The **Eclipse Café** serves up hearty, traditional breakfasts and lunches: omelettes, sandwiches, burgers, pies and cakes. You'll leave full and so will your wallet. ~ 139 West Alder Street, Sequim; 360-683-2760. BUDGET.

The undisputed winner in the northern Olympic Peninsula fine-dining sweepstakes is **C'est Si Bon**. The decor is modern and dramatic, with handsome oil paintings and full picture windows allowing panoramas of the Olympic Range. The cuisine, on the other hand, is classical French: tournedos with crabmeat and a shallot sauce, coquilles St. Jacques, veal Normande with apples and calvados. There are French wines and desserts, too. Dinner only. Closed Monday. ~ 23 Cedar Park Drive, four miles east of Port Angeles; phone/fax 360-452-8888; www.cestsibon-french cuisine.com. DELUXE.

A New England reader raved about the clam linguine at the charming **Bella Italia**. In addition to a variety of pasta, this inti-mate, candlelit eatery whips up Tuscan steak, *cioppino* and veal Marsala. But the menu here reaches beyond typical Italian fare, and you're likely to find the peninsula's freshest and most cre-ative seafood dishes here. The restaurant also has an extensive wine selection. ~ 117-B East 1st Street, Port Angeles; 360-457-5442, fax 360-457-6112; www.bellaitaliapa.com, e-mail bella@ olypen.com. MODERATE TO DELUXE.

Port Angeles Crabhouse, located in the Red Lion Hotel, of-fers sweeping waterfront views in a casually elegant decor of etched glass and tapestry-covered booth seating. Simple and straightforward seafood dishes such as cracked Dungeness crab and grilled salmon are the specialties. ~ 221 North Lincoln Street,

Port Angeles; 360-457-0424, fax 360-452-4734. MODERATE TO
ULTRA-DELUXE.

Practically next door is the **First Street Haven**, one of the best
places around for quick and tasty breakfasts and lunches. Have
a homemade quiche and salad, along with baked goods and the
house coffee, and you'll be set for the day. Breakfast and lunch
only. ~ 107 East 1st Street, Port Angeles; 360-457-0352, fax 360-
452-8502. BUDGET.

BEACHES
& PARKS

SEQUIM BAY STATE PARK
Shellfish (clams, oysters and crabs) as well as fishing for salmon
and halibut are the main attractions at this park on Sequim Bay,
sheltered from rough seas by two spits at its mouth and from
heavy rains by the Olympic rain shadow. There's a beach; you'll
also find restrooms and picnic areas. Day-use fee, $5. ~ Route
101, four miles east of Sequim; 360-683-4235, fax 360-681-5054.

▲ There are 60 standard sites ($15 per night), 16 RV hook-
up sites ($21 per night) and 3 primitive sites ($10 per night). Reservations: 888-226-7688.

DUNGENESS RECREATION AREA   The
Dungeness Spit is a national wildlife refuge, but a recreation area
trail provides access. Marine birds and seals are among the impressive wildlife to be seen; the Dungeness crab is internationally
famous as a fine food. There are restrooms, showers and picnic
areas. ~ Located at the base of the Dungeness Spit, five miles west
of Sequim on Route 101, then four miles north on Kitchen-Dick
Road; phone/fax 360-683-5847.

▲ There are 66 sites (no hookups); $14 per night.

HIDDEN ►

SALT CREEK RECREATION AREA
One of the finest tidepool sanctuaries on the Olympic Peninsula is this three-mile stretch of rocky beach. Starfish, sea urchins,
anemones, mussels, barnacles and other invertebrate life can be
observed . . . but not removed. Anglers will find rockfish. Restrooms, picnic areas, playground and hiking trails are all here. ~
Located three miles north from Joyce (or 15 miles west from Port
Angeles) on Route 112, then another three miles north on Camp
Hayden Road; 360-928-3441, fax 360-417-2395.

▲ There are 92 sites (no hookups); $12 to $14 per night.

Olympic National Park

Rugged, glaciated mountains dominate this 1400-square-mile park, with rushing rivers tumbling from their slopes. The rainier western slopes harbor an extraordinary rainforest, and a separate 57-mile-long coastal strip preserves remarkable tidepools and marvelous ocean scenery. Wildlife in the park includes the rare Roosevelt elk, as well as deer, black bears, cougars, bobcats, a great many smaller mammals and scores of bird species. Besides the main part of the park, which encompasses the entire mountain wilderness in the center of the peninsula and can be entered from the north or west, Olympic National Park includes a separate Coastal Unit spanning more than 50 miles of Pacific headlands and beaches.

The first residents of the peninsula and coast were tribes like the Makah, Ozette and Quileute, whose descendants still inhabit the area today. A seafaring people noted for their woodcarving, they lived in a series of longhouses facing the sea and are known to have inhabited this region for as long as 2500 years.

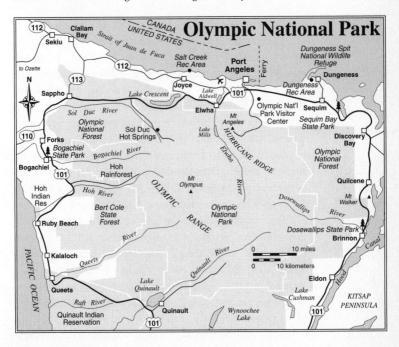

Olympic National Park was annexed to the national park system in 1938. But long before that, Washingtonians had discovered its natural wonders. A fledgling tourism industry grew, with lodges constructed at several strategic locations around the park, including lakes Crescent and Quinault, Sol Duc Hot Springs and Kalaloch, overlooking the Pacific. Coastal communities were also building a visitor infrastructure, and quiet beach resorts soon emerged.

SIGHTS

There is no lack of facilities throughout the park: picnic areas, hotels, restaurants and groceries. For general information on the park, call the **Olympic National Park Visitor Center**. ~ 360-565-3130.

The most direct route into the park from Port Angeles is the Heart of the Hills/Hurricane Ridge Road. It climbs 5200 feet in just 17 miles to the **Hurricane Ridge Lodge**, where there are breathtaking views to 7965-foot Mt. Olympus, the highest peak in the Olympic Range, and other glacier-shrouded mountains. Visitors to Hurricane Ridge can dine in the day lodge, picnic, enjoy nature walks or take longer hikes. In winter, enjoy the small downhill ski area here and many cross-country trails.

Twenty miles west of Port Angeles on Route 101 is **Lake Crescent**, one of three large lakes within park boundaries. Carved during the last Ice Age 10,000 years ago, it is nestled between steep forested hillsides. A unique subspecies of trout lures many anglers to its deep waters. There are several resorts, restaurants, campgrounds and picnic areas around the lake's shoreline. From National Park Service–administered Lake Crescent Lodge, on the southeast shore, a three-fourth-mile trail leads up Barnes Creek to the beautiful **Marymere Falls**. ~ 360-928-3211, fax 360-928-3253; www.lakecrescentlodge.com, e-mail lclodge@olypen.com.

West of Lake Crescent, the Sol Duc River Road turns south to **Sol Duc Hot Springs**, 14 miles off of Route 101. Long known to the Indians, the therapeutic mineral waters were discovered by a pioneer in 1880 and like everything else the white man touched, soon boasted an opulent resort. But the original burned to the ground in 1916 and today's refurbished resort, nestled in a valley of old-growth Douglas fir, is more rustic than elegant. The springs remain an attraction. Sol Duc is a major trailhead for backpacking trips into Olympic National Park; also located here is a ranger station. ~ 360-327-3583, fax 360-327-3593; www.north olympic.com/solduc, e-mail pamsdr@aol.com.

The largest town between Port Angeles and Hoquiam is **Forks** (population 3000), the main population center on the Olympic Coast, and the nearest to the Hoh Rainforest. (It's also Washington's rainiest town, with well over 100 inches a year.) Steelhead fishing, river rafting and mushroom gathering are major activities here, but the one most evident to visitors is the timber industry. Some days, in fact, there seem to be more log trucks on the roads than passenger cars.

The **Forks Timber Museum** is filled with exhibits of old-time logging equipment and historical photos, as well as pioneer and Indian artifacts. Interpretive trails, gardens and a logger memorial are next to the visitors center. ~ Route 101 South, Forks; 360-374-9663, fax 360-374-9253; www.forkswa.com.

On the coast 14 miles west of Forks is the 800-year-old Indian fishing village of **La Push**, center of the **Quileute Indian Reservation**. Sportfishing, camping and beach walking are popular year-round. An abandoned Coast Guard station and lighthouse here are used as a school for resident children. ~ 360-374-6163, fax 360-374-6163.

A national park road eight miles west of Forks branches off the La Push Road and follows the north shore of the Quileute River five miles to **Rialto Beach**, where spectacular piles of driftwood often accumulate. There are picnic areas and campgrounds here, and a trailhead for hikes north up the beach toward Cape Alava.

IN MEMORIAM

Much of the Olympic coastline remains undeveloped. Hikers can wander along the high-water mark or on primitive trails, some wood-planked and raised above the forest floor. Offshore reefs have taken many lives over the centuries since European exploration began, and two memorials to shipwreck victims are good destinations for intrepid hikers. Nine miles south of Ozette, the **Norwegian Memorial** remembers seamen who died in an early-20th-century shipwreck. Six miles farther south, and about three miles north of Rialto Beach opposite La Push, the **Chilean Memorial** marks the grave of 20 South American sailors who died in a 1920 wreck.

The Peninsula's Northwest Coast

Much less traveled than Route 101, Route 112 runs from near Port Angeles to Neah Bay on the northwest tip of the Olympic Peninsula. The drive takes about one and a half hours each way. Allow an additional one and a half to two hours to see the Makah Cultural and Research Center. You may wish to make this an all-day excursion by adding a side trip to Lake Ozette, one of the most hidden spots you can reach by road in Olympic National Park.

THE NORTHWEST COAST   From Port Angeles, follow Route 101 west for five miles, then turn off to the right on Route 112. For much of its length, this narrow two-lane highway runs within sight of the Strait of Juan de Fuca and partly traces the water's edge. Travel 46 miles to the sister communities of **Clallam Bay** and **Sekiu** (pronounced "C-Q"). These are prime sportfishing grounds for salmon and huge bottomfish, especially halibut. Check out the wonderful tidepools north of Clallam Bay at **Slip Point**. Just west of Sekiu, at the mouth of the Hoko River, visitors can view the remains of a 2500-year-old Makah Indian fishing village at the **Hoko Archaeological Site**.

NEAH BAY   Continue for 18 more miles past Sekiu to the highway's end at Neah Bay, the administrative center of the Makah Indian Reservation. This rather bleak little village has a few motels and a commercial fishing fleet, and visitors can book charter-fishing excursions from the harbor. Beyond the town, roads continue to stormswept beaches on Cape Flattery, strewn with driftwood and shipwrecks. Neah Bay's touristic centerpiece, the **Makah Cultural and Research Center** houses finds from the Oz-

On the west side of the national park are three more major points of entry. The **Hoh Rainforest** is 19 miles east of Route 101 via the Hoh River Road, 13 miles south of Forks. For national park information here, call the **Forks Ranger Station** (360-374-5877). There's a less well-known rainforest at the end of the **Queets River Road**, 14 miles off Route 101, 17 miles west of Quinault. Finally, **Lake Quinault**, on Route 101 at the southwestern corner of Olympic National Park, is the site of several resorts and campgrounds, including the venerable Lake Quinault Lodge. Watersports of all kinds are popular at this glacier-fed lake, surrounded by old-growth forest.

ette Dig at Cape Alava, about 20 miles down the Pacific coast. Few relics remain from the ancient culture of the Northwest Coast tribes because their wooden structures and implements rotted away quickly in the damp climate. Ozette, however, was buried 500 years ago by a mudslide that preserved it from the elements until archaeologists discovered it in the 1970s. The artifacts found there and exhibited in an atmospheric long-house setting at the cultural center include baskets, log canoes, clothing, wood carvings and whaling harpoons. Admission. ~ Bay View Avenue; 360-645-2711, fax 360-645-2656; www.makah.com.

LAKE OZETTE   Returning from Neah Bay on Route 112, two miles before you reach Sekiu a paved secondary road turns off to the south (right) and goes 20 miles to Lake Ozette, the northernmost part of Olympic National Park's Coastal Unit. The largest of the park's three lakes, it is separated from the ocean by a strip of land just three miles wide. Several trails lead from here to the sea, including the Indian Village Trail, which leads to the Ozette Dig at Cape Alava, and the Ozette Loop Trail, which weaves past 56 petroglyphs that depict various aspects of historic Makah life.

SAPPHO   Back on Route 112, six miles east of Clallam Bay Route 113 turns off to the south (right) and goes nine miles through the forest to join Route 101 at Sappho. Here you face a choice: If you turn east (left), you'll return to Port Angeles, a distance of 45 miles through Olympic National Forest and Olympic National Park, passing **Lake Crescent** and **Mary-mere Falls** (page 216) and the road to **Sol Duc Hot Springs** (page 216). If you turn west (right), Route 101 will take you through Forks to the turnoff for the **Hoh Rainforest** (pages 218, 221) and past that to the beaches of the **Olympic National Park Coastal Unit** (page 219), a total distance of 53 miles.

The **Hoh Indian Reservation** is 25 miles south of Forks, off Route 101. Of more interest to most visitors is the **Kalaloch Lodge**, 35 miles south of Forks on Route 101. A major national park facility, it affords spectacular ocean views at the southern-most end of the park's coastal strip. ~ Kalaloch Lodge: 157151 Route 101; 360-962-2271, 866-525-2562, fax 360-962-3391; www.visitkalaloch.com.

The **Olympic National Park Coastal Unit** includes some 3300 square miles of designated marine sanctuary both above and below water level. Although most of the 50-mile seacoast is unreach-able by road, trails lead down to six diverse beaches from Route

101 between Kalaloch and Ruby Beach. Here you'll find broad, log-strewn expanses of sand, gravel stretches great for beachcombing, and rocky tidepools teeming with tiny marine life.

LODGING

The rustic **Log Cabin Resort** is a historic landmark on the shores of gorgeous Lake Crescent along Route 101. Budget-watchers can stay in the main lodge; more upscale are the lakeshore chalets and cabins. There is also an RV park with full hookups on Log Cabin Creek. The handsome log lodge has a restaurant and a gift shop; all manner of boats are rented at the marina. Closed November through April. ~ 3183 East Beach Road, 21 miles west of Port Angeles; 360-928-3325, fax 360-928-2088; www.logcabinresort. net, e-mail logcabin@tenforward.com. MODERATE TO DELUXE.

The **Sol Duc Hot Springs Resort** is another historic property, originally built in 1910 around a series of hot sulphur pools 12 miles south of Route 101. The 32 cabins (six with kitchens) were rebuilt in the mid-1980s and now have indoor plumbing! The best plunge, however, after a day of hiking or fishing, remains the water in three ceramic natural mineral spring pools, kept between 98° and 104°F and cleaned nightly. There is also a full-size swimming pool. Camping sites and RV hookups are available. The resort is closed November to April. ~ Sol Duc Hot Springs Road, 44 miles west of Port Angeles; 360-327-3583, fax 360-327-3593; www.northolympic.com/solduc, e-mail pamsdr@aol. com. MODERATE TO DELUXE.

The hamlet of Sekiu flanks Route 112 on the protected shore of Clallam Bay, on the Strait of Juan de Fuca. The lone waterfront hotel here is **Van Riper's Resort and Charters**. Family owned and operated, it's a cozy getaway spot. More than half of the 16 rooms have great views of the boats on the picturesque strait. ~ 280 Front Street, Sekiu; 360-963-2334, 888-462-0803, fax 360-963-2354; www.vanripersresort.com. BUDGET TO DELUXE.

The **Cape Motel and RV Park** has eight motel rooms and two cottages; five have kitchens. Six months of the year, an RV park with restrooms is also open. ~ Bayview Avenue, Neah Bay; phone/fax 360-645-2250. BUDGET.

HIDDEN ▶

Among several low-priced bed and breakfasts in Forks is the **River Inn on the Bogachiel**, an A-frame chalet on the banks of the Bogachiel River two-and-a-half miles from town. Two bedrooms share a bath and sundecks; one has a private bathroom

The Hoh Rainforest

No matter where you go on this earth, there's only one Hoh Rainforest. It's said to be one of the only coniferous rainforests in the world. Graciously spared the logger's blade, it's been undisturbed since time began. In other words, it's a natural wonder to be cherished.

Reached by traveling 13 miles south from Forks on Route 101, then 19 miles east on Hoh River Road, this is the wettest spot in the contiguous 48 states. In fact, wet isn't the word: even the air drips like a saturated sponge, producing over 30 inches of fog drip in the summer. The average annual precipitation due to rainfall is 145 inches, more than 100 inches of which fall between October and March. But temperatures at this elevation, between 500 and 1000 feet, rarely fall below 40° in winter or rise above 85° in summer. The legacy of this mild climate is dense, layered canopies of foliage.

The forest floor is as soft and thick as a shag carpet, cloaked with mosses, bracken ferns, huge fungi and seedlings. Hovering over the lush rug are vine maple, alder and black cottonwood, some hung with moss, stretching wiry branches to taste any slivers of sunlight that may steal through the canopy. Above them, Douglas fir, Sitka spruce, Western hemlock, Western red cedar and other gigantic conifers rise 200 to 300 feet, putting a lid on the forest. In all, over 300 plant species live here, not counting 70 epiphytes (mosses, lichens and such).

Some compare this environment to a cathedral. Indeed, the soft light is like sun filtered through stained glass, and the arching branches could pass for a vaulted apse. To others, it's simply mystical. The ancient coastal Indians would have agreed.

Though there are similar rainforests in Washington, the rainforest ecology is most conveniently studied at the **Hoh Rainforest Visitor Center** and on the nature trails that surround it. ~ 360-374-6925; www.nps.gov/olym. The **Hoh River Trail** extends for 18.5 miles to the river's source in Blue Glacier, on the flank of Mt. Olympus, but the rainforest can be appreciated by most visitors on one of two loop hikes that are both about a mile long. About three-fourths of a mile in, you'll see enormous old-growth Douglas fir, spruce and hemlock, some over nine feet in girth and at least 500 years old. At about one mile, the trail drops down to Big Flat, the first of several grassy open areas. The winter grazing of Roosevelt elk, whose survival was a major reason for the creation of Olympic National Park, has opened up the forest floor. Keep your eyes open, too, for wildlife. Besides the elk, you may spot river otter or weasel. Black bears and cougars also inhabit these forests. Bald eagles and great blue heron feed on the salmon that spawn seasonally in the Hoh.

and stairs leading to the hot tub. You can fish from the shore or relax in the hot tub while keeping your eyes open for elk, deer and river otter. Full breakfast. Closed in September. ~ 2596 West Bogachiel Way, Forks; 360-374-6526, fax 360-374-6590. MODERATE.

Much nearer to shops and restaurants is the **Miller Tree Inn**. A quiet and comfortable farm homestead on one tree-filled acre, it has attractive rooms (two with half-baths) that practice an "open-house" policy not common among bed and breakfasts: children and pets are welcome (with some restrictions)! And visitors love the fresh farmhouse breakfasts. ~ 654 East Division Street, Forks; 360-374-6806, fax 360-374-6807; www.northolympic. com/millertree. MODERATE TO DELUXE.

Eight American Indian tribes are associated with the Olympic National Park and its environs.

Sixteen miles west of Forks in the Quileute Indian Reservation, surrounded by the coastal strip of Olympic National Park, is the **La Push Ocean Park Resort**. The driftwood-speckled beach is just beyond the lodgings, which fall into four categories: moderate-to ultra-deluxe-priced cabins with fully supplied kitchenettes and fireplaces; older moderate-priced townhouse units with balconies overlooking the beach; 20 budget-priced motel units with either full kitchens or kitchenettes; and rustic, budget-priced A-frames with wood stoves (haul your own fuel from the woodshed) and toilets (showers are in a communal washroom). Be warned: One reader found the cabins unsatisfactory. ~ 700 Main Street, La Push; 360-374-5267, 800-487-1267, fax 360-374-4153; www.ocean-park.org. BUDGET TO ULTRA-DELUXE.

The **Kalaloch Lodge** is perched on a bluff high above the crashing surf. Accommodations here (which may disappoint some) include 10 lodge units, 10 motel units, 20 log cabins with kitchenettes (but no utensils provided) and 18 units atop the bluff, 7 of which are duplexes. The lodge has a dining room and lounge overlooking the Pacific Ocean, as well as a general store, gas station and gift shop. ~ 157151 Route 101, 35 miles south of Forks; 360-962-2271, fax 360-962-3391; www.visitkalaloch.com. DELUXE TO ULTRA-DELUXE.

Forks also has a youth hostel, complete with the cosmopolitan atmosphere one would expect. The **Rain Forest Hostel**, like other lodgings of its ilk, offers dorm bunks and community bathrooms and kitchen. The common room is a bonus with its fireplace and library. There is also one room for a couple and one room for a family. ~ 169312 Route 101 North, 23 miles south of Forks; 360-374-2270; www.rainforesthostel.com, e-mail go2hostel@cen turytel.net. BUDGET.

If you're planning a stay in the corner of Olympic National Park that includes beauteous Lake Quinault, consider the **Lake Quinault Lodge**—especially if you can get a lakefront room in the historic cedar-shingled lodge itself. The huge building arcs around the shoreline, a totem-pole design on its massive chimney facing the water. Antiques and wicker furniture adorn the main lobby, constructed in the 1920s. There is also a sun porch, dining room and bar. There are nice rooms in a newer wing, but they lack the lodge's historic ambience. You can rent boats in the summer, hike year-round or relax in the pool or sauna. ~ 345 South Shore Road, Quinault; 360-288-2900, 800-562-6672, fax 360-288-2901; www.visitlakequinault.com. MODERATE TO ULTRA-DELUXE.

The best choice for dining in the park is the **Log Cabin Resort**. Enjoy the view of beautiful Lake Crescent, where anglers dip their lines for the unique crescenti trout, a subspecies of rainbow trout. Northwest cuisine is the specialty. ~ 3183 East Beach Road, 21 miles west of Port Angeles; 360-928-3325, fax 360-928-2088. MODERATE.

DINING

There's a dining room at the **Sol Duc Hot Springs Resort,** just behind the hot sulphur springs. As at the Log Cabin, the food is solid Northwest fare, including some vegetarian dishes and Dungeness crab from the north Olympic Coast. Closed October through April. ~ Sol Duc Hot Springs Road, 44 miles west of Port Angeles; 360-327-3583, fax 360-327-3593. MODERATE.

A mile high in the Olympic Range, 17 miles south of Port Angeles, the **Hurricane Ridge** frames glaciers in the picture windows of its coffee shop. Come for the view, but the standard American fare served here isn't half-bad either. Open daily mid-May through September, weekends mid-December to April. ~ Hurricane Ridge Road; 360-928-3211. BUDGET.

Sunsets from the **Kalaloch Lodge,** high on a bluff overlooking the ocean in the national park's coastal strip, can make even the most ordinary food taste good. Fortunately, the fresh salmon and halibut served here don't need the view for their rich flavor. A lounge adjoins the dining room. Breakfast, lunch and dinner. ~ 157151 Route 101, 35 miles south of Forks; 360-962-2271, fax 360-962-3391. MODERATE TO DELUXE.

The restaurant at the park's **Lake Quinault Lodge** faces another gorgeous lake surrounded by lush cedar forests. As you've come to expect along this coast, the seafood is excellent. Breakfast and dinner year-round. ~ 345 South Shore Road, Quinault; 360-288-2900, 800-562-6672, fax 360-288-2901; www.visit lakequinault.com. DELUXE.

Other than the national park lodges, pickings are slim in the restaurant department along this stretch of highway. A mile north of Forks, the **Smoke House Restaurant** serves standard greasy-spoon fare that should stave off hunger pangs if nothing else. ~ Route 101 at La Push Road; 360-374-6258. MODERATE.

SHOPPING　For authentic Northwest Indian crafts, you won't do better than the gift shop at the **Makah Cultural and Research Center** on the Makah Indian Reservation near Cape Flattery at the end of Route 112. ~ Bay View Avenue, Neah Bay; 360-645-2711.

BEACHES & PARKS

OLYMPIC NATIONAL PARK This spectacular national park, 922,626 acres in area and ranging in elevation from sea level to nearly 8000 feet, contains everything from permanent alpine glaciers to America's lushest rainforest (the Hoh) to rocky tidepools rich in marine life. Wildlife includes deer in the mountains, elk in the rainforest, steelhead and trout in the rivers and colorful birds everywhere. Three large lakes—Crescent (near Port Angeles), Ozette (on the coast) and Quinault (on the southwestern edge)— are especially popular visitor destinations. There are restrooms, picnic areas, hotels, restaurants and groceries. ~ Route 101 circles the park. The numerous access roads are well marked; 360-565-3000, fax 360-565-3015 (Port Angeles); ranger stations in Forks (360-374-5877), Quilcene (360-765-2200) and Sol Duc (360-327-3534).

▲ There are 17 campgrounds; $10 to $15 per night.

BOGACHIEL STATE PARK Not far from the Hoh Rainforest, this eternally damp park sits on the Bogachiel River, famous for its salmon and steelhead runs. Hiking and hunting in the adjacent forest are popular activities, although this park is more of a campsite than a day-use area. Facilities include restrooms, showers and limited picnic areas. Day-use fee, $5. ~ Route 101, six miles south of Forks; 360-374-6356.

Return of the Monster Slayers

Makah, the tribal name of Neah Bay's native people, means "generous food"—and no wonder! For 2000 years, the main protein in the Makah diet was the meat of the gray whale. Men of the tribe would chase one of the 35-ton leviathans in canoes, harpoon it, and kill it by stabbing it repeatedly with spears as it towed them through the open ocean. So vital was whaling to the Makah culture that in their 1855 treaty the U.S. government guaranteed their right to hunt whales forever—the only treaty ever made by the United States that contains such a guarantee. Thereafter, the tribe also sold whale oil to non-Indian settlers and became the wealthiest Indians in the Northwest. (They are now among the poorest.) They had to stop in the 1920s after the whales nearly disappeared from coastal waters due to industrial whaling.

In recent years, since the California gray whale population has recovered and the whales have been removed from the endangered species list, the Makah intend to hold new whale hunts on a limited scale, still in traditional hand-carved log canoes but using a specially designed rifle—hopefully a single carefully aimed shot at the same instant the harpoon is thrown— as a more humane alternative to spears. Meat from the whales would be divided among the 1800 tribal members, storing any excess in tribal freezers. Under the supervision of the National Marine Fisheries Service, the tribe is allowed to take up to 20 migrating adult whales without calves in a five-year period. After nearly five years of planning the hunt and practicing the use of the harpoon and rifle, and a year of ceremonial purification, tribal hunters killed their first whale in May 1999.

Makah whaling is the subject of one of the biggest animal rights controversies in the Northwest. Opponents interpret the language of the Makah treaty as allowing whaling only as long as non-Indians were also hunting whales, before the present international ban. They also fear that despite federal prohibitions the tribe might find the Japanese importers' $1 million offer for a single whale an irresistible temptation. Tribal leaders say whaling is a matter of cultural preservation, discipline and pride. They claim that many of the tribe's health problems may come from the loss of their traditional whale meat diet and point out that the indigenous Chukotki people of Russia's Pacific coast have been "harvesting" about 165 gray whales a year for the last 40 years, yet the whale population continues to grow. Escalating with each whale hunt, the dispute is unlikely to be resolved soon.

▲ There are 36 standard sites ($15 per night), 6 RV hookup sites ($21 per night) and 2 primitive sites ($10 per night).

▼▼▼▼▼▼▼▼▼▼▼▼▼▼

Outdoor Adventures

SPORT-FISHING

Despite charter operators' complaints that government restrictions hinder their operations, the Strait of Juan de Fuca is still one of the nation's great salmon grounds, with chinook, coho and other species running the waters during the summer months. From April to September, halibut is also big in these waters—literally: one local operator holds the state record, 268 pounds. Bottomfish like ling cod, true cod, red snapper and black bass round out the angling possibilities.

KITSAP PENINSULA The family-run **Emerald City Salmon Charter** has a 40-foot boat that accommodates up to 12 people for winter weekend and daily summer trips on the Sound. Dad skippers the boat while kids help out as deck hands. ~ 253-630-3150.

OLYMPIC COAST When **Big Salmon Fishing Resort** isn't breaking state records for halibut (288 pounds), it runs half-day charters for salmon and bottomfish. The store also sells bait and rents tackle. ~ 1251 Bay View Avenue (or Front Street), Neah Bay; 360-645-2374, 866-787-1900; www.bigsalmonresort.com.

Olson's Resort runs year-round charters out of Neah Bay and Sekiu for halibut, bottomfish and salmon (in season). ~ Sekiu; 360-963-2346; www.olsonsresort.com.

RIVER FISHING

It's not just the fish—salmon, steelhead, trout—that attract anglers to the mountain streams flowing from the Olympic Mountains. Spectacular scenery and glimpses of eagles, deer, elk and other wildlife sweeten the deal.

◆◆

DIGGIN' IN

Folks who like to shellfish will be happy in Washington. There are clams (littleneck, butter, Manila and razor), scallops, oysters (Willapa Bay is famous for its oysters), mussels and crab (Dungeness Spit, north of Sequim, is the home of the renowned Dungeness crab). Then, of course, there's that Northwest oddity, the geoduck (say "gooey-duck"), whose huge foot cannot fit within its shell. See "Shellfishing" for information on this popular activity.

PORT ANGELES AREA An hour or two away are several destinations for river fishing: the Sol Duc, Bogachiel, Hoh, Queets and Calawah rivers.

OLYMPIC NATIONAL PARK The lower Quinault River is not "overpacked" with fishermen—yet—partly because nontribal people may not fish rivers on the reservation without a Quinault guide. Contact the **Quinault Indian Nation Fish and Game Department** to receive information about available guides for drift boat or walk-in fishing. ~ 1214 Aalis Street, Taholah; 360-276-8211 ext. 227. **Three Rivers Resort & Guide Service** operates four 16-foot drift boats for two anglers on the Sol Duc, Bogachiel and Hoh rivers (another "quiet" spot). The eight-hour trips are for salmon and steelhead. Tackle, continental breakfast, and lunch are provided. ~ 7764 La Push Road, Forks; 360-374-5300.

SHELL-FISHING Before you start digging up clams or other shellfish, please remember that just like other forms of fishing, a license is required for this activity. You can pick one up at tackle shops and other locations that sell fishing licenses. Recreational harvesting of shellfish is permitted on public beaches, but you should double-check, because much of the state's tideland is privately owned. Generally, shellfishing is permitted year round; razor clams and oyster harvests are restricted by season and location. Call the **Washington State Department of Fish and Wildlife** for information. ~ 360-902-2700. You can also call the **Shellfish Rule Change** hotline. ~ 866-880-5431. You must also check with the Health Department's **Red Tide Hotline** to find out which waters are unhealthy for shellfish harvesting. ~ 360-753-5992.

RIVER RUNNING The Elwha River flows from the Olympic Mountains into the Strait of Juan de Fuca. Along the way, there are some Class II whitewater rapids—not quite a thrill ride, but enough excitement for good family fun (it's the only commercially rafted whitewater on the peninsula). Besides that, there's plenty of wildlife to see—elk, osprey, bald eagles, deer, harlequin ducks—as well as a view of a glacier. **Olympic Raft and Kayak** runs a couple of trips daily, each lasting about two and a half hours. The trips down the Class II Elwha and Class I Hoh rivers are on rafts. Both beginning and experienced rafters can partake. ~ 123 Lake Aldwell Road, Port Angeles; 360-452-1443, 888-452-1443; www.raftandkayak.com.

KAYAKING   Experienced or novice, kayakers who paddle around a mountain lake, through coastal marshlands or under sea cliffs will be rewarded not only with good exercise but also with the opportunity to observe abundant wildlife in a wilderness setting. Companies offering guided tours generally operate during the warmer months (May through September). But think about this: Many kayakers swear the best time to paddle is in the rain.

KITSAP PENINSULA   Kayak rentals and instruction are the specialty of **Olympic Outdoor Center**. Custom group trips for eight or more take paddlers throughout the Puget Sound. ~ 18971 Front Street, Poulsbo; 360-697-6095; www.kayakproshop.com.

PORT TOWNSEND AREA   Nearby Bird Island is a popular half-day sea-kayaking destination for the guided tours operated by **Kayak Port Townsend**. Rentals are available. ~ 435 Water Street at Monroe Street, Port Townsend; 360-385-6240, 800-853-2252; www.kayakpt.com.

The Dungeness crab was the first commercially harvested shellfish on the Olympic coast.

Port Townsend is a sea-kayaking center; call **Sport Townsend** where you can buy backpacks and kayaks. ~ 1044 Water Street, Port Townsend; 360-379-9711.

Olympic Outdoor Center offers three-hour sea-kayaking tours on Saturday. The center also rents kayaks and offers classes. ~ 18971 Front Street, Poulsbo; 360-697-6095; www.kayakproshop.com.

PORT ANGELES AREA   For kayak rentals and sales in Port Angeles, try **Sound Bikes and Kayaks**. ~ 120 East Front Street, Port Angeles; 360-457-1240; www.soundbikeskayaks.com.

You may have Lake Aldwell all to yourself, aside from the waterfowl nesting along its shores, when you join a two-hour guided tour of this clear blue lake. **Olympic Raft and Kayak** uses the more stable sea kayaks for these lake tours. The service also offers a four-hour trip in the saltwater Freshwater Bay just west of Port Angeles, which teems with bald eagles, otters and endangered marbled murrelets. ~ 123 Lake Aldwell Road, Port Angeles; 360-452-1443, 888-452-1443; www.raftandkayak.com.

WHALE WATCHING   California gray whales and humpbacks head back up to Alaskan waters between March and May. Orcas, or killer whales, are frequently seen in the waters of the Strait of Juan de Fuca, and we land-based mammals can't seem to get enough of the spectacle.

Many fishing charter operators convert to whale-watching cruises during these months. See "Sportfishing" above for charters.

The only skiing on the Olympic Peninsula is **Hurricane Ridge Ski Area**, 17 miles south of Port Angeles, in Olympic National Park. Here skiers will find a few downhill runs and several cross-country trails starting from the visitors center. There are two rope tows and a T-bar lift on site. The Hurricane Hill Road cross-country trail (1.5 miles one way) is probably the easiest of the area's six trails; the most challenging is the Hurricane Ridge Trail to Mt. Angeles, a steep three-mile route that's often icy. Rentals of down-hill, cross-country and snowshoeing equipment are also available. Open December through March, weekends and weather permitting only. Contact the **Olympic National Park Visitor Center**. ~ 3002 Mt. Angeles Road, Port Angeles; 360-565-3130, for road conditions 360-565-3131; www.portangeles.org.

SKIING

For ski lift information, call the **Hurricane Ridge Winter Sports Club**. ~ 360-457-4519.

Llama lovers will be delighted to accompany an Andean pack an-imal into the Olympics, thanks to **Kit's Llamas**. ~ P.O. Box 116, Olalla, WA 98359; 253-857-5274; www.northolympic.com/llamas. **Deli Llama Wilderness Adventures** leads one- to seven-day trips into the Olympic and North Cascades National Parks. ~ 360-757-4212; www.delillama.com. **Olympak Llamas** offers extended trips to neighboring national parks that include all meals. ~ 1614 Dan Kelly Road, Port Angeles; 360-452-5867.

LLAMA TREKKING

Bay views, ocean views, mountain views—take your pick. They're part and parcel with the courses in this region, all of which rent power carts, push carts and clubs.

GOLF

PORT TOWNSEND AREA   The public 18-hole **Chevy Chase Golf Club** is set in the woods above Discovery Bay. It is a fairly flat course, although it can get a bit mushy after winter rains. ~ 7401 Cape George Road, Port Townsend; 360-385-0704.

The public, double-teed, nine-hole **Port Townsend Golf Club** is located in town. It's considered the driest winter course in the area (it gets only 17 inches of rain), with rolling terrain, small greens and a driving range. ~ 1948 Blaine Street, Port Townsend; 360-385-4547.

Golf Digest has named the semiprivate 27-hole Port Ludlow Golf Course designed by Robert Muir Graves one of the best in the country. Although housing flanks one section, the spectacular views of Ludlow Bay and abundant wildlife prompt comments like "Amazing" and "It's like golfing in a national park" from local duffers. ~ 751 Highland Drive, Port Ludlow; 360-437-0272.

PORT ANGELES AREA   Although the 18-hole private **Sunland Golf and Country Club** goes through a housing development, it's well treed and fairly flat. Call for reciprocal play times. ~ 109 Hilltop Drive, Sequim; 360-683-6800. **Dungeness Golf Course** offers a semiprivate, 18-hole course. The number-three hole, called "Old Crabbie," has ten contracts guarding the crab-shaped green. ~ 1965 Woodcock Road, Sequim; 360-683-6344.

BIKING   Except along the southwestern shore areas, bicycling this part of Washington requires strength and stamina. There's spectacular beauty here, but there's also lots of rain and challenging terrain.

KITSAP PENINSULA   Cyclists find the moderate **Poulsbo–Port Gamble Loop,** with its 20 miles featuring outstanding views of Hood Canal, the Cascade Range and the Olympic Mountains, a worthwhile ride.

PORT TOWNSEND AREA   Recreational bicyclists will probably enjoy a ride through **Fort Worden State Park,** which overlooks the Strait of Juan de Fuca, in Port Townsend.

OLYMPIC COAST   A recommended road tour is the 85-mile **Upper Peninsula Tour** from Sequim to Neah Bay. The 55-mile trip down Route 101 from **Port Angeles to Forks** is also recommended. A paved six-mile trail loops the Port Angeles waterfront. The trail is flat, mostly following the shoreline, with picnic tables and other stopping spots along the way. On a clear day, you can see across the strait to Victoria.

Bike Rentals   **Mt. Constance Mountain Shoppe** rents and sells full-suspension mountain bikes and accessories, does repairs, and offers occasional bike tours. ~ 1550 Northeast Riddell Road, Bremerton; 360-377-0668; www.mountainshoppe.com.

In Port Townsend, rent mountain bikes, tandems, running strollers, bike trailers and road bikes at **Port Townsend Cyclery.** ~ 252 Tyler Street, Port Townsend; 360-385-6470; www.olympus. net/ptcyclery. **Sound Bikes and Kayaks** rents hybrids and mountain bikes. ~ 120 East Front Street, Port Angeles; 360-457-1240; www.soundbikeskayaks.com.

All distances listed for hiking trails are one way unless otherwise noted.

KITSAP PENINSULA Located southwest of Bremerton, **Gold Mountain Hike** (4 miles) is a moderate-to-strenuous climb with a 1200-foot elevation gain. You will survey the twisting waterways of Southern Puget Sound and Hood Canal from a 1761-foot point that also offers vistas from the Olympics to the Cascades and Edmonds to Olympia. The best access is from Holly Road at the trailhead called Wildcat.

PORT TOWNSEND AREA **Mount Walker Trail** (2 miles) ascends the Olympics' easternmost peak (2804 feet) through a rhododendron forest. The view from the summit, across Hood Canal and the Kitsap Peninsula to Seattle and the Cascades, is unforgettable. The trailhead is one-fifth mile off Route 101 at Walker Pass, five miles south of Quilcene.

PORT ANGELES AREA **Dungeness Spit Trail** (5.5 miles) extends down the outside of the longest natural sandspit in the United States, and back the inside. The spit is a national wildlife refuge with a lighthouse at its seaward end. The trail begins and ends at the Dungeness Recreation Area.

OLYMPIC NATIONAL PARK Olympic National Park and adjacent areas of Olympic National Forest are rich in backpacking opportunities. Most trails follow rivers into the high country, with its peaks and alpine lakes. **Obstruction Point Trail** (7.4 miles) leads from the Deer Park Campground to Obstruction Point, following a 6500-foot ridgeline.

AUTHOR FAVORITE

One of the most unforgettable hikes I've experienced is the **Hoh River Trail** (17.5 miles), which wanders through lush, primeval rainforest teeming with deer from the Hoh Ranger Station to Glacier Meadows, at the base of the Blue Glacier on 7965-foot Mt. Olympus, the park's highest point. (Afterwards, I felt like a very tired Greek god.)

The **West Fork of the Dosewallips-Anderson Pass** trail (9 miles) starts at the Dosewallips Ranger Station on the park's eastern boundary, follows the Dosewallips River to its source in the Anderson Glacier, then goes down the East Fork of the Quinault to the Graves Creek Campground.

Seven Lakes Basin Loop (22.5 miles) has several trail options, starting and ending at Sol Duc Hot Springs.

Coastal areas of the Olympic Peninsula have hiking trails as well. **Cape Alava Loop** (11 miles) crosses from the Ozette Ranger Station to Cape Alava; follows the shoreline south to Sand Point, from which there is beach access to shipwreck memorials farther south; and returns northeast to the ranger station. Prehistoric petroglyphs and an ancient Indian village can be seen en route.

▼▼▼▼▼▼▼▼▼▼▼
Transportation

CAR

Traveling from Seattle, most Olympic Peninsula visitors take either the Seattle–Winslow ferry (to Route 305) or the Edmonds–Kingston ferry (to Route 104), joining 101 just south of Discovery Bay. **Route 305** runs northwest across Bainbridge Island and onto Kitsap Peninsula to Poulsbo. From Tacoma, the practical route is **Route 16** across the Narrows Bridge. From the north, the Keystone ferry to Port Townsend has its eastern terminus midway down lanky Whidbey Island, off Route 20. Northbound travelers can reach the area either through Astoria, on Route 101, or via several routes that branch off Route 5 north of Portland.

Route 101 is the main artery of the Olympic Peninsula and Washington coastal region, virtually encircling the entire land mass. Branching off Route 5 in Olympia, at the foot of Puget Sound, it runs north to Discovery Bay, where **Route 20** turns off to Port Townsend; west through Port Angeles to Sappho; then zigzags to Astoria, Oregon, and points south. Remarkably, when you reach Aberdeen, 292 miles after you start traveling on 101, you're just 36 miles from where you started!

AIR

William R. Fairchild International Airport, near Port Angeles, links the northern Olympic Peninsula with major cities throughout the United States and western Canada via Horizon Air Lines. ~ 360-417-3433.

FERRY

Washington State Ferries serves the Olympic Peninsula directly from Whidbey Island to Port Townsend and indirectly across Puget

Sound (via the Kitsap Peninsula) from Seattle and Edmonds. ~ 206-464-6400. The **Black Ball Transport** offers direct daily service between Port Angeles and Victoria, B.C. ~ 360-457-4491; www.ferrytovictoria.com. **Victoria Rapid Transit** provides foot-passenger service mid-May through September. ~ 360-452-8088, 800-633-1589; www.victoriaexpress.com. Some smaller cruise lines may make stops in Port Angeles.

Shuttle service to the northern Kitsap Peninsula is available through the **Bremerton-Kitsap Airporter**. ~ 360-876-1737.

CAR RENTALS

In Port Angeles, **Budget Car and Truck Rental** can be found in town. ~ 800-527-0700. Or try **Dan Wilder Auto Center**. ~ 800-927-9372.

PUBLIC TRANSIT

In the Kitsap Peninsula area, **Kitsap Transit** provides routed service in Poulsbo, Bremerton, Kingston, Port Orchard and Bainbridge Island; otherwise, you will have to depend on car or taxis for transportation around the peninsula. ~ 800-501-7433; www.kitsaptransit.org. Shuttle service to the northern Kitsap Peninsula is available through the **Bremerton-Kitsap Airporter**. ~ 360-876-1737.

For local bus service in the northern Olympic Peninsula, including Port Angeles and Sequim, contact **Clallam Transit System** in Port Angeles. ~ 360-452-4511, 800-858-3747; www.clallamtransit.com. Port Townsend, Sequim and eastern Jefferson County are served by **Jefferson Transit**. ~ 360-385-4777, 800-371-0497; www.jeffersontransit.com.

ELEVEN

Northern Puget Sound & the San Juan Islands

The area referred to as Northern Puget Sound begins just beyond the far northern outskirts of Seattle, where most visitors first arrive, and extends northward up the coast to the Canadian border. This awe-inspiring land once supported the American Indians, providing for all their needs with verdant woods full of deer and berries and crystal waters full of salmon, letting them live in peaceful coexistence for hundreds of years. Even the weather was kind to them here in this "rain shadow," shielded by the Olympic and Vancouver Island mountain ranges.

The traditional pursuits of logging and fishing still dominate the economies of coastal communities such as Everett and Bellingham, while other small towns such as La Conner and Mt. Vernon are still very pastoral, dependent on an agriculturally based economy. However, current booms in real estate and tourism are beginning to tilt the economic scale as more and more people discover the area's beauty.

Just offshore, the 172 named islands of the San Juans are also very pastoral, with rich soil and salubrious conditions perfectly suited to raising livestock or growing fruit. The major islands are connected to the mainland by limited ferry service, an inhibiting factor that helps preserve the pristine nature here; they have become prime territory for ecotourism and are increasingly populated with the summer homes of big-city dwellers. Lopez is by far the friendliest and most rural of the islands, followed closely by San Juan, the largest and busiest. Shaw Island is one of the smaller islands, and lovely Orcas Island, named after Spanish explorer Don Juan Vincente de Guemes Pacheco y Padilla Orcasitees y Aguayo Conde de Revilla Gigedo (whew!) rather than for orca whales, is tallest, capped by 2400-foot Mt. Constitution.

Although it's not considered part of the San Juans, serpentine Whidbey Island, with its thick southern tip reaching toward Seattle, is the largest island in Puget

Sound. Situated at Whidbey's northern tip is Fidalgo Island, home of Anacortes and the ferry terminal gateway to the San Juans.

The ferry system is severely overtaxed during the busy summer season when the San Juans are inundated with tourists, making it difficult to reach the islands at times and absolutely impossible to find accommodations if you haven't booked months in advance. The crowds drop off dramatically after Labor Day, a pleasant surprise since the weather in September and October is still lovely and the change of seasonal color against this beautiful backdrop is incredible.

Northern Puget Sound

Stretched along the fertile coastline between the Canadian border and the outer reaches of Seattle, communities along Northern Puget Sound are dependent on agriculture, logging and fishing, so the distinct pastoral feel of the area is no surprise. Verdant parks and vista spots taking in the beauty of the many islands not far offshore head the list of sightseeing musts here. But islands and shorelines are just part of the scenic and geographic mix in this region, which also includes rivers and delta wetlands, forests and picturesque farmlands.

SIGHTS

As you drive north from Seattle along Route 5, you'll cross a series of major rivers issuing from the Cascade Mountains. In order, you'll pass the Snohomish River (at Everett), the Stillaguamish (not far from Stanwood), the Skagit (at Mt. Vernon/Burlington) and the Nooksack (Bellingham). The lower reaches of these streams offer wetlands and wildlife to see, fishing villages to poke around in, a vital agricultural heritage in the Skagit and Nooksack valleys, and small towns by the handful. (In this volume, I've cut off the description of this region just north of Mt. Vernon; the region north to the Canadian border, including the burgeoning city of Bellington, is covered in Ulysses Press' *Hidden Washington* book.)

If you plan to catch the Mukilteo ferry to Clinton on Whidbey Island, be sure to allow enough time to visit the historic **Mukilteo Lighthouse** built in 1906. There are picnic tables above a small rocky beach cluttered with driftwood and a big grassy field for kite-flying adjacent to the lighthouse in little Mukilteo State Park. Open April through September, weekend afternoons only. ~ Mukilteo; 425-513-9602.

In Everett you'll find your best vantage point from the dock behind **Marina Village**, a sparkling complex of upscale shops, microbreweries and restaurants located in the second-largest marina on the West Coast. ~ 1728 West Marine View Drive, Everett.

In summer, a free pontoon boat ride will shuttle you from the 10th Street boat launch to picturesque **Jetty Island** for guided nature walks, birdwatching, campfires, a hands-on "Squirmy, Squiggly and Squishy" program to teach children about small marine animals and one of the only warm saltwater beaches on the Sound. For reservations, call 425-257-8300, fax 425-257-8325.

The **Firefighter's Museum** offers a storefront display of antique early-20th-century firefighting equipment. The collection is set up for 24-hour, through-the-window viewing. ~ 13th Street Dock, Everett.

The **Everett Area Chamber of Commerce** can provide you with more information. ~ 11400 Airport Road, Everett; 425-438-1487; www.everettchamber.com.

On the hillside above the marina, ornate **mansions** of the lumber barons that once ruled the economy here line Grand and Rucker streets from 16th Street north. None are open to tour, but a slow drive up and down these avenues will give you a feel for the history of the city.

On the south side of town you can take a **Boeing Everett factory tour**, which showcases the Boeing airplane company and the Everett product line, the 747, 767 and 777. It starts with a video about how airplanes are built, then takes visitors through the largest building in the world by volume (472,000,000 cubic feet). Visitors will see airplanes in various stages of pre-flight and flight-testing. Children must be 50 inches tall. Tours are weekdays, on a first-come, first-served basis; fee. Groups of ten or more people may make a reservation. Admission. ~ Tour Center, State Road 526, Everett; 800-464-1476, fax 425-342-7787; www.boeing.com.

The **Skagit Valley** has become a year-round retreat for city visitors, as nourishing to the soul in winter as it is inspiring to the adventurous spirit in summer. Indeed, artists and writers have been gathering in the Skagit for decades, including members of the famed "Northwest School" beginning in the 1930s— Mark Tobey, Morris Graves, Kenneth Callahan, Clayton James, Guy Anderson and many others. They were drawn by the Skagit's enchanting blend of meandering river levees and farm fields, bayous and bays, nearby islands and distant misty mountains, along with the extraordinary quality of the valley's ever-changing light. The farmlands, estuaries and tide flats attract several species of hawks and is one of the best places in all of North America to go "hawkwatching." See the "Scenic Drive" for more information.

DINING

◀ **HIDDEN**

The history of **Charles at Smugglers Cove** is as good as the food, making it doubly worth the drive out to Mukilteo. This red-brick mansion-turned-restaurant was purportedly owned at one time by Mafia kingpin Al Capone. Today the owners traffick in fresh seafood and steaks with French flair; their bouillabaisse, châteaubriand, rack of lamb and prawns in tarragon butter are out-

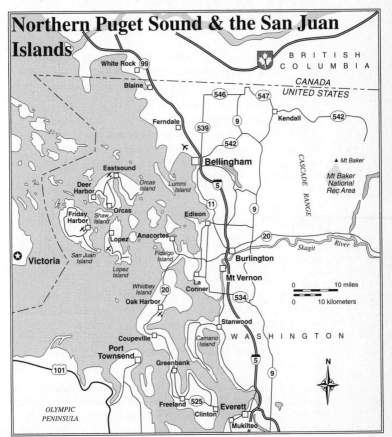

Text continued on page 240.

Island-hopping to the San Juans

The trip through the San Juan Islands is the longest and most beautiful cruise the Washington State Ferries network has to offer. It's not expensive, but in recent years, as both tourism and population in the Puget Sound area have grown enormously, the San Juan ferries have become so overburdened that even island residents have a hard time getting home during the summer months and on sunny weekends. If visiting during the off-season is out of the question, the best strategy is to arrive in Anacortes the afternoon before, sleep early and get in line for the ferry by dawn. The ferry schedule changes seasonally so obtain a current one at any ferry terminal or toll booth. Study the San Juan Island schedule carefully—it's complicated.

Day 1
- Leaving Seattle, head north on Route 5 to **Edmonds** (Exit 189), where a 30-minute ferry trip will take you to **Kingston** on the Olympic Peninsula (16 to 20 sailings daily from 5:50 a.m. to 1 a.m.).

- Drive eight miles north on Route 104 for a look at picturesque, New England–like **Port Gamble** (Chapter Ten, page 198). Another 25 miles north via Routes 104, 19 and 20 brings you to **Port Townsend** (Chapter Ten, page 203), a quaintly Victorian village on the northwest tip of the peninsula. Along the way, you might stop for lunch at the **Chimacum Café** (page 207), or you can catch a quick bite on the ferry.

- Take the ferry across to Keystone on **Whidbey Island** (page 240), a 30-minute trip (ten sailings daily from 7:45 a.m. to 9:30 p.m.).

- Follow Route 20 for 40 miles up the northern half of Whidbey Island, visiting **Coupeville** (page 245), yet another picture-perfect historic town, along the way.

- Before crossing **Deception Pass** from Whidbey Island to **Fidalgo Island** (page 252), be sure to walk out on the bridge for a magnificent seascape view. You've almost reached today's destination, so if you have time and feel like stretching your legs, the beaches and hiking trails of **Deception Pass State Park** (page 252) are the place to do it.

- Crossing the bridge, drive another six miles to the town of **Anacortes** (page 253) and check into your lodging for the evening. Dine out, then go to bed early so you can catch the dawn ferry well rested.

Day 2 • Be at the Anacortes ferry dock no later than (yawn!) 5:15 a.m. to catch the first ferry of the day to **Orcas Island** (page 264). Otherwise you can expect to wait in line for *at least* three hours to get on another one. The trip to Orcas Island takes about one hour with intermediate stops at Lopez and Shaw islands; there are 10 to 12 sailings daily from 5:45 a.m. to 9:15 p.m. or later; vehicles for Orcas load 20 minutes before sailing.

• Have breakfast on the ferry or upon arrival on Orcas Island.

• Check into your accommodations and buy food for a picnic lunch.

• Head for **Moran State Park** (page 267), the largest and finest park in the Washington State Parks system. Take in the view from the top of Mount Constitution, the highest point in the San Juans. Then take your pick of many hiking possibilities.

• By mid-afternoon you may be ready for a nap.

• For dinner this evening, try a seafood feast at the **Orchard House Restaurant** (page 267) at the Deer Harbor Inn.

Day 3 • It's not quite as critical to catch the first ferry from Orcas to **San Juan Island** (page 258) because any of the ferries, which run from 7:25 a.m. to 9:50 p.m. or later, is likely to unload as many vehicles at Orcas as are waiting to load. The trip to Friday Harbor takes about 30 minutes.

• Visit the **Whale Museum** (page 272).

• Take a driving tour around San Juan Island. On opposite sides of the island you'll find the sites of two historic forts of **San Juan Island National Historical Park** (page 258), where U.S. and British armies faced off in the anticlimactic "Pig War" over control of the San Juans. Several coastal beaches and parks along the way offer opportunities for picnicking and wildlife viewing. You may even see bald eagles or orca whales.

• As evening nears, catch a ferry back to Anacortes. The trip takes one to one and a half hours, depending on whether the ferry makes intermediate stops, and there are eight or nine sailings daily from 6 a.m. to 7:45 p.m.

• Back in Anacortes, you're less than an hour away from Seattle via Route 5.

standing, and the setting in the elegant dining rooms or on the sheltered deck is splendid. No lunch Friday and Saturday. Closed Sunday. ~ 8340 53rd Avenue West, Mukilteo; 425-347-2700, fax 425-531-8981. DELUXE.

Anthony's Home Port is the spot for seafood when it comes to waterfront dining in Everett. Prime picks on the seasonal menu include Whidbey Island mussels, grilled steak and prawns, Dungeness crab cakes, pan-fried scallops sprinkled with gremolatta, and six varieties of fresh oysters. Their four-course Sunset Dinner (served Monday through Friday from 4:30 to 6 p.m.) is a bargain and includes everything from appetizer to dessert. You can dine alfresco on the deck or pick a spot in the considerably less breezy dining room or lounge. ~ 1725 West Marine View Drive, Everett; 425-252-3333, fax 425-252-7847. MODERATE TO DELUXE.

SHOPPING   In Everett, the **Everett Public Market** is the prime browsing spot for antiques as well as Northwest arts and crafts. The market also houses a natural foods co-op that offers organically grown fruits and vegetables. ~ 2804 Grand Avenue, Everett; 425-252-1089.

BEACHES & PARKS   **MUKILTEO LIGHTHOUSE PARK** 🏊 🛥 🎣 🚤 🛳 ⚓ A swath of beach adjacent to the Whidbey Island–Mukilteo Ferry facilities on Puget Sound, Mukilteo Lighthouse Park is a day-use-only facility known primarily as a prime salmon-fishing spot with public boat launch (fee). Noble little Elliott Point Lighthouse, also known as Mukilteo Lighthouse, on the tip will keep shutterbugs happy; it's also a fine spot for beachcombing or picnicking while waiting for the ferry to Whidbey Island. There are restrooms, picnic grounds and floats. Day-use fee, $5. ~ Take the Mukilteo exit off Route 5 and follow the signs to the ferry; 425-353-2923, fax 360-652-1785.

Whidbey Island

Whidbey Island, stretching north to south along the mainland, is the longest island in the continental United States aside from Long Island. This slender, serpentine bit of land is covered in a rolling patchwork of loganberry farms, pasturelands, sprawling state parks, hidden heritage sites and historic small towns. The artistic hamlet of Langley near Whidbey's southern tip is a hotspot for weekend escapes from Seattle.

Text continued on page 244.

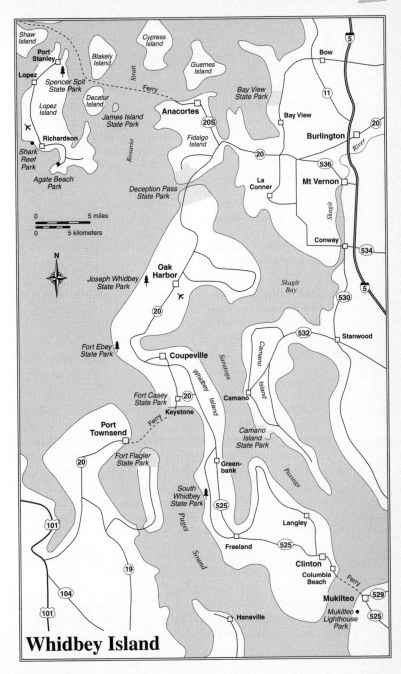

Whidbey Island

A Visit to the Skagit Valley

Someday, the Skagit Valley may become as famous as the well-known tourist attractions that surround it. But for now, out-of-state visitors tend to speed through this 25-mile-wide floodplain, missing its beauty as they hurry to or from the San Juan Islands, the Olympic Peninsula, Whidbey Island, North Cascades National Park, or Vancouver and Victoria, B.C. Alas, they're missing something special. About halfway between Seattle and Vancouver (and an hour's drive or so from either city via Route 5), this valley is very likely the most glorious union of countryside and seashore in the Northwest. It's centered on the largest, most pristine river delta on Puget Sound, whose sweeping estuary—an important stop on the Pacific Flyway—nurtures an extraordinary diversity of marine life and waterfowl. With topsoil up to several feet deep, the Skagit is the world's third-most fertile river delta, according to Skagitonians to Preserve Farmland.

MT. VERNON   Mt. Vernon, situated on the broad banks of the Skagit River, has done little to capitalize on its superior riverside location. But it does claim the liveliest "main street" in the valley. The true main street is signed as 1st Street here; it is lined with a variety of vintage architecture in both brick and wood dating to the turn of the century.

BLOOMING BUSINESS   Each spring, the fields of the Skagit Valley are alive with color as the tulips and daffodils begin to appear. **The Skagit Valley Tulip Festival Office** provides a guide to the festival that runs the entire month of April. ~ 100 East Montgomery Street, Suite 250, Mt. Vernon; 360-428-5959, fax 360-428-6753; www.tulipfestival.org. There are interesting gardens to view year-round. The prettiest is **RoozenGaarde** with display gardens and a great little gift shop. ~ 15867 Beaver Marsh Road, Mt. Vernon; 360-424-8531, fax 360-424-4920; www.tulips.com.

LA CONNER   West of Mt. Vernon, across the channel from the Swinomish Indian Reservation, La Conner is in the running for the title of quaintest little waterfront town in the Puget Sound area. Built on pilings above the bank of Swinomish Channel, La Conner got its start in the 1880s as a market center for farmers in the Skagit Flats. Now a historic district, this small village of fewer than 800 people is easy to explore on foot and, with its many well-preserved homes and buildings, offers a glimpse of turn-of-the-20th-century life.

SKAGIT COUNTY HISTORICAL MUSEUM   Park your car at the **La Conner Chamber of Commerce**. ~ Morris Street between 3rd and 4th streets; 360-466-4778, 888-642-9284, fax 360-466-0204; www.laconner-chamber.com. Walk a short distance up 4th Street to the top of the hill to visit the Skagit County Historical Museum, where you'll find a collection of automobiles, farm and fishing equipment, vintage clothing, household furnishings and photographs. Exhibits in the south wing focus on how early settlers made their living and include a Northwest Coast Indian display. Closed Monday. Admission. ~ 501 4th Street; 360-466-3365, fax 360-466-1611; www.skagitcounty.net/museum, e-mail museum@co.skagit.wa.us.

GACHES MANSION   From the museum, head south along 4th Street, which turns a corner and becomes Calhoun Street. Follow Calhoun downhill toward the channel for two blocks to the Gaches Mansion. This grand Victorian home was built in 1891 by a local merchant who wanted the finest house in town. The mansion houses the **La Conner Quilt Museum**, the Pacific Northwest's only quilt museum. Closed Monday and Tuesday, and the first two weeks of January. Admission. ~ 703 2nd Street South; 360-466-4288, fax 360-757-3573; www.laconnerquilts.com, e-mail lacquiltm@aol.com.

MAGNUS ANDERSON CABIN   Stroll a block south of the Gaches Mansion to see the Magnus Anderson Cabin next to city hall. The oldest structure in Skagit County, the 1869 cabin was moved here from a solitary location on the north fork of the Skagit River to save it from decay. ~ 2nd and Douglas streets.

MUSEUM OF NORTHWEST ART   Walk one more block west to 1st Street, then proceed north. This time-capsule waterfront street has been gentrified with boutiques, galleries and restaurants yet still retains a palpable air of history. Two longish blocks up the street you'll find the Museum of Northwest Art, which exhibits the works of regional painters and sculptors, presenting a cohesive look at the distinctive school of visual arts that has developed in the Pacific Northwest—an often surrealistic blend of Northwest Coast Indian and Asian motifs. Admission. ~ 121 South 1st Street; 360-466-4446, fax 360-466-7431; www.museumofnwart.org.

LA CONNER SERVICES   Opened in 1977, **La Conner Country Inn** was the first inn in these parts. It's still a favorite with long-time visitors, partly because several of its 28 rooms are so comfortable. ~ 107 South 2nd Street, La Conner; 360-466-3101, fax 360-466-5902; www.laconner lodging.com. MODERATE TO DELUXE. Few tourists ever discover **Marina Bistro**, located off the beaten shopping track in the marina just north of town. But local anglers and working folk know it well. The lack of tourist attention means you get good café food at budget prices. ~ 611 North 3rd Street, La Conner; 360-466-0331, fax 360-466-2410. BUDGET. Shopping is a major drawing card of little La Conner, with most of the boutiques and galleries concentrated along 1st and Morris streets.

SIGHTS   Most of the sights in **Langley** are concentrated along 1st and 2nd streets, where falsefront shops house small galleries, boutiques and restaurants. There's a lovely stretch of public beach flanked by a concrete wall adorned in Northwest Indian motifs just below **Seawall Park** (look for the totem pole on 1st Street), and a wonderful bronze statue by local artist Georgia Gerber above a second stairwell leading down to the beach.

In the spring months, you'll find a colorful tulip display at **Holland Gardens**. During the balance of the year come to see the beautiful floral displays that make this small garden a local favorite. ~ Corner of Southeast 6th and Ely streets, Oak Harbor.

Beautiful greenery typifies Whidbey Island, and one Greenbank area establishment offers visitors a close look at cultivating the landscape. The famous **Meerkerk Rhododendron Gardens** feature hundreds of varieties of these showy bushes—with 2000 species spread across 53 acres—which find Whidbey's climate one of the best on earth. Magnolia, maple and cherry trees add to the beauty of this spot, which is also a test garden. April and May are the peak months for blooms. Admission. ~ Just off Route 525 south of Greenbank; 360-678-1912; www.meerkerkgardens.org, e-mail meerkerk@whidbey.net.

Only a few wine grapes ripen in Puget Sound's cool climate; **Whidbey Island Vineyard & Winery** specializes in clean, crisp vintages, such as Madeleine Angevine and Siegerrebe, that are rarely grown elsewhere. Closed Tuesday in summer, and Monday through Wednesday the rest of the year. ~ 5237 South Langley Road; 360-221-2040, fax 360-221-4941; www.whidbeyisland winery.com, e-mail winery@whidbeyislandwinery.com.

Ebey's Landing National Historical Reserve, the first such reserve in the country, lies midway up Whidbey Island. The reserve

sights

AUTHOR FAVORITE

Spanning the "Grand Canyon of Puget Sound," **Deception Pass Bridge** links Whidbey with Fidalgo Island. Most visitors just drive slowly by, taking in the sights. But if you want a little more excitement, stroll out onto the bridge for vertigo-inducing views—straight down into the swift, churning currents of Deception Pass. You can also walk down to the shore on the footpaths of Pass Island to watch the streaming waters up close and personal.

takes in 19,000 acres that include Fort Ebey and Fort Casey state parks and the historic town of **Coupeville**, where falsefront buildings line Front Street above the wharf. Here you'll find Alexander Blockhouse (Alexander and Front streets) and Davis Blockhouse (Sunnyside Cemetery Road), built by early settlers for protection against possible Indian attacks, and a good collection of pioneer agricultural artifacts and historical displays in the **Island County Historical Museum** (908 Northwest Alexander Street, Coupeville; 360-678-3310). Reduced hours in winter. Admission. ~ Ebey's Landing National Historical Reserve, P.O. Box 774, Coupeville, WA 98239; 360-678-6084; www.nps.gov/ebla.

Built in 1901, **Admiralty Head Lighthouse** at Fort Casey State Park features an interpretive center offering history on the region's military past. You'll also enjoy excellent views of Puget Sound. Hours vary; call ahead. ~ 1280 Engle Road, Coupeville; 360-679-7391, fax 360-240-5503.

The big draw on Whidbey has always been bed-and-breakfast inns, over 100 of them at last count. Your choices run the gamut from log cabins on the beach to posh retreats tucked into the forest. For a comprehensive list, contact the **South Whidbey Visitor Information and Accommodation Referral Service**. ~ P.O. Box 403, 208 Anthes, Langley, WA 98260; 360-221-6765, fax 360-221-6468.

LODGING

The beautiful **Inn at Langley** has perfected the fine art of hospitality at a polished property worthy of its magnificent waterfront setting. With a decorator's color palette taken directly from the beach, rooms in shades of gray, cream, tan and brown accented by lots of natural wood are elegant, presenting a delicate balance of modern art and furnishings, and are decked out with every possible amenity (fireplace, jacuzzi, Krups coffee set and large deck to take advantage of the view). A serene oriental garden set in front of the grand dining room is an added touch. Continental breakfast. ~ 400 1st Street, Langley; phone/fax 360-221-3033; www. innatlangley.com. ULTRA-DELUXE.

◀ HIDDEN

Whidbey Inn overlooks Saratoga Passage and boasts six rooms with a view. On the main shopping street, this long-established bed and breakfast also is close to shopping and other attractions. Although the rooms are not huge, they feel more cozy than cramped, and large antique-decorated suites with fireplaces also are available. Full breakfast is delivered to your room. ~ 106 1st Street, Langley; phone/fax 360-221-7115, 888-313-2070; www. whidbeyinn.com, e-mail whdbyinn@whidbeyinn.com. MODERATE TO ULTRA-DELUXE.

Though it's inland a few miles from Langley, Lone Lake offers its own special sense of solitude and repose. A 100-acre lake that offers excellent swimming in the summer, Lone Lake is great for trout fishing, birdwatching, canoeing or just sitting quietly on the dock watching evening fall. **Lone Lake Cottage and Breakfast** offers two spacious cottages with kitchens, a tiny houseboat and a lakefront suite—all with jacuzzis and fireplaces. Many birds—exotic birds inside the main house's aviary, and ducks, pheasant, peacocks, quail and swans—populate the premises. Canoes, rowboats and bikes are available free for guest use. Continental breakfast. ~ 5206 South Bayview Road, Langley; phone/fax 360-321-5325; www.lonelake.com. DELUXE.

HIDDEN ▶

Cliff House is an architecturally stunning two-story structure of wood and sweeping panes of glass set on a wooded bluff overlooking Puget Sound. Guests have the run of the two-bedroom house, with its open central atrium, wonderful gourmet kitchen, sunken sitting area with fireplace and wraparound cedar deck with large jacuzzi. A stairway leads down to miles of empty beach. There is also a separate small cottage with one bedroom. ~ 727 Windmill Drive, Freeland; 360-331-1566, 800-450-7142; www.cliffhouse.net, e-mail wink@whidbey.com. ULTRA-DELUXE.

Built as officer's housing just prior to World War I, the **Fort Casey Inn** has been converted into inviting cottages overlooking Puget Sound. Its access to Fort Casey State Park and Crockett Bay makes this inn a prime location for outdoor recreation. Each of its ten units features a plethora of patriotic military memorabilia, including walls decked out with nostalgic postcards sent by soldiers overseas to their sweethearts at home. All have a bath and a living room, and most have a large kitchen with a breakfast nook as well as cast-iron gas fireplaces. A favorite with children, Fort Casey Inn is a historical treasure and a delightful retreat rolled into one. ~ 1124 South Engle Road, Coupeville; 360-678-5050, 866-661-6604; www.fortcaseyinn.com. BUDGET TO DELUXE.

The **Captain Whidbey Inn**, a well-preserved and maintained log inn on Penn Cove, is a fine example of the type of Northwest retreat all the rage years ago and now coming back into fashion.

This walk into the past offers several cozy, antique furnished rooms that share two baths and waterfront views; two rows of spacious, pine-paneled rooms with baths and a few private cottages with fireplaces. A full breakfast is served in the dining room where the wooden floors creek nostalgically and the massive stone fireplace chases away the chill. This is one of only a handful of waterside accommodations in the region; to enjoy the water fully, arrange for an afternoon sail with Captain John Colby Stone, the third-generation descendant of the original innkeeper. Full breakfast. ~ 2072 West Captain Whidbey Inn Road, Coupeville; 360-678-4097, 800-366-4097, fax 360-678-4110; www.captainwhidbey.com, e-mail info@captainwhidbey.com. MODERATE TO ULTRA-DELUXE.

> Of Washington State's nearly 400 bed-and-breakfast inns, over 100 are on Whidbey Island.

The **Coupeville Inn** has a French mansard–style roof that adds a touch of class to this otherwise straightforward two-story inn with a condo unit (subject to availability) that sleeps up to four. Breakfast featuring homemade muffins is included in the room rates. Of the two dozen rooms, most have balconies, about half have water views. Possibly the best motel value on the island, given the free continental breakfast and excellent location. ~ 200 Northwest Coveland Street, Coupeville; 360-678-6668, 800-247-6162, fax 360-678-3059; www.coupeville.com. BUDGET TO MODERATE.

The **Auld Holland Inn** is a reasonably priced roadside motel with flair, from the flowering window boxes on the European exterior to the immaculately clean, antique-filled rooms. Some rooms have fireplaces and princess canopied beds. For those seeking budget prices, there are 24 mobile home units with two or three bedrooms tucked behind the full-sized windmill housing the motel's office. If you're looking for more luxury, there are six deluxe-priced units furnished with jacuzzis and fireplaces. Continental breakfast. ~ 33575 Route 20, Oak Harbor; 360-675-2288, 800-228-0148, fax 360-675-2817; www.auldhollandinn.com, e-mail dutchvillage@oakharbor.net. BUDGET TO DELUXE.

Since 1989, **Cafe Langley** has served Mediterranean favorites such as spanikopita, moussaka, dolmades and lamb shish kabobs along with fresh seafood (Penn Cove mussels, grilled salmon and halibut), pastas and steaks. The atmosphere here is airy Mediterranean,

DINING

with stucco-like walls, exposed beams and an assortment of exotic fish etched on a glass partition. There are often people waiting in the park across the street for a table in this popular café. ~ 113 1st Street, Langley; 360-221-3090, fax 360-221-8542. MODERATE TO DELUXE.

The **Doghouse Tavern** is the place to go for great ribs, burgers, fish-and-chips and chowder. A totem on the side of this waterfront building points the way to their separate family dining room in case you've got the kids along. ~ 230 1st Street, Langley; 360-221-9825. BUDGET TO MODERATE.

The chef provides a floor show as well as fine cuisine at the **Inn at Langley**. The dining area is a huge country kitchen where gleaming copper pots and pans hang from the ceiling and each table has a view of the culinary action. Served on weekend nights only, the dinners consist of five courses emphasizing regional flavors such as duck breast with loganberries or baked salmon with apples, leeks and chanterelles. ~ 400 1st Street, Langley; phone/fax 360-221-3033; www.innatlangley.com, e-mail info@innatlangley.com. ULTRA-DELUXE.

The **Star Bistro Cafe and Bar**, a trendy little café with art deco decor, is a popular meeting spot for lunch, dinner and drinks. Their pastas, salads and Northwest wines are particularly good, fresh mussels are always available and the grilled pesto King salmon on a french roll is inventive and tasty. On a calm day you can dine alfresco on the second-floor heated deck with a great view of the Saratoga Passage. No dinner on Monday. ~ 201½ 1st Street, Langley; 360-221-2627, fax 360-221-5853; www.star-bistro.com, e-mail bistro@whidbey.com. MODERATE.

Award-winning **Rosi's Garden** serves a blend of Northwest and gourmet Italian cuisine. On the menu you'll find grilled asparagus salad, pasta primavera, raspberry salmon and rack of

AUTHOR FAVORITE

Toby's Tavern serves up a cheeseburger that was rated tops by actress Kathleen Turner, who starred in the film *War of the Roses*, which was filmed partly in and around Coupeville in 1989. Good fish-and-chips, Penn Cove steamed mussels and an upscale atmosphere add a touch of class to this waterfront watering hole. ~ 8 Northwest Front Street, Coupeville; 360-678-4222. BUDGET TO MODERATE.

lamb. Save room for the decadent desserts. Seating in the front room of this historic Victorian is intimate, yet the atmosphere is casual; it's like dining at your favorite grandma's house. ~ 602 North Main Street, Coupeville; 360-678-3989, fax 360-678-4487. MODERATE TO DELUXE.

Christopher's Front Street Cafe specializes in "creative contemporary cuisine" with a menu that changes seasonally. The emphasis is on fresh, local fare, especially seafood, and runs the gamut from superb Penn Cove mussels, to beef and chicken, vegetarian dishes, and pasta; regional wines and microbrews are also available. Closed Wednesday. ~ 23 Front Street, Coupeville; 360-678-5480, fax 360-678-1827. BUDGET TO DELUXE.

At **Kasteel Franssen**, lace table dressings, antiques, tapestries and fine-art reproductions of Rembrandt and other masters set a romantic European tone well suited to this Northwest French restaurant. Special dishes include ostrich in pinot noir–shallot tarragon demi-glace, Ellensburg rack of lamb as well as others that feature venison, pheasant and other wild game. Dinner only. Closed Sunday from September through May. ~ 33575 Route 20, Oak Harbor; 360-675-0724, fax 306-675-2817. MODERATE TO DELUXE.

SHOPPING   There's plenty to keep shoppers and browsers busy on Whidbey Island, especially in artsy Langley and historic Coupeville. The best art galleries are concentrated in Langley. **Museo** specializes in art glass made by local Whidbey Island artists. ~ 215 1st Street, Langley; 360-221-7737. The **Gaskill/Olson Gallery** showcases bronzes, paintings, sculpture and pottery. Closed Wednesday. ~ 302 1st Street, Langley; 360-221-2978. **Soleil** carries double-sided aluminum-alloy pieces by Arthur Court, silver, bone, pewter and glass jewelry, candles, stationery, photo albums and soaps. ~ 308 1st Street, Langley; 360-221-0383. The **Hellebore Glass Gallery** has fine handblown glass created on the premises. Closed Tuesday in winter. ~ 308 1st Street, Langley; 360-221-2067.

There's an array of charming shops in the revitalized waterfront district of Coupeville. You'll find wonderful antiques and collectibles at **Elk Horn Trading Company**. ~ 15 Front Street, Coupeville; 360-678-2250. Nautical gifts, artifacts and sportswear can be found at **Nautical 'N' Nice**. ~ 22 Front Street, Coupeville; 360-678-3565.

Just three miles south of Coupeville is **Salmagundi Farms**, which specializes in estate liquidations, tag sales and auctions. It's listed on the National Historic Register and filled with antiques and old farm equipment. Open weekends only. ~ 19162 South Route 20; 360-678-5888.

NIGHTLIFE   **Hong Kong Gardens** has a pool table and deejays every Saturday night. ~ 9324 State Route 525, Clinton; 360-341-2828.

For local color in a friendly tavern try the cozy pub in Captain Whidbey Inn's **Cove Restaurant**, where the walls are adorned with wine bottles and travel souvenirs from around the world. Closed Monday and Tuesday from Labor Day to Memorial Day. ~ 2072 West Captain Whidbey Inn Road, Coupeville; 360-678-9325.

Or drop by **Toby's Tavern**, where they filmed the bar scene from the movie *War of the Roses*. ~ 8 Northwest Front Street, Coupeville; 360-678-4222.

BEACHES & PARKS   **SOUTH WHIDBEY STATE PARK** 🏃 🏊 ⚓ There are 340 acres with 4500 feet of rocky shoreline to explore in this lovely state park. Hikers here will enjoy the one-and-a-quarter-mile loop trail through an old-growth stand of fir and cedar. Anglers seek silver salmon, and climbing is popular. Black-tailed deer, bald eagles and osprey are among the many creatures here. Only the hardy will venture into the cold waters of Admiralty Inlet for a dip. There are restrooms, showers, picnic tables, shelter and fireplaces. Day-use fee, $5. ~ Take Route 525 nine miles north of Clinton to Bush Point Road, which after six miles becomes Smuggler's Cove Road; 360-331-4559, fax 360-331-5202.

▲ There are 45 standard sites ($16 per night) and 9 RV hookup sites ($22 per night). Closed December through February. Reservations: 888-226-7688.

FORT CASEY STATE PARK 🏃 🚣 🚤 ⚓ History buffs and children will enjoy exploring the military fortification of this 137-acre park. While most of the big guns are gone, you'll still find panoramic views of the Olympic Mountains across the Strait of Juan de Fuca from the top of the concrete bunkers built into the escarpment. Wild roses and other flowers line the paths to the museum housed in pretty Admiralty Head Lighthouse and the beachside campground that overlooks the Keystone Harbor ferry terminal. Scuba enthusiasts swarm to the underwater trail through the park's marine wildlife sanctuary off Keystone Harbor, and anglers try for salmon and steelhead. Facilities include restrooms, showers, picnic tables, fireplaces and an underwater marine park. Day-use fee, $5. ~ At Coupeville turn south off Route 20 onto Engle Road and follow the Keystone Ferry signs to the park; phone/fax 360-678-4519.

▲ There are 35 standard sites ($16 per night) and 3 primitive sites ($10 per night).

FORT EBEY STATE PARK The massive guns are long gone from this coastal World War II fortification, but there are still bunker tunnels and pillboxes to be explored. The picturesque beach at Partridge Point is the hands-down favorite of the islanders; at low tide it's possible to walk the five-mile beach stretch to Fort Casey. Anglers cast a rod for bass and salmon on Lake Pondilla. There are restrooms, showers, picnic tables, fireplaces and nature trails. ~ From Route 20 turn west onto Libbey Road, then south onto Hill Valley Drive and follow the signs; 360-678-4636, fax 360-678-2982.

> In Deception Pass State Park, you'll find beaver dams and muskrats at Cranberry Lake's south shore.

▲ There are 44 standard sites ($16 per night), 4 RV hookup sites ($22 per night) and 3 primitive sites ($10 per night). The secluded campsites under a canopy of Douglas fir are much nicer than the crowded sites at nearby Fort Casey. Reservations: 888-226-7688.

JOSEPH WHIDBEY STATE PARK This small park has remained a secluded treasure, known only to locals, until recently signed on Route 20. Famous for its mile or so of sandy beach, it is just right for sunset strolls or picnics with views westward across Admiralty Inlet to the Olympic Mountains. There's no overnight camping. Closed October through March. ~ Swantown Road, three miles west of Oak Harbor; 360-678-4636, fax 360-678-2982.

OAK HARBOR CITY BEACH PARK A full-scale windmill and an A-6 Intruder, first used in Vietnam and donated by the Navy, are just two of the features of this day-use park on Oak Harbor Bay next to the sewage processing plant (not a deterrent, believe it or not). A sandy beach slopes down from the lighted walking path bordering expansive green fields suitable for flying kites or playing frisbee. Anglers will find salmon, bottomfish and bass. There are two wading pools in summer and a protected swimming area. There are bathhouses, picnic tables, ball fields, tennis and volleyball courts and a playground. ~ Located in downtown Oak Harbor off Pioneer Parkway, east of Route 20; watch for the windmill; 360-679-5551, fax 360-679-3902.

▲ An RV park with 56 full hookups and hot showers can be accessed at Beeksma Drive or City Beach Street. An overflow area has campsites with no hookups.

DECEPTION PASS STATE PARK

🛶 The most popular state park in Washington, it encompasses over 4800 acres laced with eight and a half miles of hiking trails through forested hills and wetland areas and along rocky headlands. There are several delightful sandy stretches for picnics or beachcombing. Breathtaking views from the 976-foot steel bridge spanning the pass attract photographers from around the world. There's swimming on Cranberry Lake in the summer and flyfishing for trout on Pass Lake. Facilities include restrooms, showers, bathhouses, picnic tables, kitchens, shelters, fireplaces, a concession stand, an environmental learning center and an underwater park. ~ Take the Mukilteo ferry to Whidbey Island and follow Route 525 and Route 20 to the park on the northern tip of the island; 360-675-2417, fax 360-675-8991.

▲ There are 178 standard sites ($15 per night), 83 RV hookup sites ($22 per night) and 5 primitive sites ($10 per night). Reservations: 888-226-7688.

Fidalgo Island

A two-hour drive northwest of Seattle, Anacortes on Fidalgo Island is a good place to enjoy folk art, ride a charming excursion train and see impressive murals. Quiet inns and waterfront restaurants make this town a pleasant retreat.

But Anacortes is only the beginning of adventures on this charming island. Often called the first of the San Juans, Fidalgo is actually linked to the mainland by the Route 20 bridge over Swinomish Channel in the Skagit Valley, and to Whidbey Island by another bridge. Access is easy. Nevertheless, you can still find quiet beaches and parks to explore. Lonely trails wind through an enormous forest reserve to superb viewpoints. A mini "Lake District" clusters more than half a dozen splendid lakes. And a marvelous resort complex—Scimitar Ridge Ranch—combines a working Northwest horse ranch and a deluxe campground that includes covered wagons outfitted for camping.

Because of its ferry terminal, **Anacortes** is known as "the gateway to the San Juans," but don't just zip on through because there's plenty to see and do here. One of the best ways to get acquainted with the city and its history is to make a walking tour of downtown to view the 40 life-size murals attached to many of the historical buildings. As part of the **Anacortes Mural Project**, these murals are reproductions of early-20th-century photographs depicting everyday scenes and early pioneers of the town. A tour map of the murals is available from the **Anacortes Chamber of Commerce**. ~ 819 Commercial Avenue, Anacortes; 360-293-3832; www.anacortes.org, e-mail anacortes@sos.net.

SIGHTS

In front of the Anacortes History Museum there's a highly amusing (but non-functional) drinking fountain with varying levels suited for dogs, cats, horses and humans, which was donated to the city by the Women's Temperance Union.

Another reminder of earlier days is the **W. T. Preston**, a dry-docked sternwheeler that once plied the waters of the Sound breaking up log jams. Closed weekdays April, May and September, and from October through March. ~ 7th Street and R Avenue, Anacortes; 360-293-1916; www.anacorteshistorymuseum.org.

At the **Anacortes Museum**, you'll find an entertaining collection of memorabilia from Anacortes, Fidalgo and Guemes islands. Closed Tuesday and Wednesday. ~ 1305 8th Street, Anacortes; 360-293-1915, fax 360-293-1929; www.anacorteshistorymuseum.org.

The **Anacortes Community Forest Lands** is a 2200-acre treasure of fishing and swimming lakes, wildlife wetlands, and tall conifers climbing the slopes of 1270-foot Mt. Erie, about five miles south of downtown Anacortes. Some 20 miles of foot trails offer days of wandering. For maps and information, stop at the Anacortes Chamber of Commerce. ~ 819 Commercial Avenue, Anacortes; 360-293-3832; www.anacortes.org, e-mail anacortes@sos.net.

You can also simply drive to the top of Mt. Erie and enjoy a series of vista points carved into its rocky summit that look out in all directions of the compass from the Cascades to the Olympics, across the San Juans, over Skagit Bay to Whidbey and all the way to Mt. Rainier.

Within the park and all around it are a handful of lakes—Heart, Erie, Campbell, Whistle, Cranberry, Pass. You can swing past Campbell Lake and Pass Lake (good fishing) on Route 20 between Anacortes and Deception Pass. And you can visit Heart and Erie (picnicking, fishing) from Mt. Erie Road leading into the park. Whistle and Cranberry (good fishing) are reached by foot trail.

LODGING
At the **Holiday Motel** one of the only motels that keeps its prices low even during high season, you get what you pay for. Aging rooms are very basic but tidy, with nicked furnishings in both the cramped bedroom and separate sitting room. ~ 2903 Commercial Avenue, Anacortes; 360-293-6511. BUDGET.

The **Anaco Bay Inn** is a step up, with 18 spacious, well-appointed rooms, all featuring a cozy fireplace. Some rooms have kitchens while others offer jetted tubs—the Honeymoon Suite, of course, has both. Four two-bedroom suites are also available. A public jacuzzi, a library and laundry facilities round out the amenities. An expanded continental breakfast is included. ~ 916 33rd Street, Anacortes; 360-299-3320, 877-299-3320, fax 360-299-3336; www.anacobayinn.com, e-mail anacobay@fidalgo.net. MODERATE.

In the late 1800s, the bustling city of Anacortes was also referred to as the "Magic City," "Liverpool of the West" and "New York of the West."

At the **Nantucket Inn**, the proprietress was welcoming weary travelers into her home long before bed and breakfasts came into fashion. Each of the comfortable guest rooms is furnished in lovingly polished family antiques and cozy quilts; all five have private baths. There is even a spa. ~ 3402 Commercial Avenue, Anacortes; 360-293-6007, 888-293-6007, fax 360-299-4339; www.whidbey.com/nantucket, e-mail nantucketinnnw@msn.com. MODERATE TO DELUXE.

DINING
The **Deception Cafe & Grill** serves traditional hand-breaded oysters and prawns, grilled burgers and mouth-watering pies. Look for this unpretentious roadside establishment on the hill four miles north of Deception Pass. Closed Monday and Tuesday. ~ 1541 Route 20, Anacortes; 360-293-9250. BUDGET TO MODERATE.

Potted plants, taped classical music and tablecloths soften the rough edges of **Charlie's**, a hash house overlooking the ferry terminal and water. Captive diners, here during the long wait for the ferry, choose from soups, salads, sandwiches and seafood at lunch and pasta, steak and seafood for dinner. ~ 5407 Ferry Terminal Road, Anacortes; 360-293-7377, fax 360-293-6124. MODERATE TO DELUXE.

At the fascinating and fun **Bunnies by the Bay** you can tour the workshop where they create designer stuffed animals (not taxidermy) to complement any decor scheme. ~ 3115 V Place, Anacortes; 360-293-8037. The same business also has a retail outlet store at 2320 Commercial Avenue as well as one in La Conner. **SHOPPING**

Most of the great shops on Fidalgo Island are scattered along Anacortes' Commercial Avenue. **Left Bank Antiques,** housed in two floors of a renovated church, absolutely bulges with American and European antiques and architectural items. ~ 1904 Commercial Avenue, Anacortes; 360-293-3022.

The historic **Marine Supply and Hardware** is packed to the rafters with nautical antiques and memorabilia. Closed Sunday. ~ 202 Commercial Avenue, Anacortes; 360-293-3014. ◄ *HIDDEN*

Resist the temptation to buy smoked salmon to take home until you visit **SeaBear Smokehouse**, which has been producing authentic smoked salmons since 1957. Not only does the smokehouse sell smoked salmon, smokehouse chili and smoked salmon chowder, it also offers tours Tuesday through Saturday. Pose with a salmon, learn to fillet, or just taste the goods. ~ 605 30th Street, Anacortes. Take 22nd Street east toward the Anacortes Marina, turn right onto T Avenue and you'll find the warehouse in an industrial complex a block down on the right; 360-293-4661; www.seabear.com.

▼▼▼▼▼▼▼▼▼▼▼▼▼▼
Lopez & Shaw Islands

Life on pastoral Lopez and Shaw islands is slow and amiable; residents wave to everyone and are truly disappointed if you don't wave back. Lopez didn't earn its nickname as the "Friendly Island" for nothing. Even better, these two islands remain much less developed than San Juan and Orcas islands.

The history of Lopez Island is well mapped out at the **Lopez Historical Museum** with its exhibit of pioneer farming and fishing implements, stone, bone and antler artifacts and fairly large maritime collection. While you're here, pick up a historical landmark tour guide to the many fine examples of Early American and **SIGHTS**

American Indian architecture scattered around the island. Closed October through April. ~ 28 Washburn Place, Lopez Village; 360-468-2049.

Stroll out to **Agate Beach Park** on MacKaye Harbor Road to watch the sunset. Another good sunset view spot is **Shark Reef Park** on Shark Reef Road, where you might see some harbor seals, heron and, if you're lucky, a whale or two.

Shaw Island is one of only four of the San Juan Islands that can be reached by ferry, but most visitors to the San Juans miss it. You need to stay on the ferry from Anacortes and get off at Shaw, one stop beyond Lopez Island. Those who do make the trip are in for a treat. Stop by the general store near the ferry landing for picnic supplies before heading out to **South Beach County Park** on Squaw Bay Road, two miles to the south.

Both the general store and ferry landing on Shaw Island are operated by Franciscan nuns.

Afterward, continue east along Squaw Bay Road, turn north on Hoffman Cove Road and make your way to the picturesque little red schoolhouse. Park by the school and cross the street to see the **Shaw Island Historical Museum,** a tiny log cabin housing a hodgepodge of pioneer memorabilia. Open limited hours on Tuesday, Thursday and Saturday. ~ Schoolhouse Corner; 360-468-4068.

LODGING

The **Lopez Islander,** once a dog-eared motel, has turned upscale. All of the 28 rooms have been refurbished and two suites have been added (moderate to deluxe). The marina has been upgraded (new floats and piers, a seaplane dock). An ambitious outings program for guests includes opportunities to bike, kayak and fish. ~ 2864 Fisherman Bay Road, Lopez Village; 360-468-2233, 800-736-3434, fax 360-468-3382; www.lopezislander.com. MODERATE TO DELUXE.

Edenwild, a welcome addition to the scant list of lodgings on the island, is a two-story Victorian. The eight guest rooms are pretty, with blond-wood floors, claw-foot tubs and antique furnishings; three rooms have romantic fireplaces, one is handicapped accessible and four have views of Fisherman's Bay or San Juan Channel. Included in the room rates is breakfast, served in the sunny dining nook or on the delightful garden terrace. Apéritifs and truffles are served in the rooms. ~ 132 Lopez Road, Lopez Village; 360-468-3238, 800-606-0662, fax 360-468-

4080; www.edenwildinn.com, e-mail edenwild@rockisland.com.
DELUXE TO ULTRA-DELUXE.

The best bet on Lopez Island is the **Inn at Swifts Bay**, a de- ◄ *HIDDEN*
lightful bed and breakfast in an elegant Tudor home. Posh best
describes the interior, with a comfortable mix of modern, Williams
Sonoma–style furnishings and antique reproductions adorned in
crocheted antimacassars and needlepoint pillows. There are two
rooms sharing one bath, as well as three suites with private en-
trances and baths; each room has a gas-lit fireplace. A hot tub,
an exercise studio and a sauna are on the premises. The leisurely
gourmet breakfast is without a doubt the most delicious morning repast available in the islands. ~ Port Stanley Road; 360-
468-3636, 800-903-9536, fax 360-468-3637; www.swiftsbay.
com, e-mail inn@swiftsbay.com. MODERATE TO ULTRA-DELUXE.

The **Bay Cafe** has an imaginative menu featuring fresh North- **DINING**
west products. There are always daily specials to choose from,
and regular entrées include Creole prawns, spinach ravioli and
citrus soy–marinated chicken breast. Check out the surprising
garlic cheesecake. Reservations are essential, especially during
summer. Closed Tuesday in fall, and Monday through Wednesday in winter. ~ Lopez Village Road; 360-468-3700, fax 360-468-
4000; www.bay-cafe.com. MODERATE TO DELUXE.

Located next to the Lopez Village Market in a handsome
Cape Cod–style building with weathered shingles and a terrace
overlooking the water, the **Love Dog Cafe** uses fresh ingredients
to create an eclectic blend of world cuisine. The seasonal menu
changes regularly, offering anything from simple, juicy burgers to
pesto cappelini to Alaskan halibut. Breakfasts include many just-
baked goods. The casual, warm atmosphere draws a real local
crowd—hang out with a book or borrow a boardgame and enjoy
the easy rhythm of island life. ~ 360-468-2150. BUDGET TO DELUXE.

The **Lopez Islander Restaurant** is a true waterfront restaurant, looking west across Fisherman Bay to spectacular evening
sunsets. In summer, ask for a table on the outdoor dining patio.
Specialties of the house include an award-winning clam chowder
and a daily fresh sheet of local seafood—salmon and halibut, for
example. No lunch in winter. ~ 2864 Fisherman Bay Road, Lopez
Village; 360-468-2234, fax 360-468-3382; www.lopezislander.
com. BUDGET TO DELUXE.

SHOPPING   For the most part, shopping here is limited to establishments in Lopez Village. **Archipelago** sells cotton T-shirts and women's casual apparel. ~ 360-468-3222. **Islehaven Books and Borzoi** stocks an admirable selection of new books and regional music. ~ 360-468-2132. For fine art, visit **Chimera Gallery**, the cooperative showcase for prints, paintings, weaving, pottery, handblown glass and jewelry produced by local artists. ~ 360-468-3265.

BEACHES & PARKS   **SPENCER SPIT STATE PARK** 🚶 🚴 ⛴ 🎣 🏕 🛶 This long stretch of silky sand on Lopez Island encloses an intriguing saltwater lagoon. The mile-long beach invites clamming, crabbing, shrimping, bottom fishing, wading and swimming during warm summer months. Facilities include restrooms, beach firepits and picnic shelters. ~ Take the ferry from Anacortes to Lopez Island, then follow the five-mile route to the park on the eastern shore of the island; 360-468-2251, fax 360-468-3176.

▲ There are 37 standard sites ($16 per night) and 7 primitive sites ($10 per night). Closed November through February. Reservations: 888-226-7688.

▼▼▼▼▼▼▼▼▼▼▼
San Juan Island

San Juan Island, the namesake of the archipelago, is a popular resort destination centered around the town of Friday Harbor. This 20-mile-long island has a colorful past stemming from a boundary dispute between the United States and Great Britain. The tension over who was entitled to the islands was embodied in American and British farmers whose warring over, get this, a pig, nearly sent the two countries to the battlefield. When an American farmer shot a British homesteader's pig caught rooting in his garden, ill feelings quickly escalated. Fortunately, cooler heads prevailed so that what is now referred to as the "Pig War" of 1859 only resulted in one casualty: the pig.

SIGHTS   The history of this little-known war is chronicled through interpretive centers in the **San Juan Island National Historical Park**, which is divided into English Camp and American Camp. Located on West Valley Road at the north end of the island is **English Camp**, which features barracks, a formal garden, cemetery, guardhouse, hospital and commissary. **American Camp**, on Cattle Point Road at the south end of the island, is where the officers and laundress' quarters, and the Hudson Bay Company

SAN JUAN ISLAND SIGHTS

Farm Site remain. ~ 360-378-2240, fax 360-378-2615; www.
nps.gov/sajh.

San Juan Historical Museum is located on the 1891 James King
farmstead. The museum complex consists of the original farmhouse, milk house and carriage house, as well as the original
county jail. A variety of memorabilia is displayed throughout, including American Indian baskets and stone implements, an antique diving suit, period furniture and clothing. A great place to
learn about the region's maritime history, the museum also features
an excellent collection highlighting the region's proud past. Closed
Monday through Wednesday in summer; limited hours in winter,
so call ahead. ~ 405 Price Street, Friday Harbor; phone/fax 360-
378-3949; www.sjmuseum.org, e-mail curator@sjmuseum.org.

Oyster lovers and birdwatchers should make the trip down
the dusty road to **Westcott Bay Sea Farms**, where they'll find saltwater bins of live oysters and clams and an array of birds at-   ◄ HIDDEN

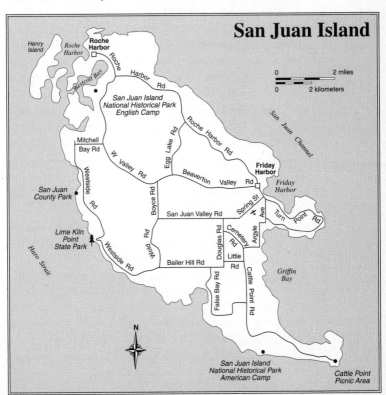

tracted to the oyster beds that stretch out into the bay. Closed Sunday in winter. ~ 904 Westcott Drive, Friday Harbor; 360-378-2489, fax 360-378-6388; www.westcottbay.com, e-mail sandy@westcottbay.com.

The lavender fields at **Pelindaba Farms** are awash with color in the summertime, the best time to visit this working organic farm. An old farmhouse serves as the general store here, offering all things lavender, from soaps and essential oils to honey, pepper and even vinegar. Docent-led tours allow you to view the farming and distilling operations. Closed January. ~ 33 Hawthorne Lane, Friday Harbor; 360-378-4248, fax 360-378-6606; www.pelindaba.com, e-mail admin@pelindaba.com.

Believe it or not, Friday Harbor was named after an early 1800s settler named Joe Friday.

The fir-paneled tasting room at **San Juan Vineyards** was once a one-room schoolhouse. And they still hand out lessons here—but they're a lot more fun than arithmetic. Instead, you'll learn all about the unusual varietals, like Madeleine Angevine and Siegerrebe, grown on this pretty semi-wooded patch of excellent grape-growing land. This is an up-and-coming island outpost of Washington's burgeoning wine industry. Closed in January and February except by appointment. ~ 3136 Roche Harbor Road, Friday Harbor; 360-378-9463, fax 360-378-2668; www.sanjuanvineyards.com, e-mail manager@sanjuanvineyards.com.

Afterglow Vista is the mausoleum of one of the region's wealthy families. The structure itself is fascinating; an open, Grecian-style columned complex surrounds six inscribed chairs, each containing the ashes of a family member, set before a round table of limestone. A seventh chair and column have obviously been removed, some say as part of Masonic ritual, others believe because a member of the family was disinherited or because the seventh member considered life unending. ~ Roche Harbor Resort, 4950 Reuben Tarte Memorial Drive, Roche Harbor.

LODGING
Conveniently located one and a half blocks from the ferry terminal, **Harrison House Suites** provides home-away-from-home comfort in five spacious suites. The suites, set in a turn-of-the-20th-century Craftsman and a 1930s cottage, sleep from two to fourteen guests and include private baths and kitchens. Most have sundecks and two have private outdoor hot tubs while one features a wood stove and upright piano. In addition, laundry facil-

ities are available. For those without the luxury of an in-room whirlpool, relax in the outdoor hot tub. Transportation from the ferry can be provided by request. Continental breakfast is complimentary; full gourmet breakfast costs extra. ~ 235 C Street, Friday Harbor; 360-378-3587, 800-407-7933, fax 360-378-2270; www.san-juan-lodging.com, e-mail hhsuites@rockisland.com. MODERATE TO ULTRA-DELUXE.

Named for its view, **Olympic Lights** is a remodeled 1895 farmhouse set on five grassy, breeze-tossed acres overlooking the Olympic Peninsula across the Strait of Juan de Fuca. Guests kick off their shoes before heading up to the cream-carpeted second floor with four comfortably appointed, pastel-shaded rooms; a fifth room on the ground floor is also available. You'll find no frilly, Victoriana clutter here, just a peaceful night snuggled under down comforters topped off by a farm-fresh breakfast. ~ 146 Starlight Way, Friday Harbor; 360-378-3186, 888-211-6195, fax 360-378-2097; www.olympiclights.com, e-mail olympiclights@ rockisland.com. DELUXE.

If you've dreamed of life on the water, you'll appreciate the **Wharfside Bed and Breakfast,** a 60-foot, two-masted sailboat with two guest rooms. The forward stateroom with a double bed and two bunks feels cozy, while the aft stateroom with queen bed is a little roomier. The rates include a three-course breakfast. Pets and children are welcome. ~ Port of Friday Harbor; 360-378-5661, 800-899-3030; www.fridayharborlodging.com, e-mail slow season@rockisland.com. DELUXE TO ULTRA-DELUXE.

Friday's is a renovated historic inn with 15 individually decorated rooms, all with down comforters and wildlife art. You can stay in the Orca Room and soak in the private jacuzzi. All this romance is conveniently located in the heart of Friday Harbor. Continental breakfast. ~ 35 1st Street, Friday Harbor; 360-378-5848, 800-352-2632, fax 360-378-2881; www.friday-harbor. com, e-mail stay@friday-harbor.com. DELUXE TO ULTRA-DELUXE.

Set in the rolling West Valley near English Camp National Park and surrounded by a working ranch, **States Inn** is a bit of Sleepy Hollow in San Juan. Each of the ten rooms has a decor that hints at its namesake state—tiny Rhode Island comes closest, with shells and brass dolphins on the fireplace mantle, various renditions of ships on the walls and copies of the New England publication *Yankee* to peruse. The friendly and informative innkeepers and the multicourse country breakfasts make up for the slight sulphur odor of the tap water. The inn is also disabled-accessible, hard to find in the islands. Full breakfast. ~ 2687 West Valley Road, Friday Harbor; 360-378-6240, 866-602-2737, fax 360-378-6241; www.statesinn.com, e-mail info@statesinn.com. MODERATE TO DELUXE.

Roche Harbor Resort has something for everyone. You can check in to the 1886 **Hotel de Haro**, where gingerbread trim, parlor beds, antiques and a roaring fireplace bring back memories of the good old days. In addition to this three-story, 20-room establishment, nine former workers' cottages have been converted into two-bedroom units, ideal for families. The cottages are convenient to the swimming pool. For contemporary lodging, choose one- to three-room harbor-view condominiums. ~ Roche Harbor Resort, 4950 Reuben Tarte Memorial Drive, Roche Harbor; 360-378-2155, 800-451-8910, fax 360-378-6809; www.rocheharbor.com, e-mail roche@rocheharbor.com. MODERATE TO ULTRA-DELUXE.

DINING

The Blue Dolphin is an unpretentious diner serving hearty portions of home-cooked breakfast favorites like biscuits and gravy, eggs Benedict, blueberry pancakes and chicken-fried steak. No dinner. ~ 185 1st Street, Friday Harbor; 360-378-6116. BUDGET.

Among the best restaurants on the island, the rustic look and rural setting of the **Duck Soup Inn** hardly hints at the creative, though somewhat limited, bill of fare. Several seafood and beef options are available, but why not try the inn's namesake—Southwest duck stew seasoned with chipotle chiles, lime and cilantro? For starters, there are appetizers such as Westcott Bay manila clams steamed in a vindaloo curry broth or prosciutto and pear bruschetta, as well as fine Northwestern wines. Dinner only. ~ 50 Duck Soup Lane, Friday Harbor; 360-378-4878; www.ducksoupinn.com. DELUXE.

SHOPPING

Most of the shops are located within blocks of Friday Harbor, giving you plenty to do while waiting for the ferry. Near Sunshine Alley, **Dolphin Art** sells original screenprint art on cotton sportswear. ~ 165 1st Street; 360-378-3531.

Art lovers visiting Friday Harbor will want to stop by several galleries. **Waterworks Gallery** features a collection of contemporary eclectic Northwest art in media such as glass, pottery, oil and

watercolor. ~ 315 Spring Street, Friday Harbor; 360-378-3060.
Garuda & I carries an amazing selection of ethnic arts, beads, crafts, musical instruments as well as jewelry from Indian, Asian and local artisans. ~ 60 1st Street, Friday Harbor; 360-378-3733.

On San Juan Island, **Herb's Tavern** is the local sidle-up-to-the-bar joint with pool tables. ~ 80 1st Street, Friday Harbor; 360-378-7076. You'll find pool tables, a dart board and several TVs at **Haley's Bait Shop**, a smoke-free sports bar and grill. ~ 175 Spring Street, Friday Harbor; 360-378-4434. The **Roche Harbor Resort Madrona Bar** has weekend dancing to live music in the summer. ~ 248 Reuben Memorial Drive, Roche Harbor; 360-378-2155.

NIGHTLIFE

SAN JUAN COUNTY PARK Orca whales frequently pass by the rocky shoreline of this 12-acre park on the western edge of San Juan Island. Because of its location on Smallpox Bay, the park is a haven for kayakers and scuba divers who enjoy the easy waters in the shallow bay or the more challenging shelf that drops steeply off about 80 feet out. Swimming is good in the shallow, protected bay; fishing is fair for bottomfish, rockfish, salmon and crab. There are restrooms, picnic tables and fire pits. ~ On Westside Road just north of Lime Kiln Point State Park; 360-378-8420, fax 360-378-6405.

BEACHES & PARKS

Lime Kiln Point State Park is named for an early lime kiln operation, with remnants of old structures still visible to the north of the lighthouse.

▲ There are 19 standard sites ($22 per night), two mooring buoys ($8 per night) and one premium site ($32 per night, nine-person minimum). Reservations: 360-378-1842.

LIME KILN POINT STATE PARK Situated on a rocky bluff overlooking Haro Strait, this is the prime whale-watching spot on San Juan Island. A footpath takes you to picturesque Lime Kiln Lighthouse, listed on the National Register of Historic Places. Restrooms, picnic tables and interpretive displays are found here. There is no drinking water for the public. ~ Off Westside Road on the western shore of San Juan Island; 360-378-2044.

CATTLE POINT PICNIC AREA Though it takes a precarious scramble down a rocky ledge to reach it and picnic tables on the bluff above lend little privacy, this gravelly half-moon is arguably the prettiest public beach on San Juan Island. Anglers will find bottomfish and salmon. Facilities include picnic tables, shelter, restrooms, interpretive signs and a nature trail. ~ Follow Cattle Point Road through American Camp and on to the southern tip of the island. ~ 360-856-3500, fax 360-856-2150.

FOURTH OF JULY BEACH This secluded, gravelly crescent is where the locals head when they're looking for privacy. There are often bald eagles nesting in the nearby trees, a poignant sign of this aptly named stretch. The shallow, little bay area extends out a long way and is suitable for wading on hot days. Anglers can try for bottomfish and salmon. There are pit toilets, picnic tables and a fenced grassy area off the parking lot suitable for frisbee. Large groups should call American Camp for a permit (360-378-2902). ~ Located on the northeastern edge of American Camp; 360-378-2240, fax 360-378-2615.

Orcas Island

Trendy, artsy-craftsy and lovely to look at, Orcas Island is a resort that caters to everyone from backpackers to the well-to-do. A nature sanctuary pocketed with charming towns, the island also boasts more sun than some of its neighbors.

SIGHTS

One of Orcas Island's leading landmarks is **Rosario Resort**. Even if you're not planning to stay here during your trip, make sure to visit the original mansion here for a fantastic evening show that includes music performed on a 1910 Steinway grand piano and an amazing pipe organ along with entertaining narration and slides of life on the island in the early 1900s. Call ahead for show schedule. ~ 1400 Rosario Road, Eastsound; 360-376-2222, fax 360-376-2289; www.rosarioresort.com.

HIDDEN ►

Of the many small historical museums in the San Juans, the **Orcas Island Historical Museum** is our favorite. Six interconnected log cabins of prominent early settlers house a fine assemblage of relics and antiques, American Indian art and local contemporary art that maps the history and growth of industry on the island. Closed Monday and from October through April. Admission. ~ North Beach Road, Eastsound; 360-376-4849; www.orcasisland. org/~history, e-mail orcasmuseum@rockisland.com.

HIDDEN ►

Madrona Point, a pretty madrone tree–dotted waterside park saved from condo development by the Lummi Indians and local residents, is a fine spot for a picnic. It's at the end of the un-

marked road just past Christina's Restaurant in Eastsound. No
dogs are allowed.

One of Orcas Island's best-kept secrets is Doug and Jeri Smart's **LODGING**
Little House on the Farm, a no-host home for rent that looks so
homey passersby just assume the Smarts live in it. The house ◄ *HIDDEN*
nicely accommodates four people who have the run of it, from
the two bedrooms with queen-size beds to the reading room, full
kitchen, stone fireplace in the living room and jacuzzi. Decorated
with Victorian country furnishings, the house sits on 27 acres of
fenced pastures and woodlands complete with grazing horses.
Carriages are on display in the yard. ~ 180 West Beach Road,
Eastsound; 360-376-5306, 877-376-9423; www.walkinghorse
farm.com, e-mail stay@walkinghorsefarm.com. ULTRA-DELUXE.

The **Outlook Inn** is right in Eastsound, overlooking the bay
and close to the town's many shops and restaurants. A classic
turn-of-the-20th-century maritime inn, it's been restored with
light pine and fir floors and wood furnishings helping bring in
the light off the harbor. In addition to the original inn, there are
16 contemporary suites. The inn's restaurant serves hearty, mar-
itime-style breakfasts, with salmon and oyster omelettes typical.
~ Main Street, Eastsound; 360-376-2200, 888-688-5665, fax 360-
376-2256; www.outlook-inn.com, e-mail info@outlook-inn.com.
MODERATE TO ULTRA-DELUXE.

It's not unusual to find semi-tame deer roaming around the
ample grounds of **Rosario Resort,** tucked away on Cascade Bay
on the east side of the horseshoe of Orcas Island. The motel-style

AUTHOR FAVORITE

A stay at **Turtleback Farm Inn** is like stepping into the much-loved story
The Wind in the Willows, surrounded as it is by acres of forest and farm tracts
full of animals as far as the eye can see. Rooms in this lovely, late-19th-cen-
tury farmhouse vary in size and setup, but all 11 rooms have a charming
mix of contemporary and antique furniture, cozy quilts and antique fixtures in private baths. Full breakfast. ~ 1981 Crow Valley Road, Eastsound; 360-376-4914, 800-376-4914, fax 360-376-5329; www.turtle
backinn.com, e-mail info@turtlebackinn.com. MODERATE TO ULTRA-
DELUXE.

rooms scattered along the waterfront or perched on the hillside overlooking the bay are spacious and comfortable, and some feature fireplaces, jacuzzis and private balconies. Three pools, a fitness room and sauna round out the amenities. ~ 1400 Rosario Road, Eastsound; 360-376-2222, 800-562-8820, fax 360-376-2289; www.rosariorockresorts.com. ULTRA-DELUXE.

Accommodations at the funky **Doe Bay Village Resort** include yurts and rustic cabins with 33 units total. There are shared central bathrooms, a community kitchen and a small seasonal café on the grounds of this large retreat along with a splendid three-tiered sauna and three mineral baths perched on a covered deck. Be aware of the strict seven-day, advance-notice cancellation policy. ~ Star Route 86, Olga; 360-376-2291, fax 360-376-5809; www.doebay.com. BUDGET TO MODERATE.

DINING

Pegged as "adventurous world cuisine," **The Sunflower Café** is a favorite among locals and tourists alike. Owners Chris and Julie Hogle showcase an eclectic menu that includes delicious soups, meat, seafood and vegetarian fare. They utilize only the freshest ingredients; much of the food is grown in their two organic gardens. The waitstaff is friendly and professional, and the presentation is first class with fine china, silver and linen napkins. The menu changes frequently depending on seasonal availability. Call ahead for hours and reservations. ~ Main Street (in the Outlook Inn), Eastsound; 360-376-2335; www.thesunflower cafe.com. DELUXE.

Bilbo's Festivo specializes in Tex-Mex fare. A margarita or cerveza on the tiled garden patio surrounded by adobe walls is a great way to relax. Bilbo's serves dinner only, but opens **La Taqueria,** a lunch outlet in the courtyard, during the summer months.

MUSIC WITH A VIEW

If you're around Orcas at the end of August, don't miss the annual **Orcas Island Chamber Music Festival**. Created by a group of Seattle-based professional musicians, this event features both classical and experimental pieces performed by internationally renowned musicians. This very brief concert series always sells out, so call ahead for tickets. ~ P.O. Box 646, Eastsound, WA 98225; 360-376-6636; www.oicmf.org.

~ North Beach Road, Eastsound; 360-376-4728, fax 360-376-3692. BUDGET TO MODERATE.

The **Orchard House Restaurant** on the grounds of the Deer Harbor Inn, tucked away in an expanse of orchard grove peering out over Deer Harbor and the Olympic Range, is where locals come for that special night out. The daily menu is chalked on the board; rock cod, coho salmon and choice steaks are prime picks. For diners on the deck, this is a great spot to watch the sunset. Dinner only; reservations recommended. ~ 33 Inn Lane, Deer Harbor; 360-376-4110, fax 360-376-2237; www.deerharborinn.com, e-mail stay@deerharborinn.com. MODERATE TO DELUXE.

You'll find several interesting shops in Eastsound. **Darvill's Rare Print Shop** carries antique maps, etchings and fine prints and has a connected bookstore. ~ 296 Main Street, Eastsound; 360-376-2351.   **SHOPPING**

An 1866 cabin houses **Crow Valley Pottery & Gallery**, a long-established studio that got its start making ceramic wind bells inspired by Northwest tribal arts. It has expanded to represent numerous island artists and craftspeople working in art glass, metal sculpture, watercolors, jewelry, pastels and more. ~ 2274 Orcas Road, Eastsound; 360-376-4260; www.crowvalleypottery.com.

Don't spend all your time and money in Eastsound because you won't want to miss **Orcas Island Pottery**, the oldest existing ◀ *HIDDEN* craft studio on Orcas. You can watch potters at work through the windows of the studio. ~ 338 Old Pottery Road, off West Beach Road, Eastsound; 360-376-2813.

At a bend in Horseshoe Highway as you reach Olga is **Orcas**   ◀ *HIDDEN* **Island Artworks**, the cooperative art gallery showcasing fine arts, handicrafts and furniture all produced by local hands. Closed January and February. ~ 360-376-4408.

Moran Lounge is the place to go for live entertainment on the weekends and great sunsets. ~ Rosario Resort, 1400 Rosario Road, Eastsound; 360-376-2222. For convivial pub action, step into the **Lower Tavern** and amuse yourself with darts and pool. Beer and wine only. ~ Prune Alley and Main Street, Eastsound; 360-376-4848.   **NIGHTLIFE**

MORAN STATE PARK 🚶 🚴 🎣 🏕️ 🏊 Washington's fifth-largest park consists of 5000 verdant acres dotted with five   **BEACHES & PARKS**

freshwater lakes and crowned by sweeping Mt. Constitution. The view from the stone tower at the peak of Mt. Constitution takes in the San Juans, Mt. Baker and Vancouver, B.C. There are miles of forest trails connecting the four mountain lakes, numerous waterfalls and five campgrounds. There is fishing for rainbow, cutthroat and kokanee trout on several lakes, with boat rentals available. Facilities include restrooms, showers, kitchen shelters and picnic tables. ~ Located near Eastsound, accessible by state ferry from Anacortes; 360-376-2326, fax 360-376-2360.

▲ There are 151 standard sites ($16 per night) and 15 primitive sites ($10 per night). Reservations: 888-226-7688.

HIDDEN ►   **OBSTRUCTION PASS STATE PARK** 🏃 ⛵ 🚣 This primitive, heavily forested locale on the southeastern tip of Orcas Island is tricky to get to, so the crowds are kept to a minimum, a reward for those who care to search it out. The area has a hiking trail, several free campsites and a beach with cold water for brave swimmers. Anglers will find bottomfish and rockfish. There are vault toilets, picnic tables, three mooring buoys and trails. ~ From the town of Olga follow Doe Bay Road east, turn right on Obstruction Pass Road and keep right until you hit the parking area. From there it's a half-mile hike to the campground; 360-376-2326, fax 360-376-2360.

▲ There are nine free primitive sites; hike-in only.

OTHER PARKS   Many of the smaller islands are preserved as state parks including **Doe, Jones, Clark, Sucia, Stuart, Posey, Blind, James, Matia, Patos** and **Turn.** They are accessible by boat only and in most cases have a few primitive campsites, nature trails, a dock or mooring buoys off secluded beaches, but no water (except Jones, Stuart and Sucia, in season) or facilities except for composting toilets. Costs are $5 for mooring buoys, $5 for camping, $8 for boats under 26 feet and $11 for boats over 26 feet to dock overnight. Washington watertrail sites cost $7 per night and must be reached by a human-powered beachable watercraft.

▼▼▼▼▼▼▼▼▼▼▼▼▼▼
Outdoor Adventures

BOATING

Spending time on the water is a part of daily life here, and certainly something that visitors should not miss. In fact, many of the 100-plus islands of the San Juans are accessible only by boat. Rental options are numerous.

In the islands, try **North Isle Sailing**, which offers sea cruises around Whidbey, the San Juans and Canada. Trips last from a half day to a week. ~ 1856 North Swantown Road, Oak Harbor; 360-675-8360. **Penmare Marine Co.** rents 15- to 60-foot yachts. ~ 2011 Skyline Way, Anacortes; 360-293-4839.

Skipper Ward Fay of **Northwest Classic Day Sails** offers sunset and day sails in a classic 1940s Blanchard Sloop "Aura" from Deer Harbor in Orcas Island Wednesday through Sunday. Excursions range from three to eight hours. Personalized as well as dinner trips to Friday Harbor are available. ~ 360-376-5581 from May 1st through September 30th; www.classicdaysails.com, e-mail wardfay@rockisland.com.

SPORT-FISHING

Catching some salmon is the hoped-for reward when you head out on a fishing charter through Northern Puget Sound and the San Juan Islands. As a bonus, you're also likely to encounter seals, eagles and whales as you sail past islands wooded with red-bark madrone trees.

In winter, of course, the temperature on the water can get chilly and the water a bit choppy. All the charter fishing services listed here provide boats with heated, enclosed cabins to keep you comfortable. Charter fees include bait and tackle, but do not include a fishing license or food and drink.

In Everett, Gary Krein is president of the Charter Boat Association of Puget Sound and owner of **All Star Charters**. He operates a 28-foot fiberglass-bottom boat that can carry up to six peo-

SOUND BITE

With thousands of miles of tidal coastline, Puget Sound and the San Juan Islands once boasted some of the best sportfishing opportunities in North America. These days, the fish—especially salmon—are in great peril from various abuses. For the present, there are still five varieties of Pacific salmon (chinook, coho, chum, pink and sockeye), and anglers can also try for cod, flounder, halibut, ling, rockfish, sea perch, squid and sturgeon. Scuba divers often concentrate their efforts on harvesting abalone, crab, octopus, shrimp and squid, while shellfishers are rewarded with butter and razor clams. Clamming and fishing licenses are required and are available in sporting goods stores.

ple each, and encourages "angler participation" on his full-day trips (two daily in summer, one in winter). The boat comes fully equipped with electronic fishfinding equipment that seeks out the salmon and bottomfish. Bait and tackle are included. ~ Port of Everett; 425-252-4188, 800-214-1595; www.allstarfishing.com.

In 1996, San Juan County outlawed jet skis. Locals complained that the serenity of the San Juans was disrupted by the incessant buzzing of cityfolk zipping around on their waterfront.

Mike Dunnigan is the skipper of **Sea Hawk Salmon Charters**. He runs year-round, exclusive eight-hour charters for up to four people to fish for salmon, bottomfish and halibut. Bait and tackle are included. ~ Capsante Marina, Anacortes; 360-424-1350.

SAN JUAN ISLANDS Trophy Charters will pick anglers up from the other islands before heading out on a four- to six-hour fishing trip seeking salmon and bottomfish in a 29-foot bayliner that holds six. Captain Monty runs a fast boat (up to 30 mph), so travel time is reduced. ~ Friday Harbor; 360-378-2110.

KAYAKING   For nonadventurers who want an outdoor experience that's a lot of fun but not extremely challenging, a guided water excursion in a sea kayak may be just the thing. No previous kayaking experience is necessary to join one of these groups for a paddling tour of sea caves around Deception Pass State Park on Whidbey Island; or off San Juan Island, where you are likely to see whales, seals and other marine wildlife. Unless noted, the operators listed here generally offer a regular schedule of excursions from April–May to September–October. Cost for a sea kayak excursion ranges from $30 to $60. Most operators can also arrange overnight or longer trips.

LOPEZ ISLAND Lopez Kayaks offers morning and afternoon sea-kayaking tours in double kayaks for eight people to Mac-Kaye Harbor, which is also popular with seals. If you have experience, you can also rent a kayak for your own use without joining a tour or buy your own vessel, accessories or related books. ~ 2845 Fisherman Bay Road; 360-468-2847.

SAN JUAN ISLAND Since the waters just off the west side of San Juan Island are in the main whale-migration corridor, your chances of seeing whales are good. If not, there's plenty of other wildlife to view, notably seals and bald eagles. (The highest density of bald-eagle nestings in the lower 48 states is in the San Juan Islands.)

There are also kelp forests, jutting cliffs, sea caves and rocky out-croppings. A biologist or scientist accompanies the day excursions led by **Sea Quest Kayak Expeditions** for groups of four to twelve. There are also camping trips lasting from two to five days that go through primary orca viewing areas. ~ Friday Harbor; 360-378-5767. **Crystal Seas Kayaking** escorts up to eight people on morning or afternoon sunset excursions. You can also arrange custom camping trips from two to six days. Paddlers will see eagles, seals and whales. ~ Friday Harbor; 360-378-7899.

ORCAS ISLAND **Osprey Tours** brings a different, historical twist to half-day and full-day sea-kayaking tours. Following the Alaskan Eskimo tradition, owner Randy Monge makes these wood-frame kayaks with bifurcated (T-shaped) bows, which, he says, split the water and provide lift going through waves. Monge also gives each kayaker an Aleutian whale-hunter's hat, shaped like a conical visor that resembles a bird's beak. The hats helped disguise Aleutian hunters and, acting like a hearing aid, collected sound. ~ West Beach; 360-376-3677. For lessons or tours contact **Shearwater Sea Kayak Tours**, which offers half- and full-day tours. Custom overnight trips can also be arranged. Shearwater has also sold accessories and clothing since 1982, making it the oldest outfitter on the islands. ~ P.O. Box 787, Eastsound, WA 98245; 360-376-4699.

The protected waters of Puget Sound hold untold treasures for the diver: craggy rock walls, ledges and caves of this sunken mountain range and enormous forests of bull kelp provide homes for a multitude of marine life. Giant Pacific octopus thrive in these waters, as do sea anemones and hundreds of species of fish.

SCUBA DIVING

"Within 15 minutes of Friday Harbor on San Juan Island, there are hundreds of great dive spots," says one local diver who grew up in the area. The west side of San Juan Island and the south side of Lopez Island are particular favorites, largely because the absence of silt means the water is cleaner and therefore clearer. There are also lots of ledges along these rocky coasts, which abound with exceptional wall-dive spots. Acres of bull kelp forests, with their teeming marine life, are also popular dive spots. But just as these waters hold great beauty, they can also be treacherous with tremendous tidal changes and strong currents.

Text continued on page 274.

Whale Watching in the San Juan Islands

Here in the waters of the San Juan archipelago there are three resident pods, or extended families, of *Orcinus Orca*, otherwise known as "killer" whales. Because they are so frequently and easily spotted in the protected waters, these gentle black and white giants have been carefully studied by scientists since 1976.

Their research is documented at the **Whale Museum**, where you can learn more about whales. A photo collection with names and pod numbers will help you identify some of the 80 or so resident orcas, distinguished by their grayish saddle patches and nicks, scars or tears in the dorsal fins. Displays and videos explain the difference between breaching, spyhopping, tail-lobbing and other typical orca behavior and the many vocalization patterns that scientists can only guess at the significance. Call ahead for winter hours. Admission. ~ 62 1st Street North, Friday Harbor; 360-378-4710, 800-946-7227, fax 360-378-5790; www.whalemuseum.org.

The Whale Museum also has an orca adoption program set up to help fund the ongoing research and all sorts of whale-related educational material, art and souvenirs available in their gift shop. They operate a 24-hour hotline (Washington only, 800-562-8832) for whale sightings and marine mammal strandings as well.

From May to September you can often see the whales from shore when they range closest to the islands to feed on migrating salmon. The best shoreline viewing spots are **Lime Kiln Point** on San Juan Island or **Shark Reef Park** on Lopez Island. Sightings drop dramatically in the winter as the pods disperse from the core area in search of prey.

If you want to get a closer look, put on your parka and sunglasses, grab your binoculars and camera and climb aboard one of the

wildlife cruises that ply the waters between the islands. Even if you don't see any orca during the trip, you will almost certainly spot other interesting forms of wildlife such as sleek, gray minke whales, Dall's porpoises (which look like miniature orca), splotchy brown harbor seals, bald eagles, great blue heron, cormorants or tufted puffin.

Mosquito Fleet Enterprises offers full-day whale-watching tours on cruisers that hold from 68 to 149 people. The boats leave the Everett Marina from April to October. ~ 1724 West Marine View Drive, Everett; 425-252-6800.

Deer Harbor Charters offers four-hour whale-watching tours from April to October on a 36-foot boat that carries 20 people from Deer Harbor Resort or on a 47-foot boat that carries 30 people from Rosario Resort. Both boats have a naturalist guide. ~ P.O. Box 303, Deer Harbor, WA 98243; 360-376-5989, 800-544-5758; www.deerharborcharters.com.

Western Prince Cruises has similar naturalist-accompanied wildlife tours on a half-day basis. Boats include a 46-footer that holds 30 people and a 22-footer that holds six people. ~ Friday Harbor; 360-378-5315, 800-757-6722; www.orcawhalewatch.com. **Viking Cruises** offer three-hour nature tours to Deception Pass from La Conner. Their three-day excursion to Rosario Resort in Eastsound combines a crabfeast and pipe-organ concert with whale-watching trips. The captain claims an 80 percent success rate for spotting whales. ~ 109 North 1st Street, La Conner; 360-466-2639, 888-207-2333; www.vikingcruises.com. You can also try **San Juan Boat Tours Inc.** for a three-hour whale-sighting excursion aboard a 100-foot tour vessel. ~ Friday Harbor; 360-378-3499, 800-232-6722; www.whaletour.com.

Happy spotting!

WHIDBEY ISLAND   Besides air fills, diving lessons and rental of wetsuits and other equipment, **Whidbey Island Dive Center** offers half- to full-day dive charters using two tanks per dive. One popular spot for experienced divers is under the bridge at Deception Pass State Park, where currents reach seven knots—"a diving rush." For the less experienced, the charter to the diving sanctuary off Keystone Jetty is an excellent spot to view marine life. The Dive Center also teaches all types of certification. ~ 1020 Northeast 7th Avenue #1, Oak Harbor; 360-675-1112; www. whidbeydive.com.

SAN JUAN ISLAND   **Island Dive & Water Sports** is a full-service dive shop, retail and rental. It specializes in daily half-day charters, guaranteeing you at least two dives using one tank per dive, in different locations during the trip. One might be a vertical wall dive, another may be in a grotto filled with marine life. Its vessels can accommodate up to 18 divers. Open-water certification classes are also available. ~ 2-A Spring Street Landing, Friday Harbor; 360-378-2772, 800-303-8386; www.dive sanjuan.com. **Underwater Sports Inc.** offers full-day chartered trips to the islands, night dives, rentals, open-water certification, classes and air fills. ~ 205 East Casino Road, Everett; 425-355-3338; www.underwatersports.com.

Useless Bay is so named because it's too shallow to provide anchorage for any but small boats.

SHELL-FISHING   Many of the public parks and tidelands in north Puget Sound offer clamming opportunities in season. Licenses are necessary, and it's imperative to check first with the **Red Tide Hotline**. Shellfish poisoning can be deadly. ~ 800-562-5632.

HIDDEN ►   One of the best beaches is on Whidbey Island. **Double Bluff State Tidelands** is a long beach stretch looking south across Useless Bay. This is a fine place for a walk; the beach stretches two miles to the headland, and the southern exposure means it's warm on almost any sunny day.

It's also a top-notch spot during low tides to dig for steamer clams and for the native Washington butter clam, which is excellent for steaming or chowder. Clams and mussels are available year-round, but there are no oysters. ~ At the end of Double Bluff Road, turn west off State Route 525 about ten miles west of Clinton, a mile north of the Langley turnoff.

Saddle up for a gentle, leisurely ride around an 85-acre ranch or take in the scenic beauty of the San Juan Islands.

WHIDBEY ISLAND Put on jeans and a pair of sturdy leather shoes (leave your Birkenstocks and sneakers at home) for a guided trail ride through the hilly, wooded **Madrona Ridge Ranch**. Please call ahead (evenings are best) to arrange a one-and-a-half-hour ride; groups are limited to up to people at a time. Riding lessons are available for all ages, but the trail rides are for teens and adults only. Nonriders can enjoy nature walks and the nearby beach. ~ Madrona Way, Coupeville; 360-678-4124.

SAN JUAN ISLAND On the western side of San Juan Island, **Saddle Up Trailriding** offers hour-long horseback rides three times daily, June through September, around a 62-acre ranch. Call ahead to schedule rides in May and October. ~ 2687 West Valley Road, Friday Harbor; 360-378-4243; www.saddleuptrail riding.com.

Award-winning design, lush scenery and the Northwest's only par-5 to an island green are among the distinctions of golf courses in this part of the state.

A good choice is the **Walter E. Hall Memorial Golf Course,** an 18-hole public facility with well-kept grounds, a restaurant and cart rentals. ~ 1226 West Casino Road, Everett; 425-353-4653.

FIDALGO ISLAND **Similk Beach Golf Course** is a public 18-hole facility that rents carts. ~ 1250 Christiansen Road, Anacortes; 360-293-3444.

LOPEZ ISLAND The nine-hole **Lopez Island Golf Course** is a private, flat course. ~ Airport Road, Lopez Island; 360-468-2679.

SAN JUAN ISLAND It's only nine holes, but the **San Juan Golf and Country Club** "plays like 18." Private, but open to the public, the course is set on a wooded, rolling tract next to Griffin Bay. Cart rentals are available. ~ 806 Golf Course Road, Friday Harbor; 360-378-2254.

ORCAS ISLAND For a distinctive, lesser-known golf experience, try the **Orcas Island Golf Club,** a quaint, challenging 9-hole public course that plays like an 18-hole course. The regular nine alternates tees on the back nine to make play a little more interesting. The pro shop and clubhouse are like a touch of Scotland, and wildlife abounds. ~ 2171 Orcas Road, Eastsound; 360-376-4400.

◄ HIDDEN

TENNIS No need to leave your racquet at home with so many public courts to take advantage of. In Everett, you'll find six first-come, first-served lighted courts at **Clark Park**. ~ 2400 Lombard Street.

On Whidbey Island, you can use the four lighted courts at **Coupeville High School** at South Main Street or the four clay courts at **Oak Harbor City Park** at 1501 City Beach Street. On Fidalgo Island, try the six courts at **Anacortes High School facility**. ~ 20th Street and J Avenue. Though **Lopez High School** is your only option on Lopez Island, the school has two hardtop courts and is building four more. ~ Center Road. On San Juan, try the four courts at the **Friday Harbor High School** at Guard Street or head out to the **Roche Harbor Resort** at Roche Harbor Road.

BIKING If you plan to bike on the San Juan Islands, it's important to remember that the islands' narrow roads don't have special lanes or other provisions for cyclists. Lopez Island is probably the best bet for the occasional bicyclist: you'll be able to bike long, flat country roads, rather than the steeper, twisting roads of some of the other islands. You can rent a bike on the island or in Anacortes before ferrying over for the day.

The hardy cyclist might prefer a 20-mile hilly and winding route around San Juan Island or 16 miles of steep, twisting roads beginning at the ferry landing on Orcas Island.

For bike trails here and in other parts of the state, contact the **Washington Department of Transportation** to request a route map and informative brochure, or call 360-705-7277 for the Bicycle Hotline. ~ P.O. Box 47393, Olympia, WA 98504.

NORTHERN PUGET SOUND Some of the best country bike routes in the state can be found in the **Skagit Valley**. Use the backroads east, northeast and southeast of La Conner to fashion loop tours from a few miles to over 20.

The **Waterfront Loop** in Everett takes you past the majestic old homes of early lumber barons and through the Everett Marina Village.

WHIDBEY ISLAND Those looking for a long-distance ride will enjoy the 50-mile Island County Tour, which begins at Columbia Beach on Whidbey Island and continues on to Deception Pass at the northern tip of the island. This trip is moderately strenuous, with high traffic on a good portion of the ride, but the spectacular views of the Strait of Juan de Fuca and the Saratoga Passage are reward enough.

SAN JUAN ISLAND The slightly difficult, 30-mile **San Juan Island Loop** leads along hilly, winding roads through Friday Harbor, Roche Harbor, San Juan Island National Historical Park and along the San Juan Channel.

ORCAS ISLAND The **Horseshoe Route** is by far the most difficult island bike route, with 16 miles of steep, twisting roads beginning at the ferry landing in Orcas, continuing through Eastsound, then on to Olga. An alternative route for the very hardy starts in Olga, passes through Moran State Park and ends in Doe Bay, with a possible challenging 3.5-mile sidetrip up and back down Mt. Constitution.

Bike Rentals For mountain-bike sales and repairs in the Northern Puget Sound region, contact **The Bicycle Center**. ~ 4718 Evergreen Way, Everett; 425-252-1441.

Located just off Route 20, the main drag into Anacortes, the **Skagit Cycle Center** rents bikes (and helmets) by the hour, day, week or month. The center's location is ideal for cyclists heading to the San Juans ferry or just pedaling around nearby Skagit Valley. ~ 8608 South March's Point Road, Anacortes; 360-588-8776.

Most people coming to Lopez Island who want to bicycle bring their own bikes. Otherwise, head for **Lopez Bicycle Works**, which rents, repairs and sells mountain bikes, touring bikes and hybrids and will let you drop off the bike at the ferry landing when you leave for the day. ~ Fisherman's Bay Road; 360-468-2847.

For bike rentals on San Juan Island, contact **Island Bicycles**, which offers mountain bikes, hybrids and road bikes, as well as bike sales, repairs and friendly advice. ~ 380 Argyle Avenue, Friday Harbor; 360-378-4941; www.islandbicycles.com.

AUTHOR FAVORITE

On Lopez Island, the easiest and most popular bike route here is the **Lopez Island Perimeter Loop**, 32 miles of gently rolling hills and narrow, paved roads passing by Fisherman's Bay, Shark Reef Park, MacKaye Harbor and Agate Beach on the west side of the island and Mud Bay, Lopez Sound and Shoal Bay on the east side.

Rent, buy or repair mountain bikes and hybrids on Orcas Island at **Dolphin Bay Bicycles,** which also offers custom tours for 10 to 30 people. ~ Ferry Landing; 360-376-4157. Mountain bikes, road bikes, tandems, bike trailers and trail-a-bikes can be found for sale or rent at **Wildlife Cycles,** which also does repairs and offers off-road tours. ~ North Beach Road, Eastsound; 360-376-4708; www.wildlifecycles.com.

HIKING   All distances listed for hiking trails are one way unless otherwise noted.

NORTHERN PUGET SOUND   On the **Langus Riverfront Park Nature Trail** (2.5 miles) in Everett, hikers are likely to spot red-tailed hawk or gray heron as they make their way through towering spruce, red cedar and dogwood trees along the banks of the Snohomish River, past Union Slough and on toward Spencer Island, a protected haven for nesting ducks.

WHIDBEY ISLAND   The most picturesque hikes on Whidbey Island are found in and around Fort Ebey State Park. The **Ebey's Landing Loop Trail** (3.5 miles) has some steep sections on the bluff above the beach, but carry your camera anyway to capture the views of pastoral Ebey's Prairie in one direction and Mt. Rainier and the Olympic Mountains framed by wind-sculpted pines and fir in the other. Trimmed in wild roses, the trail swings around Perego's Lagoon and back along the driftwood-strewn beach. Be aware that the trail passes over some private property.

The **Partridge Point Trail** (3.5 miles) in Fort Ebey State Park climbs through a mix of coastal wildflowers on a windswept bluff rising 150 feet above the water with wide views of Port Townsend, Admiralty Inlet, Protection Island and Discovery Bay. A fenced path at the southern end drops down the headland to the cobbly beach below.

There are numerous trails to choose from in Deception Pass State Park. Locals prefer **Rosario Head Trail** (.3 mile) on the Fidalgo Island side, stretching over the very steep promontory between Rosario Bay and Bowman Bay with sweeping views of the San Juans, Rosario Strait and the Strait of Juan de Fuca, and continuing on the **Lighthouse Point Trail** (1.5 miles), which extends farther along the rocky bluff, past the lighthouse and into a dense stand of fir and cedar. On the Whidbey Island side of the bridge, climb the steep switchback on **Goose Rock Perimeter Trail** (3.5 miles) and you might see great blue heron on Coronet Bay, then follow the path down under the bridge next to the swirling waters of the pass and on to quiet North Beach to see the totem pole located at West Point where North and West beaches converge. Heartier hikers might want to tackle the **Goose Rock Summit Trail** (.5 mile), with an altitude gain of some 450 feet for an unparalleled view of Deception Pass and the Cascades.

FIDALGO ISLAND   In Anacortes, your best bet is to head for the **Washington Park Loop Road** (3 miles), located on Fidalgo Head at the end of Sunset Avenue four miles west of downtown. Rewarding views on this easy, paved path with a few moderate slopes include incredible glimpses of the San Juan Islands, Burrows Pass and Burrows Island. You'll also find quiet, cool stretches through dense woods and access to beaches and romantic, hidden outcroppings suitable for a glass of champagne to toast the breathtaking sunsets.

Boeing means big. The largest aerospace, electronic and computer business in the U.S. employs nearly 80,000 people in the Puget Sound area alone.

LOPEZ ISLAND   On Lopez, ideal hiking choices include the **Shark Reef Park Trail** (.5 mile), a mossy path that meanders through a fragrant forest area and along a rock promontory looking out over tidal pools, a large kelp bed, a jutting haul out spot for seals and across the channel to San Juan Island. Spencer Spit State Park's **Beach Trail** (2 miles) travels down the spit and around the salt marsh lagoon alive with migratory birds; at the end of the spit is a reproduction of a historic log cabin built by early settlers, a fine spot for a picnic or brief rest stop with a nice view of the tiny islands offshore.

SAN JUAN ISLAND   Two of the best hiking alternatives on San Juan are the established hiking trails of the San Juan Island National Historical Park. The **Lagoon Trail** (.5 mile) in American Camp is actually two trails intertwined, starting from a parking area above Old Town (referred to on maps as First) Lagoon and passing through a dense stand of Douglas fir connecting the lovely, protected cove beaches of Jakle's Lagoon and Third Lagoon. The highlight of the short but steep **Mt. Young Trail** (.75 mile) in English Camp are the plates identifying the many islands dotting the waters as far as the eye can see. If you want a closer view of the water, you can take the flat, easy **Bell Point Trail** (2 miles), also in English Camp, which runs along the edge of the coast.

ORCAS ISLAND Unless you plan to spend an extended period of time here, there's little chance of covering the many hiking trails that twist through Moran State Park on Orcas Island connecting view spots, mountain lakes, waterfalls and campgrounds. The **Mountain Loop** (3.9 miles) is fairly easy and takes in sights such as drooping log cabins and a dam and footbridge at the south end of Mountain Lake. For a little more challenge, try a section of the two-part **Twin Lakes Trail**: one part (2.2 miles) heads up the valley at the north end of Mountain Lake; the other (3.7 miles) takes you from the summit of Mt. Constitution along a rocky ledge to Twin Lakes and the Mountain Lake Campground, with occasional views through the thick trees. If you're a waterfall lover, take the **Cascade Creek Trail** (4.3 miles) from the south end of Mountain Lake past Cascade and Rustic falls and on to Cascade Lake.

Transportation

CAR

Route 5, also known as the Pacific Highway, parallels the Northern Puget Sound coastline all the way up to the Canadian border. **Route 20** from Burlington takes you into Anacortes, the main jump-off point for ferry service to the San Juan Islands, and south to Coupeville on Whidbey Island.

AIR

Visitors flying into the Northern Puget Sound area usually arrive at **Seattle-Tacoma International Airport** (see "Transportation" in Chapter Two for more information).

Charter and regularly scheduled commuter flights are available into the tiny **Friday Harbor Airport** through Northwest Sea Planes, Island Air and West Isle Air. ~ 360-378-2688. Small commuter airports with limited scheduled service include **Anacortes Airport**, **Eastsound Airport** and **Lopez Airport**; all are served by West Isle Air.

FERRY

Washington State Ferries, which are part of the state highway system, provide transportation to the main islands of the San Juans —Lopez, Orcas, Shaw and Friday Harbor on San Juan—departing from the Anacortes Ferry Terminal (Ferry Terminal Road; 888-808-7977 in Washington). Schedules change several times per year, with added service in the summer to take care of the heavy influx of tourists. The system is burdened during peak summer months, so arrive at the terminal early and be prepared to wait patiently (sometimes three hours or more) in very long lines if you plan to take your car along; walk-on passengers seldom wait long. ~ 206-464-6400.

Greyhound Bus Lines (800-231-2222; www.greyhound.com) provides regular service into Everett and Mt. Vernon. Stations are in Everett at 3201 Smith Avenue, 425-252-2143; and in Mt. Vernon at 1101 South 2nd Street, 360-336-5111.

BUS

Amtrak offers service into Everett on the Puget Sound shoreline via the "Empire Builder," which originates in Chicago and makes its final stop in Seattle before retracing its route. West Coast connections through Seattle on the "Coast Starlight" are also available. ~ 3201 Smith Avenue, Everett; 800-872-7245; www.am trak.com.

TRAIN

Seattle-Tacoma International Airport has several car-rental agencies (see "Transportation" in Chapter Two for more information).

CAR RENTALS

Skagit Transit services the Mt. Vernon, Sedro Woolley, Anacortes and Burlington areas. ~ 360-757-4433. In Everett you can get just about anywhere for 75 cents via **Everett Transit**. ~ 425-353-7433. **Island Transit** covers Whidbey Island, with scheduled stops at Deception Pass, Oak Harbor, Coupeville, the Keystone Ferry, Greenbank, Freeland, Langley and the Clinton Ferry. ~ 360-678-7771. In smaller towns like La Conner and Mt. Vernon and on most of the islands there are no public transportation systems set up; check the Yellow Pages for taxi service.

PUBLIC TRANSIT

For service from the Friday Harbor Airport contact **San Juan Taxi Service** (360-378-3550). **Triangle Vans** (360-293-3979) serves the Anacortes Airport.

TAXIS

Index

Lodging Index

Dining Index

HIDDEN GUIDES

Adventure travel or a relaxing vacation?—"Hidden" guidebooks are the only travel books in the business to provide detailed information on both. Aimed at environmentally aware travelers, our motto is "Where Vacations Meet Adventures." These books combine details on unique hotels, restaurants and sightseeing with information on camping, sports and hiking for the outdoor enthusiast.

THE NEW KEY GUIDES

Based on the concept of ecotourism, The New Key Guides are dedicated to the preservation of Central America's rare and endangered species, architecture and archaeology. Filled with helpful tips, they give travelers everything they need to know about these exotic destinations.

PARADISE FAMILY GUIDES

Ideal for families traveling with kids of any age—toddlers to teenagers—Paradise Family Guides offer a blend of travel information unlike any other guides to the Hawaiian islands. With vacation ideas and tropical adventures that are sure to satisfy both action-hungry youngsters and relaxation-seeking parents, these guides meet the specific needs of each and every family member.

Ulysses Press books are available at bookstores everywhere. If any of the following titles are unavailable at your local bookstore, ask the bookseller to order them.

You can also order books directly from Ulysses Press
P.O. Box 3440, Berkeley, CA 94703
800-377-2542 or 510-601-8301
fax: 510-601-8307
www.ulyssespress.com
e-mail: ulysses@ulyssespress.com

HIDDEN GUIDEBOOKS

____ Hidden Arizona, $16.95
____ Hidden Bahamas, $14.95
____ Hidden Baja, $14.95
____ Hidden Belize, $15.95
____ Hidden Big Island of Hawaii, $13.95
____ Hidden Boston & Cape Cod, $14.95
____ Hidden British Columbia, $18.95
____ Hidden Cancún & the Yucatán, $16.95
____ Hidden Carolinas, $17.95
____ Hidden Coast of California, $18.95
____ Hidden Colorado, $15.95
____ Hidden Disneyland, $13.95
____ Hidden Florida, $18.95
____ Hidden Florida Keys & Everglades, $13.95
____ Hidden Georgia, $16.95
____ Hidden Guatemala, $16.95
____ Hidden Hawaii, $18.95
____ Hidden Idaho, $14.95
____ Hidden Kauai, $13.95

____ Hidden Los Angeles, $14.95
____ Hidden Maui, $13.95
____ Hidden Montana, $15.95
____ Hidden New England, $18.95
____ Hidden New Mexico, $15.95
____ Hidden Oahu, $13.95
____ Hidden Oregon, $15.95
____ Hidden Pacific Northwest, $18.95
____ Hidden Salt Lake City, $14.95
____ Hidden San Francisco & Northern California, $18.95
____ Hidden Seattle, $13.95
____ Hidden Southern California, $18.95
____ Hidden Southwest, $19.95
____ Hidden Tahiti, $17.95
____ Hidden Tennessee, $16.95
____ Hidden Utah, $16.95
____ Hidden Walt Disney World, $13.95
____ Hidden Washington, $15.95
____ Hidden Wine Country, $13.95
____ Hidden Wyoming, $15.95

THE NEW KEY GUIDEBOOKS

____ The New Key to Costa Rica, $18.95

____ The New Key to Ecuador and the Galápagos, $17.95

PARADISE FAMILY GUIDES

____ Paradise Family Guides: Kaua'i, $16.95
____ Paradise Family Guides: Maui, $16.95

____ Paradise Family Guides: Big Island of Hawai'i, $16.95

Mark the book(s) you're ordering and enter the total cost here ➯ [   ]

California residents add 8.25% sales tax here ➯ [   ]

Shipping, check box for your preferred method and enter cost here ➯ [   ]

❑ BOOK RATE   **FREE! FREE! FREE!**

❑ PRIORITY MAIL/UPS GROUND   cost of postage

❑ UPS OVERNIGHT OR 2-DAY AIR   cost of postage

Billing, enter total amount due here and check method of payment ➯ [   ]

❑ CHECK   ❑ MONEY ORDER

❑ VISA/MASTERCARD _____ EXP. DATE_____

NAME _____ PHONE_____

ADDRESS _____

CITY_____ STATE _____ ZIP _____

ABOUT THE AUTHOR

JOHN GOTTBERG was raised in the Pacific Northwest and has lived in Seattle intermittently since 1977. He has been an editor and writer for both of the city's major daily newspapers, the *Times* and the *Post-Intelligencer*, and earned his second degree at the University of Washington. The author of 20 books, including Ulysses' *Hidden Montana* and *Hidden Wyoming*, he also has been an editor for *The Los Angeles Times* and for international travel publishers as far-flung as Singapore and Paris. In addition to freelance book and magazine work, he teaches online travel-writing classes for the Gotham Writers' Workshop.